PITTSBURGH THEOLOGICAL MONOGRAPH SERIES

Dikran Y. Hadidian

General Editor

33

INTERGERINI PARIETIS SEPTUM (Eph. 2:14)

Essays presented to Markus Barth
on his sixty-fifth birthday

Intergerini Parietis Septvm

Septvm

(Eph. 2:14)

Essays presented to
MARKUS BARTH
on his sixty-fifth birthday

edited by
Dikran Y. Hadidian

THE PICKWICK PRESS

Pittsburgh, Pennsylvania

1981

Library of Congress Cataloging in Publication Data
Main entry under title:

Intergerini parietis septum (Eph. 2:14)

   (Pittsburgh theological monograph series ; 33)
   Includes one essay in French and one in German.
   "Bibliography of Markus Barth": p.
   Includes bibliographical references.
   1. Theology--Addresses, essays, lectures.
2. Bath, Markus--Addresses, essays, lectures.
I. Barth, Markus.   II. Hadidian, Dikran Y.   III. Se-
ries.
BR50.I57   230   81-284
ISBN 0-915138-42-5   AACR1

© 1981 by
THE PICKWICK PRESS
Pittsburgh, Pa.

Tabula Gratulatoria

James Luther Adams, Cambridge, Massachusetts

James B. Adamson, Santa Rosa, California

Heinrich Baltensweiler, Binningen, Switzerland

Denis Baly, Gambier, Ohio

Ernest Best, Glasgow, Scotland

Raymond E. Brown, New York, New York

Fritz Buri, Basel, Switzerland

Carnegie Samuel Calian, Pittsburgh, Pennsylvania

William S. Campbell, Birmingham, England

Bruno Corsani, Rome, Italy

C. E. B. Cranfield, Durham City, England

David Daube, Berkeley, California

Charles Dickinson, Charleston, West Virginia

École Biblique et Archeologique Française de Jerusalem, Israel

Richard A. Edwards, Milwaukee, Wisconsin

Mircea Eliade, Chicago, Illinois

E. Earle Ellis, New Brunswick, New Jersey

William R. Farmer, Dallas, Texas

W. Ward Gasque, Berkeley, California

D. H. Gollwitzer, Berlin, West Germany

Erich Grässer, Witten-Bommern, West Germany

Ferdinand Hahn, München, West Germany

Richard B. Hardie Jr., Little Rock, Arkansas

Kristin and Frederick Herzog, Durham, North Carolina

Morna D. Hooker, Cambridge, England
Jared J. Jackson, Pittsburgh, Pennsylvania
Eberhard Jüngel, Tübingen, West Germany
David MacLachlan, Musquodoboit Harbour, Nova Scotia, Canada
George W. MacRae, Cambridge, Massachusetts
Ralph P. Martin, Pasadena, California
Ulrich Mauser, Pittsburgh, Pennsylvania
Bruce M. Metzger, Princeton, New Jersey
C. F. D. Moule, East Sussex, England
Petr Pokorný, Prague, Czechoslovakia
Norman W. Porteous, Edinburgh, Scotland
James L. Price Jr., Durham, North Carolina
Bo Reicke, Basel, Switzerland
Eugene Ruckstuhl, Lucerne, Switzerland
H. M. Rumscheidt, Halifax, Nova Scotia, Canada
Martin H. Scharlemann, St. Louis, Missouri
Martin Anton Schmidt, Basel, Switzerland
Leonard Swidler, Philadelphia, Pennsylvania
Katsumi Takizawe, Najme, Japan
Shemaryahu Talmon, Jerusalem, Israel
T. F. Torrance, Edinburgh, Scotland
Günter Wagner, Rüschlikon, Switzerland
Bob Wallace, Maysville, North Carolina
Roy Bowen Ward, Oxford, Ohio
Ulrich Wilckens, Hamburg, West Germany
Amos N. Wilder, Cambridge, Massachusetts
Archibald M. Woodruff III, Albuquerque, New Mexico
Wilhelm Wuellner, Berkeley, California

CONTENTS

FOREWORD

Markus Barth attains his sixty-fifth birthday this year. With this volume a small group out of a larger circle of colleagues and friends bring their congratulations and honor him on this occasion. Others have also joined this group, and their names appear at the end of this volume. There are a few who could not meet the deadline for the publication of this festschrift but their initial positive response to the invitation to participate in this work will in itself be sufficient to indicate their respect for Markus Barth.

As a colleague of Markus Barth for five years at Pittsburgh Theological Seminary, I came to respect him for many reasons: for his meticulous and painstakingly exhaustive scholarship in New Testament studies (e.g. his commentary on the Ephesians!), with doors wide open to so many other disciplines; for his gentleness and patience with students by not overpowering them with his knowledge; for his humanity--the love for friends, food and spirits and good conversation, and a great love for the Alps and climbing; for relentless energy in fighting for academic excellence and an "irrelevant" theological curriculum!

Who can forget his disarming smile and laughter or his devotion to his pipe and tobacco?

One admires his loyalty and great awe for his father, Karl Barth, and yet he kept his own identity by being, if need be, an 'un-Barthian Barth' (see A. C. Cochrane's article in this volume) and thus his father found in his son, Markus, a scholar worth listening to and learning from.

I consider it a great privilege and honor to be able to plan this volume as a tribute to a humble scholar who, in reality, has all the academic and family credentials to be proud and arrogant. But he chooses through his life and scholarship, spoken and written, to break down walls and barriers of race, religion and color. Hence the title of this volume: INTERGERINI PARIETIS SEPTUM (Eph. 2:14).

Pentecost, 1980   Dikran Y. Hadidian

BIBLIOGRAPHY OF MARKUS BARTH

1937

"Die Gestapo gegen die Bekenntniskirche," *BN*, June 19/20, 1937

"Die Verfolgung der Evangelischen Kirche in Deutschland," *BN*, June 21, 1937

"Der Kempf der Bekennenden Kirche," *Christkatholische Jugend* 3 (1937), 10

"Der politische Friede in der Botschaft der Kirche," *Zofingia* 78 (Zurich 1937), 133-7

1938

"Unterschriftensammlung für Pfarrer Niemöller an der Basler Universität," *BN*, Febr 28, 1938

1939

"Möglichkeiten zur kritischen Würdigung britischer Theologie I - II," *KBrefS* 95 (Basel 1939), 389-91, 405-8

"P. T. Forsyth: The Theologian for the Practical Man," *The Congregational Quarterly* (London 1939), 436-42

1940

"Ueber britische' Theologie," *Der Quäker* 17 (Bad Pyrmont 1940), 19

1945

Das Abendmahl, Passamahl, Bundesmahl und Messiasmahl, *Theol-Stud* 18 (1945)

1946

"Arbeitstagung in Bad Boll," *EPD* 12 (1946), 3-12

Der Augenzeuge, eine Untersuchung über die Wahrnehmung des Menschensohnes durch die Apostel (Zurich: *EVZ*, 1946)

1947

"Projet de constitution ecclésiastique pour l'Eglise Réformée de Bâle-Campagne," *Verbum Caro* 1 (Neuchâtel 1947), 32-43

"Gemeindeaufbau in biblischer Sicht," *Der Kirchenfreund* 81 (Zurich 1947), 81-85

1948

"Gebete für die Gottesdienste in den reformierten Kirchen des Kantons Baselland am Bettag," Sept 15 (Liestal 1948)

"Is. 63:7-16," *MPT* 37 (Goettingen 1948), 58-61

1949

"Is. 55:6-11," *MPT* 38 (1949), 79-82

"Entmythologisierung I - II," *KBrefS* 105 (1949), 114-7, 130-33

"Jesus Christus, der grosse Hohepriester des Neuen Bundes," *Der Kirchenfreund* 86 (1949), 145-50

"Luke 2:41-52," *GPM* 4 (1949), 46-50

"Rev 22:12-20," *GPM* 4 (1949), 56-62

1950

"Der Andere," *Leben und Glauben*, 25 (Laupen-Bern 1950), 1

Review "Werner Bieder, Die Vorstellung von der Höllenfahrt Jesu Christi," *KBrefS* 106 (1950), 171-72.

Review "Christian Maurer, Ignatius von Antiochien und das Johannesevangelium," *KBrefS* 106 (1950), 188-9

Review "Hannelies Schulte, Der Begriff der Offenbarung im Neuen Testament," *KBrefS* 106 (1950), 203-6

"Advent--1950!" *Baselbieter Kirchenbote* 43

"John 6:1-15," *GPM* 5 (1950), 102-6

"Luke 10:23-37," *GPM* 5 (1950), 234-9

Der Zeugendienst der Gemeinde in der Welt, TheolExH 21 (1950)

"Matt 22:15-22," *GPM* 5 (1950), 290-6

"2 Cor 12:1-10," *GPM* 5 (1950), 64-7

1951

"Um eine Verfassung der Reformierten Kirche in Baselland I-II," *Landschäftler* Jan 18 and 19 (Liestal 1951)

"Mitteilungen aus Deutschland," *EPD* 16 (1951), 4

"James 1:22-27," *GPM* 6 (1951), 119-22

"Gal 3:15-20," *GPM* 6 (1951), 183-6

"Um eine Verfassung der Reformierten Kirche in Baselland," *Reformierte Kirchenzeitung* 22 (Wuppertal-Barmen 1951), 329-38

"Die Auferstehungsordnung," *Der Kirchenfreund* 85 (1951), 262-6

Die Taufe -- ein Sakrament? Ein exegetischer Beitrag zum Gespräch über die kirchliche Taufe (Zurich: *EVZ*, 1951)

1952

"Matt 10:32-39," *GPM* 7 (1952), 176-9

Review "Franz J. Leenhardt, Pédobaptisme Catholique et Pédobaptisme Réformé," *KBrefS* 108 (1952), 43

"Die christliche Taufe -- ein Zauber?" *Bekennende Kirche auf dem Weg* 3 (Darmstadt 1952), 17-22

Review "Max Geiger, Die Basler Kirche und Theologie im Zeitalter der Hochorthodoxie," *KBrefS* 108 (1952), 268-9

"Rom 1:13-25," *GPM* 7 (1952), 47-51

"Vorwort," to Martin Niemöller, *Des Christen Weg zwischen Ost und West* (Basel: Bibelschule, 1952)

1953

"Acts 1:10-14," *MPT* 42 (1953), 125-7

"Mission and Misery in Europe's Churches," *CC* 70 (1953), 1290-2

1954

"Acts 4:32-35," *MPT* 43 (1954), 257-61

"The Christ in Israel's History," *Theology Today* 11 (Princeton 1954), 342-53

1955

"Die Methode von Bultmann's Theologie des Neuen Testamentes," *TZ* 11 (Basel 1955), 1-19

Review "G. Ebeling, Geschichtlichkeit als theologisches Problem," *Für Arbeit und Besinnung* 9 (Stuttgart 1955)

"Speaking of Sin (Rom 1:19-3:20)," *SJT* 8 (Edinburgh 1955), 288-96

Review "G. B. Verity, Life in Christ," *JBL* 74 (1955), 206-7

1956

Review "A. Wilder, New Testament Faith for Today," *CTSReg* 461 (1956), 77

Sermon on Luke 23:39-43: "For Criminals Only," *Divinity School News* 23 (Chicago 1956), 1-7

Review "H. Traub, Botschaft und Geschichte," *Für Arbeit und Besinnung* 10 (1955), 323

Review "H. A. Guy, The Origin of the Gospel of Mark," *CTSReg* 46 (1956), 16

Review "O. Cullmann, The State in the New Testament," *CC* 73 (1956), 1423-4

1957

Review "E. Goodspeed, The Key to Ephesians," *CC* 74 (1957), 18

Review "B. Gärtner, Areopagus Speech and Natural Revelation," *JR* 37 (1957), 45-6

Review "R. Bultmann, Theology of the New Testament II," *JR* 37 (1957), 46-8

"La Méthode de Bultmann dans la Théologie du Nouveau Testament," [trsl. of "The Christ in Israel's History"], *ETR* 31 (Montpellier 1956), 3-25

"A New Man is Born," (John 1:1-18), *Reformed Review* 10 (Holland, Mich. 1957), 1-11

"Karl Barth," *The New Christian Advocate* 1 (Chicago 1957), 16-20

Sermon on Psalm 72, "The Justice of God," *The Pulpit* 28 (Chicago 1957), No 7, 6-7, 21-3

"Introduction to Demythologizing," *JR* 37 (1957), 145-53

"Reflection on Another Doctrine," *Comprendre* 17-18 (Venice 1957), 129-35

Review "F. J. Leenhardt, Ceci est mon corps" and "N. Clark, Approach to a Theology of Sacraments," *JR* 37 (1957), 222-5

"Reflections on U.S. Foreign Policy," *Christianity and Crisis* 17 (New York 1957), 132-4

1958

Review "W. A. Visser't Hooft, Renewal of the Church" and "A. Nygren, Christ and His Church," *International Review of Missions* (London 1958), 100-3

Review "J. M. Robinson, Das Geschichtsverständnis des Markusevangeliums," *JR* 38 (1958), 54-5

"A Chapter on the Church -- the Body of Christ (1 Cor 12)," *Int* 12 (1958), 131-56

"Contribution to a Portrait of God," *The Pulpit* 29 (1958), No 8, 8-9

"Weakness or Value of the Baptist Position," *Foundations* (Rochester, N. Y. 1958), 62-8

Review "O. Cullmann, Christologie des Neuen Testamentes," *JR* 39 (1958), 268-71

1959

The Broken Wall, A Study of Ephesians (Philadelphia: Judson Press 1959; reprint London: Collins 1960)

Review "R. Bultmann, The Presence of Eternity," *JR* 39 (1959), 61-2

Review "K. Stendahl, The Scrolls and the New Testament," *CTSReg* 49 (1959), 12-4

"Baptism and Evangelism," *SJT* 10 (1959), 32-40

"Christ and Law," *Oklahoma Law Review*, Vol. 12:67, (1959), 67-85

"The Church and Israel in Paul's Epistle to the Ephesians (a summary)," *The Student World* 52 (1959), 68-80

"Taufe," *Evangelisches Kirchenlexikon* II, (Göttingen: Vandenhoeck & Ruprecht 1959), 1283-95

Review "A. Toynbee, Christianity Among the Religions of the World," *JBL* 78 (1959), 99-101

Sermon on Rom 8:28, "Predestination to Conformity," *The Pulpit* 30 (1959), No 6, 8-10, 22-23

"The Preacher and the Authority of the Bible," *Foundations* 2 (1959), 230-4

"Israel und die Kirche im Epheserbrief," *Stimme der Gemeinde* 11 (Wiesbaden 1959), 561-6

"Israel und die Kirche im Brief des Paulus an die Epheser," *TheolExH* NF 75 (Munich: Kaiser 1959)

Review "R. R. Niebuhr, Resurrection and Historical Reason," *CTSReg* 49 (1959), 58-60

Review "O. Cullmann, Christology of the New Testament," *CC* 76 (1959), 1503-4

1960

Review "J. G. Davies, He Ascended into Heaven," *Theology Today* 16 (1960), 539-43

"Marriage is Not the Chief End of Man" (on racially mixed marriages), *Social Progress* (Philadelphia, Febr 1960), 5-7

Review, "J. Jeremias, Die Kindertaufe in den ersten vier Jahrhunderten," *ThLZ* 85 (1960), 42-4

Review "J. Huby, S. Paul (Romans)," *JBL* 79 (1960), 85-6

Sermon on Psalm 16, "Here is the Man," *The Pulpit* 31 (1960), No 6, 22-4

"Love Breaks Down All Divisions," *U. S. News and World Report*, 116-7

1961

Sermon on Rom 1:16-17, "Nought for Your Shame," *The Pulpit* 33 (1961), No 3, 18-21

Solidarität mit den Sünderu, [German revised ed. of *The Broken Wall*], (Kassel: Oncken, 1961)

Was Christ's Death a Sacrifice? SJT Occasional Papers 9 (Edinburgh: Oliver and Boyd 1961)

"Das Kreuz: Versöhnung für Feinde," *Die Gemeinde* 13 (Kassel 1961), 4-6

"Letter to the Editor," *Bulletin of the Department of the World Presbyterian Alliance* 2 (1961), No 2, 12-5

"On God's Existence," *Religious Experience and Truth*, a Symposium ed. by S. Hook (New York: University Press 1961), 220-3

Review "H. Mentz, Taufe und Kirche in ihrem ursprünglichen Zusammenhang," *ThLZ* 86 (1961), 851-2

1962

"The Cowboy in the Sunday School I-II," *Religious Education* 17 (New York 1962), 39-52, 120-7

"The Blake Proposal: Pool of the Rich or Pilgrimage of Servants?" *McCormick Quarterly* 15 (Chicago 1962), No 3, 3-8; reprint in *The Challenge to Reunion*, eds. R. M. Brown and D. H. Scoll (New York: McGraw-Hill 1963), 190-7

"The Old Testament in Hebrews," *Current Issues in New Testament Interpretation*, Fs Otto Piper, eds. F. Klassen and G. Snyder (New York: Harper and Bros. 1962), 207-10

Review "J. Jeremias, *Infant Baptism in the First Four Centuries*" and "K. Aland, *Die Säuglingstaufe im Neuen Testament und in der alten Kirche*," *Int* 16 (1962), 207-10

"Reflections of God's Glory (Comments on an Unknown Flemish Artist's Landscape)," *Crossroads* 13 (1962), No 1, 3-4

Vom Geheimnis der Bibel, TheolExH NF 100 (Munich: Kaiser 1962)

"Erfüllung des Gesetzes," translation of Wilber Katz, "Fulfillment of the Law," *EvTh* 22 (1962), 494-500

"Call for the Repeal of the McCarran Act," *Louise Pettibone-Smith Journal* (Oct. 12, 1962), New York

1963

"Evangelical Theology, A Guide to the Lectures of Karl Barth,"
(Waco, Texas: World Records 1963)

"Conversion and Conversation" (Israel and the Church in Paul's
Epistle to the Ephesians), *Int* 17 (1963), 3-24

Sermon on Luke 21:25-28, "Christ Will Come Again," *Foundations*
6 (1963), 64-71

Review "M. E. Dahl: Resurrection of the Body," *JR* 43 (1963),
59-60

"Just a Property and Trade Agreement?" [reprint of part of
"The Blake Proposal..."], *Presbyterian Life*, March 15 (Philadelphia 1963), 21

"The Freedom of God," *The Empirical Theology of H. N. Wieman*,
ed. R. W. Bretall (New York: Macmillan 1963), 288-98

"The Church According to the Epistle to the Ephesians," *The
Ecumenical Dialogue at Cornell University 1960-1962* (Ithaca,
N. Y.:   Cornell United Rel. Work 1962), 7-49, 70-2

"What Can the Church Do in Correction?" *Concern* 5 (Washington
1963), No 13, 12-14; reprint *Social Progress* 54 (Philadelphia
1964), No 5, 40-4

"Paul, Apostle or Apostate?" Review "H. J. Schoeps: Paul"
and "C. K. Barrett, From First Adam to Last," *Judaism* 12 (New
York 1962), 370-5

"La démocratie occidentale à l'épreuve," *Comprendre* 25 (Venice
1963), 158-61

Sermon on Is. 40:3, "In the Wilderness Prepare the Way of the
Lord," *The Pulpit* 34 (1963), No 9, 10-13

1964

(With Verne Fletcher) *Acquittal by Resurrection* (New York:
Holt, Rinehart and Winston, 1964)

"The Challenge of the Apostle Paul," *JES* 1 (1964), 58-81

(With J. Taubes) "Letter to the Editor" (concerning Kittel-Friedrich *Theological Dictionary to the New Testament*), *New York Times Book Review* (April 12, 1964)

"Salvation from the Jews?" *JES* 1 (1964), 323-6

Conversation with the Bible (New York: Holt, Rinehart and Winston, 1964)

"What is the Gospel?" *International Review of Missions* 53 (Geneva 1964), 441-8; reprint ed. R. S. Rosales, *The Evangelism in Depth Program in Latin American Mission* (Mexico: Son-teos 1968), 27-34

"Introduction," eds. Goppelt-Thielicke-Müller/Schwefe, *The Easter Message Today* (New York: Nelson & Son, 1964), 9-25

Review "R. Bultmann, The History of the Synoptic Tradition," *CC* 81 (1964), 1434

"Sola Scriptura," ed. L. Swidler, *Scripture and Ecumenism* (Pittsburgh: Duquesne University Press, 1965), 75-94

1965

"What can a Jew Believe about Jesus and Still Remain a Jew?" *JES* 2 (1965), 382-405; reprint (in part) *Newsletter WCC* (May 1965), No 2; reprint *Reflection* (New York: Commission on Interfaith Activities, April 1967)

"Preaching on Pentecost," *Preaching on Pentecost*, ed. A. M. Potter (Philadelphia: Fortress Press, 1965), 1-9

"The Latest Church Ideology, A Critique of G. Winter, *New Creation as Metropolis*," *Int* 19 (1965), 435-56

1966

"Jew and Gentile, White Man and Negro," *Katallagete* (Nashville, Tenn. 1965), No 2, 27-31

"Que peut croire un Juif au sujet de Jésus - tout en restant Juif?" [trsl. of "What Can a Jew Believe..."], *VAV, Revue de dialogue* 1 (Paris 1966), 17-46

"Christians and Jews Today," [reprint (in part) of *The Broken Wall*], *Crossroads* (1966), No 2, 65-69

"Gottes und des Nächsten Recht," ed. M. Geiger, *Parrhesia*, Fs Karl Barth (Zurich: EVZ, 1966), 447-69

"Natural Law in the Teachings of St. Paul," ed. E. Smith, *Church-State Relations in Ecumenical Perspective* (Pittsburgh: Duquesne University, 1966), 113-51

"Church and Communism in East Germany I - II," *CC* 83 (1966), 1440-3, 1469-72

"Ein Brief aus USA," *Die Rheinpfalz* (Ludwigshafen, Germany, Dec. 24, 1966)

1967

"Everybody's Bible," response to an article by Rev. W. M. Abbot, *Pittsburgh Press*, Family Magazine (Febr 26, 1967), 11

Review "C. Spicq, Théologie morale du Nouveau Testament," *JBL* 86 (1967), 101-4

"Dialogue is not Enough, A Report on the Jewish-Christian Harvard Conference in Oct. 1966," *JES* 4 (1967), 115-20; reprint *Encounter Today* 2 (Paris 1967), No 4, 145-50

"Did God Die at Auschwitz?" Review "R. Rubenstein, After Auschwitz," *The Pittsburgh Point* 1 (Apr 6, 1967), 6

"The Kerygma of Galatians," *Int* 21 (1967), 131-46

"Kirche und Kommunismus in Ostdeutschland," [trsl. of "Church and Communism..."] *Pastoralblätter* 107 (1967), No 5, 258-74

"Interview," ed. P. Garfield OB, *Theologians at Work* (New York: Macmillan, 1967), 385-405

"Developing Dialogue between Marxists and Christians," *JES* 4 (1967), 385-405

Jesus, Paulus und die Juden, TheolStud 91 (1967)

"Die Grenzen blossen Dialogs," [trsl. of "Dialogue is Not Enough..."], *Jüdisch-christliches Forum*, No 39 (Basel 1967), 66-70

"Was kann ein Jude von Jesus glauben - und dennoch ein Jude bleiben?" [trsl. of "What Can a Jew Believe..."], *Freiburger Rundbriefe* 19 (1967), 87-96

"The Scope of Law: Man, Morals or Money?" Review "ed. M. Radcliffe, The Good Samaritan and the Law," *Wisconsin Law Review* (1967), No 4, 961-9

1968

"Marxisten und Christen im Gespräch," [trsl. of "Developing Dialogue Between Marxists and Christians"], *EvTh* 28 (1968), 83-107

Review "N. Kehl, Der Christushymnus Kolosser 1, 12-20," *CBQ* 30 (1968), 106-10

Review "J. Bligh SJ, Galatians in Greek," *CBQ* 30 (1968), 75-83

"Was Paul an Anti-Semite?" *JES* 5 (1968), 78-104

"Justification: From Text to Sermon on Gal 2:11-21," *Int* 22 (1968), 147-57

"Jew and Gentile, the Social Character of Justification in Paul," [trsl. of "Gottes und des Nächsten Recht"], *JES* 5 (1968), 241-67

"Shall Israel Go it Alone?" *JES* 5 (1968), 446-52

"Gefangene - Christen - Menschen," *Wort und Gemeinde*, Fs Eduard Thurneysen (Zurich: EVZ, 1968), 331-51; reprint *Bausteine* (Kantonale Strafanstalt Saxenrieth, Switzerland, July 1968)

"Zur Taufe - zur Kindertaufe," *Pastoralblätter* 57 (1968), No 9, 375-77

"Evolution du dialogue entre Marxistes et Chrétiens," [trsl. of "Developing Dialogue Between Marxists and Christians"], *Comprendre* 31-32 (1968), 119-35

1969

"Sieben Sätze zur Taufe im Neuen Testament," ed. D. Schellong, *Warum Christen ihre Kinder nicht mehr taufen lassen* (Frankfurt: Stimme-Verlag, 1969), 74-107

Rechtfertigung, TheolStud 90 (1969); reprint, including discussion, *Analecta Biblica* 42 (Rome 1970), 137-209

The Letter to the Galatians. Four lectures on tape in the series ed. Maryknoll Seminary, *The New Testament for Today* (Maryknoll, N. Y. 1969)

The Letters to the Colossians and Ephesians. Six lectures on tape in the series ed. Maryknoll Seminary, *The New Testament for Today* (Maryknoll, N. Y. 1969)

"Israel im Alleingang?" [trsl. of "Shall Israel Go it Alone?"], *Junge Kirche* 30 (Dortmund 1969), 588-92

"The Faith of the Messiah," *Heythrop Journal* 10 (1969), 363-70

Israel and the Church (Richmond, Va.: John Knox Press, 1969)

"What Did the Bible Mean? Why Was Jesus Baptized?" *Asheville Citizen-Times* (Dec 7, 1969) 6A

1970

"Albert Speer and the Miracle of Forgiveness," *CC* 87 (1970), 1537-8

1971

"Papal Fallibility," Review "H. Küng, Infallible?" *Saturday Review* (Apr 10, 1971), 17-19

"Whither Biblical Theology?" Review "Br. Childs, Biblical Theology in Crisis," *Int* 25 (1971), 350-4

"Gott vergibt - die Oeffentlichkeit nicht," Review "A. Speer, Erinnerungen," *Südwestdeutscher Rundfunk* (Apr 1971), copyrighted MS, 12-15

Justification [trsl. of *Rechtfertigung* by A. M. Woodruff] (Grand Rapids, Mich.: Eerdmans, 1971)

1972

"Die Parusie im Epheserbrief - Eph 4,13," eds. B. Reicke and
H. Baltensweiler, *Neues Testament und Geschichte*, Fs Oscar
Cullmann (Zurich: TVZ, 1972), 239-50

"The Old Testament in the New Testament," *Biblia Universal* I
(Barcelona: Labor & Fides, 1972)

"Response" to a discussion on the theology of K. Barth, *Union
Seminary Quarterly Review* 28 (1972) 72-3

1973

"On Palestinians in Israel," *JES* 10 (1973), 121-7; reprint
Newsletter WCC (Geneva 1973), No 2, 3-8

De Jood Jesus en het Geloof der Jooden, [trsl. of "What Can a
Jew Believe..."] (Kampen: H. Kok B.V., 1973)

"Die Stellung des Paulus zu Gesetz und Ordnung," *EvTh* 33
(1973), 496-526; reprint W. G. Kümmel etc., *Die Israelfrage
nach Römer 9-11*, ser. mon. *Benedictina* 3 (Rome 1977), 245-
87

1974

"Current Discussion on the Political Character of Karl Barth's
Theology," ed. M. Rumscheidt, *Footnotes to a Theology*, suppl.
SR (Toronto 1974), 77-94

Contributions to discussion, ed. L. di Lorenzi, *Battesimo e
Gusticia in Rom 6 e 8*, ser. mon. *Benedictina* (Rome 1974), 27-
31, 61, 65-6, 74-6, 106-8, 114-6, 121-3, 162, 168, 174, 193-4,
197-8

Ephesians I - II, Anchor Bible 34 and 34A (New York: Doubleday, 1974)

"Ein Pfarrer," in memory of Eduard Thurneysen, *Neue Zürcher
Zeitung* (Nov 2/3, 1974), 66

1975

"Sakral und Profan," *Reformatio* 24 (Zurich 1975), 228-42

"Bleibt ein Weg für Israel?" *BN*, Apr 19 (1975), 7-8

"Biblical Preaching Today," *Review and Expositor* 72 (Dallas 1975), 161-7; reprint *The New Pulpit Digest* 55 (1975), 17-20

Der Jude Jesus, Israel und die Palästinenser (Zurich: TVZ, 1975)

"Der theologische Antisemitismus," letter to the editor, *Allgemeine jüdische Wochenzeitung*, Aug 1 (Düsseldorf 1975), 5

1976

"Israel, die Palastinenser und wir," *National Zeitung*, Febr 7 (Basel 1976), Weekend suppl., 1-5

"Kolosser 4,2-6," *GPM* 30 (1976), 225-33

"Auferstehung. Die historisch-kritische Bearbeitung der neutestamentlichen Auferstehungszeugnisse," *KBrefS* 132 (1976), 114-6

"Die Einheit des Gottesvolkes," [selections from "Das Volk Gottes"], *Zur Debatte* 6 (Katholische Akademie Bayern 1976), 13-14

"Die Einheit des Galater- und Epheserbriefs," Review "F. Mussner, Der Galaterbrief" und "A. Van Roon, The Authenticity of Ephesians," *TZ* 32 (Basel 1976), 78-91

"Exegetische Anfrage an das Gesetzesverständnis Luthers und Barths," ed. B. Klappert, *Promissio und Bund* (Goettingen, Vandenhoeck & Ruprecht, 1976), 256-66

Review "K. M. Fischer, Tendenz und Absicht des Epheserbriefes," *ThLZ* 101 (1975), 355-9

Contributions to discussion, ed. L. di Lorenzi, *The Law of the Spirit in Rom 7 and 8*, ser. mon. *Benedictina* (Rome 1976), 48, 63-6, 108-10, 112, 161-2

"Baptism," *Interpreters Dictionary of the Bible*, suppl. vol. (1976), 85-89

1977

"Das Volk Gottes," M. Barth, J. Blank, J. Bloch, F. Mussner, R. J. Z. Werblowski, *Paulus, Apostat oder Apostel* (Regensburg: Pustet, 1977), 45-134

1978

Sermon on Colossians 1:15-20, "Ein Lob Jesu Christi," *Basler Predigten* 42 (Basel 1978), No 2

"Herausforderung Traditionalismus," *KBrefS* 134 (1978), 114-5

Review "E. Schweizer, Der Brief an die Kolosser," *TZ* 34 (1978), 110-3

"Theologians at Bat for Peace in Mideast," Interview by D. Virtue, *The Province*, July 22 (Vancouver 1978), 14

1979

"Der gute Jude Paulus," *Richte unsere Füsse auf den Weg des Friedens*, Fs Helmut Gollwitzer (Munich: Kaiser, 1979), 107-37

Excerpts from a letter to J. Moltmann, ed. M. S. Welker, *Diskussion über Jürgen Moltmanns Buch Der Gekreuzigte Gott* (Munich: Kaiser, 1979), 160-2

Review "K. Stendhal, Der Jude Paulus und wir Heiden," *KBrefS* 135 (1975), 122-3

"Ps. 16. Leben dem Tode zum Trotz," ed. W. Strolz, *Aus den Psalmen leben* (Freiburg: Herder, 1979), 39-48

Sermon on Ephesians 3:2-6, "Gnade für die Andern," *Basler Predigten* 43 (1979), No 10

Contributions to discussion, ed. L. di Lorenzi, *Dimensions de la vie Chrétienne (Rom 12-13)*, ser. mon. *Benedictina* (Rome 1979), 136-7, 146-7, 174-5, 212-3, 217-8

"The Dishonest Steward and His Lord, Reflections on Luke 16: 1-13" in *From Faith to Faith, Essays in Honor of Donald G. Miller on His Seventieth Birthday*, ed. Dikran Y. Hadidian (Pittsburgh: Pickwick Press, 1979), 65-73

"Epheser 3, 2-3a, 5-6," *GPM* 34 (1979), 66-76

"St. Paul - A Good Jew," *Horizons in Biblical Theology, an International Dialogue*, I (1979), 7-45

1980

"The State of the Free, Romans 13:1-7 in the Context of Paul's Theology" in *Reformatio Perennis; Essays on Calvin and the Reformation in Honor of Ford Lewis Battles*, ed. B. A. Gerrish in collaboration with Robert Benedetto (Pittsburgh: Pickwick Press, 1980), pp. 173-194

CONTRIBUTORS

C. K. Barrett, Professor of Divinity, Department of Theology, University of Durham, Durham, England

Ford Lewis Battles, Late Visiting Professor of Church History, Calvin Theological Seminary, Grand Rapids, Michigan

Arthur C. Cochrane, Distinguished Visiting Ecumenical Professor of Systematic Theology, Wartburg Theological Seminary, Dubuque, Iowa

Oscar Cullmann, Professor of New Testament Studies, Emeritus, The University of Basel, Switzerland

W. D. Davies, George Washington Ivey Professor of Advanced Studies and Research in Christian Origins, Duke Divinity School, Durham, North Carolina

David Demson, Professor of Systematic Theology, Emmanuel College of Victoria University in the University of Toronto, Toronto, Canada

Donald E. Gowan, Professor of Old Testament, Pittsburgh Theological Seminary, Pittsburgh, Pennsylvania

Alfred M. Johnson, Jr., Cary, North Carolina

Paul Lehmann, Charles A. Briggs Professor of Systematic Theology, Emeritus, Union Theological Seminary in New York City

Joseph L. Mihelic, Professor Emeritus, Archivist, University of Dubuque Theological Seminary, Dubuque, Iowa

Donald G. Miller, Formerly President, Pittsburgh Theological Seminary, Pittsburgh, Pennsylvania

Paul S. Minear, Winkley Professor Emeritus of Biblical Theology, Yale University Divinity School, New Haven, Connecticut

Robert S. Paul, Professor of Ecclesiastical History and Christian Thought, Austin Presbyterian Theological Seminary, Austin, Texas

Dietrich Ritschl, Professor of Systematic Theology, University of Mainz, Mainz, Germany

Eduard Schweizer, Professor of New Testament Exegesis and Theology, University of Zurich, Zurich, Switzerland

Phillip Sigal, Adjunct Faculty, Pittsburgh Theological Seminary, Pittsburgh, Pennsylvania

H. Eberhard von Waldow, Professor of Old Testament, Pittsburgh Theological Seminary, Pittsburgh, Pennsylvania

ABBREVIATIONS

AB	Anchor Bible
BBB	Bonner biblische Beiträge
BHK	Biblia hebraica, Hg. v. Rudolf Kittel
BK	Biblischer Kommentar
BN	Basler Nachrichten
BZAW	Beihefte zur Zeitschrift für die altestament- liche Wissenschaft
CBQ	Catholic Biblical Quarterly
CTSReg	Chicago Theological Seminary Register
EPD	Evangelischer Pressedienst der Schweiz
ETR	Études theologiques et religieuses
EvTh	Evangelische Theologie
EvZ	Evangelischer Verlag, Zollikon (today, TVZ)
FRLANT	Forschungen zur Religion und Literatur des Alten und Neuen Testaments
Fs	Festschrift (in honor of)
GPM	Göttinger Predigtmeditationen
IKZ	Internationale kirchliche Zeitschrift
Interp.	Interpretation
JBL	Journal of Biblical Literature
JES	Journal of Ecumenical Studies
JR	Journal of Religion
MPT	Monatschrift für Pastoraltheologie
NF	Neue Folge
NTS	New Testament Studies
SBT	Studies in Biblical Theology
SJT	Scottish Journal of Theology
SR	Studies in Religion
TheolExH	Theologische Existenz heute
TDNT	Theological Dictionary of the New Testament
ThSt (B)	Theologische Studien, Hg. v. Karl Barth
TZ	Theologische Zeitschrift

VTSup	Vetus Testamentum, Supplements
WCC	World Council of Churches
WMANT	Wissenschaftliche Monographien zum Alten und Neuen Testament
ZAW	Zeitschrift für die altestamentliche Wissenschaft

WHAT IS NEW TESTAMENT THEOLOGY?
SOME REFLECTIONS

C. K. Barrett

Few who remember Cambridge theology between the wars are likely to question the outstanding significance of Sir Edwyn Hoskyns's lectures on the Theology and Ethics of the New Testament. "It is no dishonour to the Divinity Professors to record how men, and women, came to Cambridge for the sake of Hoskyns."[1] Hoskyns died, still a young man, in 1937; I had the good fortune to hear him lecture in his last year, 1936-1937, and then, and later, to be supervised by his pupil, Noel Davey, perhaps a more profound though less extrovert theologian than Hoskyns himself. I can bear witness to the truth of a further remark contained in Charles Smyth's Memoir, which I have already quoted. "You may generally recognise a pupil of Hoskyns by the fact that, when he says 'theology', what he means is 'New Testament theology'" (p. xx). I need not say that this does not mean that either Hoskyns, or his pupils, were unaware of the existence, and the significance, of other subdivisions of the total theological undertaking: Systematic Theology, Philosophical Theology, Moral Theology, and the like. The translator of Karl Barth, even though it was the Commentary on Romans that was translated, and at a time when the *Kirchliche Dogmatik* had scarcely begun to appear,[2] is hardly likely to have continued in ignorance of the discipline of Dogmatics, even if he had known little about it to begin with. The fact is rather that in Hoskyns's hands New Testament theology was so fascinating, absorbing, exciting, that most of us, though from time to time we had to turn our attention to other fields, knew that the New Testament was the one area in which we had to work. After 42 years the fascination and the excitement remain.

"When he says 'theology', what he means is 'New Testament theology'." But what does he mean when he says "New Testament theology"? I do not recall that Hoskyns ever told us.[3] Perhaps it was enough that wherever you opened the New Testament, whether at the Synoptic Gospels, or Paul, or 2 Peter, you found that it was talking theology; but that will scarcely suffice for a definition of a fundamental department of theological study. It is a curious fact, indicative, it may be, of national characteristics, that English-speaking, and especially English, theologians, though they have not been unmindful of the theology of the New Testament, have produced very few "New Testament Theologies".[4] I must myself confess that though I have for many years lectured on the theology of the New Testament it is only recently, and in part under the stimulus of younger scholars, such as, notably, Robert Morgan,[5] not to mention friends and colleagues in other countries,[6] that I have come to ask myself what New Testament theology is. Hence this paper, which is no more than a groping towards an answer to the question that it poses.

New Testament theology as a separate discipline is a relatively new department of theological study. Through most of Christian history theologians have taken it for granted that theology that was not biblical could not be Christian; at the same time they have recognized that the task of theology was not completed by the repetition, or even the rearrangement, of the words of Scripture. Athanasius, for example, in defending the use of such unscriptural terms as ἐκ τῆς οὐσίας and ὁμοούσιος, declared that it was the business of the bishops in council to "collect the sense of the Scriptures",[7] and collecting evidently included repacking the material in new bags bearing new labels. The substance of the scriptural message had to be collected from the various places in which it was expressed and re-expressed in a new terminology suitable to the controversies and to the philosophical habits of speech and mind of the age. But this did not mean that theology was divided into two distinct operations, biblical theology and dogmatic theology. It is arguable that in the Middle Ages there was a tendency for the biblical element in Christian thought to diminish and for the non-biblical philosophical element to increase, for the dogmatic tail to wag the biblical dog. It would be wrong, indeed ludicrous, to claim that theologians such as Anselm and Thomas abandoned the final authority of Scripture,[8] but it is certainly true that the Reformation rested upon a reassertion of this authority and a critical application of it: if current ecclesiastical practices and current ecclesiastical thought were not consistent with Scripture, so much the worse for them; they must be abandoned or amended. *Sola Scriptura*, as a critical principle, was not new; at least, *Scriptura* was not new. But it was enforced with a new rigour, and discovered to be creative as well as critical. This however did not establish Biblical Theology as an autonomous branch of theological study. It was reasserted that all theology must be fundamentally biblical, and the effect of this was rather to suppress than to encourage a special activity of biblical theology.[9]

It is not to the period of the Reformation but rather to

that of the Enlightenment[10] that we must look for the origins
of "New Testament theology". There were several reasons for
the development of biblical theology at this time. One was
discontent with the limitations imposed by dogmatic orthodoxy.
This had now been developing among Protestants as well as
Catholics for many years, and scepticism and pietism joined
forces in the desire for something simpler and less hidebound.
The best way of blowing away the cobwebs of the ages was simply to go back through the centuries to the origins of Christian dogma, thus cutting off masses of what seemed to be unnecessary, and clogging, accretions. It is not accidental
that the study of biblical theology, and the use of that term,
go back to about the same period as the origins of what we
call the quest of the historical Jesus.[11] "Back to Jesus" was
in fact the "back to the theology of the Bible" movement in
its most radical form. Those who wished to be free from the
fetters of current dogmatics, and those who sought a warmer
and more intimate faith in communion with the Lord, might combine in the study of the apostles and their witness to Jesus.
All this, of course, grossly simplifies a complex picture; at
the moment I am drawing attention to a negative motive in the
movement towards a New Testament theology, distinct from what
theology had become.

There was a positive side too. *Dogmengeschichte* as a
discipline, a historical discipline, arose at the time of the
Enlightenment. "Die Dogmengeschichte ist ein Kind der deut-
schen Aufklärungszeit."[12] The context of this pronouncement
goes on to mention, among others, Lessing (1729-1781) and Semler (1725-1791), who were notable figures in the early Quest
and in the development of New Testament theology.[13] The development of *Dogmengeschichte* was part of a general development of historical awareness which contributed to the view
that there might be a theology of the Bible with a historical
distinctiveness as well as a special authority. It is at least
approximately true that at about the same time, or a little
later, scholars became aware of "the theology of" other periods
too. Migne published the great *Patrologiae*,[14] recognizing the
patristic period as an isolable entity in a far fuller way than
the more dogmatic, less historical, classical Anglican appeal
to the authority of the great councils of the undivided church.
G. J. Planck began in 1781 to publish what was (as far as I
know) the first history of Protestant Theology; Dorner's better known history followed in the next century.[15] My point is
a simple one: a clearer, sharper, more critical awareness of
history was among the factors that led to the recognition that
the New Testament marked off a period of history which might
be expected to have a theology of its own and to be worth in-
vestigating for that reason.[16]

Negative and positive motives for the study of New Testament theology thus combined with each other, as well as with the polemical motive of proving that one brand of dogmatics was correct over against all the rest. It is not my intention to take the history of New Testament theology further[17] but, on this basis, to resume the inquiry into what New Testament theology is. In this sketch of origins at least three possibilities have presented themselves. (i) New Testament theology is the foundation of dogmatics, the basis of Systematic Theology, still requiring to be rethought and reformulated in the light of the philosophical fashions of the day but providing, as it were, the basic material which the systematic theologian will recycle. (ii) It is a way of escape from dogma, an escape into an ampler, freer air. (iii) It is a totally independent historical discipline.[18] I see no reason why any one of these propositions should be taken to represent the whole truth to the exclusion of the other two.

It is of primary importance that New Testament theology should retain full independence as a critical historical process. Hoskyns, as I have said, did not define New Testament theology; but in *The Riddle*[19] Noel Davey, after quoting the second article of the Nicene Creed, wrote,

> When the Catholic Christian kneels at the words *incarnatus est* or at the words *and was incarnate*, he marks with proper solemnity his recognition that the Christian Religion has its origin neither in general religious experience, nor in some peculiar esoteric mysticism, nor in a dogma, and he declares his faith to rest upon a particular event in history. Nor is the Catholic Christian peculiar in this concentration of faith. This is Christian Orthodoxy, both Catholic and Protestant. In consequence, the Christian Religion is not merely open to historical investigation, but demands it, and its piety depends upon it. Inadequate or false reconstruction of the history of Jesus of Nazareth cuts at the heart of Christianity. The critical and historical study of the New Testament is therefore the prime activity of the Church. (p. 10)

This passage does not mention New Testament theology, but it does provide a pointer to the sort of thing that New Testament theology may turn out to be; and it is clear that it is rooted in critical historical study of the New Testament. In fact, this passage makes the same claim that Wrede makes, though with a quite different application. Wrede was one of the earliest and most radical members of the *religionsgeschicht-liche Schule*; Hoskyns and Davey rejected "religion" and "religious experience" as the basis and content of Christianity (notwithstanding the repeated use in the passage quoted above of the term "the Christian Religion"). Further, the core of the New Testament is not a religious experience but a historical event; but this event is such that the critical study of it generates theology. The historian begins by asserting the crown rights of his own subject: history is and must be independent, and the historian serves but one mistress. Yet precisely in practising his own trade as a historian he finds that he becomes, whether he will or no, a theologian. Thus Wrede himself, as a historian, discovered that his sources (the gospels) were theologically rather than historically motivated; and this is not the end of the story.[20] If the record of what religious men do in the interests of their religion is *Religionsgeschichte*, then the New Testament historian must practise *Religionsgeschichte*, but his proper subject, pursued with all the integrity and rigour proper to historical investigation, turns out to be not *Religionsgeschichte* but theology.

New Testament theology is thus generated internally; I mean, within the general field of New Testament studies, as a kind of by-product, and (unless we are to withdraw to the mere collection of *dicta probantia*) it cannot be divorced from the literary criticism by which the books of the New Testament are analysed and the historical criticism by which the events of the New Testament period are assessed in regard to their historical probability and arranged in plausible sequence and relation to one another. Yet, notwithstanding its origins, it turns out to belong within the operation of the Faculty of Divinity, and it is proper to consider its relation with other aspects of theological study. Whether it is best regarded as the foundation of dogmatics or as an escape from dogmatics[21] is a question that may be deferred until we have turned over the facts and examined them further.

Let us begin by allowing that both New Testament theology and Systematic Theology exist. How may they be compared with each other? The former may be characterized by the word process, the latter by the word result. I do not mean by this that the work of Systematic Theology is ever finished; by definition it never is. Each generation, each distinct intellectual climate, calls for its own Systematics, precisely because Systematics involves the relation between unchanging truth and varying philosophical modes. We await the next 13-

volume set of *Kirchliche Dogmatik*. Yet Systematics means the production of a system, and this is a result, an end-product, and if it is not relatively final--final, that is, in relation to the environment for which it was designed--it has simply failed to achieve that which it was designed to accomplish. A truly satisfactory Systematics would be the system of Christian truth appropriate to today's date. Over against this, New Testament theology is a matter of process.[22] May we then think of it as the process that leads to the systematic result? There is some value in this suggestion, but in truth New Testament theology is both less and more, and cannot simply be dropped in some middle point between the text of the New Testament and modern reconstruction of the New Testament message. There is a famous passage in which K. Barth contrasts the great commentators on Romans in the early years of the twentieth century with Calvin.[23]

> For example, place the work of Jülicher
> side by side with that of Calvin: how
> energetically Calvin, having first es-
> tablished what stands in the text, sets
> himself to re-think the whole material
> and to wrestle with it, till the walls
> which separate the sixteenth century
> from the first become transparent!
> Paul speaks, and the man of the six-
> teenth century hears.

Here is one contrast: Jülicher and his company (we will not stop to ask if Barth is entirely fair to them, or whether the walls that separate the first century from the twentieth are not very much thicker than those that separate it from the sixteenth) are content to take up the language of the New Testament and adduce parallels to it from Greek philosophy, Hellenistic Judaism, and the Rabbis (how fortunate we are to have the rich fields of Qumran and Nag Hammadi to draw on too!), and suppose that they have thereby done their duty to the text, whereas Calvin inquires what the text has to say to him in his own age. There is another contrast: that between Calvin and the man who is not content until he hears the text speaking the language of his own time--Luther, for example, who is not happy till he hears the text pronouncing judgement on the Papacy and the Scholastics,--and, it may be, Barth himself (here and there in *Romans*) till he can hear Paul speaking in terms of Kierkegaardian existentialism. Where does authentic New Testament theology, not badly represented, perhaps, by Calvin, though I think the work has to be done rather differently today, stand?

Part of the answer to this question is negative. It is the business of New Testament theology to check the systematic theologian when his enthusiasm runs away with him. Consider a very familiar New Testament term, kingdom of God. It is well known that this has been subjected to classical misinterpretations; for example, "the corporate human God-consciousness which is the existence of God in human nature and which comes into being as a result of Christ's God-consciousness."[24] When we read this we know that it is time to call up all the information acquired by the first-year student of theology--'$a$donai malak; malkutha dash$e$maya; and so on--to demonstrate that though Schleiermacher may be saying something true and important he is not saying anything that Jesus could conceivably have communicated to his fellow Jews in first-century Palestine. For him and for them the kingdom belonged to the realm of eschatology. But what does that mean? There are two questions, or groups of questions, here. The first group asks what were the eschatological beliefs of Jesus' audience, and how Jesus appropriated, negated, or modified them so as to create a new eschatological world view. The second group of questions inquires what, if anything, this eschatological world view can mean to a new generation that has abandoned the presuppositions of eschatology in that it no longer finds it possible to contemplate or assign any meaning to a "last day" whether near or distant. It may seem that the wheel has come full circle from Schleiermacher when Perrin writes at the end of a later book,[25] "Kingdom of God is a symbol evoking a myth; the hermeneutical possibilities vary enormously according to the viability of the myth and the functional possibilities of the symbol." Schleiermacher and Perrin are not saying the same thing, but each has abandoned biblical language (except for the actual symbol, kingdom of God, which is being defined) in favour of terminology appropriate to his own time.

The practitioner of biblical theology can hardly allow himself so free a hand. Yet the quotation from Perrin may serve the useful purpose of pointing us on from the negative to the positive function of biblical theology. Perrin's recognition of a variety of hermeneutical possibilities lying beyond his own work indicates the kind of service New Testament theology may perform. There is an analogy to the point I have in mind in what Albert Schweitzer said about Paul. Paul, according to Schweitzer,[26] did not hellenize Christianity, but did express it in a form in which it could be hellenized--brought, that is, into direct relation with, and set out in terms of, the philosophies and culture patterns of the hellenistic world into which it had been introduced. Whether Schweitzer was right or wrong about Paul does not concern us; we may however claim that it is not the business of the New Testament theologian as such to deal directly with the thought

forms of his own time, but that it is his business so to liberate the contents of the New Testament from their original setting that they may be made intelligible and thus applied in a
new one--or rather in an indefinite number of new ones. How,
it may be asked, is this liberation to be achieved? An answer
to this question must wait till a later point in the discussion.

I have used the word "process" to describe New Testament
theology, and outlined one sense in which the word may be understood. A second observation, which may take the argument
further, is that the New Testament itself is a process; that
is, it describes a historical process. It begins with the
story of Jesus, running back to and indeed before his birth
and continuing up to his death. It proceeds with the resurrection and the story of the early church, reaching in explicit narrative as far as about A.D. 60, and, by implication, to
the end of the century. This is not a long stretch of time
compared with what might be involved in, say, "The Theology of
the Middle Ages", but it is the classical and formative period;
it would perhaps not at this stage be right to say, the authoritative period.[27] I shall consider two aspects of it. The
first is the great watershed which, on the Christian view,
divides all history in two: the death and resurrection of
Jesus. In the New Testament this separates the story of the
life and teaching of Jesus of Nazareth from the history of the
primitive church--separates, but also unites them. The second
aspect of the period that will be considered is the story of
the church itself.

The first of these points may be introduced by quoting
two well known propositions; they are often used, but are too
important to be neglected. There is Loisy's dictum: "Jesus
foretold the kingdom, and it was the Church that came."[28] Before the epigram is dismissed the critic should take the simple step of consulting the concordance under the words βασι-
λεία, so common in the Synoptic Gospels and relatively rare
elsewhere, and ἐκκλησία, hardly occurring in the gospels and
frequent in the rest of the New Testament. Moreover, though
the synoptic teaching on the kingdom is more complex than
Loisy appears to allow, it does include a vivid urgent eschatological element--there are some of those who stand here who
shall not taste death till they see the kingdom of God come in
power (Mark 9.1)--which suggests an outlook that was already
becoming an embarrassment in the first century and has in the
twentieth, after 1900 years of Christian history, become frank-
ly impossible. Is there a historical continuity between Jesus
and the church? The second proposition is Bultmann's: "Die
Verkündigung Jesu gehört zu den Voraussetzungen der Theologie
des Neuen Testaments und ist nicht ein Teil dieser selbst."[29]

This leads us to put our question in a different way: Is there a theological continuity between Jesus and the church? Examination of these questions may in the end contribute to an answer to the wider question, What is New Testament theology?

In a short paper the material available at this point must be handled selectively. We shall take the fact that, in the gospels, the ministry of Jesus ends with the account of a supper that he took with his disciples shortly before his arrest.[30] From one point of view this was a failure. To eat with someone, especially to be united with him by blood, was to pledge an absolute loyalty. This the disciples recognized. "If I should have to die with you, I will not deny you," said Peter; and so said they all (Mark 14.31). Correspondingly, the horror of the betrayal was that it was "one of you", εἷς ἐξ ὑμῶν, who shall betray me, "he who is eating with me", ὁ ἐσθίων μετ' ἐμοῦ (Mark 14.18). But they did break their commitment, betray, deny, and desert him, and Jesus died, not in the company of his friends but alone. This of course is not the end of the gospel story, and before long the meals were resumed; the followers of Jesus continued to hold their supper party, and it was a κυριακὸν δεῖπνον because the κύριος was there; and Paul taught them at their supper to recall what the Lord had done in the night in which he was betrayed (1 Cor. 11. 23). Yet it was not the Last Supper they observed. That was rightly defined as the last, the end-point of a series, and though a new series related with the former might begin, the last was the last. It is akin to the mishnaic distinction between the "Passover of Egypt", which could never happen again, and the "Passover of the generations that followed after" (Pesahim 9.5). The continuing supper provided a connection with the past, but the connection was neither simple identity nor bare recollection. The same words might be spoken, the same actions performed, but they were spoken and performed in a new context, in a different eschatological setting, between the resurrection of Jesus as the firstfruits of those who slept, and his coming.

It would be possible, and perhaps profitable, to follow this observation in an exposition either of the Last Supper itself or of eucharistic theology. This however is not the present task. I wish rather to draw out the analogy between the act of eating and drinking, transposed into a new period in the eschatological process, and the tradition of the words and deeds of Jesus, used, as it was after the resurrection, for theological rather than purely historical purposes. The event that revolutionized the supper by putting it into a new setting necessarily affected the teaching of Jesus too, which could no more be repeated identically than the supper. Even when the words were most accurately remembered they took on a new meaning.

The resurrection proved to the disciples in a way they could not doubt that Jesus had been right in the great issues-- such as kingdom of God and Torah--of his ministry, and immediately they began to find new ways of expressing the fact that he had been right. These found their way progressively into the tradition. They began to label him with dignified titles-- χριστός, κύριος, υἱὸς τοῦ θεοῦ--and to work out in theological terms the effect and significance of his death. They did not discard the historical tradition, but they could see that merely to repeat it would not make the point that had to be made. What had been reticent and allusive had to become explicit and challenging. It was necessary now to preach "Jesus *and* the resurrection",[31] though this had not been prepared for and was certainly not a ready-made form of the Gospel. The propositional form of the preaching, like the structural form of the church, was not laid down in advance, and both had to be improvised in a new period of history whose very existence had not been foreseen; for this reason much in both was bound to be provisional. There is another pointer here to the nature of New Testament theology, at once permanently authoritative and transitional.

It is true that the gospels themselves are preaching. Units of tradition were used for this purpose, but it may well be that on this point Bultmann (who thought that the material was used for a variety of catechetical purposes) was more nearly right than Dibelius (who thought it was used in mission preaching).[32] If preaching, as we encounter it in Acts and Paul, means preaching Jesus and the resurrection, then the gospels are preaching if they are read as wholes, up to and including their last chapters; the individual pericope is complete only when put by the preacher in the new post-resurrection context. In the gospels themselves we see signs of this process; it constitutes the principal difference between the Synoptics and John. Perhaps we may conclude that the Synoptic Gospels (not quite the same thing as "Die Verkündigung Jesu", though related to it) are New Testament theology when we take them in their entirety; that the teaching of Jesus is New Testament theology when it is transposed out of its pre-crucifixion setting and placed where it can be seen in the light of the resurrection. For this reason we may be glad of all the modifications--even if they amount to historical falsifications--that entered the tradition in the course of its transmission.

There is a further inference of great importance. What we see in the process I have just described, whereby units of tra-

dition were given a new form and context which made them usable
as preaching material, is New Testament theology, beginning
within the New Testament itself--very notably in the relation
between John and the Synoptic Gospels[33]--and from this we may
infer what the task of New Testament theology is. Its function
is to relate all parts of the New Testament to its (the New
Testament's) centre, and to interpret them in the light of that
centre. What is the centre of the New Testament? That is a
question that each New Testament theologian must in the end
answer for himself, and until there is an agreed answer New
Testament theologies will differ not only in detail but in
fundamental conception. Our own generation has seen two outstanding opinions. For Bultmann the centre was justification
by faith; this led him to interpret the New Testament as an
anthropology, with existentialism as his hermeneutical principle. More recent theologians[34] have focused on Jesus, and New
Testament theology becomes essentially a Christology. In fact,
the two centres, justification by faith (*sola fide*), and Jesus
crucified and risen (*solus Christus*), are if not identical at
least so closely related as to be indivisible. This was already seen by Luther,[35] and (to pursue the geometrical image)
an ellipse based on these two points as foci will turn out to
be not very different from a circle. But the image matters
little; what is important is the establishing of the principle
on which New Testament theology works.

We have now considered, and drawn certain conclusions
from, one aspect of that historical process which the New
Testament describes. We must now turn to the second, the
story of the post-resurrection church. I propose to mention
two related senses in which this story bears upon New Testament theology. In the first place, the history itself is the
record not of peaceful development but of strife and controversy; in the second place, and arising out of the controversy,
the books that make up the New Testament bear traces of dis-
agreement, or at least of diversity, to such an extent that we
are bound to ask whether "the theology of the New Testament"
is a proper expression; should we not rather speak of "the
theologies of the New Testament"?

I may at this point recall a remark that I made earlier.
I said that when applied to the New Testament critical and historical study itself becomes a theological operation. It might
seem enough to say that the New Testament is such a thoroughly
theological work that any method of study is bound to unearth
theology in it; but there is more than this. It is critical
historical investigation that brings to light the controversies
that underlie the New Testament, and critical literary investigation that lays bare the various literary units and groups
that constitute the New Testament. Thus these processes bring

to light both the intensity and conviction, and the variety,
that are characteristic of New Testament thought.

At present, however, I am concerned not with these characteristics but with the bare facts, and of these the first is
that the New Testament is a record of strife and controversy.
This is familiar to all students of the New Testament, though
I suspect that they do not always recognize the violence of
the strife and the heat of the controversy--the fact, for
example, that Paul alleges that the majority of Christian
preachers are untrustworthy cheats (2 Cor. 2.17; cf. 4.2), and
that the false brothers (who must at least have claimed to be
Christians) appear to have threatened his life (2 Cor. 11.24-
6).[36] No wonder; they were in truth servants of Satan (2 Cor.
11.15). Paul's apostleship was disputed (1 Cor. 9.2; 15.8f.);
but he could stand up for himself, and when envoys from James
turned Peter from the straight path he did not hesitate to resist him (Gal. 2.11). So much by way of illustration; a serious New Testament history would have to be both fuller and more
cautious. It must not be assumed that Paul's opponents in
Galatia, Corinth, and Jerusalem were the same; we must distinguish between Pillars, such as James and Cephas, and false
apostles. What is important is that it was out of this clash
of opinion and personality that Paul's theology grew. It has
been said that we should not heed Galatians as a source for
Paul's view of the law; it springs out of a controversy and
therefore expresses a biased, one-sided opinion. I cannot accept so low a view of Paul's intelligence and integrity--or,
as it seems to me, so low a view of Scripture. The opposite
is the truth. Paul said what he had to say, neither more nor
less. He may say it more violently in Galatians than in Romans, but what he says he means, and the effect of controversy
is to sharpen the edge of his argument. We may be grateful to
the false brothers for the statement of the doctrine of justification that they elicited, to those in Corinth who challenged
Paul's apostleship for the exposition they provoked of what it
means to be an apostle, to those in Colossae who did not "hold
fast the Head" and thereby made Paul work out afresh a Christology in which Christ is head of both universe and church.

It is not simply that controversy sharpens men's wits,
though this is true, and doubtless Paul's mind acquired a
keener edge as he debated with Judaizers, Gnostics, and others.
Controversy develops a special kind of theology, a critical
theology which is seen already in the New Testament and especially in Paul and John. It is a function of theology to
submit systems of thought, including well-meant systems of religious thought, to critical examination, to probe and to inquire; to say on occasion a sharp No. Truth is best defined
over against error; creeds may need the sting of anathemas in

their tail. This observation is needed as a supplement to W. Bauer's study of orthodoxy and heresy in the early church.[37] If it is true that Paul conducted no heresy hunts it is equally true--and this is the point of the preceding paragraph-- that he was constantly at work establishing truth over against what he took to be error. This is not the same thing as drawing a straight line and excommunicating all who stand on the wrong side of it; that is a static, Maginot-line kind of warfare, whereas Paul's battles, and those of the New Testament in general, are full of movement, with a good deal of overlapping and interlocking of opposed forces.

It is the critical historical study of the New Testament that brings this critical theology to light as the creative thought of the New Testament period; an uncritical, unhistorical reading will miss it. It is of vital importance to the New Testament theologian that he should pursue this historical study and by entering into the history of the New Testament grasp the genesis of its theology. Yet, when all is done, we are not contemporaries of the apostles; we do not stand in Jerusalem or on Mars' Hill and join in the debates there. Our contact with these debates is literary, and we must therefore turn to the second aspect of the post-resurrection history. The New Testament consists of a considerable number of books which are, to say the least, not identical in their approach to and expression of theological truth. We have a variety of sources, and it is this variety that makes critical thought possible for us, whether in the realm of history or of theology.

The shortest way of illustrating this will be to consider Luke-Acts. For its first readers this was probably all the New Testament they had. Mark had been absorbed into the longer gospel, and could therefore be discarded; the author of Acts shows no knowledge of Paul's letters, and it would be surprising if his readers were aware of them. At this point critical thought is not impossible, but it is both difficult and limited. If Acts, for example, is read on its own it is possible to ask such outworn questions as How did Christianity reach Damascus? and such not uninteresting historico-theological questions as whether Peter's vision (10.9-16) originally had to do with clean and unclean animals or with clean and unclean men, and whether the decree of 15.29 deals with the challenge of 15.1,5 or with some other matter; but it is only when the Pauline epistles are brought into the discussion that questions about the opposition in Galatia and in Corinth, and the issues of the law, and of natural theology and heathen worship, become vivid and significant. It is by the comparison of document with document that we engage in the work of critical history and of critical theology too. Not that the comparison of one

New Testament document with another opens the way to the kind of dispute Paul had with his enemies;[38] the New Testament writers are on the same side, even though, like the armies in *King John*, in attacking the same city from opposite points they sometimes succeed in shooting at each other. The point is that critical, question-asking history provides an approach to the more difficult concept of critical, question-asking theology; and not only so, in New Testament study the two are inseparable. They belong together and can only be forced apart by violence.

The immediate practical consequence of this is to be found in the lay-out of a book on New Testament theology. This must in some way express the variety of New Testament thought. There is, of course, no single "right" way of setting out the sections and chapters of a book, but broadly speaking one may say that Bultmann's method, in which the proclamation of Jesus, the *kerygma* of the primitive church, the *kerygma* of the Hellenistic church, the theology of Paul, the theology of John, and the development towards the ancient church, are successively studied, is correct, and that of Alan Richardson's *Introduction to the Theology of the New Testament* (London, 1958), which results in a topically arranged book resembling a systematic theology, is wrong.

More important is the fact that we here return (see p. 11) to the principle by which each theological statement is related to the "centre"; this now appears however in a fuller and more complex form. There the centre was defined in doctrinal terms; it may now be sought (though probably not found) in personal, or rather literary terms. Is the centre of New Testament theology to be found in Paul? or in John? or should we simply say, corresponding to the *Solus Christus*, in Jesus? Clearly the word "centre" will not do. Paul must be related to Jesus, and to John; John must be related to the synoptic tradition, and to Paul; Hebrews must be related to John and to Paul; and so on. This is not only an essential process in a critical theology; it provides a vital clue to that liberation of New Testament theology desiderated above (p. 8). The New Testament theologian traces the development of Christian thought from its origins--or presuppositions--in the ministry of Jesus through a variety of religious and intellectual contexts. This should enable him to distinguish between the essential and the peripheral, the constant and the variable; more than this, he should learn a great deal about proper and improper kinds of variation and adaptation. There is sufficient variety in the New Testament for general principles both positive and negative[39] to be established. For example, the New Testament gives us clear enough hints about the extent to which the mythical element in it may be demythologized, and the handling of the

synoptic tradition in John[40] provides a pointer to the way in
which primitive eschatology has to be modified as time runs
out. In yet another sense, New Testament theology is a matter
of process. It does not simply reproduce the content of the
New Testament; it does not simply differentiate between the
various theologies in the New Testament, or attempt a neat
harmony of them; it describes and analyses the process by
which one theology, or mode of theology, is transposed into
another, and thus on the one hand liberates the essential theological content of the New Testament from the various settings
in which it was formulated, and on the other hand indicates to
the systematic theologian the methods by which and the limits
within which he may set to work to reformulate Christian truth
in the current idiom--reminding him, however, at the same time,
that however successful he may be he is not adding to the canon.

It is time to draw these reflections, which are no more
than a preliminary attempt to answer the question at the head
of this paper, to a close. I do this under three heads.

First, it may be asked what authority a New Testament theology thus conceived may have. It has been described in terms
of a critical process, involving historical reconstruction with
all its manifold uncertainties. If conflict and variety play
an essential part in it, can it be in any sense authoritative?
We may begin (but it is only a beginning) by returning to the
Enlightenment and to Pietism. There is a sense in which Biblical Theology has always meant a release from authority, a sense
in which it has always signified a turning to the immediate and
personal in religion. It would be a mistake to regard either
of these motivations as simply misleading. Indeed, they suggest the first point--a negative one, it is true, yet impor-
tant--that is to be made here. The authority of New Testament
theology means deliverance from various false authorities to
which from time to time Christian life has been subjected.
This could be illustrated not only from the period of the
Reformation, but also, as I have said, from that of Enlightenment and Pietism. More important than these illustrations,
and indeed the most fundamental observation of all, is that
the New Testament itself reveals precisely this kind of deliverance. The gospels record a conflict between two kinds of
authority, the authority of law as administered by Jewish institutions and the liberating authority of Jesus. It is essentially the same conflict, though transposed to different
circumstances, that flares up in the story of Paul. The false
brothers, to whom not even for a moment would he yield, crept
in "to spy out our liberty which we have in Christ, in order
that they might enslave us" (Gal. 2.4); at the same time, Paul
does not stand for anarchy--he has authority, but it is author-

ity "for building you up and not for throwing you down" (2 Cor. 10.8; 13.10). Whatever is to be said about the authority of a theology based on the New Testament, it is not the kind of authority that lies in the rigid constitution of an ecclesiastical body which men question at their peril. Equally it is not the authority of a worked out and carefully formulated set of dogmatic propositions, which those who do not accept must be expelled from the community. This kind of authority makes itself felt on the margin of the New Testament (2, 3 John), but it is not to be found at the centre, where Paul, contending to the last ditch for the purity of the Gospel, asks only if a man loves the Lord (1 Cor. 16.22), and proposes only the corresponding formula, κύριος Ἰησοῦς (1 Cor. 12.3).

Two points may be added to this note on the authority of New Testament theology. (a) "There is a riddle in the New Testament. And it is a riddle neither of literary criticism, nor of date and authorship, nor of the historicity of this or that episode. The riddle is a theological riddle, which is insoluble apart from the solution of a historical problem. What was the relation between Jesus of Nazareth and the Primitive Christian Church? That is the riddle."[41] Since the theological riddle is bound up with the historical problem the answer can be found only in New Testament theology. There are no independent historical traditions about Jesus of Nazareth that are of any value; the witness of the New Testament church enshrined in the New Testament books is decisive and authoritative. This does not in itself mean that the New Testament witness is right; we may reject it as mistaken. It does not mean that it is unitary; as we have seen, the New Testament is marked by variety. It does not mean that it is self-evident; we have to search for it with all the tools of the trade. It does not mean that, when we find it, we shall find it expressed in terminology that pleases us; the whole task of reformulation remains. It means simply that if we do not like the account, given by the New Testament and brought out in New Testament theology, of the relation between the New Testament church and Jesus, we must lump it; there is nowhere else to go. This is the sort of authority New Testament theology has.

(b) The authority of the New Testament (and thus of New Testament theology so far as it is genuine) is creative. I have already quoted Paul's "authority for building you up, not for throwing you down". The same man wrote to the same church, "You are the seal of my apostleship in the Lord" (1 Cor. 9.2). Their very existence was a visible token of his apostleship, of his authority (though in the context he might well have disclaimed the word) as an apostle. Authority *within* the New Testament does not consist in occupying a position of dignity but in accomplishing a task. The authority *of* the New Testament does not consist in a doctrine of inspiration but in its apostolic effectiveness. The authority of New Testament theology within the whole theological operation does not consist in having the last word, but in having the first, creative word.

So Professor X's "Theology of the New Testament" has no authority save that which is conferred on it by its faithfulness to its subject-matter and theme; but New Testament theology--as a process, an unachieved process--has a paradoxical authority of its own. The second and third concluding points may now be set out in little space. The second follows from what I have just written, and I need do no more than recall the argument (p. 8) that it is the task of New Testament theology to set the theological content of the New Testament free so that it can be re-expressed in the language of any age and place. It is often supposed that the contribution of New Testament scholars to Christian preaching consists in turning the Greek of their text into plain, easy English (or whatever it may be). The truth is the reverse of this. The New Testament scholar must put the New Testament into English as difficult, as full of problems and offence, as the original Greek; the smoother, the easier, the more inoffensive his rendering the greater his failure. Releasing the New Testament for assimilation in the modern world does not mean presenting something that the modern world will be glad to hear, and New Testament theology means making available the full content of New Testament thought and conviction in all its offensiveness.

It follows, and this is the third concluding point, that New Testament theology must be a free and independent operation (see p. 4). It does not set out to please either the church or the world; it will often offend both. This is essentially a theological observation, but its effect is to make New Testament theology academically respectable, and to do so more effectively than Wrede's arguments, which stood on a different foundation. Any trimming of the sails to prevailing winds would be treachery both to scholarship and to the subject-matter of the discipline itself. There are no limits to the questions that may be asked, or to the sources to which the questions may be directed. Provided that the principle of judgement "by the centre" (pp. 10-11, 14-15) is maintained there is no reason why there should be any trouble over the precise limits of the canon; it will soon enough appear that Ignatius is further from the centre than John.[42] It does however follow from this that New Testament theology is indeed theology, and not *Religionsgeschichte*; and the theology turns out to be one that expresses its integrity in a firm criticism of religion--as Hoskyns never tired of saying. But this is

only part of the fact that New Testament theology is always
critical theology.

NOTES

1. Charles Smyth, in *Cambridge Sermons*, by Edwyn Clement Hoskyns (London, 1938), p. xix.

2. Hoskyns's translation of Barth's Commentary on Romans was published in 1933 (Oxford); the first volume of *Christliche Dogmatik* appeared in 1928, revised as *Kirchliche Dogmatik* in 1932.

3. This will to some extent be remedied when (it is hoped in the summer of 1980) S.P.C.K. publish *Crucifixion-- Resurrection: A Study of the Essential Pattern of New Testament Theology and Ethics*, begun by Hoskyns, continued by Davey, and edited by G. S. Wakefield.

4. O. Merk, in *Biblische Theologie des Neuen Testaments in ihrer Anfangszeit* (Marburg, 1972), a book to which I am much indebted, in sketching "Probleme neutestamentlicher Theologie seit F. C. Baur" devotes 5 out of 34 pages to "die Entwicklung im angelsächsischen Sprachbereich". The proportion is both correct and misleading. See my review in *Journal of Theological Studies* 28 (1977), pp. 245-7.

5. Robert Morgan, *The Nature of New Testament Theology* (Studies in Biblical Theology, Second Series, 25; London, 1973). This book contains a long and very valuable essay by Morgan, together with translations of W. Wrede's *Über Aufgabe und Methode der sogenannten neutestamentlichen Theologie* (1897) and A. Schlatter's "Die Theologie des Neuen Testaments und die Dogmatik" (1909).

6. Of whom, let it here be gratefully said, by no means the least or least valued is Markus Barth. I wish I had known him at the time when I was hearing Hoskyns in Cambridge and he was reading theology in Bern and Basel.

7. συναγαγεῖν ἐκ τῶν γραφῶν τὴν διάνοιαν (*de Decretis Nicenis* 20), said with special reference to the hypocrisy of their adversaries (Arians).

8. For example, Anselm, *Cur Deus Homo* I 18 (388A): Certus enim sum, si quid dico quod sacrae Scripturae absque dubio contradicat, quia falsum est; nec illud tenere volo si cognovero; Thomas, *Summa Theologica*, Qn 1, Art. 1,2: Necessarium fuit homini ad salutem, quod ei nota fierent quaedam per revelationem divinam, quae rationem humanam excedunt;--see the whole context.

9. Collections of *dicta probantia* (see, e.g., Merk, op. cit. 15f., and elsewhere) can hardly be called theologies.

10. See Merk, op. cit. 21-8.

11. A. Schweitzer, *The Quest of the Historical Jesus* (E. T., London, 1910, 1936). Schweitzer begins his account with Reimarus (1694-1768).

12. F. Loofs, *Leitfaden zum Studium der Dogmengeschichte*, 5th edition edited by K. Aland, 1. Teil (Halle-Saale, 1951), p. 1.

13. It was G. E. Lessing who published the "Wolfenbüttel Fragments" (of Reimarus's work) in 1778. J. S. Semler replied to this in 1779.

14. The Latin series began in 1844; the Greek concluded in 1866.

15. I. A. Dorner, *A History of Protestant Theology* (Edinburgh, 1871), a translation of *Geschichte der protestant-ischen Theologie* (Munich, 1864).

16. It is no coincidence that F. C. Baur, whose critical sense of history was unsurpassed, contributed both to *Dogmengeschichte* in general and to New Testament theology as well. The first edition of his *Lehrbuch der christlichen Dogmengeschichte* appeared in 1847. *Vorlesungen über die christliche Dogmengeschichte* was published posthumously (1865-7), and so was *Vorlesungen über neutestamentliche Theologie* (1864).

17. See, in addition to Merk, op. cit., the Epilegomena in R. Bultmann, *Theologie des Neuen Testaments*[7] (Tübingen, 1977), pp. 585-99; N. A. Dahl, in *Theologische Rundschau* 22 (1954), pp. 21-49; G. Bornkamm, in *Theologische Rundschau* 29 (1963), pp. 33-141; G. E. Ladd, *A Theology of the New Testament* (Guildford and London, 1975), pp. 13-33.

18. This is the view of Wrede; see the book by Morgan (note 5). So for example: "How the systematic theologian gets on with its results and deals with them--that is his own affair. Like every other real science, New Testament theology has its goal simply in itself, and is totally indifferent to all dogma and systematic theology" (p. 69).

19. E. Hoskyns and N. Davey, *The Riddle of the New Testament* (London, 1931).

20. See *Expository Times* 87 (1975-6), pp. 8f.

21. See (i) and (ii) on p. 4; also pp. 15-17.

22. It is, I trust, unnecessary to point out that I am not talking about "process theology".

23. K. Barth, *The Epistle to the Romans* (E. T. by E. C. Hoskyns, Oxford, 1933), p. 7.

24. Not Schleiermacher himself, but Norman Perrin summarizing Schleiermacher in *The Kingdom of God in the Teaching of Jesus* (London, 1963), p. 14.

25. *Jesus and the Language of the Kingdom* (Philadelphia, 1976), p. 203.

26. *The Mysticism of Paul the Apostle* (E. T., London, 1931), especially p. 334: "Paul did not Hellenize Christianity; but he prepared the way for its Hellenization."

27. On the question of authority see below, pp. 15-17.

28. A. Loisy, *The Gospel and the Church* (E. T., London, 1903), p. 166.

29. Bultmann, op. cit., 1.

30. In what follows I shall draw upon what I have written in *Jesus and the Gospel Tradition* (London, 1967), pp. 50f.

31. The words are precisely those of Acts 17.18, but significantly enough the same sense, in similar wording, is found at Rom. 10.9.

32. R. Bultmann, *Die Geschichte der synoptischen Tradition*[2] (Göttingen, 1931), p. 64: "Apologetik und Polemik wie Gemeindebildung und Disziplin sind ebenso in Rechnung zu setzen und daneben schriftgelehrte Arbeit." M. Dibelius, *From Tradition to Gospel* (E. T., London, 1934), p. 13: "Missionary purpose was the cause and preaching was the means of spreading abroad that which the disciples of Jesus possessed as recollections." Bultmann does not exclude preaching as part of the setting in life of the gospel material. On the difference see especially P. Vielhauer, *Geschichte der urchristlichen Literatur* (Berlin, 1975), pp. 285-9.

33. This point is not dependent on the view (which I hold; see *The Gospel according to St John*[2] [London, 1978], pp. 42-6; *Expository Times* 85 [1973-4], pp. 228-33) that John probably knew Mark.

34. See my "Christocentric or Theocentric? Observations on the Theological Method of the Fourth Gospel", in *La Notion biblique de Dieu*, edited by J. Coppens (Bibliotheca Ephemeridum Theologicarum Lovaniensium XLI; Gembloux, 1976), especially pp. 361-3. I go on in this paper to show that for John Christology is not the last word; the gospel is in the strictest sense *theo*logical.

35. See for example the 1522 Preface in which, though he praises the Epistle of James, he sets side by side the two complaints that it ascribes righteousness to works, and makes no mention of the suffering, resurrection, and Spirit of Christ.

36. See my *Second Epistle to the Corinthians* (London, 1973), pp. 299f.

37. W. Bauer, *Rechtgläubigkeit und Ketzerei im ältesten Christentum* (Tübingen, 1934; second edition, 1964; E. T., Philadelphia, 1971).

38. James (see note 35) is not really an exception, though there may well be misunderstanding of Paul on the part of the writer, or of other persons known to him.

39. Again (see notes 35, 38), James comes to mind; see also E. Käsemann's discussion of 2 Peter (in *Exegetische Versuche und Besinnungen I* [Göttingen, 1960], pp. 135-57).

40. See note 33; I am not assuming a literary connection, though such a connection may well exist.

41. *The Riddle of the New Testament* (note 19, above), p. 14.

42. This is not intended as a complete answer to the problem of the canon, only as a claim that *in practice* no harm but good results if we look at all the literary products of the apostolic and sub-apostolic ages.

2

NOTES ON JOHN CALVIN, JUSTITIA
AND THE OLD TESTAMENT LAW

Ford L. Battles

Notanda etiam est justitiae definitio:
Ut faciant quod in oculis Dei rectum est;
quod carnis rationi et judicio opponitur.

(Dt 6:1, Schipper, 1.344)

INTRODUCTION

Roman Law is a vast field, one in which many great writers in jurisprudence have dealt far better than I can do with the concept of *justitia*. Furthermore, the harmonization of Roman and Mosaic legislation was the work of centuries, both in actual codification and in commentary as well. Roman Law itself in its final and classic form is a marriage of the two streams, perhaps unequal partners, but nevertheless (beginning with the Theodosian Code of AD 438 and culminating in the Code of Justinian of AD 530ff) a new creation. After its inauguration the perception of neither Hebraic nor Graeco-Roman institutions could ever be the same again.

In our own Reformed tradition--as distinct from the Roman Catholic, the Lutheran and the Anabaptist traditions--the Mosaic legislation has been viewed from the vantage point of 16th Century humanistic legal scholarship as understood by John Calvin and as applied to Mosaic exegesis by him. Central to his exposition of law is the passion for justice--social, political and religious. It seemed therefore good to me to examine the Mosaic and Graeco-Roman elements in Calvin's view of justice.

A. *Calvin's Study of Roman Law and Its Bearing Upon His Understanding of Jewish Law.*

In a paper entitled "Calvin's Humanistic Education",[1] I dealt summarily with the fortunes of Western European legal education in the middle ages and renaissance, and contrasted the traditional narrow glossator handling of the Code of Justinian with the new humanist effort to understand Roman Law within its broad cultural context. Calvin's teachers represented the best of both traditions: Pierre de l'Etoile for the older school, Andrea Alciati and Guillaume Budé for the new humanist school of legal exegesis.

Calvin's first steps in exegesis were taken not in the Scriptures but in the Law. His earliest exegesis is reflected in his youthful *Commentary on Seneca's De Clementia*. At the heart of his interpretation of Roman Law and institutions is the classic concept of *epieikeia*, to which we shall turn shortly. When his conversion occurred, Calvin undertook an intensive study of Scriptures, giving particular attention to the relation of law and grace. That his view of the law contrasts with that of Luther may be attributed at once to his different temperament and also to the contrasting way he was introduced to Roman Law.

Without further elaboration, we can confidently state that what Calvin wrote about the Mosaic law in general, and on justice and equity in particular, was profoundly affected by his early studies in Roman law at the Universities of Orléans and Bourges.

B. *Contrasting 16th Century Attitudes toward Law.*

What was the milieu into which Calvin launched his first theological essay, *The Institution of the Christian Religion*, in 1536? Elsewhere I have pointed out that Calvin found himself at a mid-point between the theological extremes of Papalism and Anabaptism.[2] More narrowly, in the Eucharist, he found himself midway between Luther and Zwingli. In respect to the legal institutions of his own day he found himself at yet another midpoint. At the one end of the continuum was the repudiation of law courts, and all they stood for, by the Anabaptists; at the other was a small group of Lutheran theologians (with whom Melanchthon was at least sympathetic) who desired to supplant the inherited legal structures by the Mosaic Code, a sort of 16th C. counterpart to the Biblical theocratic dreams of Zionists or Koranic dreams of the modern state of Pakistan at its inception.

For Calvin both these extreme views were wrong. Both rejected juridical institutions and processes, but for opposite reasons and with opposite intent. Calvin's conception of justice and his handling of the Law, both Mosaic and Roman, is shaped, by 1536, in response to these extremes. The Anabaptists took literally Paul's advice to quarreling Christians

not to have recourse to the law court, and Jesus' strictures
against the swearing of oaths. The Mosaic restitutionists apparently took literally Jesus' assertion that he came not to
set aside the law but to fulfill it; they read Paul's praise
of the Jewish law without his distinctive teaching on its
primary function for Christians. Thus both advocated radical
dismemberment of the existing system of justice.

Some other way of approaching the law must be found, a
way that asserted the God-given character of the contrasting
legal systems of the nations, and at the same time the binding
character of the essence of the Mosaic law for Christians.
This task was central to Calvin's whole career. Its outwork-
ing may be seen not only in his theological and exegetical
writings, but also in his framing of constitutions and regulations for the city of Geneva, and in the day-to-day moral
discipline of the citizens. The chief literary sources for
this to which one must turn in this brief paper are the following: (1) The *Seneca Commentary* for the earliest evidence
of his assimilation of legal concepts; (2) The *Institutes*,
particularly the first and last Latin editions (1536 and
1559) for the analysis of Jewish and extra-Jewish law; (3)
The *Harmony of the Four Last Books of Moses* (1563) for the
exposition of the Mosaic codes. We shall deal with these
in reverse order.

II. CALVIN'S ANALYSIS OF THE LAW

A. *The Tripartite Character and Purpose of the Law*.

When, in the first century of our era, Christianity began
to disassociate itself from its parent Judaism, and the flood
of Gentile converts (excused from much of Jewish ceremonial
and ritual) raised questions about the continuing force of the
Mosaic legislation, some groups took the radical line of re-
pudiating the whole Old Testament--the Gnostics; others clung
in varying degrees to the Mosaic regulations. Stimulated by
the pagan critique of Christianity, and following in the foot-
steps of Paul and the Epistle to the Hebrews, the second century Apologists inaugurated an analysis of the Mosaic code calculated to sort out the elements still in force from those
which had been set aside. The distinction between moral and
ceremonial law, with a typological or allegorical interpretation of the latter, was gradually worked out by the Fathers.
In its completed form, this Christian analysis of Moses became tripartite: the heart of it was the moral law, center-
ing in the Decalogue, with its Gentile analogue of the natural

law residing in the conscience (see Romans, ch. 1); the ceremonial law was abrogated as far as literal observance was concerned but still valid as a typology of the new dispensation
to come in Christ; finally, the judical law (in the civil and
criminal sphere) was merely the Jewish counterpart of comparable laws in other societies. So thought Thomas Aquinas, Melanchthon, and Calvin. By thus sorting out the Mosaic legislation, Christians could read the Old Testament within the
civil and ecclesiastical structures of their own time. This
analysis however made a split between secular and religious
in the Christian understanding of the Mosaic Code which was
most certainly not characteristic of Mosaism in its pristine
form.

B. *Calvin's Four-fold Grouping of the Mosaic Codes.*

Modern liberal Biblical Criticism handles the Pentateuch
as incorporating layers of tradition from various periods, the
work of human compliation. Earlier exegetes took more serious-
ly the claim of Mosaic authorship and sought in other ways to
concord or at least explain the discordant canons of Torah.
There is a certain analogy between the critical problems of
the Pentateuch and of the Gospels. Calvin grappled with both
through the constructing of a *Harmony*.

He brought to the Torah the same capacity for grouping
the scattered and often confusing legal traditions of a culture under coherent categories. Concerning Torah, Calvin
makes the following assumptions:

(1)   Exodus, Leviticus, Numbers and Deuteronomy contain
      two principal parts--the Historical narrative and
      the Doctrine;

(2)   The purpose is to instruct the Church (seen as tak-
      ing its origin in the OT) in true piety (including
      faith and prayer), as well as in the fear and wor-
      ship of God;

(3)   The intent is to provide a rule for a just and holy
      life, with exhortation of individuals in the perfor-
      mance of their assigned duties;

(4)   Moses related all this in an unconnected form, as
      opportunity occurred;

(5)   The clue to the whole is the Decalogue but for those
      unable to discern the teaching of the other laws or
      to classify them under their appropriate categories,

the exegete here sets before them the plan of Moses so they may profit by his writings.

Calvin harmonizes the doctrinal contents of Exodus-Deuteronomy under four heads: (1) Preface, (2) Decalogue, (3) Supplements to the two Tables of the Decalogue, (4) The End and Use of the Law. (An outline of his *Harmony* is appended.) Let us briefly examine these.

The Preface is intended to prepare the minds for the reception of the Law. Statements concerning the dignity of the Law are to conduce to the due reverencing of God. Therefore they are set before the precepts of the Law. The Second and Prime Head is, of course, the Decalogue itself. Both in *Inst.* 2.7-8 and in the *Harmony*, Calvin divides the two tables 1-4 (to God), 5-10 (to God through neighbor), and groups all else under the Commandments. The Commandments are a divinely given, brief, but comprehensively summarized Rule of a Just and Holy Life. To these must be affixed other precepts not physically connected with the Commandments in the text, but bearing the same sense. In his arrangement Calvin affixes them to their respective commandments. The Third Head comprises the Supplements or Appendices. The Supplements to the Commandments of the First Table have to do with the outward exercises of worship; those to the commandments of the Second Table are the political laws. The purpose of these supplements is to aid in the observance of the moral law; they do not add or take away from what is laid down in the Ten Commandments, but are helps to the worship owed to God and *to the promotion of justice toward men*. The supplements, while they constitute in Calvin's analysis of the Law a third category of material, are distributed in the *Harmony* under their respective Commandments.

The Fourth category concerns itself with the end and use of the Law. With Paul, Calvin accepts Christ as the end of the Law. The motivating force of threats and promises prepares us for instruction in *justitia* by showing us our guilt and inducing us to seek after the remedy. Only when we recognize ourselves inexcusable before God and void of all confidence in our own *justitia*, can we reach our goal. The law, recalling to us our fallen condition but also God's fatherly adoption, is our tutor unto Christ.

C. *The Uses of the Law.*

Already in his *Commentary on Seneca's De Clementia* (1532) Calvin worked through Plato's, Aulus Gellius' and Seneca's teaching on the uses of punishment. These are reset within a Christian context in the *Institution* of 1536. According to the classical scheme, punishment serves (1) to reform the man who is punished; (2) by punishing him, to make the rest better; (3) by removing bad men, to let the rest live in greater security and at the same time to protect the dignity and authority of him against whom the sin has been committed (*Comm. Sen. De Clem.*, 1.22.1). While not taking these 'uses' of punishment over directly into either his scheme of the Uses of the Law (*Inst.* 1536:88-90; *Inst.* 1559:2.2.6ff) or of the Uses of Church Discipline (*Inst.* 1559:4.12.5ff) one can see how Calvin read the Mosaic Law through a classical Christian gloss. Your attention is called to the diagram (Appendix 1).

A detailed study of these parallels (which is not the purpose of this paper) would reveal that Calvin's view of *justitia*, as it is manifested in the discipline of society, is a composite of classical and Biblical elements.

D. *The Common Ends of Hebrew and Gentile Law.*

Earlier it was pointed out that Calvin sought a position on law and legal institutions between Anabaptist Rejection and Mosaic Restoration, two prominent tendencies of his time. In refuting these two views and in formulating his own, Calvin assumes amid all the diversity of laws in the nations of the world that there is an underlying unity. All laws, he asserts, may be analyzed under two aspects: (1) the actual constitution of the law, (2) the equity on which the constitution is founded and rests. The constitution, or (as we might call it) the form of the law, varies somewhat according to the particular circumstances under which it was originally framed and to which it initially referred. However, the important thing is not so much these culturally induced differences among the corresponding common laws of nations; rather they are to be adjudged according to the degree to which they press toward the goal of equity. Equity, the goal and rule and limit of all laws, is prescribed in the moral law--the testimony of natural law and of the conscience which God has engraved upon the minds of mankind. In *Inst.* 4.20.16 Calvin examines the varied punishments meted out by different legal systems for common offenses forbidden in Commandments 8, 9, 6 and 7:

> "God's law forbids stealing. The penalties meted out to thieves in the Jewish state are to be seen in Exodus (Ex. 22: 1-4). The very ancient laws of other nations punished theft with double restitution; the laws which followed these distinguished between theft, manifest and

not manifest. Some proceeded to banish-
ment, others to flogging, others finally
to capital punishment. False testimony
was punished by damages similar and equal
to injury among the Jews (Deut. 19:18-21);
elsewhere, only by deep disgrace; in some
nations, by hanging; in others, by the
cross. All codes equally avenge murder
with blood, but with different kinds of
death. Against adulterers some nations
levy severer, others, lighter punishments.
Yet we see how, with such diversity, all
laws tend to the same end. For, together
with one voice, they pronounce punishment
against those crimes which God's eternal
law has condemned, namely, murder, theft,
adultery and false witness. But they do
not agree on the manner of punishment.
Nor is this either necessary or expedient. There are countries which, unless
they deal cruelly with murderers by way
of horrible examples, must immediately
perish from slaughters and robberies.
There are ages that demand increasingly
harsh penalties. If any disturbance
occurs in a commonwealth, the evils
that usually arise from it must be corrected by new ordinances. In time of
war, in the clatter of arms, all hu-
maneness would disappear unless some
uncommon fear of punishment were introduced. In drought, in pestilence, unless greater severity is used, everything will go to ruin. There are nations inclined to a particular vice,
unless it be most sharply repressed.
How malicious and hateful toward public
welfare would a man be who is offended
by such diversity, which is perfectly
adapted to maintain the observance of
God's law?" (*Inst.* 1559:4.21.16)

While in this passage Calvin is specifically concerned
to refute the Mosaic restorationists, he is also providing a
principle for the harmonization of the judicial laws of all
nations (including the Jews) and for the Christian determination of what constitutes a just or an unjust law.

II. EPIEIKEIA: CLUE TO THE CONCEPT OF JUSTICE

In the *Nicomachean Ethics* (5.10) Aristotle distinguishes between *epieikeia* and *kata ton nomon dikaion*, or, to use the Latin terms, *aequitas* and *summum jus*. In law and in the interpretation and judicial application of law, we may describe these as clemency and the letter of the law. But all laws, however imperfect, are to be judged by the intention of the lawgiver. Equity endeavors to penetrate beneath the surface, the literal language of the law, the time-bound form in which the law was originally cast, to the spirit and intent of the original. This principle is used by Calvin very effectively in examining Jesus' interiorization of the Decalogue in the Sermon on the Mount, to which we shall shortly turn.

But Calvin's first use of the distinction is at various points in the *Commentary on Seneca's De Clementia*. He became acquainted with in it Budé's *Annotationes in Pandectas*, a partial commentary on the *Digest* of Justinian. Calvin adverts to the principle in commenting on Seneca's statement, "to use authority over slaves with moderation", with copious reference to classical authors. (See Battles-Hugo, pp. 269ff.) Again, when Seneca speaks of guiltless persons who fall under punishment not through their own fault but through misfortune: if such persons "...are subjected to strict severity they can legitimately be punished, if to equity, legitimately condoned" (Battles-Hugo, pp. 69ff). Equity is also appealed to by Calvin in interpreting Seneca's closing words, "Clemency may therefore assess the damages at any value it pleases." Such a principle gives flexibility to the judge in applying the law: the justest way to administer the law is not to be governed by its letter, but to show compassion in pronouncing sentences (Battles-Hugo, pp. 379ff).

This classical principle is carried over, after Calvin's conversion, to his Christian understanding of all law and becomes a prime rule of Scriptural exegesis. In *Inst.* 2.2.21f he teaches that in his fallen state man still retains enough of reason to distinguish him from brute beasts. One area in which this is seen is in man's retention of "some seed of political order". Here is set forth the theological rationale for the unity of human law to which we referred above:

> "...since man is by nature a social animal,
> he tends through natural instinct to fos-
> ter and preserve society. Consequently, we
> observe that there exist in all men's minds
> universal impressions of a certain civic
> fair dealing and order. Hence no man is

to be found who does not understand that
every sort of human organization must be
regulated by laws, and who does not comprehend the principles of those laws. Hence
arises that unvarying consent of all nations and of individual mortals with regard to laws. For their seeds have, without teacher or lawgiver, been implanted in
all men.

I do not dwell upon the dissension and conflicts that immediately spring up. Some,
like thieves and robbers, desire to over-
turn all law and right, to break all legal
restraints, to let their lust alone mas-
querade as law. Others think unjust what
some have sanctioned as just (an even com-
moner fault), and contend that what some
have forbidden is praiseworthy. Such persons hate laws not because they do not
know them to be good and holy; but raging
with headlong lust, they fight against
manifest reason. What they approve of in
their understanding they hate on account
of their lust. Quarrels of this latter
sort do not nullify the original conception of equity." (*Inst.* 1559:2.2.13)

Again, in his "Treatise on the Christian Life" (*Inst.* 3.
6-10) wherein he sets forth the twin principles of self-re-
nunciation and the bearing of the cross, Calvin shows the
place of equity in a well-ordered life. Basing his discussion on Titus 2:11-14, he states:

"Thus, with reference to both Tables of the
Law, he commands us to put off our own nature and to deny whatever our reason and
will dictate. Now he limits all actions of
life to three parts: soberness, righteousness, and godliness. Of these, soberness
doubtless denotes chastity and temperance
as well as a pure and frugal use of temporal
goods, and patience in poverty. Now righteousness embraces all the duties of equity
in order that to each one be rendered what
is his own (cf. Rom. 13:7) There follows
godliness, which joins us in true holiness
with God when we are separated from the in-
iquities of the world. When these things

are joined together by an inseparable bond,
they bring about complete perfection."
(*Inst.* 1559:3.7.3)

Yet, nothing is more difficult than to attain such perfection.
In *Inst.* 3.5.7 Calvin is faced with denying the reference of
Matthew 5:25f to purgatory, as made by the Roman Catholics.
In this passage, he asserts, "...Christ, in order to urge his
followers more cogently to equity and concord, meant to show
the many dangers and evils to which men expose themselves who
obstinately prefer the letter of the law rather than to act
out of equity and goodness."

Equity, then, is the prime principle for Calvin in understanding true justice. The social justice sought, for example,
by the Civil Rights Movement, in direct conflict with unjust
laws, if examined under the rule of equity, would demonstrate
the superiority of *aequitas* over *summum jus*. It is this principle that should animate the framers of laws as well as the
judges whose verdicts stand upon laws. It is upon this foundation that all human laws and their just application must rest.
In this sense all human law is a great unity.

But these remarks do not exhaust Calvin's use of *equity*.
The sublimest task to which it is put in his system is the
harmonization of Decalogue and Sermon on the Mount. Through
epieikeia, Calvin penetrates to the intent of the lawgiver of
the Decalogue, an intent implicit in the Old Testament law but
made explicit in Jesus' reading of the Commandments. Murder
is more than a physical act: murder is committed in the heart
before the hand does the deed, or even when the outward deed
is never done. Working through the Second Table of the Decalogue, Calvin shows how Jesus "interiorizes" the Decalogue,
transforming it from a moral code to an ethic of intention.
The divine pedagogy exhibited in the Mosaic code operates by
synecdoche: the part stands for the whole. The lawgiver has
selected the most heinous instance in every class of offense
to shock his hearers into a grasp of the class as a whole.
Murder stands for all the feelings of enmity, envy and rage
that boil within and poison our relations with our fellows:
inwardly we commit murder against the objects of our hatred.
The very shock of "Thou shall not kill", moves us to a broader
and deeper examination of our moral state. So it goes with
the other precepts as well. Through the classical principle
of *epieikeia*, Calvin has plumbed the depths of the Decalogue
and delineated at the same time the true Christian concept of
justitia. For example, in the Sixth Commandment he sees this
positive purpose: the Lord having bound mankind together in
a certain unity, each man ought to concern himself with the

safety of all (*Inst.* 2.8.39). We must reverence God's image in man, embracing our flesh in him. Thus unthinkable is murder, of which we are guilty not only in the act but in the plan, and even in the wish to kill (*Inst.* 2.8.40).

NOTES

1. F. L. Battles, "Calvin's Humanistic Education," unpublished essay, 1972, especially pp. 10ff.

2. *Institutions, 1536*, tr. F. L. Battles (1975), Introduction, p.

Appendix 1: Uses of Punishment,

The 3 Uses of the Law *Inst. 1536:88-90*	*The 3 Uses of the Law* *Inst. 2:7:6ff; cf. 4:20:14-21*
III It warns the believers, too, in whose hearts the Spirit of God already lives & reigns, what is right & pleasing in God's sight.	III The Pedagogical: admonishes believers & urges them on in well-doing (pars. 12-13)
II It serves at least by fear of punishment to restrain certain men who, unless compelled, are untouched by any concern for what is right and just: this necessary for the public community of men for whose tranquility the Lord so provided in guarding against complete and violent confusion.	II The Restraining: restrains malefactors and those who are not yet believers (10f) (a) protects community from unjust men[4] (b) deters those not yet regenerate i) brings those confident of their own self-righteousness to humility before God ii) restrains those uncontrolled in their own lust
I While showing God's righteousness, i.e., what God requires of us, it admonishes each one of his unrighteousness and convicts him of his sin	I The Punitive: mirrors our sin before God & leaves us inexcusable (pars. 6-9) (a) those to be redeemed thus realize their empty-handedness before God (b) the wicked are terrified, but because of their obstinancy of heart

Law and Church Discipline

The 3 Uses of Punishment
Comm. Sen De Clem. 1:22:1

The 3 Uses of Church
Discipline
Inst. 4:12:5ff

I   To reform the man
    that is punished[1]
    (125.7-26)

III To overcome men
    with shame for
    their baseness,
    that they may be-
    gin to repent

II By punishing him to
    make the rest better[2]
    (125.26-37)

II To keep the good
    from being cor-
    rupted by the com-
    pany of the wicked

I   To banish the
    wicked from the
    fellowship

IIIa By removing bad men,
     to let the rest live
     in greater security
     (Seneca, *De Clem.*,
     1:22:1/Calv. *Comm.*
     125.37-126.1)

IIIb To protect the digni-
     ty & authority of him
     against whom the sin
     has been committed[3]
     (Aulus Gellius, *Noc-
     tes Atticae* 7(6).14)

Notes

1. Greek: nouthesia,
   kolasis parainesis;
   Latin monitio, ani-
   madversio

2. Greek: paradeigma;
   Latin: exemplum

3. Latin: timoria

4. Cf. *Inst.* 4:20:19

36

Appendix 2

Outline of Calvin's Commentary on a Harmony of the Last Four Books of Moses

Key

*   Initial numbers refer to pages in Schipper edition *Joannes
     Calvini Opera Omnia*, Vol. 1 (Amsterdam, 1671).
** First number in parenthesis after each division refers to
     Calvin Translation Society edition, *Commentary on the Four
     Last Books of Moses arranged in his Form of a Harmony by
     John Calvin*, 4 vols. (Edinburgh, 1852-55).

3

MARKUS BARTH--AN UN-BARTHIAN BARTHIAN
THE PLACE OF THE DOCTRINE OF BAPTISM
IN THE CHURCH DOGMATICS[1]

Arthur C. Cochrane

When in 1936 Karl Barth delivered the Gifford Lectures in Aberdeen, Scotland, on *The Knowledge of God and The Service of God* (an exposition of the Scots Confession of Faith 1560), he was an un-Calvinistic Calvinist, particularly with respect to the doctrines of election and the civil government. On that occasion he gave me a photograph of himself signed: "Karl Barth--kein Barthianer". In the preface to IV, 4 the father wrote that "in the face of the exegetical conclusions in my son's book (Markus Barth, *Die Taufe ein Sakrament* ? 1951), I have had to abandon the 'sacramental' understanding of baptism, which I still maintained fundamentally in 1943.... Without following him closely, without cashing in to a large extent on his work, I could hardly have made the reorientation in my own doctrine of baptism." These sentences reveal that Markus, though a Barthian "after the flesh", was not a Barthian, and that Karl also was not a Barthian. Both wanted to learn from each other and from others what it means to be a faithful teacher in the Church of Jesus Christ as attested in Holy Scripture.

In this paper we cannot go into the exegesis of either the father or the son. Instead we shall endeavor to show that the son was the first to grasp the implications of the father's christology for ecclesiology and Christian ethics. We wish to show that their doctrine of baptism is not an aberration or *non sequitur* from the *Church Dogmatics* but is a logical outcome of its basic theological premises; that it was inevitable that the father's doctrine should come out as it did, even though he himself did not consciously realize it as late as 1951.

* *

GOD IS NOT MAN AND MAN IS NOT GOD

A fundamental tenet of Barth's whole theology is that God is not man and man is not God, and there is no way from man to God: only a gracious coming of God to man. Armed with what Soren Kierkegaard called an 'infinite qualitative, distinction between time and eternity', the early Barth attacked the anthropocentric theology of the 19th century with its roots in Schleiermacher's innate God-consciousness. To this so-called dialectical period belong Barth's commentary on *The Epistle to the Romans* and *The Word of God and The Word of Man*. One must not think, however, that Barth abandoned this basic principle when he embarked upon the *Church Dogmatics*. On the contrary, he sharpened the distinction by a categorical rejection of the Roman Catholic *analogia entis*, for which he later substituted an *analogia relationis*--a concept he took over from Bonhoeffer. He sharpened the distinction by taking leave of the remnants of an existential anthropology in his earlier writings, and by a concentration upon a christological, or rather Trinitarian rethinking of all Christian doctrines.

Barth teaches that the doctrine of the Trinity, as the answer to the question who God is, is a transcript of the earliest Christian confession: Jesus is Lord. God is antecedently in himself and in his works *ad extra*, the one and only God in three modes of being Father, Son and Holy Spirit. He is at once the Revealer, the revelation and revealedness. As the Triune God He is distinguished from all the gods of religion and philosophy, as well as from all heavenly and earthly creatures and from all *vestigia trinitatis*. That God is not man and man is not God has now been made clear in the doctrine of the Trinity.

The distinction is made still more evident in the doctrine of God in which the reality and perfections of God are expounded not in terms of an abstract concept of being but strictly in terms of God's act in revelation, and therefore in trinitarian categories. For example, God's love is not human love raised to the nth degree; it is God's act of seeking and creating fellowship, first in his own triune being and then with man in Jesus Christ. God was not obliged to create man in order to have someone or something to love. In Himself He is the Subject and Object of His loving.

On the other hand, though God is self-sufficient in himself, he does not will to be alone; he wills to elect man in Jesus Christ as his covenant partner before the foundation of the world. He wills to establish an everlasting covenant of grace with man which consists of two parts: God's election

of grace and God's commandment. God takes the initiative. He
chooses man not only to bestow upon him the riches of his love
and grace but in order that man may serve and glorify him in a
life of obedience of faith.

Here emerges a basic characteristic of Barth's theology:
the priority of Gospel to law or of dogmatics to ethics, as
well as their unity. First election as the sum and essence of
the good news, then the commandment as God's claim, decision
and judgment upon man. But God's law has nothing in common
with a distorted, perverted "law of works" or of "sin and
death", emptied of grace. On the contrary, the divine commandment is holy, just and good, yes sweeter than the honey-
comb because its ground and content is Christ and because, in
contrast to all other laws, it *liberates*. It frees man for
obedience. It frees man to be a hearer and doer of the perfect law of liberty.

The distinction between God and man is maintained. In
Christ God elects and man is elected; God commands and man
obeys. Yet man is not treated as a robot or automaton. Man
is chosen to be a free, active, responsible and responsive
creature.

The same train of thought is followed in the volumes on
the doctrine of creation. God's work of creation is described
as the external basis of the history of the covenant and the
covenant as the internal basis of creation. Man is created to
live in the unity of soul and body in a vertical relation to
God as his covenant-partner and in a horizontal relationship
with his fellow-human beings. Man is not created male or
female but male *and* female, that is, in the image or creaturely analogue of the covenant of grace. Man's co-humanity is
the *analogia relationis* we mentioned earlier. Moreover, God
graciously preserves and governs his creature. God's activity
precedes, accompanies and follows creaturely activity, yet not
in such a way as to treat people as pawns in the hands of a
master chess player but as the ground and guarantee of the
freedom of the creature.

Thus the doctrine of creation, like the doctrine of God,
concludes with a volume on special ethics--the Commandment of
God the Creator. Man is not required to repeat or even to cooperate in God's creative and preserving work, but rather to
affirm and attest God's work by his own free, human decision
and work. Man is responsible to and is to respond and correspond to God's work--free for God, free for his fellow-man,
free to respect and protect life. There is nothing divine
about marriage and procreation, about the labor of human hands
and minds. Man does not become like God with his science and

culture, his knowledge of good and evil. The distinction, but also the relation, between God's work and man's work, between dogmatics and ethics, is rigorously maintained.

In the doctrine of reconciliation the truth that God is not man and man is not God is deepened immeasurably. For in the light of christology--the humiliation of the Son of God, the exaltation of the Son of man, and Jesus Christ the true witness and mediator--man is revealed to be a proud, slothful, and false creature. In his thoughts, words and deeds he is altogether a lost sinner. Man's justification, sanctification and calling is exclusively God's gracious work. By the awakening, quickening and enlightening power of the Holy Spirit the Church comes to know her being as the body of Christ, is gathered, built up, and sent forth in mission, and certain individuals are made free for faith, love and hope. In no sense is the church a reconciling or redemptive community.

Actually what Barth writes about the church and its ministry and about the faith, love and hope of its members already falls under the head of ethics. For Barth insists: "The confession of Christians, their suffering, their repentance, their prayers, their humility, their works, baptism too, and the Lord's Supper can and should attest this event but only attest it. The event itself, the event of the death of man, is that of the death of Jesus Christ on Golgotha: no other event, no earlier and no later, no event which simply prepares the way for it, no effect which has to give to it the character of an actual event. This is the one *mysterium*, the one sacrament, and the one existential fact before and after which there is no room for any other of the same rank" (C.D. IV, 1, pp. 295f.). "The event of the incarnation...is the great Christian mystery and sacrament beside which there is, in the strict and proper sense, no other" (C.D. IV, 2, p. 40; cf. pp. 50, 55, 107).

Concerning faith, love and hope Barth wrote: "One thing is clear: the New Testament speaks of 'mystery' in the singular or in the plural exclusively with reference to *God's* action and revealing in history, but *not* with reference to human reactions corresponding to it. The πίστις of whose mystery I Tim. 3:9 speaks, is obviously the *fides quae* and not the *fides qua creditur*, and the case is similar with the μυστήριον τῆς εὐσεβείας in I Tim. 3:16. Faith as a human work is never called a 'mystery', nor the obedience of Christians, their love, their hope, etc. Nor are the existence and function of the ἐκκλησία, its proclamation of the Gospel or of its tradition as such. Nor are Baptism and the Lord's Supper so called. Would this omission have been possible if the New Testament community had been aware that certain human attitudes, actions

and institutions were freighted with the divine word and act,
if it had ascribed to baptism in particular the quality of a
bearer and mediator of grace, salvation, and its manifestation?" (C.D. IV, 4, p. 108f.).

Certainly there were mysteries of this kind in ancient
Greece and then in the mystery religions. By means of secret
cultic rites the godhead was presented to participants and
therewith salvation, namely, a life that conquers death, was
mediated to them. From the second century onwards recollection of what the New Testament denotes as *mysterion* gradually
fades and the concept is applied to the action of the Church
and especially to what it does in baptism and the Lord's Supper. Pagan mysteries were explained either as malicious imi-
tations or as anticipations of the Christian mysteries. *Mysterion* was translated as *sacramentum*.

It was, therefore, quite in keeping with the *Church Dogmatics* as a whole, and in keeping with the distinction he had
consistently[2] maintained between God's work and man's work
that Barth planned that Volume IV, 4 should contain a special
ethics from the standpoint of the reconciliation of the world
with God effected in Jesus Christ. It was to present *Christian ethics* as the free and active response of man to the divine word and work of grace, dealing with baptism, prayer and
the Lord's Supper. It would deal with the specific works of
faith, love and hope which God the Reconciler has commanded.
Unfortunately we have only the fragment of baptism. But in
the preface Barth has indicated the direction he would have
taken with prayer and the Lord's Supper.[3] Presumably if he
had lived long enough to expound the doctrine of the consum-
mation of all things he would have ended with a volume on a
special ethics as the commandment of God the Redeemer. And
what would he have dealt with? I do not know but I fancy that
he would have dealt with the State—with human political activity—not in order to build the kingdom of God on earth but
a creaturely *polis* as a reflection of the kingdom that is
coming in glory.

In the light of the *Church Dogmatics* as a whole it is not
surprising that Barth insists time and again that in baptism
there is no doing of God's work by man (pp. 19f., 24, 33, 68,
71ff., 89f., 101f., 118, 128, 144f., 158ff.). Baptism with
the Spirit is God's work; baptism with water is a human work.
Both John the Baptist and Jesus made a clear distinction between baptism with the Spirit which only Christ can bestow and
baptism with water which human beings may administer and receive (Mk. 1:8; Mt. 3:11; Lk. 3:16; Jn. 1:33; Acts 1:5).

I said that with one exception Barth consistently main-

tained the distinction between divine and human work. That
exception is in Volume I, 2 where Barth is discussing the
Holy Spirit as the subjective reality and possibility of
revelation. His teaching was sound with respect to the
Spirit's work in relation to the Son. But when he ventured
to define the objective reality of the Spirit in terms of
sign-events such as the history of Israel, preaching and the
sacraments, he departed from the qualitative distinction between God and man which he previously and subsequently maintained. Barth was not wrong in insisting that the Spirit
creates signs, testimonies and witnesses to Christ. However,
when the Spirit's work is identified with the human witness,
then preaching, Baptism and the Lord's Supper become the
means, the channels and mediators of grace and salvation.
Christians become not merely co-workers with God but co-re-
deemers. As Barth delved deeper into christology, he was to
correct this early Calvinistic aberration.

Barth's rejection of a sacramental view of baptism, especially of infant baptism, was consistent with the basic
premises of his theology. This cannot be said of Luther's
and Calvin's defense of infant baptism. As Barth points out,
the main themes of Luther's theology--Law and Gospel, justification by faith alone, the freedom of a Christian man--hardly
prepare us for the statement--that a small child becomes a
Christian in baptism. And if one considers Calvin's theology
as a whole, who having read the decisive third book of the
Institutes and particularly the first chapter on faith, would
expect to find in the fourth book so forcible a defense of infant baptism? Indeed, who is able to reconcile what Calvin
wrote about baptism in IV, 15 with what he wrote about infant
baptism in IV, 16? The fact is that both Luther and Calvin
and their followers became involved in strange inconsistencies
and speculations, as Paul K. Jewett has shown on his provocative book, *Infant Baptism and the Covenant of Grace* (Eerdmans,
1978).

* *

THE PROBLEM OF THE PRESENCE OF CHRIST

The nagging question persists. Has not Barth been too
consistent? Has he not so reduced preaching, Baptism and the
Lord's Supper to a purely human work that Christ is no longer
present? Are they bare signs that point to nothing? Are they

just memorials of a past crucified and risen Lord, of an absentee Christ in heaven? Were not the mystery religions formally right, even if the dying and rising god was not Jesus of Nazareth? Was it not necessary and right for the church to regard the sacraments as mysteries by and in which Christ is made present? Do not Jesus Christ and his death, or the benefits or merits of his death, need to be conveyed, communicated and applied to us and appropriated by us through the ministry of the Church? Does not Christ need to be re-presented, realized and actualized by cultic acts of preaching, Baptism and the Supper? Is not baptism a necessary means of regeneration and salvation as Luther and the Augsburg Confession teach? Or at least is it not a cognitive means of salvation as Calvin taught?

Barth answers in the negative for the simple reason that Christ is already present. In the preface to IV, 4 Barth states that the Lord's Supper is "the thanksgiving which responds to the presence of Jesus Christ in His self-sacrifice and which looks forward to His future" (p. ix). Parenthetically we observe that the 16th century debates about Christ's presence had to do with the Lord's Supper and not with Baptism and preaching. However, the problem of his presence has to do with all forms of the church's ministry. How does Barth understand Christ's presence?

There are two passages in the *Church Dogmatics* where Barth deals with this question at length. The first is in connection with the doctrine of God's omnipresence in C.D. II, 1. In a lengthy excursus he is able to criticize and correct both Lutheran and Reformed christologies which arose over the issue of Christ's presence in the Supper.

Barth contended that the Lutherans erred in that they failed to *distinguish* the three ways in which God is omnipresent and the Reformed erred in that they failed to *connect* the three ways in which he is omnipresent. First, God is present to himself as the Triune God. In the eternal Godhead the Father is present to the Son and the Son to the Father, and the Spirit is present to both. Thus God in himself is not spaceless nor is he infinite creaturely space. God has his own uncreated space. Jesus Christ, as the eternal Son or Word of God, was always at the right hand of God—before, during and after the Incarnation. Secondly, God has a special presence in the world in Jesus Christ. In virtue of the Incarnation God's own uncreated space adopted creaturely space into unity with itself, so that the creature in its finite space is included in God's own space. This special presence is his work of reconciliation and revelation within creation. Thirdly, in virtue of God's special presence in Jesus Christ,

there is God's general presence in the whole of creation. For
all things are created and preserved by God's Word which is
none other than the Word of reconciliation and revelation.

When the Reformers taught that "according to his manhood,
Christ is not upon earth, but according to his Godhead his
majesty, his grace and Holy Spirit He is at no time from us"
(*Heidelberg Cat. Ques.* 47), the Lutherans protested—rightly ·
Barth believes—that the Reformers had destroyed the unity of
the two natures and had thereby denied a real presence of
Christ in the church and in the world. It has to be admitted
that unintentionally Reformed christology tended toward the
error of Nestorianism. The Lutherans, on the other hand, interpreted the right hand of God, not as God's own proper place,
but in terms of God's general presence in the world, that is,
in terms of infinite creaturely space. The Reformers protested—rightly Barth believes—that the true humanity of
Christ had disappeared in his divinity. Thus Lutheran christology unintentionally tended toward the error of Monophysit-
ism.

A correct statement of the special presence of God in
Jesus Christ in the Church and the world must affirm the unity
and distinction of divine and creaturely space. It must affirm the real presence of the one, whole Jesus Christ, in his
humanity and divinity, his humiliation and exaltation, where
two or three are gathered together, that is, in the power of
his self-revelation through the Spirit, and secretly—but no
less really—in the least of his hungry, thirsty, naked, sick
and imprisoned brethren.

Note that here Barth does not mention a special sacramental presence. Nor does he explain *how* Christ who died, rose
and ascended into heaven nearly two thousand years ago is
truly present today. That comes much later in the christology
of the doctrine of reconciliation. In my opinion perhaps the
most crucial section in the whole of the *Church Dogmatics* is
the section entitled, "The Verdict of the Father" (IV, 1, pp.
283-357). There Barth carries on a debate with Gotthold Ephraim Lessing and with the theology of G. Thomasius and R.
Bultmann, and with the traditional understanding of christology in Roman Catholicism and Protestantism. It affords the
deepest reason for his rejection of sacramentalism.

Barth is wrestling with the Lessing's question about "the
ugly, broad ditch" of the eighteen hundred years between
Christ's resurrection and us. Lessing's question, as re-
phrased by Barth, was how can we be reached and affected by
what happened back then. "How can that which happened once,
even if it did happen for us, be recognized today as having

happened for us, seeing it does not happen today? How can that which happened once have happened for us when we who live today were not there and could not experience it ourselves?" (IV, 1, p. 287). Barth answered that the resurrection is not just a past event. The resurrection is God's declaration, God's proof, that Jesus Christ is not a prisoner of a dead past or of a past death, but is alive and present forever more. Jesus Christ is present as the creative and reconciling word and work of God once and for all times, whether men and women know it or not. The New Testament speaks of the life, death and resurrection of Jesus not as an ideal, principle or potentiality that has to be subsequently realized and actualized but as a concrete deed of God in time that has radically altered the situation of all men in all times and places. "Jesus Christ is the same yesterday and today and forever" (Heb. 13:8). He who is, who declares, "Lo, I am with you always" (Mt. 28:20), is He who was and who is to come (Rev. 1:8).

The problem of an "ugly, broad ditch" of eighteen hundred years *before* Christ's incarnation did not bother Lessing. But it did bother the Jews to whom Jesus said that Abraham saw my day and was glad. "The Jews then said to him, 'You are not yet fifty years old, and have you seen Abraham?' Jesus said to them, 'Truly, truly I say to you, before Abraham was, I am'" (Jn. 8:56-58). Thus the assumption of Lessing and the Jews of an "ugly, broad ditch" was a false assumption and the question of leaping over it either forward or backward was a spurious question. There was no ditch that had to be bridged for the simple reason that no ditch existed. The event of the incarnation (which embraces Christ's death and resurrection) is the event in which God's space and time assumed creaturely space and time into unity with itself, so that there is no time and space where God in Christ is not contemporaneous with man. Unlike all other deities and personages Jesus Christ does not need to be made present by cultic acts.

Moreover, the living, present Christ is the bearer and dispenser of the Holy Spirit by which he so discloses himself to people that they come to faith, love and hope in him. The apostles receive power to be witnesses to Christ in Jerusalem and to the end of the earth (Acts 1:8) and those who receive their witness receive power to believe and confess Christ. But they do not receive power to mediate Christ and therefore to convert and save others. In I Timothy 2:5-7 Paul makes a sharp distinction between the one mediator between God and men, the man Christ Jesus, who gave himself a ransom for all, *and* the testimony to which was born at the proper time. Paul does not think of himself or his words as mediating salvation but simply as one appointed a preacher and apostle, a teacher of the Gentiles.

No, Barth does not deny the presence of Christ. On the contrary, he affirms it more clearly and strongly then the Reformers managed to do. For he grounds it in christology and pneumatology. It is the living presence of Christ here and now that calls ,forth and enables Christians to respond with their human confession and witness.

* *

In this paper I have been content to note two salient features of Barth's doctrine of baptism and to show their consistency with theological premises which inform his whole theology. Nevertheless, for the sake of clarity it is necessary to point out--especially in view of the religious climate in America today--that Barth dissociates himself not only from baptismal sacramentalists but also from certain Separatist or charismatic groups who also reject a sacramental view of water baptism, but who replace the external work of water baptism "by an 'inner work' in the form of experiences, illuminations, exaltations or raptures. This work as such is then invested with the sacramental interpretation denied to water baptism, and it is thus identified with the baptism of the Spirit. Hence the problem of the sacramental significance of water baptism which was supposed to be set aside in this understanding is not set aside at all in practice. It immediately reappears in another form. Here again there is no place for the man who obeys the work and word of God. The answer which he is liberated to give to that which 'eye hath not seen, nor ear heard, neither have entered into the heart of man', to that which may be known only by God's revelation through his Spirit (I Cor. 2:9f.), is fundamentally eliminated again by an exclusive interest in a divine factor which is grasped in the human" (C.D. IV, 4, p. 106).

Thus in a quite different way the distinction between God's work and human work is obliterated. God's saving work is done in, with and under human experience. After all, there is no essential difference between those who see Baptism and the Lord's Supper as a divine work and those who see God's saving work in an experience of being changed or born again. When were we born again? In baptism? In an ecstatic experience? No, on Golgotha! According to Jesus' conversation with Nicodemus, to be "born of the Spirit" means to "see" or "enter" the kingdom of God and that means to believe that on Golgotha, the Son of Man was lifted up as Moses lifted up the serpent in the

wilderness, that whoever *believes* in him may have eternal life
(Jn. 3:1-14).

Moreover, Barth is well aware of the dangers which threaten "baptism which presupposes and includes the free decision and confession of the candidate, namely, hypocritical and imaginary conversions, scrupulosity, the rise of Pharisaical sects of baptized believers" (p. 192). In the face of this danger he writes: "There can naturally be no question of arbitrarily trying to separate the sheep and the goats, believers from unbelievers, the righteous from the unrighteous, the converted from the unconverted, true Christians from purely nominal Christians....the baptizing community...can lay no claim to divine knowledge. It must steer clear of all anxiously probing legalism" (*ibid.*). On the other hand, "the free willingness and readiness of these candidates will consist basically in the recognition and confession of their profound solidarity with unbelievers, with the unconverted, with the unrighteous, in the light of the divine judgment which strikes both and also of the divine grace which is addressed to both" (*ibid.*). Where this confession is made the Christian community will not refuse to baptize. Yet, Barth asks, are the dangers which threaten baptism really eliminated by infant baptism in which one passively becomes a Christian without his or her consent?[4]

NOTES

1. A paper prepared for a *Festschrift* in honor of Markus Barth and delivered at a meeting of the Midwest section of the Karl Barth Society of North America in Chicago, October 26-27, 1979.

2. With one exception which I will refer to presently.

3. In my book, *Eating and Drinking with Jesus. An Ethical and Biblical Inquiry*, I endeavored to follow Barth's direction. A friend of mine has told me that he is embarking on a book on prayer. Courageous man! I suspect that prayer needs to be de-mythologized as much as baptism and the Supper. I hope he avoids talking about the sacrament or mystery of prayer and about prayer as a means of grace. And if he writes about the power of prayer he had better handle it with kid gloves. Incidently Barth teaches that prayer in a hope in Christ's promise of forgiveness and redemption is as integral to baptism as obedience to his command to repent, believe and confess (cf. Lk. 3:21; Acts 22:16; I Peter 3:21).

4. Obviously Barth's theological premises need to be tested by a careful exegesis of Scripture, especially of texts that *could* be interpreted sacramentally. This has been done, first by the son and then by the father. Cf. for example the latter's exegesis of Mark 16:16 and I Peter 3:21 which speak of baptism as saving, along with texts that speak about saving one's soul. (Mk. 8:35), saving the soul of another (Jas. 5:20), and working out one's own salvation (Phil. 2:22) and of the saving power ascribed to preaching (I Cor. 1:21; I Thess. 2:16) and especially to faith (Lk. 7:50, 8:12; Rom. 10:9). Barth declares that this can, may and should be done, not because human work has the power of God (Rom. 1:18) within it, but because it is grounded in it, because it is made possible by it, because it takes place in correspondence with it (IV, 4, p. 122). When in the footnote on p. 43 of this paper I spoke of handling the saving power of prayer with kid gloves, I had in mind Jas. 5:15ff. When texts are taken out of the context of the Scriptural witness to Jesus Christ, they can be used to prove justification and salvation by human works, including preaching, baptism and the Lord's Supper.

4

LA PRIÈRE "AU NOM DE JÉSUS"
SELON L'ÉVANGILE DE JEAN
(XIII,31 - XVI)

Oscar Cullmann

Depuis les temps les plus anciens l'Eglise a l'habitude de terminer ses prières par les mots que nous trouvons souvent dans les Epîtres pauliniennes: "par Jésus-Christ notre Seigneur" et qui trop souvent ne sont plus aujourd'hui qu'une formule dont le sens est oublié, alors qu'ils sont propres à rendre nos prières beaucoup plus ferventes, plus vivantes. Ils est d'autant plus nécessaire d'étudier à fond ce que signifie la recommandation que le Christ, avant de quitter la terre, fait aux disciples avec une insistance particulière, de prier désormais le Père "en son nom".[1] Elle fait partie des "consolations" destinées à les convaincre qu'il ne les laissera pas "orphelins" après son départ (chap. 14,18). Sa présence permanente parmi eux sera réalisée de différentes manières: par l'amour des uns pour les autres qui, étant l'amour même du Christ, les unira avec lui (chap. 13,34s.); par l'envoi du Saint Esprit le "Consolateur" (*parakletos*); enfin précisément par la prière au nom du Christ qui, dans ce contexte, apparaît comme la grande consolation assurant sa présence au milieu d'eux. Cette présence équivant en elle-même à l'exaucement de la prière.

Plusieurs fois la nécessité du lien de la prière avec le nom du Christ est répétée: chap. 14,13: "Ce que vous demanderez *en mon nom*, je le ferai"; chap. 14,14: "ce que vous me demandez *en mon nom*, c'est moi qui le ferai"; chap. 15,16: "ce que vous demandez au Père *en mon nom*, il vous le donne"; chap. 16,23: "ce que vous demandez au père, il vous le donnera *en mon nom*"; chap. 16,24: "jusqu'à présent vous n'avez rien demandé *en mon nom*."

Pour nous rendre compte de la signification exacte de cette recommandation de prier "en son nom", nous devons connaître d'abord le sens du *"nom"*, ensuite celui de l'expression *"au nom de"*, puis plus précisément des mots *"au nom du Christ"*.

Nous ne pouvons pas entrer dans le détail des résultats des travaux consacrés au problème du "nom" dans les différentes religions. Je me borne à ce qui est propre à éclairer la question dont nous nous occupons, et je ne citerai que les plus importants parmi les nombreux textes qui entrent en ligne de compte.[2]

Le "nom" désigne d'une manière générale tout ce qui caractérise celui qui le porte, l'ensemble de ses attributs, l'essence profonde de son être et ses fonctions fondamentales (Matth. 10,41).[3] Par son "nom", la divinité manifeste sa présence et sa puissance, tout le côté tourné vers l'homme. Dans l'Ancien Testament, le nom de Dieu est dans le temple (1.Rois 8,29). Le mot hébraïque pour "nom" (*šem*) peut devenir la désignation pour Dieu, son nom lui-même ne devant pas être prononcé. "Sanctifier son nom" (Notre Père, Matth. 6,9) c'est répandre, en écartant toute profanation par le péché, la vénération de tous les attributs qu'il comporte.

Dans le Nouveau Testament, le nom de Dieu est lié à l'oeuvre qu'il accomplit par le Christ: sa présence, sa puissance, tout son être. Nous pouvons aussi dire vice-versa que le nom du Christ, sa personne et son oeuvre, est identique avec le nom du Père en ce qui concerne l'oeuvre du salut (Jean 17,6,26). Ainsi précisément dans l'évangile de Jean, chap. 12, 28, Jésus prie Dieu de "glorifier son nom (de Dieu)" en permettant au Fils d'achever sa mission sur la terre, et dans la prière sacerdotale, chap. 17,1, il dira: "glorifie ton fils", exactement dans le sens de "glorifie ton nom". L'unité si fortement soulignée dans le quatrième évangile entre le Père et le Fils est donc en rapport avec la manifestation du nom de Dieu en Jésus-Christ.

Le nom du Christ est exprimé par l'appellation "Fils de Dieu" dans Hébr. 1,4ss., et surtout par l'appellation "Seigneur" (*Kyrios*) dans l'hymne christologique de Phil. 2,6ss.: "le nom qui est au-dessus de tout nom" est conféré par Dieu au Christ, qui est "plus qu'élevé" à la suite de son "obéissance jusqu'à la mort sur la croix" (Phil. 2,8-10), et le v. 11 spécifie que c'est le nom de *Kyrios*, en hébreu *Adonaj*, qui désigne Dieu lui-même; toute la puissance divine est donnée au Christ à qui tous les êtres sont désormais soumis. Ainsi cette conception du nom du Christ, liée à celle du nom de Dieu, fait dire à Pierre dans les Actes 4,12 qu'"aucun autre nom de peut être donné pourque nous soyons sauvés que le nom de Jésus-Christ le Nazaréen". Dans l'Apocalypse l'église de Pergame est louée par ce qu'elle "garde ferme le nom" (Apoc. 2,13). Ce nom doit être annoncé partout (Actes 9,15). "Croire au nom de Jésus-Christ" (Jean 1,12; 2,23; 1.Jean 5,13 etc.), c'est croire à sa messianité, à l'oeuvre accomplie par lui en parfaite unité avec le Père. C'est la raison pour laquelle l'expression "ceux qui invoquent le nom du Christ" (1.Cor. 1,2; Rom. 10,13;

Actes 2,21), qui implique aussi la souffrance pour ce nom (Mc. 13,13), est une des premières appellations des chrétiens.[4]

Que signifie d'une façon générale la formule agir ou parler *au nom de* quelqu'un" qui nous rapproche de l'expression johannique "prier *au nom* du Christ"? Elle peut vouloir dire: agir ou parler à la place de celui qui porte le nom, mais plus souvent c'est ce dernier qui est censé être présent auprès de (ou même en) celui qui agit ou parle "en son nom". Ainsi dans Dt. 18,18 Dieu dit à Moïse en visant le prophète qu'il suscitera: "si quelqu'un n'ecoute pas la parole qu'il dira en mon nom, c'est moi qui lui demanderai compte."[5] L'expression "au nom de" évoque donc la *présence* spirituelle du porteur du nom. Les significations "par la puissance de", "sur l'ordre de" (Mc. 11,10 par.; Jean 5,43), le sens plus juridique de "se réclamant de", "en appelant à" en sont dérivés. Quelquefois la présence spirituelle peut se réduire à un simple souvenir, comme dans certaines prières juives rappelant les noms des patriarches. Parfois plusieurs de ces significations s'appliquent à un même texte.

Nous retrouvons cette même variété de sens dans l'emploi de la formule néo-testamentaire "au nom de *Jésus-Christ*". Elle évoque en tout cas tout ce que nous avons dit du "nom" du Christ. On agit et parle au nom du Christ, lorsqu'on le fait en recourant à sa personne et à son oeuvre rendues présentes. Ainsi Jésus peut dire dans Jean 14,26, le Père enverra le Saint Esprit "en mon nom". La signification précise de la formule peut varier selon le contexte: dans les récits de miracles: "par la puissance du Christ" ou même "sur son ordre" (par ex. Actes 3,6; Luc. 10,17): à propos du baptême c'est l'idée d'"appartenance au Christ" qui prédomine. La préposition grecque pour "dans" peut changer[6] sans que le sens en soit fondamentalement différent.

On a essayé de considérer l'expression au nom de Jésus comme telle comme une formule magique, comme si le fait seul de la prononcer avait été censé produire l'effet miraculeux, ce qui en rapprocherait l'usage de certaines pratiques courantes dans le paganisme.[7] Il est exact que l'exemple qui en abusent, en prophétisant ou en accomplissant des miracles au nom de Jésus, des faux prophètes (Matth. 7,22) pourrait parler en faveur de cette thèse. Mais comme le dira l'apôtre Paul à propos de la confession du "Seigneur" (*Kyrios*), la "confession de la bouche" doit être accompagnée de "la foi du coeur" (Rom. 10,9). Ainsi dans Mc. 9,38s. celui qui chasse les démons sans faire partie du groupe des disciples, n'est pas, selon la réponse de Jésus (v. 39) dépourvu d'un rapport intérieur avec lui, et dans Actes 3,16 Pierre dit que c'est par la *foi* en le nom de Jésus que ce nom a produit la guérison.

Cette foi en l'efficacité actuelle de l'oeuvre accomplie
par Jésus incarné et en l'efficacité du rôle du Christ élevé
à la droite de Dieu implique la conviction de sa *présence* parmi les siens promise pour le temps après sa mort. D'une façon
ou d'une autre elle est à l'arrière-plan de la plupart des
textes cités. La promesse est explicitée dans Matth. 18,20:
"là ou deux ou trois sont réunis 'en mon nom' je suis au
milieu d'eux." L'exhortation que S. Paul adresse aux Thessa-
loniciens dans 2. Thess. 3,6, et la décision relative au grave
cas d'inceste, 1.Cor. 5,4, se fait "au nom du Seigneur Jésus-
Christ", c'est-à-dire en présence du Christ glorifié. "Tout
ce que les membres de la communauté entreprennent en paroles
et en actes doit se faire au nom du Seigneur Jésus", c'est-
à-dire en sa présence (Col. 3,16; Eph. 5,20), aussi les actions de grâce (*eucharistountes*).

Nous arrivons ainsi, après ce long, mais indispensable
détour, à la *prière au nom du Christ dans le quatrième évangile*. Nous devrons nous souvenir de toutes les significations
que nous avons trouvées dans le Nouveau Testament pour la conception du "nom" et surtout pour l'expression "au nom du
Christ". La diversité des aspects s'applique aussi à la
prière. Mais le cadre de l'évangile de Jean et plus spécialement des discours d'adieux dans lequel la recommandation
se trouve (chap. 14,13-14; 15,7,16; 16,23,24) lui donnent une
profondeur particulière. Pour comprendre l'insistance sur la
nécessité de prier au nom du Christ, il faut connaître d'une
part les idées johanniques sur l'unité entre le Père et le
Fils et sur le rôle du Saint Esprit, d'autre part il faut
tenir compte de la situation caractérisée par la départ du
Christ.

"Jusqu'à présent vous n'avez rien demandé en mon nom,"
dit Jésus au chap. 16,23. C'est que cette prière n'était pas
nécessaire tant que Jésus était avec les disciples sur la
terre en chair et en os. Lorsqu'ils priaient Dieu, Jésus
incarné se trouvait auprès d'eux. Désormais, son oeuvre terrestre étant accomplie, sa *présence spirituelle* sera nécessaire, lorsqu'ils prieront le Père. Elle devra donc être in-
voquée. C'est dire que "prier en son nom" signifie d'abord:
prier en implorant sa présence.

Cela présuppose que nous avons besoin d'une aide lorsque
nous prions. Cette idée paulinienne que l'homme est incapable
par ses propres moyens de parler à Dieu,[8] est aussi impliquée
ici. Nous ne pouvons pas prier en notre propre nom, nous devons prier au nom du Christ.[9]

Dans presque tous les textes que nous avons cités, cette
prière au nom du Christ s'adresse au *Père*, dans un seul, chap.

14,14 (et pas dans tous les manuscrits) au Christ. Tout en
priant le Père, nous devons concentrer en même temps notre
pensée sur le Christ, sa personne et son oeuvre. *Nous devons
le voir pour ainsi dire à côté de nous*, afin que notre prière
ne soit pas un monologue. Car nous devons nous rappeler
l'idée johannique, si fondamentale, soulignée précisément
dans les discours d'adieux: *nous connaissons le Père par le
Christ*. Lorsque au chap. 14,8ss. Philippe demande au Christ:
"montre-nous le Père", il obtient la réponse: "celui qui m'a
vu, a vu le Père". Nous retrouvons la prière "en vérité" du
chap. 4,24, c'est-à-dire dans la vraie connaissance de Dieu
révélée en Jésus-Christ. Sur le plan du Nouveau Testament, on
ne saurait se représenter Dieu *en tant qu'il nous regarde* sans
se représenter en même temps Jésus-Christ, son action passée
et actuelle rendue présentes pour nous. Car nous avons vu
que, dans le Nouveau Testament, le "nom" de Dieu c'est Dieu
en tant qu'il est tourné vers l'homme, et c'est précisément
ainsi que le Prologue de l'évangile de Jean décrit la fonction
et l'être du Logos, du Verbe: il est Dieu qui parle, qui
agit, qui se révèle.

Nos prières deviendront plus ferventes, de vrais dia-
logues, si nous prenons davantage au sérieux les mots "par
Jésus-Christ", si vraiment nous voyons Jésus-Christ se tenant
à côté de nous dans nos prières pour intercéder pour nous,
pour nous assister dans nos prières. Nous prions Dieu en
celui qui par son humanité est tout à fait proche de nous et
que nous pouvons nous représenter selon le témoignage des
évangiles. Ainsi la nécessité de l'incarnation de Dieu de-
vient manifeste dans la prière au nom du Christ.

Dans Jean 14,12 nous trouvons cette affirmation hardie du
Christ selon laquelle, après sa mort, les siens accompliront
non seulement les mêmes, mais de plus grandes oeuvres que
celles qu'il a accomplies pendant sa vie terrestre, et cela
non pas *bien qu'il* les quitte, mais *parce qu'il* les quitte:
"*car* je vais auprès du Père". Ce verset est suivi immediate-
ment de la promesse, même répétée au v. 14, de l'exaucement
"de la prière en son nom". C'est dire que sa présence spirituelle rendra infiniment plus efficaces aussi toutes les
prières des disciples.

Dans le contexte des discours d'adieux, cette présence du
Christ se manifeste par celle du *Saint Esprit*-Consolateur. Il
y a un lien étroit entre le Christ et le Saint Esprit: "c'est
de ce qui est à moi qu'il prend" (chap. 16,14). Il est envoyé
par le Père "au nom du Christ" (chap. 14,26). Ici cela signifie: sur la demande du Christ: "je demanderai au Père, et il
vous l'enverra" (chap. 14,16). Bien que le rapport de cet envoi du Saint Esprit avec la prière, si important pour l'apôtre

Paul (Rom. 8,12ss.) ne soit pas explicitement établi dans ces chapitres, il est clairement suggéré par toute l'argumentation de l'instruction qu'ils contiennent et dans laquelle la promesse de la venue du Saint Esprit alterne avec celle de l'exaucement de la prière au nom du Christ.[10] La présence permanente du Saint Esprit ("pour toujours" *eis ton aiôna*, chap. 14,16) correspond à celle de la présence du Christ dans "la prière en son nom". C'est le Saint Esprit ("Esprit de vérité" chap. 14,17; 16,13) "qui conduira (les disciples) dans toute la vérité" (chap. 16,13), cette vérité dans laquelle "les vrais adorateurs doivent adorer le Père" (chap. 4,23s.). C'est lui qui doit inspirer le contenu de notre prière, et ainsi ce sera une prière "selon la volonté" du fils de Dieu, dont parle la première epître de Jean (chap. 5,14) et à propos de laquelle il est dit qu'"il nous écoute".[11] "Selon sa volonté": c'est là ce que S. Paul appelle prier "comme il faut" (Rom. 8,26).

D'autre part il convient de rappeler que le mot grec employé dans les discours d'adieux pour désigner le Saint Esprit (*Parakletos*) signifie aussi "avocat", celui qui "intercède". Dans 1.Jean 2,1 Jésus-Christ lui-même est appelé Parakletos. Il intercede pour nous auprès du Père, mais ici l'intercession ne se rapporte pas spécialement au contenu de nos prières. Ce rapport est présupposé cependant dans Jean 11,22 où Marthe dit à Jésus au sujet de Lazare: "Je sais que tout ce que tu demandes à Dieu, il te le donnera", et au v. 42 du même chapitre le Christ dit lui-même au Père: "Je savais que tu m'écoutes toujours."[12] Il s'agit de l'intercession pour Lazare.

L'*exaucement* de l'intercession du Christ garantit l'exaucement de la prière que les siens font "en son nom". *Car sa présence, l'union avec lui est en elle-même l'exaucement de toute prière particulière.* Pour cette raison, les nombreux textes que nous avons cités n'invitent pas seulement à prier au nom du Christ, mais ils promettent tous l'exaucement: chap. 14,13 et 14: "ce que vous demanderez en mon nom, *je le ferai*"; chap. 15,7: "si vous restez en moi..., ce que vous voulez demander, *vous sera accordé*"; chap. 15,16: "ce que vous demanderez au Père en mon nom, *il vous le donnera*"; chap. 16,23: "ce que vous demanderez au Père, *il vous le donnera en mon nom*"; chap. 16,24: "demandez, et *vous recevrez*".

Avec quelques variantes, la même promesse d'exaucement se retrouve dans les évangiles synoptiques, dans Matth. 7,7: "demandez, il *vous sera donné*..."; Matth. 7,8 par.: "quiconque demande, *reçoit*"; Matth. 18,19: "si deux d'entre vous s'accordent sur la terre pour une chose quelconque qu'ils demanderont, elle leur *sera accordée* de la part de mon Père..."; Matth. 21,22 (v. Mc. 11,24): "tout ce que vous demanderez dans la

rière en croyant, *vous le recevrez*". Le grand accord exis-
ant sur ce point entre l'évangile de Jean et les évangiles
ynoptiques prouve que cette promesse si souvent répétée par
ésus dans les quatre évangiles remonte à une tradition com-
une.[13] L'addition des mots "en mon nom" dans l'évangile de
ean[14] provient, comme nous le savons maintenant, de la per-
pective des discours d'adieux.[15]

Qui exauce la prière, le Père ou le Fils? Dans l'évan-
;ile de Jean c'est une question sans importance. De même que
a prière s'adresse généralement au Père, mais qu'exceptionel-
ement elle peut être adressée au Fils,[16] cette alternance que
ious constatons, dans les textes cités, aussi en ce qui con-
erne l'exaucement, s'explique précisément par tout ce qu'im-
liquent les mots "en mon nom", en rapport avec l'idée johan-
ique que le Père est reconnu dans le Fils.[17]

A propos des miracles accomplis "au nom du Christ", nous
vons vu[18] qu'il ne suffit pas de prononcer la formule. Sans
a foi pas de miracle; de même sans la foi pas d'exaucement.
)ans les textes parallèles des synoptiques cités tout à
.'heure (Mc. 11,24; Matth. 21,22), l'exaucement est empressé-
ient lié à la foi qui transporte des montagnes, au fait de
croire qu'on a (déjà) reçu" ce qui fait l'objet de la prière.
après ce que nous avons dit des miracles "au nom du Christ",
.l ne fait pas de doute que la foi est présupposée aussi dans
es textes johanniques sur la prière, bienque cette condition
i'y soit pas mentionnée. Elle est impliquée par la condition
ondamentale de l'exaucement de la prière "au nom du Christ":
être *uni* avec le Christ comme les sarments sont attachés au
:ep (chap. 15,1ss.).[19]

Les disciples doivent "rester dans *l'amour du Christ*"
(chap. 15,10). Cela signifie aussi que pour prire au nom du
;hrist, ils doivent s'aimer les *uns les autres* selon "le com-
nandement nouveau" qui introduit les discours d'adieux (chap.
.3,34s.). Cet aspect de l'union avec le Christ, l'amour con-
lition essentielle de l'exaucement, est mentionné expressé-
nent dans le texte synoptique cité Matth. 18,19 "si deux
l'entre vous s'accordent" pour leur demande, elle leur sera
accordée.

NOTES

1.   Col. 3,17 (Eph. 5,20) prouve que l'expression "par Jésus-Christ" est identique avec "au nom du Seigneur Jésus".

2.   Voir l'article *onoma* dans ThWb Kittel.

3.   Voir le jugement divin sur les hommes dont les "noms" sont inscrits dans les cieux" (Luc. 10,20), dans "le livre de vie" (Apoc. 3,5; Phil. 4,3).

4.   Voir sur cette appellation qui inclut en même temps une prière et une confession, mon article "All who call upon the name of our Lord Jesus Christ", Journal of Ecumenical Studies, Pittsburgh, 1964.

5.   R. Schnackenburg, Das Johannesevangelium III, 1975, p. 82 cite ce texte précisément à propos de Jean 14,13.

6.   Dans Matth. 7,22 il y a seulement le datif sans préposition.   Pour le baptême il y a surtout *eis*, avec la nuance "en vue de" (Matth. 28,19; Actes 8,16; 19,5; 1.Cor. 1, 13ss.); mais aussi *en* (Actes 10,48) et *epi* (Actes 2,38, variante B C D: *en*).

7.   Voir W. Heitmüller, Im Namen Jesu, eine sprach- und religionsgeschichtliche Untersuchung zum Neuen Testament, 1903.

8.   Voir mon article "La prière selon les Epîtres pauliniennes", ThZ 1979, p. 90ss.

9.   Au chap. 15,7 les mots "en mon nom" manquent: "ce que vous voulez demander, vous sera accordé".   Mais la promesse est précédée des mots: "si vous restez en moi...".   Cela confirme que l'expression "en mon nom" qui est contenue dans tous les textes parallèles, vise effectivement l'union du disciple qui prie, avec le Christ.

10.   Tel est aussi l'avis de R. Schnackenburg, Das Johannesevangelium III, 1975, p. 181, p. 40.

11.   Le verset précédent (13) s'adresse d'ailleurs à ceux qui croient *au nom* du Fils de Dieu.

12.   Peut-être faut-il comprendre à partir de là le verset 16,26[b] qui a priori n'est pas clair.   Après avoir répété que

les disciples le prieront en son nom, le Christ dit: "je ne
vous dis pas que je demanderai au Père (je le prierai) pour
vous". "Car", continue-t-il (v. 27) "le Père lui-même vous
aime parce que vous m'avez aimé". Le sens pourrait être
celui-ci: Le Christ est si intimement lié avec le Père que
celui-ci exauce toujours *toute* prière prononcée *au nom du
Christ* sans que le Christ ait à intervenir expressément (voir
chap. 11,42). Autrement dit: toute prière au nom du Christ
implique une intercession du Christ en sorte que Dieu est mis
en rapport direct avec celui qui prie. - Autrefois j'ai pro-
posé une explication tout à fait différente qui ne serait pas
impossible, à savoir de comprendre ce verset 26 comme une
question: "ne vous dis-je pas que prierai le Père pour vous?"
        La difficulté du passage provient du fait que le
verbe *erotān* a la double signification de "questionner" et
"demander" dans le sens de "prier" pour lequel il y a comme
synonyme courant dans ces chapitres *aitein*.

13. C. H. Dodd, p. 349ss. admet également comme base com-
mune, une forme primitive plus ancienne.

14. Dans 15,7 et 16,24 où ils manquent, ils sont mani-
festement sous entendus. D'autre part il convient de souligner-
ner que Matth. 18,19 est suivi de la parole sur la présence de
Jésus au milieu de "ceux qui sont rassemblés *en son nom*". Le
parallelisme avec les textes johanniques est frappant. Car
bien que "en mon nom" soit rattaché à "rassemblés", le contexts (verset précédent!) parle de la *prière*.

15. V. plus haut p. 55.

16. V. plus haut p. 56.

17. V. plus haut p. 52. En 16,23 le Père *exaucera* "au
nom du Christ". Les mots ont ici le même sens que dans la
parole sur l'envoi du Paraklet par le Père "au nom du Christ"
(chap. 16,26) et impliquent l'intercession du Christ.

18. Voir plus haut p. 53.

19. De même "l'observation des commandements" indiquée
comme motif de l'exaucement (1.Jean 3,22), ainsi que la nécessité déjà mentionnée de prier "selon la volonté" du Fils de
Dieu (1.Jean 5,14) ne sont que des aspects particuliers du
fait d'être uni au Christ.

5

THE TERRITORIAL DIMENSION OF JUDAISM

W. D. Davies

We shall here attempt to assess the nature and place within Judaism of the doctrine which in various ways asserts there is a special relationship (later to be described) among the God of Israel, the People of Israel, and the Land of Israel. Is that relationship primary or secondary, dispensable or indispensable? Was the territorial doctrine of Judaism one which could be ignored as necessity dictated, simply accidental and peripheral, or an aspect of Judaism without which it would cease to be itself?[*]

At first encounter the question would seem to be easily open to strict historical investigation and an unequivocal answer. Sources for the understanding of Judaism are abundant: the practice of Jews as it bears upon *Eretz Israel* has been and is open to public and private scrutiny. One would have thought that the proposed question could long ago have been settled. In the course of Jewish history and especially in this century, however, certain unavoidable factors have impinged upon Judaism which have both clouded and clarified the issue and compelled caution.

I

THE MARKED THEOLOGICAL TRADITION

Let us begin with the doctrine itself. Despite the vicissitudes of Jewish history, the sacred documents on which religious Jews have rested--the Tanak, the Mishnah, the Mid-

---

[*]My friend Markus Barth has long corresponded and discussed with me this and similar themes. This tribute is offered to him with deep gratitude for his personal stimulus and for his enthusiasm for the continued dialogue between Christians and Jews.

rashim and the Talmud--the liturgies which they have constantly celebrated, and the observances which they have kept across
the centuries all point to The Land as an essential aspect of
Judaism. The reader is referred to our work on *The Gospel and
the Land; Early Christianity and Jewish Territorial Doctrine*
(Berkeley, 1974) for a fuller treatment of the evidence.[1]
Here we merely summarize the main points of the evidence in
defence of the position indicated.

A. *The Evidence of the Classical Sources of Judaism.*
It would be impossible within the limits of this article to
examine the different ways in which the importance of the doctrine of The Land emerges in the Tanak. It finds its fundamental expression in the Pentateuch,[2] but is also abundantly
reflected in the other documents of the Tanak. Two elements
in the understanding of The Land are central. First, The Land
is regarded as promised, or more accurately, as sworn by Yahweh to the people of Israel. The history of the tradition concerning Yahweh's promise, on which there is no widespread critical agreement, is complex. The most probable development
seems to be from the recognition of a promise of a territorial
patrimony to Abraham, to that of a more extensive territory to
the people of Israel probably under the impact of Davidic imperial ambitions. Alongside the belief in the promise, the
conviction prevailed that this promised land belonged especially to Yahweh. Not only did it necessarily belong to Him, as
did all lands which He had called into being, but it was His
peculiar possession to give to His own people: the election
of the people was bound up with His promise to give His own
land to them.[3] Out of the combination (nay--fusion)[4] of the
three elements which were involved in the promise--God, the
People, and The Land--there emerged what has to be regarded as
an essential belief of religious Jews of the first century and
later, that is, of the indissolubility or eternity of the connection between these three realities.

    This belief comes to clearest expression in the Rabbinic
sources, the Mishnah, the Midrashim, and the Talmud. This is
remarkable and significant because across many centuries the
Sages, the authors and preservers of those sources, for very
good reasons had increasingly suspected any disturbing concentration on hopes for a return to The Land in any messianic
context as a delusion and snare likely to distract their
people from the essential task of living obedience to the
Torah. As we shall later insist, they had accepted the need
to acquiesce in the exiled life and to cooperate in foreign
lands with foreign rulers. But paradoxically, they continued
to shower their praises on The Land, emphatically expressing
their concern for it, and recognizing the ultimate indissolu-

bility of Israel's connection with it. The initial stimulus
for this concern has been especially connected with the destruction of The Land by the Romans in the war from 66 to 70
C.E. Conditions in Palestine after 70 C.E. were economically
very difficult. As a result there developed an increasing
tendency for Jews to emigrate from Palestine to neighbouring
countries, especially Syria. The need to encourage Jews to
remain in The Land, and not to depart from areas in it where
they were permitted to live, was so urgent that the Pharisaic
leaders adopted a policy of extolling the virtues of The Land
and encouraging settlement in it.[5] But important as they were,
economic factors are not to be regarded as the sole or even
main reason for the emergence of the doctrine with which we
are concerned. As we have indicated, the roots of the emphasis on The Land are deep in the Tanak. The Tannaitic and
other sources build on the Scriptures even though they respond
also to economic and political realities. They point to the
significance of The Land in the most unambiguous way. There
is a kind of "umbilical cord" between Israel and The Land.[6]
It is no accident that one-third of the Mishnah, the Pharisaic
legal code, is connected with The Land. Nine-tenths of the
first order of the Mishnah, *Zeraim* (Seeds), of the fifth order,
Kodashim (Hallowed Things), and of the sixth order, *Tohoroth*
(Cleannesses), deal with laws concerning The Land, and there
is much of the same in the other parts of the Mishnah. This
is no accident, because the connection between Israel and The
Land was not fortuitous, but part of the divine purpose or
guidance, as was the Law itself. The choice of Israel and the
Temple and of The Land was deliberate, the result of Yahweh's
planning. The connection between Yahweh, Israel, The Land,
Sinai, the Temple is primordial: it is grounded in a necessity of the divine purpose and is, therefore, inseverable (Lev
Rabbah 13:2). And it is no wonder that the Rabbis heaped upon
The Land terms of honor and endearment. For them The Land of
Israel is called simply *Hâ-âretz*, The Land; all countries outside it are *hûtz lâ-âretz*, outside The Land. In T. B. Berakoth 5a we read: "It has been taught: R. Simeon b. Yohai
says: The Holy One, blessed be He, gave Israel three pre-
cious gifts, and all of them were given only through sufferings. These are: The Torah, the Land of Israel, and the
World to Come...."

We have seen that behind the glorification of The Land
stood passages in the Scriptures. But, in addition to this,
two factors could not but increasingly stamp The Land upon the
consciousness of Israel. The first is that the Law itself, by
which Jews lived, was so tied to The Land that it could not
but recall The Land. As we have already stated, one-third of
the Mishnah deals with The Land and all the agricultural laws
in it, as those of Scripture itself do. Consider Lev. 19:23,

23:10 and 22, 25:2 and Deut. 26:1. These verses make it clear
that the agricultural laws are to apply "in the land". Further, only in Palestine could there be cities of refuge, which
were so important in the civil law (Num. 35:9f., Deut. 4:41f.,
19:1f.). True, there are laws not contingent upon The Land;
and the distinction between these and their opposite was
clearly recognized. But the reward for the observance of the
laws was "life in the land", as is implied in Mishnah Kiddushin 1:9-10. The Law itself, therefore, to use current terminology, might be regarded as an effective symbol of The Land:
it served as a perpetual call to The Land.

But, secondly, precisely because it was The Land to which
the Law most applied, The Land gained in sanctity. In Mishnah
Kiddushin 1:9-10--in the references to the land, the walled
cities of the land, the wall of Jersualem, the Temple Mount,
the Rampart, the Court of Women, the Court of the Israelites,
etc.--it is the connection with an enactment of the Law that
determines the degree of its holiness. And, for our purposes
especially, it is noteworthy that it is the applicability of
the Law to The Land in 1:6 that assures its special holiness.
The implication is that Jewish sanctity is only fully possible
in The Land: outside The Land only strictly personal laws can
be fulfilled, that is, the moral law, sexual law, Sabbath law,
circumcision, dietary laws, etc. Of necessity, outside The
Land territorial laws have to be neglected. The exiled life
is, therefore, an emaciated life, even though, through suffering, it atones. A passage in R. B. Sotah 14a expresses this
point of view in dealing with Moses' failure to enter The Land.
Moses, outside The Land, is a suffering servant who atones.

In the light of the above, it is not surprising that both
the gift of prophecy--the gift of the Holy Spirit--and the gift
of resurrection of the dead were by some connected with The
Land. For example, Mekilta Pisha I reveals both the affirmation of Israel as the only land fit for prophecy and the dwelling of the Shekinah, and efforts made to deal with the difficulties such a position confronted: for example, the fact that
Yahweh had appeared outside The Land.

Again, in the view of some Rabbis, the resurrection was
to take place first in The Land, and the benefits of The Land
in death are many (Gen. Rabbah 96:5). Some urged that those
who died outside The Land would not rise: but even an alien
(Canaanitish) slave girl who dwelt in The Land might expect to
share in the resurrection (T. B. Ketuboth 111a). At the end
of the second century Rabbi Meir, at his death, required that
his remains should be cast into the sea off the Palestinian
coast, lest he be buried in foreign soil. There is no space
or necessity here to enlarge further. The desire to die in

The Land, to possess the soil, to make pilgrimages to it, all these manifestations of attachment to The Land history attests. Enough has been written to indicate that the primary documents of Judaism--the Tanak and Tannaitic Midrashim, and the Talmud-- are unequivocal in their recognition that The Land is essential to the true fulfillment of the life to which Israel was called.

B. *The Liturgy and the Observance.* The liturgical practice of the Synagogue points to the same witness. Throughout the centuries, beginning with the fall of Jerusalem in C.E. 70, the conscious cultivation of the memory of The Land, concentrated in Jerusalem and the Temple, has continued in Judaism. The Rabbis at Jamnia, in demanding that the *Tefillah* or *Shemoneh Esreh* should be said three times a day, morning, afternoon, and evening (Mishnah Berakoth 4:1ff.), had in mind, among other things, the perpetual remembrances of Jerusalem and The Land. The *Shemoneh Esreh* for the morning and afternoon service corresponded to the morning and afternoon daily whole-offerings in the Temple. There was no time fixed for the evening *Shemoneh Esreh*, but on Sabbaths and Festivals the *Shemoneh Esreh* was to be said four times (there being demanded an Additional Tefillah corresponding to the "Addition Offering" presented on those days in the ancient Temple). Three times daily, then, the Jew was required to pray; among other things, he was required to repeat the 14th Benediction (dated by Dugmore in 168-165 B.C.), the 16th (possibly pre-Maccabean), and the 18th (C.E. 40-70). These read as follows:

> Be merciful, O Lord our God, in Thy great mercy, towards Israel Thy people, and towards Jerusalem Thy city, and towards Zion the abiding place of Thy glory, and towards Thy temple and Thy habitation, and towards the kingdom of the house of David, the righteous anointed one. Blessed art Thou, O Lord God of David, the builder of Jerusalem. *Benediction* 14.

> Accept [us], O Lord our God, and dwell in Zion; and may Thy servants serve Thee in Jerusalem. Blessed art Thou, O Lord, whom in reverent fear we serve [or, worship]. *Benediction* 16.

> Bestow Thy peace upon Israel Thy people and upon Thy city and upon Thine inheritance, and bless us, all of us together. Blessed art Thou, O Lord, who makest peace. *Benediction* 18.

That there was a deliberate concern with Jerusalem appears
from the text in Mishnah Berakoth 4:1ff., where the rules concerning the *Shemoneh Esreh*, indicated above, are set forth,
and where Mishnah Berakoth 4:5 states that, according to R.
Joshua (C.E. 80-120):

> If [a man] was riding on an ass [when the
> time for the prayer is upon him] he should
> dismount [to say the Tefillah: Danby].
> If he cannot dismount he should turn his
> face [toward Jerusalem]; and if he cannot
> turn his face, he should direct his heart
> toward the Holy of Holies.

The centrality of the land is clear. The same is also emphasized in Num. Rabbah 23:7 on Num. 34:2. The deliberate recalling of the Temple and, thereby of Jerusalem and the land,
in the liturgy also appears from Mishnah Rosh-ha-Shanah 4:1-3
and T. B. Baba Bathra 60b.

Again other elements in the Jewish liturgy came to be
zêker leḥorebbân, that is, in memory of the destruction. For
three weeks of sorrow, ending on the ninth day of the month of
Ab, which is given over entirely, for twenty-four hours, to
fasting, Jews annually recall the destruction of their land.
So much has that event become the quintessence of the suffering of Jewry that the 9th of Ab is recognized as a day on
which disasters recurred again and again to the Jewish people.
Connected with it, significantly, was the decree that the
fathers should not enter the promised land. The passage in
T. B. Ta-anith 29a, which states this, cannot easily be dated.
But it is traced to an unknown Rabbi whose words are explained
by R. Hama b. Hananiah (C.E. 279-320). The pertinent passage
is in Mishnah Ta'anith 4:6-7. As a matter of history only the
fall of Betar (the Beth Tor of the text), the last stronghold
of Bar Cocheba, captured by the Romans in C.E. 135, possibly
occurred on the 9th of Ab. The first Temple was burnt on the
7th of Ab (2 Kings 25:8-9) or on the 10th of that month (Jer.
52:12): the second Temple fell on the 10th (see the dictionaries). The essential feature of the liturgy for the 9th of
Ab (which is the only twenty-four hour fast, apart from the
Day of Atonement) was the reading of Lamentations and dirges.
Later, on the fast of the 9th of Ab, an addition which concen-
trates on Jerusalem still further was made to the service.
The Prayer, as used today, begins with the words:

> O Lord God, comfort the mourners of Zion;
> Comfort those who grieve for Jerusalem.

It ends with:

> Praised are You, who comforts Zion;
> Praised are You, who rebuilds Jerusalem.

So far, in showing how the sentiment for the land remained powerfully active in Judaism after C.E. 70, we have mostly adduced materials from the Haggadah and the liturgy of Rabbinic Judaism. There was also a more specifically halakic approach to the question of the Land. The ramifications of this development we are unfortunately not competent to trace. We can only refer to two items. In the Jerusalem Talmud, in Kilayyim VII:5, ed. Krotoshin (or Venice) 31a, line 32 (Venice, line 25), Orla 1:2, ed. Krotoshin 61a, line 11 (Venice, line 9), there is a law which is quoted as giving to Israel, under Jewish law, a legal right to the Land. The law is translated by Lieberman as: "Though soil cannot be stolen, a man can forfeit his right to this soil by giving up hope of ever regaining it." The argument is that "Israel" "never for a moment gave up hope of regaining the soil of Palestine. Never did they renounce their right to Palestine and never have they ceased claiming it in their prayers and in their teachings. It is on this foundation that [Jews] now claim that Eretz Israel belongs to [them]" (S. Lieberman, Proceedings of the Rabbinical Assembly of America, Vol. 12, 1949). Not unrelated to this law is that of $ha^{a}zak\bar{a}h$ (prescription) in which the legal right of Israel to the Land was sought. (See *Baba Bathra* 28a, and notes in the Soncino translation for $hh^{a}zakah$.) But how early such attempts were and how significant in the discussion of the relationship between Israel and Eretz Israel in the period of our concern we cannot determine. The history of the halakic understanding of that relationship lies beyond the scope of this study, as does the relative place of Haggadah and Halakah in Judaism. (The debate on this question is clarified in J. Neusner, *The Journal of Religion* 59/1, 1979, pp. 71-86, especially pp. 83-84. There Neusner urges that "Halakah is Judaism's primary expression of Theology". Heschel would qualify this.)

Be that as it may be, it is in the Haggadah and the liturgy that the full force of the sentiment for The Land is to be felt. It cannot properly be seen except through Jewish eyes, nor felt except through Jewish words, such as those so powerfully uttered by Abraham Heschel in a book, *Israel: An Echo of Eternity* (New York, 1969), which is more a lyrical outburst than a critical study, and in A. Néher's moving essay, "Israël, terre mystique de l'Absolu" in *L'Existence Juive* (Paris, 1962).

So far we have referred to the evidence of the classical sources of Judaism.[7] The same theological conviction that there is an inseverable connection between Israel, The Land and its God continued to be cherished throughout the medieval period and down to the modern. A rough division has been drawn between two periods. The first stretches up to the last revolt of Jews in the Roman Empire in the hope of re-establishing a Jewish State which followed upon the imposition of harsh anti-Jewish statutes under Justinian (483-565 C.E.), and later the brief three-year reign of Nehemiah, a Messianic figure, in Jerusalem from 614 to 617 C.E. It is legitimate to recognize up to that time a living, if intermittent, hope and violent activity directed towards the actual return of The Land politically to Israel. From then on, especially after the Arab Conquest of The Land in 638 and the building up of the Mosque of Omar on the site of the Temple (in 687-691; a mosque that was to be a center for the Islamic faith), there was, it has been suggested, a change. From then on Jewish devotion to The Land came to express itself for a long period not so much in political activity for the re-establishment of the State of Israel as in voluntary individual pilgrimages and immigrations to The Land.[8] But the division suggested between the two periods indicated must not be made watertight. On the one hand, in the earlier period the Tannaitic and Amoraic sages were wary of political attempts to re-establish the kingdom of Israel in its own land. On the other hand, in the Middle Ages, there was much apocalyptic-messianic speculation and probably much activity aimed at such a re-establishment: the history of this has been largely lost, so that its full strength must remain conjectural even if likely. The extent to which apocalyptic-messianism persisted, to break out finally in Sabbatianism in the 17th century, is only now being recognized, under the influence of the work of Gershom Scholem.[9] It fed into the Zionist movement of our times. What we can be certain of is that *Eretz Israel*, as an object of devotion and intense and religious concern continued to exercise the imagination of Jews after the Fall of Jerusalem in 70 C.E. and after the Arab Conquest: it remained part of the communal consciousness of Jews. In this connection, two facts need to be borne in mind. First, the devotion to The Land, to which we refer, is not to be simply equated with the imaginative notions of other peoples about an ideal land--such as the "Elysium" of Homer, the Afallon of Celtic mythology, the Innisfree of Yeats. Rather it was concentrated on an actual land with a well known history, a land known to be barren and rugged and to offer no easy life although it was transfused because of its chosenness to be Yahweh's own and Israel's as an inheritance from Him. Secondly, the influence of the familiar or customary division of History at the advent of Christ into two periods, B.C. and A.D.,[10] has often tended to create the unconscious assumption among Gentiles that after the first century, Jews *as a people* ceased to have a common history.[11] No less a scholar than Martin Noth saw Israel's history as having come to a ghastly end with the Bar Kokba revolt.[12] But the Jews continued as a people, not simply as a conglomerate of individuals, after that tragic event. The Talmud, the primary document of Judaism in the Middle Ages and afterwards to the present time, concerns itself with the way in which the people of Israel should walk. The Talmud has a communal national reference in its application of the Torah to the actualities of the Jews' existence. Its contents, formation and preservation, presuppose the continuance of the self-conscious unity of the people of Israel. It is this that explains the character of the Talmud: it adds Gemara to Mishnah and Rashi (1040-1105 C.E.) to both, to make the tradition of the past relevant to the present. It is realistically involved with the life of the Jewish people over a thousand years of its history.[13]

And in the devotional life of the Jewish community the relationship to The Land remained central.[14] To trace the various expressions of devotion to The Land among Jews across the centuries is beyond our competence. The most noteworthy is that of pilgrimage. The Law demanded that every male Israelite should make a pilgrimage to Jerusalem three times a year: at Passover, the Feast of Weeks and Tabernacles (Exod. 23:17; Deut. 16:16). During the Second Temple period even Jews of the diaspora sought to observe this demand. (See, for example, Mishnah Taanit 1:3; Jos., *Wars* 6:9; Aboth 5:4.) After the destruction of the Temple pilgrimages especially to the Wailing Wall became occasions for mourning: there were pilgrimages throughout the Middle Ages to other holy places.[15] Individual Jews witness to this, a most famous expression coming in the works of the "God-intoxicated" or "God-kissed" Jehudah Halevi, a Spanish physician born in Toledo in 1086. At the age of fifty, he left his beloved Spain on a perilous pilgrimage to Zion. He died possibly before reaching Jerusalem, but not before expressing his love for The Land and Zion in unforgettable terms such as:

> My heart is in the east, and I in the
>   uttermost west--
> How can I find savour in food? How shall
>   it be sweet to me?
> How shall I render my vows and my bonds,
>   while yet
> Zion lieth beneath the fetter of Edom,
>   and I in Arab chains?

> A light thing would it seem to me
>   to leave all the good things of Spain--
> Seeing how precious in mine eyes it is
>   to behold the dust of the desolate
>   sanctuary.[16]

It was not only single, individual pilgrims who sought The Land but groups of communities, as in the case of Rabbi Meir of Rothenburg who in 1286 C.E. sought to lead a great number of Jews from the area of the Rhine to Israel. Later, in 1523, a messianic movement which aimed at a return to The Land was led by David Reuveni and attracted the interest of communities in Egypt, Spain and Germany. The living Jewish concern to establish an earthly kingdom in Jerusalem may have contributed to the formulation of the seventeenth article of the Confession of Augsburg of 1530.[17] The justification for such a concern was made luminously clear in the astounding response to the Sabbatian movement from the Yemen to Western Europe.[18]

These data to which historians point us cannot be ignored. The relative weight which should be given to the purely *religious* interest in The Land which led individuals and groups to journey to Israel from a desire to experience the mystical or spiritual power of The Land, as over against a political concern to escape and to right the wrongs of exile, we are not competent to assess. Certainly many pious Jews had no directly political concern: their sole aim was to recognize that in The Land a relationship to the eternal was possible as nowhere else. A striking illustration of spiritual concentration on The Land is provided by Rabbi Naḥman of Bratzlov (1772-80), who journeyed to Israel. He asserted that what he had known *before* that journey was insignificant. *Before* there had been confusion; after "he held the Law whole". But all he had desired was direct contact with The Land. This he achieved by simply stepping ashore at Haifa. He desired to return immediately. (Under pressure he stayed and visited Tiberias, but never even went up to Jerusalem.) Again, the celebrated Maharal of Prague (Rabbi Yehuda Liwa of Loew--Ben Bezalel, 1515-1609) understood the nature and role of nations to be ordained by God, as part of the natural order. Nations were intended to cohere rather than to be scattered. Nevertheless, he did not urge a political re-establishment of a state of Israel in The Land: that he left to God. Exile no less than restoration was in His will; the latter *would* come in His good time, but only then. (The promise of The Land would endure eternally: Return was ultimately assured [Lev. 26:44-45].)

To the kind of devotion we have indicated is due that, despite the very real geographical and political obstacles, at no
time since the first century has The Land of Israel been wholly
without a Jewish presence, however diminished. The numbers of
Jews living in The Land throughout the centuries have been very
variously estimated, but James Parkes rightly insisted that
Jews in Palestine across the centuries were forgotten by historians. It is certain that in the nineteenth century, first
under the influence of Rabbi Elijah, Ben Solomon Salman of Vilna, known as the Vilna Gaon (1720-1797), a number of parties of
Jews, soon to be joined by many others, went to Safed in 1808
and 1809. These sought not simply contact with The Land of
which they claimed that "Even in its ruins none can compare
with it",[19] but permanent settlement. Regarding themselves as
representatives of all Jews, they assumed the right to appeal
to other Jews for aid and reinforcement. Some--as in the case
of Rabbi Akiba Schlessinger of Preissburg (1832-1922)--were
driven to go to The Land by the realization of the increasing
impossibility of living according to the Torah in Western society which was becoming increasingly secular. For such The
Land became an escape and a refuge from modernism and secularism, a bulwark for the preservation of the religious tradition. After these early settlements to which we have referred,
there were other efforts by religious Jews to re-enter The Land
whose history cannot be traced here. We must simply note that
the Zionist movement, despite its strongly "nationalistic",
socialistic, and political character is not to be divorced
from this devotion to The Land.[20] We shall deal with this
later.

II

AN INESCAPABLE HISTORICAL DIVERSITY

We have sought in the preceding pages to do justice to the
theological role of territory in Judaism. Jewish theology as
revealed in its major witnesses points to The Land as of the
essence of Judaism. In strictly theological terms, the Jewish
faith could be defined as "a fortunate blend" of a people, a
land and their God. But this view has been criticized because
in any blend an item may be lost, and in the particular blend
referred to, the essential and distinctive significance of The
Land, it has been claimed, could be lost. As in discussions
of the Trinity the personal identity of each member is carefully preserved and not simply "blended", so in our understanding
of Judaism the distinct or separable significance of The Land
must be fully recognized. Judaism held to an election of a

people and of its election to a particular land: Werblowsky
rightly speaks of "une vocation, spirituelle a la géogra-
phie".21

But Jewish theology has had, like the Christian, to find
ways of coming to terms with history. In this section we
shall indicate certain actualities of Jewish history which
must bear upon any answer to the question of the place of The
Land in Judaism.

In the first place, historically the term "Judaism" itself cannot be understood as representing a monolithic faith
in which there has been a simplistic uniformity of doctrine
either demanded or imposed or recognized about The Land, as
about other elements of belief. Certainly this was so at all
periods and in all sections of the Jewish community before 70
C.E. And, despite the overwhelming dominance of the Rabbinic
form of Judaism, the history of the Jews since that date, although not to the same degree, reveals the same fissiparous,
amorphous and unsystematized doctrinal character. The concept
of an adamant, uniform "orthodox" Judaism, which was not
stirred by dissident movements and ideas, and by mystical,
messianic yearnings which expressed themselves outside of or
in opposition to the main, strictly Rabbinic, tradition, is
no longer tenable.22 To define the place of *Eretz Israel* in
Judaism requires the frank recognition that that place has
changed or, more accurately, has received different emphases
among various groups and at different times. However persistent some views of and attachment to The Land have been, and
however uniform the testimony of the classical sources, there
has not been one unchangeable, essential doctrine universally
and uniformly recognized by the whole of Judaism. In the
Middle Ages a controversy which circled around Maimonides
(Rambam) (1135-1204) is illuminating. In his *Dalalat al
Harin*, translated into English as the *Guide to the Perplexed*,
the Great Eagle never concerned himself directly with "The
Land". Although he was so concerned in his commentary on the
Mishnah, his silence about The Land in the *Guide* caused dismay
and dispute among the Rabbis. Nahmanides (1194-1270) was led
to criticize the Great Eagle by insisting that there was a
specific *mitzwah* to settle in The Land, a *mitzwah* which Maimonides had ignored: Nahmanides notes its absence in Maimonides' *Sepher Ha-Mitzwoth*.23 In modern times Reform Judaism
in the United States, anxious to come to terms with Western
culture, was careful to avoid any emphasis on any particularistic elements in Judaism which would set Jews apart from their
Christian neighbors. Until very recently, when external and
internal pressures made themselves felt, the doctrine of The
Land tended to be ignored or spiritualized. It was an embarrassment.

The demotion of The Land, along with the Messianic idea with its disturbing potentialities, was no less evident in the liberal Judaism of nineteenth century Europe. How far the confused and confusing embarrassment with The Land went there, even among Jewish theologians, appears from Hermann Cohen. In 1880 he claimed that Judaism was already in process of forming a "cultural, historical union with Protestantism".[24] It is not surprising that he could write such paradoxical words as the following. *"The loss of the national state is already conditioned by messianism. But this is the basis of the tragedy of Jewish peoplehood in all its historic depth.* How can a people exist and fulfill its messianic task if it is deprived of the common human protection afforded by a state to its people? And yet, just this is the situation of the Jewish people, *and thus it must needs be the meaning of the history* of the Jews, if indeed this meaning lies in messianism."[25] (Our italics.) Cohen was concerned with the State and Judaism, but by implication, he here not only questioned the messianic destiny of Israel in its own land but, even if he still recognized it as a reality, he so domesticated that destiny in his Western Europe that it bore little resemblance to the dynamism of the messianism expressed in previous Jewish history. Cohen's "messianism" eradicated the Davidic Messiah and the hope of a Kingdom of God on earth--and with this any hope for The Land. That the Reform and liberal Judaism in the United States and Europe have recently reintroduced an emphasis on The Land, in response to contemporary events which they could not ignore, cannot obliterate their earlier non-territorial or anti-territorial attitude. Not unrelated to this discussion in the Reform and liberal Judaism, though not directly connected with those movements, is the insistence by such figures as Ahad Ha'Am (1856-1927) that Jews first needed to devote themselves to spiritual renewal not to the occupation of a territory. Ahad Ha'Am founded a select and secret society in 1899 "dedicated to the notion that moral and cultural preparation had to precede the material salvation of the Jews".[26]

Secondly, it is necessary to recognize that the territorial theology with which we are concerned could not but gain increasing attention and therefore emphasis among recent students of Judaism because of the pervasive influence of the Zionist movement. The ascribing of a theological concern with The Land to Jews who entertain no definable Jewish theology or even reject the tradition of their fathers has become insidiously easy, because of the Zionist climate within which so much of modern Jewry lives. The temptation to this ascription has understandably been reinforced by understandable sympathy towards the justification of this doctrine which the suffering of Jews in modern Europe so imperatively calls forth.

But sympathy by itself does not necessarily lead to historical truth. At this point it is well to emphasize the complexity and interpenetration of the many forces which combined to initiate the Zionist movement. It held together apparently irreconcilable points of view in a living tension. Any neat dichotomies between religious and political factors in Zionism are falsifications of their rich and mutually accommodating diversity. To read Gershom Scholem's autobiographical pages,[27] is to be made aware of the impossibility of presenting clean, clear lines in any picture of the Zionist movement. But this much is certain: the territorial theology of Judaism should not be directly ascribed (the qualifying adverb is important) to the many non-religious Jews who played a most significant part in Zionist history. The Zionist movement, which has played so prominent a role in our time, can be effectively dated as initiated by the Congress of Basel in 1897. It grew thereafter until, in 1948, after an abeyance of almost twenty centuries, there emerged the State of Israel. But the role of Jewish territorial doctrine and sentiment in the movement has to be carefully assessed: it can easily be exaggerated. At first it was possible for some of the leading Zionists to contemplate the establishment of a state outside The Land altogether--in Uganda, in Argentina, in newly conquered Russian territories in Asia, in Asiatic Turkey, and in North America.[28] The often silent but almost ubiquitous presence of the religious tradition, with its concentration on *Eretz Israel* caused such to change their minds and made the choice of that land as the Jewish homeland inevitable. Herzl, like other Zionist secularists, was compelled to recognize this.

But Zionism remained an expression not only, and probably not even chiefly, of the theological territorial attachment of Judaism, but even more of the nationalist and socialistic spirit of the nineteenth century. In this sense it is a typical product of that century. An examination of the history of Zionism makes its specifically religious motivation less significant than an uncritical emphasis on territorial-theology would lead one to expect. Gershom Scholem, in reply to an article by Yeuda Bourla, a novelist who died in 1970, wrote:

> I...am opposed, like thousands of other Zionists...to mixing up religious and political concepts. *I categorically deny that Zionism is a messianic movement and that it is entitled to use religious terminology to advance its political aims.*
> The redemption of the Jewish people, which as a Zionist I desire, is in no way

identical with the religious redemption I
hope for the future. I am not prepared as
a Zionist to satisfy political demands or
yearnings that exist in a strictly nonpo-
litical, religious sphere, in the sphere
of End-of-Days apocalyptics. The Zionist
ideal is one thing and the messianic ideal
is another, and the two do not touch except in pompous phraseology of mass ral-
lies, which often fuse into our youth a
spirit of new Sabbatianism that must inevitably fail. The Zionist movement is
congenitally alien to the Sabbatian movement, and the attempts to infuse Sabbatian
spirit into it has already caused it a
great deal of harm.

It seems that Scholem would here largely recognize Zionism as comparable with other nationalistic movements such as
those of Italy and many other countries in the nineteenth century. In a summary of forces which led to the triumph of
Zionism, Scholem writes with greater fullness as follows:

If Zionism triumphed--at least on the
level of historical decisions in the history
of the Jews--it owes its victory preeminent-
ly to three factors that left their imprint
on its character: it was, all in all, a
movement of the young, in which strong ro-
mantic elements inevitably played a considerable role; it was a movement of social
protest, which drew its inspiration as much
from the primordial and still vital call of
the prophets of Israel as from the slogans
of European socialism; and it was prepared
to identify itself with the fate of the
Jews in all--and I mean all--aspects of
that fate, the religious and worldly ones
in equal measure.[29]

In this admirably balanced assessment (which is as significant
for what it does not contain, i.e. apocalyptic territorial
messianism, as for what it does) Scholem, while recognizing
the role of the religious tradition, does not make it the
dominant factor. To him Zionism was essentially a socio-po-
litical protest.[30] And in the judgement of many Jews the
Congress of Basel was important not primarily because it gave
expression to a strictly religious hope for The Land, living

and creative as that was, but to a concern for the actual economic, political and social distress and often despair of Jews
in Europe; it was a response not so much to a crisis in *Judaism* and to an endemic territorial theology as to the plight of
the Jewish people.[31] To underestimate the secular character
of much of Zionism and to over-emphasize its undeniable religious dimensions is to lay oneself open to the temptation of
giving to the doctrine of The Land a significance in much of
Judaism which would be a distortion.

Again, in the third place, at first sight at least the
witness of history could be taken as suggesting that *Eretz
Israel* has not been of the essence of Judaism to the extent
that the literary sources and liturgies and observances of
pious Jews and even the political activity of non-religious
Jews would seem to suggest. Certain aspects of that history
are pertinent. We have elsewhere indicated that, although it
was assumed, there was a lack of any explicit appeal to the
doctrine of The Land in the outbreak of the Maccabean revolt
or that against Rome in 66 C.E. This is striking.[32] Even
more overlooked have been the expressions in the Maccabean
period of protests against and opposition to the Hasmonaean
rulers who had created an independent state.[33] These protests
made the later attitudes of the Pharisaic leaders in coming to
terms with Roman rule and in declaring the laws of The Land,
wherever Jews dwelt, to be Law, less innovative than has cus-
tomarily been recognized.[34] And at this point, the nature of
the Rabbinic attitude across the centuries must be fully recognized. That the doctrine of The Land remained honored among
the Rabbis cannot be doubted. But despite the facts referred
to in the preceding pages, after 70 C.E. until very recent
times, it was a doctrine more honored in word than in deed.
After 70 C.E. the powerlessness of Jews over against the Roman
authorities left the Rabbinic leaders no choice other than
that of submission and acquiescence to their divorce from "The
Land". This submission and acquiescence were to persist and
mould the life of the majority of Jews up to the present century and enabled the Rabbis to come to terms with the loss of
their Temple, City and Land. As we have seen, protests in
various forms against exile did not cease. Lurianic kabbalah,
for example, was a magnificent attempt to confront the curse
of exile, and Sabbatianism in its historical context can be
regarded as a desperate lunge at seizing the Kingdom of God
which would lead to a return to *Eretz Israel*.[35] But very
widely, both in Orthodox Judaism (by which is here meant the
main stream of Rabbinic Judaism) and in Reform Judaism in the
United States and Western Europe, the question of The Land was
eschatologically postponed either as an unacknowledged embarrassment or as a last or ultimate hope. Across the centuries
most Jews have lived on the whims of the Gentile world: they

ave not been able to afford the risk of alienating their
entile masters by giving practical expression to their vi-
ions of a territorial return to *Eretz Israel*: for most Jews,
espite some brilliant exceptions, such visions were a luxury
f Sabbath reading, dreams to be indulged in but not actively
ealized in daily life.[36] Instead the Rabbis emphasized that
he Torah itself was to become a "portable land" for Jews:[37]
t could be obeyed everywhere and could and would constitute
he centre of Jewish religious identity everywhere. Generally,
rthodox Judaism refused to indulge in political speculation
nd activity which might further a return to The Land, but ac-
epted instead an attitude of quietism. In one of the para-
oxes of history, Rabbis and Apocalyptists were here at one:
hey both preferred to wait for a Divine intervention, usually
ostponed to an indefinite future, to produce the return.[38]
rom a different point of view, as we saw, the Reform, in or-
ler to accommodate its faith to the nineteenth century and to
lake it comparable and compatible with Christianity, also pre-
erred to refuse to give to any particular place, "The Land",
a special overwhelming significance. In brief, in most Rab-
oinic writers, up to the twentieth century and in some ortho-
lox circles even up to the very present, the significance of
The Land, though never denied, has been transferred to the
'end of days". Paradoxically "The Land" retained its geographic character or actuality and was not always transcen-
lentalized, although it was largely *de facto* removed from the
realm of history altogether. And in the Reform, "The Land",
again in some circles even up to very recent times, was con-
veniently relegated to a secondary place; its geographic actuality was either sublimated or transformed into a symbol of an
ideal society located not necessarily in *Eretz Israel*. Historically then, out of necessity since 70 C.E., the doctrine
of The Land as a communal concern (it was often cherished by
individual Jews) was largely dormant or suffered a benign neglect in much of Judaism.

What happened is apparent. In their realism the Rabbis
at Jamnia had triumphed over the Zealots of Masada. They
recognized that the power of Rome was invincible: for them
Jewish survival lay in sensible, because unavoidable, political submission, and in obedience to the Torah in all aspects
of life where this was possible. The law of the country where
Jews dwelt became Law. (The principle was *dina demalkwta'
dina'*: see T. B. Nedarim 28a; T. B. Gittin 10b; T. B. Baba
Kamma 113a0b; T. B. Baba Bathra 54b.) The paradigmatic figure
was Johannan ben Zakkai, who had only asked of Vespasian permission to found a school where he could teach and establish
a house of prayer and perform all the commandments--a spiritual
center which accepted political powerlessness. For most of the
Rabbis after 70 C.E. exile became an accepted condition. For

them discretion became the better part of valour. That it is
to their discretion that Judaism owes its existence since 70
C.E. can hardly be gainsaid.[39]

In the fourth place, exile itself is the factor which
needs emphasis. Vital begins his work *The Origins of Zionism*
with the sentence: "The distinguishing characteristic of the
Jews has been their Exile." Bickerman writes of the dispersion as follows:

> "...the post-biblical period of Jewish his-
> tory, that is, that following Nehemiah...is
> marked by a unique and rewarding polarity:
> on the one hand, the Jerusalem center, and
> on the other, the plurality of centers in
> the Diaspora. The Dispersion saved Judaism
> from physical extirpation and spiritual in-
> breeding. Palestine united the dispersed
> members of the nation and gave them a sense
> of oneness. This counterpoise of histori-
> cal forces is without analogy in antiquity
> ....The Jewish Dispersion continued to con-
> sider Jerusalem as the 'metroplis' (Philo),
> turned to the Holy Land for guidance, and
> in turn, determined the destinies of its
> inhabitants."[40]

The fact of exile has been inescapable, and extraordinarily
tenacious and creative in the history of Judaism. The Talmud
itself, like much of the Tanak, was formulated outside The
Land. Surprisingly, Judaism did not produce a Theology of
Exile on any developed scale until very late. (See now, however, Thomas M. Raitt, *A Theology of Exile, Judgement and Deliverance in Jeremiah and Ezekiel*, Philadelphia, 1977, who
finds this theme developed in the Tanak.) But the presence
of large bodies of Jews outside The Land, so that (until the
twentieth century) the "exiles" became numerically and otherwise more significant than those who were in "The Land", cannot but have diminished among many Jews the centrality of The
Land and influenced their attitudes towards the doctrine concerning it. The conspicuous pre-eminence of the State of
Israel in our time can easily hide the significance of the
Exile for Judaism[41] throughout most of its history. But the
theological pre-eminence of Jews outside The Land in Jewish
history needs no documentation. Apart from all else, their
significance in the very survival of Judaism must be recognized. The loss of the Temple and The Land, the centers of
Judaism, could be sustained only because there were organized
Jewish communities scattered elsewhere.[42] Disaster even at

he center did not spell the end of Judaism but could be and
as offset and cushioned by its existence elsewhere. From
his point of view exile may be regarded as having been the
istorical condition for the survival of Judaism and Jewry.
That this did not mean a radical decline of the significance
f the primary center we shall indicate later.)[43]

The four factors which we have isolated above are to be
urther connected with what, in a previous study, we called
autionary considerations--the possible place of the "desert"
s opposed to the "land" in Judaism, the secondary role played
y Abraham outside the Pentateuch, the transcendentalizing of
he Land--(pointing to a muted role for it)--which tend to
urb the temptation to an excessive emphasis on the territo-
ial dimension of Judaism. We refer the reader to that study.
ll these factors cannot be ignored.[44]

III

A CONTRADICTION RESOLVED:
THE JEWS' INTERPRETATION OF THEIR OWN HISTORY

Our treatment so far has pinpointed what appears to be a
ontradiction: the theology of Judaism in its main expression
oints to The Land as of its essence: the history of Judaism
eems to offer serious qualifications of this. Can the contra-
iction between the Theology of Judaism and the actualities of
ts history be resolved? We suggest that the Jews' understand-
ng of their own history comes to terms precisely with this
ontradiction and resolves it in life, *solvitur ambulando*.
hat does this mean?

On previous pages we appealed to history in support of
he claim that exile as much as, if not more than, life in The
and has significantly marked Jewish history. The force of
hat appeal, we shall insist, must not be belittled. In iso-
ation, however, it is misleading, because in the Jewish ex-
erience--both religious and secular--exile has always co-
xisted with the hope of a return to The Land. Without that
ope the Jewish people would probably have gradually disinte-
rated and ceased to be. They have endured largely because of
he strength of that hope. Here the distinction between exile
nd simple dispersion is important: the two terms are easily
onfused. Statistics cannot be supplied, but many Jews
hroughout the centuries have *chosen* to live outside The Land
oluntarily, and many still do. The dispersion of such is not
xile. But in most periods most Jews have had no choice and

ultimately owe their place in the various countries of the
world to the enforced exile of their ancestors. It is with
these exiles--not simply with the dispersed--that we are here
concerned. This notion of exile must be given its full weight
and significance. That Jews outside Palestine conceived of
their existence as an exile meant that they were still bound
to their home-base, to *Eretz-Israel*, wherever they were: they
were not simply dispersed. G. Cohen has urged that this was
the fundamental reason that made possible the continuance of
the link between dispersed Jews and *Eretz Israel*. The diaspora had maintained the notion of its existence as a *galuth*,
exile. "That is to say, by the time Palestine ceased to be
the central Jewish community, its centrality had been so impressed upon the Jewish mind that it could not be uprooted."[45]
Many Jews have been sustained largely by the way in which they
have traditionally interpreted their own history as revealing
a recurring pattern of exile and return. They have understood
their existence (in the various countries of their abode) as
essentially transient or pilgrim; they have recognized that
they have had no abiding country anywhere but have always
been "en route" to The Land.

The Scriptures point to the patriarchs in search of The
Land; the settlement of The Land is followed by the descent
(a necessary "exile") into Egypt, followed by a return thence
and the re-conquest of The Land. Later there is another exile
to Babylon, and again a return in the time of Cyrus. The Hellenistic period saw the rise of a vast dispersion--both voluntary and forced--and the first century revolt against Rome was
followed by an exile which continued right down to this century, again only to lead to a return. The pattern of exile
and return, loss and restoration, is constant across the sweep
of Jewish history. Even the so-called "Non-Exilic" exile of
Jews in Moorish and Christian Spain, where Jews for long enjoyed virtual integration into the societies in which they
lived, ended in disaster and a fresh dispersion. Jews have
constantly been conditioned by the harsh actualities of their
history and their interpretation of them to think of the return. The point is that the pattern of exile and return has
been historically so inescapable that it has underlined the
belief that there is an inseverable connection between Yahweh,
His People and His Land. In Judaism, history has reinforced
Theology to deepen the consciousness of Jews that The Land was
always "there"--whether to be wrestled with in occupation or
to return to from exile. As Professor Edmund Jacob has written in a brilliant lecture: "en effet, toute l'histoire
d'Israël peut être envisagée comme une lutte pour la terre
et avec la terre, comme le combat de Jacob était une lutte
avec Dieu et pour Dieu."[46]

In Jewish tradition the Return could be conceived of in two ways. Non-religious Jews in every age could interpret the return to The Land as a political event, that is, as the restoration to Jews of political rights in their own land denied them after the collapse of the Jewish revolt in 70 C.E. (unrealistic as it must have often seemed to non-Jews). Such Jews have often understood Exile and Return in secular-political-economic terms. Not only secular Jews so thought of the Return. In principle, so also did many of the Sages. The rabbinical leaders never recognized that the conquest of *Eretz Israel* by any foreign power could be legitimized: the Romans were usurpers, their agents thieves. The Land belonged to Israel because Yahweh had promised it to her: her right to it was inalienable. So in the Mishnah it is implicitly regarded as legitimate to evade the Roman taxes (Mishnah Nedarim 3:4). The ruling powers were to be given obedience, but not cooperation--even in the interest of Law and order. To the Rabbis the return would involve control of The Land.

But to religious Jews much more was involved than this. To put it simply, to them just as exile was conceived of as the outcome of the wrath of God on a disobedient people, so too the Return was to be the manifestation of His gracious purpose for them despite their past disobedience. From this point of view the Return was to be a Redemption. What to non-religious Jews was primarily if not always exclusively of political significance, for the religious Jews was of theological significance.

This neat division between the religious and non-religious Jews, like all such divisions, is misleading. Both categories were not watertight; they interacted and were mutually stimulating as well as being very variegated. The concepts of the one permeated those of the other to make for infinite complexity. Although the secular thought in terms of Return, and the religious in terms of Redemption ultimately, because of the nature of the Tanak, often dissolved into each other. In the Zionist movement, secular, socialistic Jews constantly found themselves "at home" with the religious elements in the movement, who did not share their political views but provided a common ambience of thought on or sentiment for The Land.

Nevertheless, seeing the Return in terms of Redemption had certain discernible and definite consequences, as also did seeing it in terms of the restoration of political rights. To the religious Jews, as we have previously indicated, the various exiles the Jewish people had endured were due to the will of God. He had intervened in history to give to the disobedience to the commandments its just punishment in exile. So too,

they argued, the Return would be an act of divine intervention. The Return would be an aspect--a very important one--
of the messianic Redemption. As such it could not be engi-
neered or inaugurated by political or any other human means:
to force the coming of the Return would be impious.[47] They
best served that coming who waited in obedience for it: men
of violence would not avail to bring it in. The Rabbinic
aloofness to messianic claimants sprang not only from the
history of disillusionment with such but from this underlying,
deeply engrained attitude. As we saw, it has been claimed
that under the Rabbis Judaism condemned itself to powerlessness. But if such phraseology be used, it has also to be admitted that that powerlessness was effective in preserving
Judaism in a very hostile Christendom and must, therefore,
have had its own brand of "power". And there is more. "Orthodoxy" did recognize the dependence of the Return upon the
Divine initiative, but this did not prevent it from always re-
taining in principle that a certain human obedience could
bring that initiative into play. And in Lurianic Kabbala,
for example, this connection was particularly active.[48]

For the purpose of this essay the significance of the attitude towards their existence in foreign lands and towards
the hope of the Return which we have ascribed to religious
Jews is that despite their apparent quietism in the acceptance
of the Torah as a portable land--and this it must be emphasized is only an *Interimsethik*--the hope for the return to
Eretz Israel never vanished from their consciousness. They
remained true "in spirit" to the territorial theology of the
Tanak and with the other sources of their faith. Religious
Jews generally, especially of the most traditionalist persuasion (except perhaps in modern Germany where they often
thought themselves to have been "at home"), have regarded any
existing, present condition outside the Law as temporary. If
not always pilgrims to it in a literal sense, they have always
set their face towards The Land. This fidelity has in turn
strengthened the continuing belief in the umbilical, eternal
connection between the people of Israel and its Land and lent
to that Land a "sacred" quality. In the experience of Jews,
theology has informed the interpretation of history and history in turn has confirmed the Theology.

In reflecting on the answer finally to be given to the
question presented to us, in the light of the evidence so inadequately set forth here, an analogy from Christian ecclesiology suggests itself. In Roman Catholicism and High Church
Anglicanism the distinction has often been drawn, in discussions of the apostolic episcopate, between what is of the *esse*
and of the *bene esse* of the Christian Church. Is this distinction applicable to the way in which the main stream of

Judaism has conceived of The Land? Judaism has certainly been
compelled by the actualities of History to accept "exile" as
a permanent and major mark of its existence and as a source of
incalculable benefit. Has it implicitly recognized, despite
the witness of its classical sources and, indeed, it might be
argued, in conformity with much in them, that while life in
The Land is of the *bene esse* of all Jewish religious existence, it is not of the *esse*? Moses desired to be in The
Land so that he might have the possibility of achieving greater obedience to the Torah: that he did not enter it was a
very great deprivation. But it was not fatal to his existence
as a Jew. It is the greatest blessing to live in The Land,
but this is not absolutely essential. Philo regarded the diaspora as under the providence of God (*In Flaccum*, 4). A Jew
can remain true to his Judaism, however, inadequately, by the
standards set by the sources, as long as he is loyal to the
Torah. He can continue in his faith outside The Land, but not
outside the Torah. Not The Land but the Torah is of the essence of Judaism; it is, indeed, its relation to the Torah
that gives holiness to The Land. From this point of view it
could be argued that The Land is of the *bene esse*, not of the
esse of the Jewish faith.

Yet one is uneasy about this analogy, and that not only
because the Torah itself and the Mishnah are so overwhelmingly
concerned with The Land. The antithesis between *esse* and *bene
esse*, conceptually valid as it may seem to be, does not do justice to the place of The Land. We suggest that the way in
which the question of The Land was proposed by the editors,
that is, in terms of the essential in Judaism, may in fact itself be misleading and result in a misplacement in our answer.
The term "essence" suggests the impersonal and so is as inadequate in dealing with The Land as in dealing with Christianity,
as for example was Harnack in using the notion of the "Essence
of Christianity".[49] Néher[50] and Lacocque[51] have pointed us to
the personification of The Land in Judaism. They seem to us
to go too far in ascribing to simile and metaphor and figura-
tive language an actual personalism. But exaggerated as their
claims may be, they do guard us against impersonalism in the
understanding of the role of The Land. The Land evokes im-
mense and deep emotion among religious Jews: it is "La Terre
mystique de l'Absolu". It presents a kind of personal challenge and offers a personal anchorage. The sentiment (a term
here used in its strict psychological sense) for The Land is
so endemic among religious Jews (we are not here directly concerned with others) and so constantly reinforced by their
sacred sources, liturgies and observances that to set life in
The Land over against life outside The Land as *esse* over
against *bene esse* is to miss the point. It is better to put
the question in another way and ask: does The Land lie at the

heart of Judaism? Put in this more personal manner the question answers itself.

In another study we suggested that for Paul as for many in early Christianity, life under the Torah and in The Land was transformed into the life "in Christ", which became the Christian counterpart of the life in The Land of Judaism.[52] Few would not agree that the heart of Christianity (we avoid the term "essence") is Jesus Christ. Similarly, we must acknowledge the heart of Judaism to be the Torah. But to accept Judaism on its own terms is to recognize that near to and indeed within that heart is "The Land". In this sense, just as Christians recognize the scandal of particularity in the Incarnation, in Christ, so there is a scandal of territorial particularity in Judaism. The Land is so embedded in the heart of Judaism, the Torah, that—so its sources, worship and theology attest—it is finally inseparable from it. "Il faut...ne pas essayer de diviser des choses indivisibles."[53]

The scandal presented by a particular land is no less to be recognized than that provided by a particular Person. One may interpret the relation between Israel and The Land as a theological mystery or reject it simply as an unusually bizarre and irritating phenomenon. Many will find the "crass" materiality of the connection between Israel and The Land offensive to their "mystical" or "spiritual" sensitivities: others will find much to satisfy in the emphasis of Judaism on the need to express itself in tangible, material societary or communal form in The Land. Of its historicity in the Jewish consciousness or self identity there can, in any case, be no doubt. To accept it as a fact of historical significance is not of itself to justify it, but it is to begin to understand it, and to respect it as an aspect of Judaism's doctrine of election. "S'il y a un peuple élu, il y a aussi une terre élu."[54] The discussion of The Land drives us to the "mystery" of "Israel", that is, the eschatological purpose of God in His dealings with His people.[55]

NOTES

1. Compare R. J. Zwi Werblowsky, "Israel et Eretz Israel," in *Les Temps Modernes*, Directeur Jean-Paul Sartre (No. 253 B 15, 1967), pp. 371-393. On p. 375 Werblowsky writes of the connection with the land as an "élement essentiel". See also Martin Buber, *Israel and Palestine: the History of an Idea* (London, 1952) and *Israel and the World* (New York, 1963); the very rich chapter by G. Cohen on *Zion in Jewish Literature*, ed. A. S. Halkin (New York, 1961), pp. 38-64; "Rabbinic Theology and Ethics," a forthcoming chapter by Louis Finkelstein for *The Cambridge History of Judaism*, volume IV; Arthur Hertzberg, *The Zionist Idea* (New York, 1968); Edmund Jacob, *Israel dans la perspective biblique* (Strasbourg, 1968), and "Les Trois Racines d'une Theologie de la 'Terre' dans l'A.T." in *Revue d'Historie et de Philosophie Religieuses* 1975, no. 4, pp. 469-480; *Jüdisches Volkgelobtes Land*, eds. W. P. Eckert, N. P. Levinson, M. Stohr (München, 1970); Max Kadashin, "Aspects of the Rabbinic Concept of Israel," in *Hebrew Union College Annual*, vol. 19 (1945-46), pp. 57-96; F. W. Marquardt, *Die Juden und ihr Land* (Hamburg, 1975); A. Neher, "Israel, terre mystique de l'Absolu," *L'Existence Juive* (Paris, 1962). The numerous works of J. W. Parkes are important. A recent very stimulating treatment is by W. Brueggemann, *The Land* (Philadelphia, 1977). This deserves more attention than space allows here, as does R. Rendtorff, "Israel und seine Land" in *Theologische Existenz Heute*, n. 188, München, 1978. In "Réflexions sur la pensée nationale juive moderne," *Jerusalem Quarterly*, no. 7 (1978), pp. 3-9, Rotenstreich emphasizes the newness of Zionism or modern Jewish nationalism. It is, for him, discontinuous with traditional Jewish religious thought: "It attempts to create a new Jewish unity with living institutions rooted in the present rather than surviving to the present" (p. 5). He connects Zionism, therefore, with the collapse of the foundations of traditional Jewish life which succumbed to the attack of the Enlightenment on the traditional authorities grounded in a supra-historical authority (pp. 3-4). One can hardly agree that Zionism is so utterly new born. As will be clear from our presentation, for us Zionism is "twice-born" in the sense that it was preceded by a long tradition of concentration on The Land. On its religious dimension, see Rolf Rendtorff, "Die religiosen und geistigen Wurzeln des Zionismus" in *Aus Politik und Zeit Geschichte*, B. 49/76 (4th Dec., 1976), pp. 3-49. This does not mean that the precise forerunners of Zionism can be easily categorized; see Jacob Katz on "The Forerunners of Zionism," *The Jerusalem Quarterly, op. cit.*, pp. 10-21.

Two Hebrew terms have to be distinguished: *'adamah*, soil, land, earth, and *'eretz* which while not always to be clearly distinguished from *'adamah* bears also the meaning of a politically defined territory. It is with *'eretz* in this latter sense that we are concerned, that is, with The Land of Israel as territory. The boundaries of the promised land are never precisely defined. As does the Talmud, we use the form The Land for the promised land (*'eretz*) of Israel.

2. For the emergence and function of the Pentateuch, see J. A. Sanders, *Torah and Canon* (Philadelphia, 1972; French translation with additional response to criticisms, 1975); also "Adaptable for Life: The Nature and Function of Canon," *Magnalia Dei. Festschrift for G. Ernest Wright*, eds. F. M. Cross and others (Garden City, N.Y., 1976), pp. 531-560. Illuminating also is J. van Goudover, "Tora und Galut," in *Judisches Volkgelobtes Land, op. cit.*, pp. 197-202. As far as I am aware, the implications of Sanders' study for the question of The Land have not been adequately examined: its provocativeness can only be mentioned here. See also Truman Research Institute publication, 1970, of papers in a *Colloquium on Religion, People, Nation and Land*, Jerusalem.

3. See my *The Gospel and the Land; Early Christianity and Jewish Territorial Doctrine* (Berkeley, 1974) for the supporting evidence.

4. See G. Cohen, *op. cit.*, p. 39.

5. See my *The Setting of the Sermon on the Mount* (Cambridge University Press, 1964), pp. 295f., and literature cited there. G. Cohen, pp. 45f.

6. On all the above, for further details, see *The Gospel and the Land*, pp. 1-158.

7. G. Cohen, *Zion in Jewish Literature*, p. 41.

8. F. W. Marquardt, *op. cit.*, n. 1, p. 28.

9. *Sabbatai Svi: The Mystic Messiah, 1626-1676* (Princeton, 1973); see my reflections on this: "From Schweitzer to Scholem: Reflections on Sabbatai Svi," *Journal of Biblical Literature* 95 (1976), 529-58.

10. The lateness of the emergence of the division of history to B.C. and A.D. is not often realized: it is not followed by Jews.

11. See F. W. Marquardt, *op. cit.*, pp. 107ff.

12. M. Noth, *History of Israel* (London, 1958), pp. 448, 53f. See further G. Klein, *Anti-Judaism in Christian The-logy* (Philadelphia, 1975), pp. 15-38.

13. F. W. Marquardt, *op. cit.*, pp. 107f.

14. R. J. Zwi Werblowsky, *op. cit.*, n. 1, pp. 374-5, puts he matter in a nutshell: "On considéra comme acquis...que le euple juif a eu conscience de former un peuple à presque outes les époques de son existence historique. Une conscience e soi spécifique, c'est à dire une connaissance de son destin st un fait constant de la culture juive." We deal here with he *religious* consciousness of Jews, but ultimately it is not eparable from the historical. Werblowsky, above, and in a aper privately circulated on "Israel: The People and the and" assumes this, with much good reason and brilliance. The mpact of the figure of the Wandering Jew--an individual, al-hough he could and did serve as a symbol of the Jewish people s a whole--may have helped to blur the reality of the contin-ance of the Jewish community as a unity.

15. The Christian practice of pilgrimages to holy places, which formed the long devotional background of the Crusades, and Jewish practice were probably mutually stimulating through-out the Middle Ages. For many centuries after the Mohammedan capture of Jerusalem in 637, pilgrimages by Christians to that city continued and it is probable that the Church never gave up the hope for the recovery of the holy places from Mohamme-dan control. From the eighth century on, the Church's prac-tice of imposing a pilgrimage instead of a public penance added to the number of pilgrims. Jewish pilgrimage to The Land increased especially after Justinian (483-565). Here we can only point to the main expressions of the devotion to The Land in Judaism. The reader is referred to the standard his-tories of the themes.

16. *Selected Poems of Jehudah Halevi*, English translation by Nina Salaman, ed. H. Brody (Philadelphia, 1946[4]), p. 2. Professor Diez Macho pointed out to me that Halevi was not an isolated figure but part of a well defined tendency if not a movement. The father of Israel Zangwill provides one example of individual devotion to The Land. At an advanced age, he left his house and family to go there to die. See J. Left-wich, *Israel Zangwill*, New York, 1957, p. 163. There are countless examples of such devotion. See further T. Dreyfus, "The Commentary of Franz Rosenzweig to the Poems of R. Judah Halevi" in *Tarbiz*, vol. XLVII, 1-2 (March-October, 1978), pp. 91ff.

17. F. W. Marquardt, *Die Juden und ihr Land*, p. 131.

18. See G. Scholem, *op. cit.*

19. David Vital, *The Origins of Zionism* (Oxford, 1975), p. 7. Marquardt, *op. cit.*, pp. 131ff.

20. This remains true although the concentration on The Land among religious Jews who revered and even went to *Eretz Israel* has to be distinguished from the purely historical and geographic and archaeological interest in it of many of the Zionists. See especially D. Vital, *ibid.*, pp. 6ff. In this article we deal with Judaism and The Land, not with Jews and The Land. But the impression must not be given that these two themes can or should be effectively separated. Werblowsky illuminates the problem. He points out that in the nineteenth century assimilationist Jews were fascinated and blinded by the Enlightenment. In this enthusiasm for assimilation they shed both their religious and national identity. But they soon discovered the falsity of their hopes for being fully integrated and "normalized" in Western society. In their disillusioned reaction to the society that had erstwhile been so seductively attractive to them, they turned again to the tradition that they had shed. But for "enlightened" and "assimilationist" Jews to rediscover and to return *all at once to both their religious and national identity* was hardly possible: the rediscovery of *one* element of their tradition at a time was traumatic; to discover *both* at the same time would have been too overwhelming. So it was that the "enlightened" Jews who saw the futility of assimilation under the influence of the climate of the nineteenth century turned first to "nationalism", socialism, romanticism, to their strictly "national" tradition: they rediscovered themselves as belonging to the people of Israel, not necessarily to the religion of Israel which they still found it easy to regard as a fossilized survival. (Even Werblowsky himself seems able to think of the liturgical practice somewhat in these terms. Of the belief in the relationship between Israel and The Land he writes, *op. cit.*, p. 377: "Très souvent, il était à la fois vivant et 'gelé', comme dans une chambre froide, par les prières chaque jour répétées, les formules liturgiques et le rappel des promesses prophetiques.") All this helps to explain the insensitivity of some of the leaders both before and in the Zionist movement itself to the strictly religious dimension of relation to the Land. See Werblowsky in *Les Temps Modernes*, p. 388, see also citation in n. 14. Of Zionist leaders, he writes, "Beaucoup d'entre eux ne pouvaient faire qu'une seule découverte à la fois." This concentration on the tradition among religious Jews who revered and even went to *Eretz Israel* has to be distinguished from the purely historical and geographical interest which secular Jews, who in the nineteenth century, for reasons we shall touch upon later, showed in The

Land. For such the religious devotion to The Land symbolized
all that was particularistic, "scandalous", non-assimilable in
Judaism, even when they themselves ultimately became Zionists.

21. *Op. cit.*, p. 377.

22. The recognition of the variety of pre-Jamnian Judaism
has now become a commonplace of scholarship. It is doubtful
whether Judaism has any "dogmas", that is, doctrines as such
which are regarded as necessary for salvation as does Christianity. See my article "Torah and Dogma: A Comment," *The
Harvard Theological Review* 61 (1968), 87-105, reprinted in
*Papers from the Colloquium on Judaism and Christianity held at
Harvard Divinity School*, Oct. 17-20, 1966 (Harvard University
Press, 1968); also *The Gospel and the Land*, pp. 390-404, especially pp. 399ff.

23. Nahmanides was a Talmudist who was compelled to leave
Spain and spent his last years in Palestine. According to the
Encyclopaedia of the Jewish Religion (eds. Werblowsky and Wig-
oder, New York, 1965, p. 272 b), he was the first outstanding
Rabbi to pronounce the resettlement of the land of Israel to
be a biblical precept (*mitzwah*). It is very surprising that
such a pronouncement came so late, only in the 12th to the 13th
centuries. Doubtless it was assumed by many before the time of
Nahmanides that there was such a *mitzwah*. Nahmanides found in
Lev. 26:22 a proof of this faith. Since the loss of The Land
by Israel no other power had been able to colonize it success-
fully. The Land had refused to accept any other than the people of Israel: see his commentary on the Pentateuch. The Rabbis saw a correspondence between the history of The Land and
that of the People, see Werblowsky, private paper cited in n.
14, and Lev. 26:42. Compare J. W. Parkes, *End of an Exile*
(London, 1954), pp. 12-13. For Maimonides' view that the Messianic era would witness the return of Israel to The Land, see
A. Cohen, *The Teachings of Maimonides* (New York, 1968), pp.
225f. and the whole section on eschatology, pp. 220-240. The
contents of *The Guide to the Perplexed* could be taken to prove
that Maimonides' interests lay mainly elsewhere. But the purpose of *The Guide* must be borne in mind: it was natural for
Maimonides not to deal with The Land there. We are not competent to enter into the debate about the Great Eagle. But note
the view of Leibovitz: "Le précepte de resider en Israel a été
amplement commenté par Rambam, mais, bien qu'il soit abondam-
ment attesté dans le Midrash et la Haggadah, *il appartient au
folklore religieux*." According to Leibovitz, "On pourrait
souligner, à cet egard, que la réalité concrète du Judaïsme,
que au cours de l'histoire s'est manifestée dans l'accomplise-
ment de la Loi, n'a jamais accordé a la Terre d'Israel une
place centrale ni au plan de la pensée, ni au plan des mobiles

d'action." See *Le Monde* (Paris), 8-9 Avril, 1979, p. 2. One could wish for a more qualified statement of the case.

24. D. Vital, *op. cit.*, note 19, p. 207.

25. H. Cohen, *Religion der Vernunft aus den Quellen des Judentums* (Frankfurt, 1929), English translation by Simon Kaplan, 1972, pp. 311-12. Before we can answer this question of the relation between The Land and the state, certain clarifications are required. The words quoted from Cohen make clear that it is easy to move from the idea of a State of Israel to that of the Land of Israel or the reverse. This easy transition invites confusion. The doctrines of a State of Israel and of "the Land of Israel" are to be distinguished. That Judaism regards a "state" to be essential to its existence may legitimately be argued. To begin with, it is erroneous to think that the people of Israel in the Old Testament is to be understood as a community bound to a land and governed by a law, as a modern national state might be so tied and governed. One thing has emerged clearly from studies on law in the Hebrew Scriptures. The laws were not related primarily to the political organization of a state, but rather to a community of men in which a common allegiance to Yahweh was the constitutive element. The context or setting in life in which Israel had received the Law was the covenant, a sacral act, and the communication of the Law was connected with the celebration of the covenant which bound Israel to its God. To maintain the validity of this covenant—of which the proclamation of the Law was an essential part—Israel celebrated or commemorated it in regular feasts. The foundation of Israel lay in this religious act. "The Israelite nation had its true existence apart from and prior to the erection of their political, social and economic order in Canaan" (R. B. Y. Scott, *The Relevance of the Prophets*, New York, 1968, p. 189). The community is to be understood as a corollary of the covenant entered into at Sinai.

After 587 B.C.E., when Jerusalem fell, the idea of a state declined. The Jews became again primarily a religious community: in time priests came to rule them under God. Israel is the people of Yahweh alone. In Ezra and Nehemiah the primary, if not the only, concern is that the people should obey the Law. If we follow the traditional view of the origin of the Pharisees, it was loyalty to the Law alone that governed them, and initially it was this that moved the Maccabees also. After the Exile, the Jews became a people of the Torah: the whole history of Pharisaism is necessarily concentrated on the Torah more than on the political control of the land.

The Messianic ideas of Judaism, which have persisted from the biblical to modern times, for example in Sabbatianism, have retained a political dimension, and one aspect, the Davidic state, has remained central to them. But those ideas have often been spiritualized and transcendentalized and made symbolic. Without further elaboration we shall assume here that the doctrine of the inseverability of the Land from Yahweh and his People is not to be easily equated with the eternal connection of any state with the People and with Yahweh.

And yet despite the data to which we have referred in *The Gospel and the Land* and Scholem's apparent distinction, caution is necessary. There is the question which forcibly came to the surface, not to be re-interred, in 1848. Can a people be a people without political self-expression or the right to self-determination (two concepts not usually distinguished), that is, without being allowed to be a nation? Is the distinction between a people living in the Land of Israel and the nation of Israel ultimately a false one? Does not its full life in The Land demand that a people control its own land? And there is the exact interpretation of the Jewish evidence. The best guide to the inner life and meaning of a religious community is its liturgy. If so, in the most familiar and central prayer of Judaism, the Shemoneh Esreh, the distinction between life in the land and "national" control of the land is not recognized. In the 14th Benediction, which is usually dated in the Maccabean period, the reference to the kingdom of the House of David *(malkûth bêth David)* is unambiguous. For religious Jews, we must conclude, ultimately the land is inseparable from the state of Israel, however much the actualities of history have demanded their distinction. In this essay we are concerned not with the role of a Jewish state, but with that of the Land as such, that is, the promised land. But we must issue the *caveat* that such a distinction, although often necessarily recognized in Jewish life and thought, and therefore unavoidable in this discussion, is in the final analysis alien to the Jewish faith. To religious Jews the separation of the Land and the State is the abortive child of Jewish history not of the Jewish religious consciousness and intent. In any case despite the vicissitudes of Jewish history, the sacred documents on which religious Jews have rested--the Tanak, the Mishnah, the Midrashim, and the Talmud--the liturgies they have constantly celebrated, and the observances which they have kept across the centuries all point to "the land" as an essential aspect of Judaism.

26. D. Vital, *op. cit.*, p. 156: on Aha d Ha-'Am, pp. 188-201. One may detect echoes of Ahad Ha-'Am in Buber, see for example, *Israel and the World²*, (New York, 1965), p. 229, although there is no mistaking Buber's insistence on the need for the soil of *Eretz Israel* for his people.

27. See "With Gershom Scholem: An Interview," in *Jews and Judaism in Crisis* (New York, 1976), pp. 1-48.

28. There was a struggle among the precursors of the movement over what came to be called "territorialism", that is, th view that the specific place to which the suffering Jews of Russia and other countries should go was not important, provided they could settle in a place of their own. This territorialism was especially connected with Yehuda Leib Pinsker (1821-1891), a Russian physician from Odessa, the author of a most significant pamphlet *Auto-emancipation, Mahnruf an seine Stammesgenossen von einem russischen Juden*, 1892. For him, at first, it was not the Holy Land that the Jews needed but *a* land. It was having their own territory, not its being located in *Eretz Israel*, that was crucial. Ultimately few Jews were to follow Pinsker in this view. The thesis that in *Eretz Israel* alone would Jews cease to be "foreigners" prevailed. See on all this Vital, *op. cit.*, pp. 109-132, especially p. 131; Werblowsky, in *Les Temps Modernes*, pp. 338-389.

29. *Jews and Judaism in Crisis*, p. 44. But see above p. 71 on the impossibility of separating the religious from the national and the socialistic in Zionism.

30. *Op. cit.*, p. 375.

31. See Vital, *op. cit.*, p. 375. Vital concludes his excellent treatment with the claim that what kept Zionists together and their institutions intact was that the terrible "social reality was always stronger than the disputes about it". The misery of the Jews' conditions in the Pale of Settlement, in Galicia and Rumania could not wait for relief: it outweighed "both the force of inertia and of religious teaching". To this was added anti-Semitism in the West. With Vital's emphasis one can agree, but when he sets the force of "religious teaching" over against the need for relief, one hesitates to concur. His conclusion at this point ignores his opening chapter, which had pointed to the pervasive religious substructure of all Jewish thinking on The Land. The misery of Jews in itself would not have been creatively dynamic had it not been sustained by hope, however differently and variously expressed. Misery alone only breeds despair. Did not the endemic hope for The Land, even when denied its religious character, provide the light at the end of the tunnel which helped to sustain Jews? The history of movements of social reform and of revolutions sufficiently indicates that total misery in itself merely leads to inertia. Those movements have usually been born out of an element other than the misery itself.

32. See *The Gospel and the Land*, pp. 90-104.

33. Is. 44:28; Ezra 1:1f., The Chronicler; Jos. *Antiquities* XII. 3.3, 138f.; XIII. 13.5, 372f.; XVII. 11.1, 299f.;

Diodorus, *Bibliotheca Historica* XL. 2; cf. M. Stern, *Greek and Latin Authors on Jews and Judaism* (Jerusalem, 1974), pp. 185-36.

34. See below, p. 77f.

35. See on all this G. Scholem, *Sabbatai Svi, The Mystic Messiah, op. cit.*, n. 9.

36. G. Scholem, *ibid.*

37. This phrase, "the portable land", I learnt from Louis Finkelstein. (The Talmud is sometimes called a "portable state".)

38. On the essential quietism of Apocalypticism, see David Daube, *Civil Disobedience in Antiquity* (Edinburgh, 1972), pp. 85-86.

39. The debate on all this continues. To some Jews, such as R. L. Rubenstein, the tradition of submission historically advocated by Rabbinic Judaism has become an impossible policy or stance since the Holocaust. See, for example, his *After Auschwitz* and his *Power Struggle* (New York, 1974), pp. 171-179 in "Rabbi Yochanan's bargain". Rubenstein speaks of the "impotence" of the Jews. But to Jacob Neusner, not the abandonment of that tradition is necessary, but its more emphatic reappropriation and comprehension by Jews. For him "Studying the Torah is [we might write here "remains"] a mode of attaining transcendence through learning, not merely because God, too, studies Torah. Study of Torah is the way to the apprehension of God, the attainment of the sacred" (in a paper on "Transcendence and Worship through Learning: the Religious View of the Mishnah," *CCAR Journal* [Spring, 1978], p. 28). See also Neusner's "Toward a Jewish Renewal," in *Moment*, vol. 3, no. 6 (May, 1978), pp. 11-16. The question is how far the development of Pharisaism after 70 C.E.—which led to the elevation of Torah and Torah study into the way of holiness—was such that holiness became radically separated from a single place, the Temple, and by that very fact The Land. Baruch M. Bokser in a review of *The Gospel and the Land* even says that Rabbinic Judaism was more radically divorced from The Land than was early Christianity (*Conservative Judaism* XXX, no. 1, Fall, 1975, pp. 73-4):

> Torah, as the rabbis say it, contains
> the key to the world and to the nature of
> existence. Of course, some rabbinic cir-
> cles provided means to *remember* the Temple.
> But holiness was now divorced from a single

place. The way of Torah enabled each individual to bring holiness into daily life,
no longer by means of the Temple. The new
set of metaphors reflects a conscious dis-
continuity, in contrast to the Christian
concept which merely continued the old motif of holiness of Temple in a new way.
The holiness of a single person, Jesus,
replaces that of a single place; in faith,
the Christian community represents the
true Temple. In contrast, Torah, in the
emerging rabbinic movement, was not just
a comfort to Jews without a Temple, but
was the basis for a new piety, one quite
different from that of Christianity and
of the Second Temple.

On this theme see B. Viviano, *Study as Worship*, forthcoming in
the series *Studies in Late Antiquity*, ed. J. Neusner (Leyden);
and, by implication, G. Cohen, *op. cit.*, n. 1, pp. 45-48.

40. *From Ezra to the Last of the Maccabees*, Foundations
of Post-Biblical Judaism, Part II, translated by M. Hadas (New
York, 1962), p. 3f.

41. An interesting comment on all this comes from Israel
itself. Israelis have recently found it necessary to make a
conscious effort to counteract what is described as attitudes
towards the Diaspora which range from indifference to negation
To this end a museum has been opened in Tel Aviv designed to
depict 2,5000 years of Jewish life and to show that the Diaspora was not "a continuous story of persecution and suffering
with the Jews always in the passive role of the victim" (*New
York Times*, Sunday, May 21, 1978, p. 6). Indifference and negation generally characterize the attitude of those in a homeland to those who have left to live outside it. This attitude
was probably at work in the dispute between the "Hellenists"
and the "Hebraists" in the first century. It operates at the
present time to downgrade the significance of the exile in
Judaism. See *Le Monde*, Mars 18-19, 1979, p. 2, where Nahum
Goldmann refers to a "slogan des quelques sionistes que sou-
haitaient abolir la diaspora".

42. G. Cohen, *op. cit.*, p. 52. From this point of view
without the experience of "exile" the dispersed Jews would no
have retained The Land in their consciousness. Exile was thu
ultimately as time unrolled necessary for the preservation of
The Land.

43. This is well brought out by D. Vital, *op. cit.*, pp.

1-20, to whom I am much indebted. André Nehier also emphasizes the point in his very moving, almost lyrical essay in *L'Existence Juive* (Paris, 1962), pp. 166-76, on "Israel, terre mystique de l'Absolu." See especially p. 169: "On aurait pu croire que les urgences de l'Exil altèrent dans la pensée juive, la précellence d'Eréts et lui enlèvent certaines de ses vertus au profit des terres de la diaspora. Or il n'en est rien. Dès les premiers moments de la diaspora, tout au contraire, et à un rhythme que ira sans cesse grandissant, la pensée juive, talmudique d'abord, puis philosophique et mystique et, enfin, politique, saisait le thème biblique d'Eréts non pour l'edulcorer, mais pour lui conférer plus de poids encore, plus de gravité absolue." In the light of the preceding pages, one might venture to question the undeviating nature of the development to which Nehier points, but of the continued reality of devotion to The Land, there can be little question. Gershom Cohen finds the fundamental reason for this continuity in one fact. This was that the diaspora never abandoned the understanding of its existence as a galuth, exile. *"That is to say, by the time Palestine ceased to be the central Jewish community, its centrality had been so impressed upon the Jewish mind that it could not be uprooted.";* op. cit., p. 52, our italics.) There is another glaring reason which may possibly have been of even greater significance, that is, the fact of anti-semitism. The hostility of the Gentile world would time and again stir up the hope for The Land embedded in the tradition (see Werblowsky, in *Les Temps Modernes*, pp. 381-82).

44. See *The Gospel and the Land*, pp. 75-158.

45. See G. Cohen, op. cit., p. 48.

46. Edmund Jacob, *Israël dans la perspective biblique* (Strasbourg, 1968), p. 22.

47. See E. E. Urbach, *The Sages*, volume I, "On Redemption," pp. 649-92, especially p. 679: "'The End at its due time' is something different from liberation from the servitude of the kingdoms and cannot be attained by rebellions."

48. See G. Scholem, *Sabbatai Svi*, pp. 15-22. See my article on Sabbatai Svi (also cited above in n. 9).

49. See S. W. Sykes, *Religious Studies*, vol. 7 (1971), on "The Essence of Christianity."

50. *Op. cit., passim.*

51. A. Lacocque, "Une Terre qui decoule de Lait et de

Miel," *Revue du Dialogue*, no. 2 (1966), 28-36. The thesis that the land flowing with milk and honey gives a maternal quality to The Land as mother seems to us a *tour de force*, especially in its grammatical and lexicographical details.

52. To this concept belongs the Pauline notions of "building", "planting" and "watering" in 1 Cor. 3:6-15. See the fascinating discussion by M. A. Chevallier, *Esprit de Dieu, Paroles d'Hommes* (Neuchatel, 1966), p. 26ff. If we are correct to call the emergence in Christianity of the concept of being "in Christ" an equivalent of being in The Land, the notion of a "Return" in Christianity is thus made redundant except in the sense of a "Return to Christ". But Paul probably never wholly escaped the territorial understanding of Jerusalem and The Land as the *centrum mundi*. John certainly reveals a displacement of these centers. We find M. A. Chevallier's suggestion that the same was true of 1 Peter an excellent one, see *Mélanges offert à Marcel Simon: Paganisme, Judaïsme, Christianisme* (Paris, 1978), pp. 117-130: "Israel et L'Eglise selon Le Première Épitre de Pierre." Chevallier shows how the notion of exile and diaspora is taken up by "Peter" and reinterpreted. It is significant that he has no occasion to deal with the motif of "Return". He writes (on p. 122):

> Pas plus que le peuple des croyants en
> Jesus Christ n'a de consistent ethnique
> il n'a de réalité géographique. Jésus
> Christ n'est pas localisé comme l'était
> Jerusalem et partout où des hommes 's'ap-
> proche de lui', le temple spirituel se
> construit (2:5) de sorte que le peuple
> de Dieu est *tout entier diaspora* (1:1),
> fait 'd'étrangers' et de 'residents' au
> milieu des nations païennes (2:11).

53. Quoted by G. F. Moore, in *Judaism in the First Centuries of the Christian Era: The Age of the Tannaim*, vol. 1, p. 234 (3 volumes, Harvard University Press, 1927-30).

54. Werblowsky, *Les Temps Modernes, op. cit.*, p. 376.

55. See further my forthcoming study on this theme by the University of California Press. It is not possible to discuss in this essay what happens when the Jewish understanding of The Land comes into conflict with other inhabitants of it.

6

DIVINE POWER POLITICS
REFLECTIONS ON EZEKIEL 37

David E. Demson

The renewed emphasis in some recent Protestant writings on *theologia crucis*[1] finds solid support in the pages of the New Testament, where the manner and legitimacy of Christ's rule are attested by the accounts of Him shedding His blood for us. But one reads in the same pages of Christ as the one "who destroys every rule and every authority and every power"; of Him who "puts His enemies under His feet". While *theologia crucis* illumines the legitimacy and character of God's politics, it does not comprehend the N.T. attestation of that divine power by which the crucified tramples underfoot His enemies. A fruitful footnote to the current presentation of *theologia crucis* might be an examination of the resurrection of Jesus not only as revelation and justification, but also as divine power.

However, in the Bible a singularly luminous attestation of divine power politics precedes the proclamation of Easter. And, as far as I know, little comment has been offered on the perspicacity of the theological husbandman who connected, in what we read as Chapter 37 of Ezekiel, the dry bones vision (vss. 1-10) and its interpretation (vss. 11-14) with a political problem nearer at hand (vss. 15-23) and with the political destiny of the house of Israel (vss. 24-28). Why may this connection be regarded as perspicacious? If Professor von Rad is correct in his conclusion that the prophet everywhere envisages God as exercising His power in order that a people is brought to fulfillment as a nation,[2] then this theological/literary husbandman has not grafted together arbitrarily the attestation of God's power with an attestation of the political fulfillment of Israel, but has rather joined parts which are found together from the beginning to the end of the Ezekiel tradition.

I

If verses 1-14 are read by themselves, then the obvious point will be grasped that God manifests His power in returning Israel to life. The more specific point elaborated by the connection of verses 1-14 with verses 24-28 is that God exercises His power in order to guarantee the political fulfillment of this people. This nation will not achieve this fulfillment (nor will it be primarily its sin which prevents this); rather, God will confer this fulfillment upon it. ("My servant David shall be king over them.")

The point elaborated by the connection of the first and last portions of the chapter is not abstract, but concrete. The point concerns what the exercise of God's power reveals about the nature of political reality and power in Israel. This people as a nation is given a guarantee of fulfillment beyond judgment and is to live from the fulfillment to come. The way its life is to be shaped in the present is in the exercise of power. So what is at stake is not belief in God or God's rule in a religious way.[3] The question, rather, is: to exercise or not the power granted. Even as the issue for Israel is not religious, so also it is not moral. For David's kingship is not decided by a moral referendum, but rather is established by the bestowal of power and by the acceptance of that power (the power of fulfillment which his kingship indicates). To refuse power, and to refuse to face the issue of power as illumined by Ezekiel 37, is to return to the graves divinely opened. Israel acknowledges the power of the Lord by using power--but *this power*. Apart from this power Israel is dry bones.[4] The power by which she lives--political power since she lives as a nation--is exclusively the power of God to raise the dead. The text could hardly be clearer on this point. The people are dead apart from this power. As they are used by and use resurrection power they are alive.

II

What is not immediately clear in the text is 'the when' of this power.[5] Some reflection on the 'when' may be pertinent in trying to understand the task of those who hear of, receive and are called upon to employ this power.

The oracle states that the members of the people *are raised* from their graves; in verse 24 we hear that David *is* king over them. In the text there is no direct call to the people to exercise resurrection power. The members of the house of Israel are raised quite independently of their wishes. The volitional power of bones is, to employ the recent North American political idiom, inoperative. In the text all is well: there is fulfillment and the power that brings it is poured out.[6] To the hearers, however, the fulfillment

this prophecy is still future.[7] In the life of the hearers
the text not all is well. In fact the juxtaposition of
hat obtains in the text with what obtains in the life of its
earers creates an absurdity. It is absurd to say that dry
ones will receive sinews and flesh and be made again into an
nimated body. It is not that the figure is absurd, but rath-
r that which is represented: God's people is to arrive,
gainst all appearances, at such a fulfillment as is delin-
ated in verses 24-28. The hearer's[8] political sense directs
is attention to a world in which God's positive rule and its
ower are not evident, in which this power in His people is
ittle evident and scarcely appears to be bearing the people
owards a guaranteed fulfillment. This political sense appre-
ends the sensible situation. The throne of God, which Eze-
iel espies, defies the sensible.[9] The final verses of Eze-
iel 37 attest a guaranteed fulfillment and, by virtue of the
rafting work of the theological husbandman, the opening
erses (1-10) identify divine power as that which propels
od's people to that fulfillment. As the addressee hears of
his fulfillment and begins, perhaps, to be moved by the power
ttested, his political sense makes him aware of absurdity.
e may now enjoy the text as a literary weapon with which to
ait the sensibly minded; he may enjoy the radical implication
f the text with its symbolical suggestion of new power avail-
ble. But when the political world in which the addressee
ives is recalled by him, the radical implication appears to
e the implication of the absurd and even of the irrational.
he addressee could instruct himself that the text appears
bsurd only to the mind blinded by sin. But this kind of
justification by faith" does not accord with the primary at-
estation of Ezekiel; namely, that God, and not a man, opens
raves. The total sinfulness of Israel is attested in the
arlier portions of the book in such a fashion that no exemp-
ion of the hearer to sin blindedness is possible. Indeed,
or this reason, Ezekiel does not attribute the conception of
he figure to himself, nor (implicitly) does the husbandman
ttribute the conception of the fulfillment to Ezekiel, but
o "the hand of the Lord".[10]

The absurdity which arises when the fulfillment depicted
n the text is juxtaposed with the present situation of its
earer is an element in prophecy, which comes from "the hand
f the Lord". The fulfillment promised is not a simple one.
t follows upon the judgement of the Lord and the execution of
he judgement. The people who receive fulfillment are "dead to
egin with". And the idea that dry bones perceive dry bones
s absurd, let alone the perception that they shall be en-
leshed and vivified. The absurdity is ameliorated only to
he degree that the death of the people figured in the text is
till to be tasted in its full measure by its hearers; that is,

the text announces to the people the fulfillment beyond death and guarantees the power of that fulfillment in the moment between the judgement and the execution of that judgement. Again, the announcement of the fulfillment and of the judgement preceding it are proclaimed in the present in which the people is being divested of its flesh and sinews. The absurdity is grounded in God's rule and in the way, therefore, in which He exercises His power: He brings to nought those to whom He guarantees a fulfillment. And it is in this critical moment of His rule when it is given to be perceived that *that which is* is *now* to be brought to nought. In this moment what was perceived to be *absurd* is perceived to be real, and what was perceived to be real is perceived to be absurd.

And yet to say that this occurs is not to banish the sense of absurdity. The text speaks of David as the king over the people and of the people as obedient. To Ezekiel's hearers in exile (or in Jerusalem) this fulfillment is promise. But faith in the God who gives this promise is faith in the God who in the present is bringing the people to nought. A thinker could formulate a pattern out of this *sub specie aeternitatis*, but from within the life of the people the appearance of absurdity remains. For if one believes that God is bringing His people to nought and while doing so guarantees to it its fulfillment, the rule of God appears absurd. (If this is blasphemy it must be attributed in full measure to Ezekiel, who speaks of God giving Israel bad commands to ensure her disobedience.) The perspective of the present situation must be that a God who promises His people fulfillment, even as He brings it to death, is an absurd Promiser. The perspective of the prophecy contains no less an absurdity. Since God gives fulfillment to that which He first brings to nought, God appears to have created an absurd world. Reflection upon 'the when' of the power and fulfillment attested in prophecy has exposed the element of absurdity whether the prophecy is viewed from the perspective of the present situation of the hearer or the present situation of the hearer is viewed from the perspective of prophecy. The result of this reflection, then, encourages us to ask some questions of the text.

III

How does God redeem the present situation from absurdity? How does God redeem his prophecy from absurdity? and thereby redeem His name?

Surely it would be by the exercise now of the *power* of

the fulfillment attested in this pericope that God would redeem His prophecy from the absurdity of being pie-in-the-sky.
In the text, our husbandman has connected the attestation of
the fulfillment (vss. 24-28) with the attestation of the power
of fulfillment (vss. 1-14). By manifesting the power of fulfillment in the present situation God would redeem the prophecy of fulfillment. Moreover, the manifestation of this power
in the present would be a sign of the redemption of the present. But it is precisely this manifestation that is not evident. So, again, we must begin where God's power is in evidence: in the text. God announces through His prophet that
help for the present comes precisely at the place where there
can be no possibility of help from human powers or creaturely
authorities: death. If His people, which He brings to death,
is to live with any real hope it can only be hope in Him who
has power to raise men from the dead. He is the hope, the
only hope, for He has brought His people to the place where
there is no room for any other hope. The present situation
turns entirely and exclusively upon God and His power. The
absurdity of the present situation, as a deeper reflection
upon the text of prophecy indicates, is the absurdity which
men have always had to bear: the absurdity (to them, and indeed in their disobedience, the irksome absurdity) of being
utterly dependent upon God. Power is not of man's hands nor
of the hands of lesser powers, but is of God's hands alone.
And it would appear that because God shares His power[11] it
has come to seem absurd to His people that it has power from
His generosity rather from itself. If this is absurd to the
members of His people, then the turning of His power against
them seems to represent absurdity upon absurdity. Indeed, the
degree of absurdity perceived may rise in proportion to the
degree one has abused in practice the use of (this lent)
power. The absurdity that is in the text[12] appears to rest
finally in the mystery of a God who retains all power in order to share it with His people.

The attempt has been made to discern the root of the absurd element as it is presented in the text. How is this element overcome?

(1) *God Redeems His Prophecy*

We begin where the text begins. The house of Israel is a
valley of dry bones. God may be Israel's God and Israel may
be God's people, and God who sits on a throne may descend into
the midst of His people, but it is a descent to a dead people.
He is with His people, but with it in death. There is in the
present situation no power in the people "to praise God".[13]
Since the life of the people is a matter of God's *power*, where

there exists no will to live in praise of Him, God cuts off this power. If the people lives again it will be--and be seen to be--by God's power alone. There is no power in the people to move from death to life: from disobedience to obedience; from darkness to the light of nations (cf. vs. 28). This is the present situation as illumined by prophecy. In the face of the present situation the prophecy does not tender a bare hope. Rather the prophecy speaks of a fulfillment of fulfillments.[14] Ezekiel has recited earlier the history of fulfillments which have taken place in Israel's life. Their power is not evident at the present. *But if* God attests these earlier "acts of fulfillment" as His own, He redeems His prophecy from the bareness of pie-in-the-sky. *His* attestation of these already accomplished acts as His own would make them sureties for that fulfillment of fulfillments attested in verses 24-28. Before drawing this point to a conclusion a comment on the redemption of the present situation should be made.

(2) *God Redeems the Present Situation*

In the action of redeeming His prophecy, God would illumine the absurdity of the present situation. The man who hears and believes the prophecy understands that what is absurd in the present situation is the notion that power is of the hands of God's creatures. For in the prophecy *only the power of fulfillment* (vss. 1-14), which is bestowed by God, moves the nation (and therein the nations) to fulfillment (vss. 24-28). The perspective of the present situation deems prophecy absurd not because it considers "a return to life" intrinsically absurd. Men of eminent intellect have defended the idea of human immortality. What is absurd in prophecy according to the perspective of the present situation is that the power of the creature is envisaged as being brought to nought. Even its *coming* to nought can be accepted, but not its being brought to nought.[15]

A provisional close to the discussion of these two "acts of redemption" belongs together.

How did Ezekiel maintain his prophecy in the face of the present situation? He says (or is made to say by the husbandman): "the hand of the Lord was upon me". This is a convention of prophecy and explains nothing. It points to a religious conclusion about the redemption by God (1) of His prophecy and (2) of the present situation. The religious conclusion might be that God manifests His *power* during or even through the recitation of the prophecy (1) attesting His earlier mighty deeds as His own and thereby redeeming this prophecy of fulfillment and (2) overwhelming the notion of the prophecy's hearers that power is of their hands, and thereby redeeming the present situation from its present absurd notion of power.

It is not so much that this religious conclusion is wrong absolutely, as that it is more general and amorphous than need be, given the labours of the theological husbandman. He permits the more concrete statements to be made: *God redeems the present by making possible present enjoyment of the exercise of political power and redeems prophecy by making that enjoyment hinge entirely upon the exercise of that power in terms of the fulfillment He gives (as it is delineated in the prophecy).*

(3) *God Redeems His Good Name*

Modern theological language about God's action and man's response is not the language of Ezekiel. Dry bones are enfleshed and made alive. "David is king over them. [The people] follow my ordinances." The language is the language of God's power, which He shares with His people. The Lord who grants new life to His people does so without prior consultation with its dry bones. Because life is gift and not offer there is no account of how the present situation receives the gift. The point is *not*: who has power and who hasn't? how do you get power or lose it? Rather the point is: enjoy the power you have and exercise it for every ounce of joy in it.[16]

David's kingship is the case, indeed the political case, at hand. There is no question about his receiving or attaining his crown. It is simply for him to wear it. Similarly, it is not a question of how the people are to receive or attain peoplehood. They are to be what they already are (vs. 27). In the prophecy political power is so enjoyed by the people (rather than being sought or lost) that God enjoys placing His own dwelling place among His people.

God, who ever retains all power, does so in order to share it as political power with David and His people. Wherever *that* political power is not merely possible of enjoyment (almost everywhere), but is actually being enjoyed, God's Name is redeemed from every slander.

IV

God retains all power. Power is known rightly when it is acknowledged as God's possession, which He shares with His peo-

ple for its enjoyment. The members of His people would vainly
seek to get power and vainly fear its loss. *God retains all
power that His people may enjoy it and never have to seek it
or fear losing it.* As soon as a creature thinks to seek power
or nurtures a fear about its loss, he no longer can enjoy this
power.

To be a member of this people is to enjoy power. This is
clear, since power gives life (vss. 1-14). But this enjoyment
is clearly the enjoyment of political power, since the consequence of being raised from the dead is delineated politically,
by the theological husbandman, in verses 24-28. Of course, if
this people were only a religious community then the term "political" would have to be qualified. But it is a nation among
the nations. ("Then the nations will know that I the Lord
sanctify Israel.")

What is the source of the enjoyment of political power?
In the case of Ezekiel's contemporary hearers neither their
political power nor its enjoyment came from the political situation in which they found themselves. Rather, the political
power they could enjoy was lent them in their present by the
power of fulfillment given them by God, which fulfillment was
temporally still to come.

When Ezekiel prophesies he is constrained by God's power
to do so; he is constrained to employ God's power. When Ezekiel's hearers realize that God's power is lent them, they are
constrained to employ it.[17] This power is known, to all who
heed the work of the husbandman, as the power of fulfillment,
since the depiction of the bestowal of power (vss. 1-14) is
followed by the depiction of its consequence (vss. 24-28). A
possible corollary of the text would be that prior to the full
coming of fulfillment not only is the power of fulfillment bestowed (namely, nowadays), but signs of it are given in prophecy and are to be discerned in the world *via* the prophecy.

This fulfillment (vss. 24-28), a political fulfillment,
is evidently no natural or spiritual fulfillment. It does not
arise from the nature, history or faith of the people. The
natural (or cosmic), historical, and spiritual (or religious)
conclusion of the people is death. The fulfillment, delineated in verses 24-28, is unique and absolutely distinctive.
It arises from God's power to raise the dead. *Thus, the power
under discussion is in the world, but is not a power of the
world.* By this power alone is the people, and the individual
within it,[18] brought to fulfillment. By *this* power men enjoy
this *power*, even as they are borne--because of their own, absurd seeking for and anxiety over power--into exile and kept
there. By this power they can enjoy the political power of

exiles; namely, the yearning to return and the labouring in
order to return to their land and to their own political fulfillment. *This political power gives people the power to enjoy it and to prefer it to all other powers.* This is the
strength of this power. This aspect is hidden in the present
--epecially under its distortions--and thus suffers the charge
of absurdity.

While this power of fulfillment appears absurd to the
perspective of the present situation (as has been indicated),
it is important to remember why: because it does not appear
to be *effective* power. However, the power of fulfillment does
not have the appearance of irrationality, because it is power
entirely formed to purpose. The characteristics of this purpose are comprehended under the phrase "a covenant of peace"
(vs. 26). Neither God, nor worldly authority, nor fellow
creature, nor anything within the creature shall prevent accessibility to God (vs. 26); the world shall be enjoyed as a
home (vs. 25); David and no wrongful authority shall be prince
in perpetuity (vs. 25); the neighbour shall be a fellow child
of the fathers (vs. 25); the Lord's command, and no evil im-
pulse, shall be followed (vs. 24).

This not irrational power attested in Ezekiel (vss. 1-14)
is the power of fulfillment rather than the power of the future. The future, as the future of the present, does not have
this power. The phrase "the present" or "the present situation" as employed above, is used metaphorically to refer to
those who hear the prophecy, then and now, temporally prior
to the coming of fulfillment.[19] In this present men have
flown, do flee and shall flee this fulfillment. "The present"
is that time which is lived *out of continuity with the fulfillment.* By the exercise of that political power which is shaped
by the fulfillment attested in prophecy men also have lived,
do and will live in continuity with that fulfillment, prior to
its full coming. God's people both reach towards and flee
from its fulfillment throughout the time of its life. Real
life is the continuity of the times, the rich enjoyment of
power. "The present" does not recognize the continuity of
time with its fulfillment; it either seeks or fears to lose
power and therein can find its destiny (whether consciously or
not) only in a valley of dry bones. *It is the power of life*[20]
*which God shares with the members of His people that moves
them to defy the powers of "the present" and to reject the
brokenness of time.*[21] *This power of life is 'proved' as the
creature discovers and employs it as the power of his life.*[22]

Recent popular writing illustrates that one can "enjoy"
prophecy without really enjoying the exercise of the political
power of prophecy.[23] A certain titillation over the imagery

of Ezekiel has been evidenced by those interested in extra-
terrestrial objects. The strangeness of Ezekiel's imagery
and the strangeness of his prophecy to the present is given
confirmation. But this interest is not enjoyment of the power
of prophecy. For enjoyment of the power of prophecy stirs a
yearning and an unrest in its hearer. For *ruach Adonai* re-
moves flesh from the determination of the present (vs. 13) and
orients it upon its fulfillment, the content of prophecy (vss.
24-28). As the people are exercised by and exercise the power
of fulfillment, the beginning of fulfillment occurs; and this
beginning engenders the yearning for its full coming. Only
the present thinks to discern *this* power as only so much
wind.[24]

That the present thinks to discern this *ruach* as only
wind, although not as an irrational power, is not so deep a
difficulty as is the fact that those who know this *ruach* as
the power of fulfillment also retain a sense of absurdity
about it. For this power can be known and enjoyed as the
hearer of prophecy exercises the political power lent him by
this power. But this exercise of power never acquires the
character of a proof. The hearer of prophecy, even in his
exercise of power, can no more prove the reality of this *ruach* than he can possess or lose it. This *ruach*, unlike the
land, is not possessed or controlled by the man who exercises
and enjoys it. This has, at least, the appearance of absurdity: to know, use and enjoy a reality for which one can offer
no proof to either oneself or to another. It is God alone who
possesses and controls this *ruach*. Indeed, His summons of it
from the four winds (vs. 9) indicates that He and not His
creatures possesses it. To enjoy a power, the reality for
which no proof can be offered, remains an absurdity which can
not be dispelled. Since the Lord retains and does not give
over this power to the power of proof (even as He lends this
power) its recipient can only await its outpouring upon all
flesh. He can hope that its present enjoyment by him can
provide a clue to, if not a proof of, its reality.

The obvious and evident point that this *ruach* is *ruach
Adonai* may not be passed over. For there is something here
which can cause a difficulty for those who hear prophecy. For
while a hearer may not find it difficult to accept that he
does not give himself life, he often will find it difficult to
accept the husbandman's point that it is not the creature who
guides this life to its political fulfillment.[25] Political
fulfillment, he is told, is given, even as life is given, and
political enjoyment means enjoying the power that fulfillment
as gift confers. The hearer may want to know: where in this
is man's distinct identity? This is the difficulty he envisages: the loss of human distinctiveness. The husbandman

makes clear and rather formal the distinction between God's activity and man's: it is the distinction between ruler and ruled. The unity is expressed formally too: it is the oneness of the covenant of peace. But is this distinction too stiff for comfort? Moreover, is it lost by the husbandman in the grafting of verses 1-14 with verses 24-28? This connection proclaims that *ruach Adonai* not only makes Israel alive, but also obedient. The Ezekiel tradition from beginning to end speaks of God wielding power, bringing the people to nought, bringing the people to life and fulfillment. Where is the identity of the people in this? Where is the identity of the individual member of the people in this? Howsoever one regards the reply, it is evidently made by reference to *power*. If the husbandman represents the fulfillment rather statically, he also retains the vivid and dramatic oracle about God's exercise of power. The Lord retains His power, and yet pours it out not only upon, but also for, His people. Power is of the Lord, but it is the creature who is empowered (for fulfillment). The people is made mighty for fulfillment.[26] The concern to discern the distinctiveness of the creature in all this may be more acute than is warranted. We might well be alarmed if the language of the husbandman was religious and thus amorphous, anonymous and even, possibly, irrational. But the language of power (vss. 1-14), which might be rendered by a religious interpretation, is clearly joined with the language of politics (vss. 24-28). We hear about kingship, statutes and obedience to them, peace between parties, God's rule. More specifically: this *ruach* establishes the right political head, institutes ordinances and makes real and therefore possible obedience to them,[27] grants the people sovereignty over the land, establishes peace (which in the first place means good relations between ruler and ruled) and makes the Ruler accessible. (A Ruler who brings real peace and is accessible is to be cherished!)

While God retains the power of rule, He retains it for the enjoyment of David, the enjoyment of the people, and finally for the enjoyment of all flesh. *Our enjoyment of power is not only a use of power; it is the right use of political power.* In this enjoyment real and genuine human acts take place: real and genuine because they occur not by caprice, but according with what is true (vs. 24). The enjoyment of political power displaces anxious seeking after it and anxious fear of its loss, because in it *ruach Adonai* makes alive (vs. 14) and thus no longer hope (vs. 11) but hopelessness is lost and clean cut off.

NOTES

1. Cf. Jürgen Moltmann, *The Crucified God* (London, 1974) a translation by R. A. Wilson and John Bowden of *Der gekreuzigte Gott* (München, Second Edition, 1973) and the works of my Canadian colleague Douglas John Hall, *Lighten Our Darkness* (Philadelphia, 1976) and *The Reality of the Gospel and the Unreality of the Churches* (Philadelphia, 1975).

2. Gerhard von Rad, *Old Testament Theology, Vol. II* (London, 1975), a translation by D. M. G. Stalker of *Theologie des Altens Testaments II* (München, 1960), pp. 234-37.

3. That is, abstractly or spiritually.

4. The relation of power and fulfillment is of interest to those engaged in Christian-Marxist dialogue. A "transcendental utopia" can be so fanciful as to be incapable of engendering passion; no more can an idea of "natural transcendence" (*i.e.* the process which transcends immediate *pragmata*) engender the hope for liberation. It may be that the relation of the power of fulfillment to fulfillment as envisaged by the husbandman of the Ezekiel tradition is pertinent.

5. Cf. Professor Eichrodt's instructive comments about the dating of vss. 1-10 in: Walter Eichrodt, *Ezekiel* (Philadelphia, 1970), a translation by Cosslett Quin of *Der Prophet Hesekiel* (Göttingen, 1965-66), pp. 506-7.

6. Poured out like an invisible fluid. Cf. Eichrodt, *op. cit.*, p. 508.

7. The Christian enterprise has always to thank historical criticism for keeping it alert to the fact that during our days we are to attend to the graves until the fulfillment at which they shall be opened.

8. Ezekiel's hearer in Babylon or Jerusalem or wherever, then and now.

9. Chapter One.

10. Cf. Walther Zimmerli, *Ezechiel, Biblischer Kommentar Altes Testament XIII/1* (Neukirchen-Vluyn, 1969), p. 85.

11. David is king; a covenant of peace is given; access to God is given (vss. 26 and 27).

12. Or rather, the absurdity of the present situation in the light of the text.

13. "...praising [God] and not praising [Him] stand over against one another like life and death: praise becomes the most elementary 'token of being alive' that exists...." Thus von Rad on the Old Testament's doctrine of man, *op. cit.*, pp. 369-70.

14. Vss. 24-28 are, in fact, a summary of what has appeared earlier in the book.

15. The attempt by North American males to withstand a limitation on their power by females gives a pale glimpse of how the creature reacts to the mere suggestion that his power is going to be limited, let alone brought to nought.

16. So Jesus in the parable of the talents.

17. Cf. D. Bonhoeffer's comment: "Only he who believes is obedient, and only he who is obedient believes." in *Nachfolge* (München, 1964), p. 35, as quoted and translated by Paul Lehmann in *The Transfiguration of Politics* (New York, 1975), p. 84.

18. Chapter 18.

19. The word "temporally" is also used metaphorically; the subsequent comments should make clear just how.

20. "Come from the four winds, O breath and breathe upon these slain that they might *live*" (vs. 9b). "And I will put my Spirit within you and you shall *live*..." (vs. 14).

21. The hearer of Ezekiel's prophecy is to accept exile in order to reject exile.

22. Modern psychological theories which maintain that a human being cannot attain knowledge of himself beyond what determines him, encompass too many issues to be considered here. It may be noted, however, that the point for Ezekiel is not in the first place man's freedom and his knowledge of it, but rather God's freedom. It is God's power which raises men, frees men (by lending them power) and summons men to enjoy this power and in the enjoyment of this power to know what they are doing.

23. Cf. Erich von Daniken, *Chariots of the Gods* (New York, 1974).

24. While the perspective of the present thinks to discern this *ruach* as only wind, and not as real power, it is unable to maintain that this is irrational power. This *ruach*, which makes alive, also gives to life that genuine form which is the people as a nation. So while this nation is in exile and, by God's judgement, is being brought to nought, there is a discernible community which, being brought to nought, yearns by this *ruach* to be brought again to life and genuine life. And it is being given the power by which this shall occur!

25. Cf. Gerhard von Rad, *op. cit.*, pp. 234-37.

26. This fulfillment, of course, only follows upon the Lord's action of bringing the people to nought, as Ezekiel ever reminds his hearer.

27. This real and possible obedience is *free* obedience. These ordinances remain in God's hands, their provenance being *ruach Adonai*. God's sovereignty is to be attested thus: no creature is to fence in, catch at or harden these ordinances or their provenance. Cf. Ez. 36:26-27.

7

REFLECTIONS ON THE MOTIVE CLAUSES
IN OLD TESTAMENT LAW

Donald E. Gowan

> You've got to show how the thing was done,
> and then, if you like, bring in motive to
> back up your proof. If a thing could only
> have been done one way, and if only one
> person could have done it that way, then
> you've got your criminal, motive or no
> motive. There's How, When, Where, Why
> and Who--and when you've got How, you've
> got Who.[1]

Thus spake Lord Peter Wimsey, Dorothy Sayers' master detective,
reminding us that "Why?" is in law normally the least important
of questions. What, How, When, Where and Who are objective
questions, for which material evidence and the testimony of
witnesses can be obtained. But Why is a subjective matter, by
its nature much more difficult to determine, and indeed the
doer of the deed itself is not always certain of the real motive which lies behind the act. Sometimes, to be sure, courts
do have to decide questions of motive, e.g. when one claims to
have acted in self-defense, but normally one would expect the
law to avoid the subjective wherever possible.

When law becomes a part of theology, however, it is another matter; in the New Testament and in Rabbinic literature
why one keeps the law is just as important as the keeping of
it. Indeed, law in its narrow sense as the mere stipulation
of forbidden or required acts coupled with the penalties prescribed for disobedience, does not occur in Jewish or Christian
literature. And the foundations of Jewish and Christian ethics, the legal materials in the Old Testament, have long been
recognized as something different from a proper law code; they
are the law preached.[2] Among the non-legal features which give
the collections of law in the Old Testament their parenetic
quality are motive clauses, usually brief statements attached
to individual commandments to explain why they should be
obeyed. Despite the intrinsic interest of these clauses they
have tended to be neglected in the extensive studies of Old

Testament law which have appeared in recent years, perhaps for the reason noted at the beginning of this paper--because considerations of motive take us beyond what is strictly legal in nature, and the works alluded to tend to focus on what properly belongs in the realm of law.[3] In the law codes of the Old Testament, however, the law-giver (or preacher) not only tells the people what they must and must not do, and prescribes what must happen to transgressors of the law, but also goes on to *explain* the law to the people, to provide reasons for keeping the law which go beyond the penalties which are normally the only motivation provided by a code of law. These motive clauses may bring us as close as we can get to explicit statements about the conceptions and convictions underlying the laws of the Old Testament and the ethos they sought to preserve and protect. In considering what Israelites believed to be "motivating" we may also get some additional insights into the anthropology of the Old Testament.

This paper presents an abbreviated study of the motive clauses in the Book of the Covenant (Exod. 21-23), the Deuteronomic Code (Deut. 12-25) and the Holiness Code (Lev. 17-25), concluding with some reflections on a few of the most interesting features which have been observed.[4] It is presented to Markus Barth, former teacher and colleague, on the occasion of his sixty-fifth birthday as a small expression of thanks for all that he has done for me.

The need for a more serious consideration of the motive clauses in Old Testament law than has hitherto been available is well illustrated by the article on law in the *Theological Dictionary of the New Testament*.[5] When one reads that article after having pondered at least 90 motive clauses in the just-mentioned codes, certain statements strike one as rather peculiar. For example:

> Thus the motive for keeping this Law is simply that of obedience in so far as there is any conscious reflection on the questions of motivation. (p. 1036)

> For this reason [since covenant precedes prohibition] there is reference to punishment for violation but not to any special reward for fulfilment. (p. 1037)

> The validity of the laws [for the older historical books] is primarily based on the fact that they are divinely posited, not on their immanent goodness or utility.

> Naturally God demands what is good, but
> it is to be done because God demands it.
> (p. 1038)

From these statements it would seem obvious that there are *no*
motive clauses associated with the laws of the Old Testament!
It is not that I am proposing to engage in a critique of the
TDNT article; it was written a long time ago, and I am actually citing it here because it serves a *useful* purpose. It leads
us to consider with greater care the meaning of the many motive
clauses which do exist and to attempt to find out whether it is
possible to go beyond the helpful study of the same subject
published by Gemser in the first Supplement to *Vetus Testamentum*.[6]

TYPES OF MOTIVE CLAUSES AND THEIR FUNCTIONS

First it may be helpful to recall some of the conclusions
Gemser reached in his study:[7]

1. He could not locate any motive clauses in any of the
ancient Near Eastern law codes examined by him, so concluded
that this appears to be a distinctively Israelite feature.
The question, Why motive clauses? is accentuated by this conclusion.

2. These clauses appear in conjunction with both apodictic and casuistic forms.

3. The occurrence of rhythmic patterns in the Book of
the Covenant and the Ritual Decalogue, and perhaps also in
the Elohistic Decalogue suggests that the clauses are archaic
and traditional, not redactorial.[8]

4. The abundance of motive clauses addressed to the
people rather than to judges shows that the *Sitz im Leben* is
cultic rather than strictly legal.[9]

5. Those which appeal to common sense and to the conscience show the democratic character of Israelite law, and
the religious kind show how deeply the religious sense had
penetrated the lives of the common people.

Gemser classified the contents of the clauses as being
of four types: 1) Explanatory: e.g. Exod. 21:21 "for the
slave is his money". 2) Ethical: e.g. Exod. 22:26 (Eng.)

"for that is his only covering". 3) Religious (cultic as well
as theological): e.g. "it is an abomination to the Lord".
4) Religious-historical: e.g. Exod. 22:21 (Eng.) "for you
were strangers in the land of Egypt".

There is another way of classifying these clauses which
corresponds more closely to the different ways in which they
are formulated and which may provide more information about
the concerns which lie behind them. They group themselves
rather neatly, both as to form and function, into references
to the past, the present and the future. In what follows,
examples of each group will be given together with references
to where they occur, then some comments on the types of motivation which are provided will be offered.

1. *References to the Past:* One small group appeals to a prior
situation or to a divine act in the past to provide the reason
for the law or the motivation for keeping it. The first four
types all are introduced by $k\bar{\imath}$; the last two are formulated
differently.

a) "For you were strangers in the land of Egypt" (Exod.
22:21 [Eng.]; 23:9; Lev. 19:33-34; Deut. 23:7)

b) "You shall remember that you were a slave in the land
of Egypt and the Lord your God redeemed you." (Deut. 15:12-
15; 16:12; 24:17-18; 24:22; cf. "I am the Lord your God who
brought you out of the land of Egypt." Lev. 19:36; 25:35-38)

c) "For in it [the month Abib] you came out of Egypt"
(Exod. 23:15; Deut. 16:1; variant: "that all the days of your
life you may remember the day when you came out of the land of
Egypt" Deut. 16:3)

d) "For the Lord your God has chosen him out of all your
tribes, to stand and minister in the name of the Lord, him and
his sons for ever" (Deut. 18:4-5)

e) "Because they [Ammonites and Moabites] did not meet
you with bread and with water on the way, etc." (Deut. 23:4-
5)

f) "Remember what Amalek did to you on the way, etc."
(Deut. 25:17-19)

The initial question which is raised by these clauses
is, what kinds of appeals to past events serve to motivate

future action, and the two most obvious answers are those
which arouse the emotions of gratitude or of hatred. Hatred
presumably is the basis for Deuteronomy's references to
Israel's past treatment by the Ammonites, Moabites and Amalakites in 23:4-5 and 25:17-19. Gratitude probably lies in the
background in a good many places, but is not heavily emphasized. Appeals to history, more than the other kinds of motive clauses, need to show some obvious relationship between
the act which is commanded and the event in the past which is
cited as the reason for obedience. The most interesting set
of such analogies appears in the references to the sojourn in
Egypt.

A straightforward reasoning process appears in Deut. 15:
12-15, which provides for the release of a Hebrew slave after
six years of service. God redeemed you from slavery, therefore you must let your slaves go; and there is a clear analogy
between God's action and the action of the Israelite. That
obvious relationship seems to be broadened almost into a principle in Deut. 24:17-18, which does not deal with slaves but
with the alien, orphan and widow, yet the same motive clause
appears: "you shall remember that you were a slave in the
land of Egypt, and the Lord your God redeemed you." It would
seem that the slave has implicitly become the symbol of all
the weaker classes of society, so that God's merciful treatment of the Hebrew slaves in Egypt becomes the analogy for the
Israelite's treatment of all the weak. The same relationship
appears in the gleaning laws in Deut. 24:19-22.

A different sort of analogy is used in the clauses, "for
you were a stranger in the land of Egypt". Here, no reference
is made to what God has done as the model for human behavior.
The reasoning process is made most explicit in Exod. 23:9.
"You shall not oppress a stranger; you know the heart of a
stranger, for you were strangers in the land of Egypt." The
logic of this must be the same as that of the Golden Rule;
treat him as you would be treated. Presumably that is also
the force of Exod. 22:21 (Eng.), where the same law and motive
appear but without the explanation, "you know the heart of a
stranger".

Lev. 19:33-34 appeals to the same motive but goes a step
further, from the negative to the positive: "When a stranger
sojourns with you in your land, you shall not do him wrong.
The stranger who sojourns with you shall be to you as the native among you, and you shall love him as yourself, for you
were strangers in the land of Egypt." Here the analogy fails
to carry us as far as the law commands; to say, you know what
it's like to be a stranger, so treat the stranger as you would
be treated, does not necessarily go as far as, love him as

yourself. We have reached the point where something more than sweet reason is required.

There remains the most striking use of all; Deut. 23:7b: "You shall not abhor an Egyptian, for you were strangers in the land of Egypt." This is exactly contrary to the reasoning used in the order concerning what to do with the Ammonites, Moabites and Amalakites, i.e. essentially, treat them as they treated you. Is it because the Egyptian is no longer the arch-enemy, for Deuteronomy, that a different attitude is taken? Is it because Egypt did provide a homeland, of sorts, for the Hebrews that an analogy can be drawn with Israel as a homeland for some Egyptians in the present? Or is it simply a specific application of the general principle: "you know the heart of a stranger"? Taken by itself, this motive clause would seem to produce the opposite emotions from those desired when favorable treatment of the Egyptians is being commended. It probably could be effective only because "for you were strangers in the land of Egypt" had gathered into itself strong emotive overtones in favor of the merciful treatment of others, very likely tinged with gratitude to the God who had so treated them.

That is supported by one more use of the sojourn theme, in which there is no analogy which is immediately apparent. In Deut. 16:9-12 it is given as the reason for observing the Feast of Weeks, and no attempt is made to explain the relationship. Had it been connected with Passover (vss. 1-8), the reason would have been obvious; perhaps the best we can say about this one is that the whole complex of pilgrimage feasts had been associated with the redemption of Israel, from the Exodus to the occupation of Canaan, and the sojourn in Egypt could thus be alluded to in connection with any of them, as the beginning stage of it all. The motive clause is now used, not to commend ethical behavior, but to establish the reason for worship, and it is here where gratitude presumably is an implicit but essential factor.

2. *References to the Present:* These clauses describe a present condition (a-f) or allude to what is assumed to be a self-evident truth (g-m) as reasons for obeying the law. All of them begin with $k\bar{\imath}$ except for some of the $t\bar{o}\,'\bar{e}b\bar{a}h$ clauses (i) and most of the incest laws (g).

a) "Since he [the Levite] has no portion or inheritance with you" (Deut. 12:12; 14:27, 29)

b) "For the houses in the cities of the Levites are their

ssession among the people of Israel" (Lev. 25:33; cf. Lev.
:34)

c) "For they are my slaves, whom I brought forth out of
e land of Egypt" (Lev. 25:39-42, 47-54)

d) "For you are a people holy to the Lord" (Deut. 14:1-
21)

e) "For you are strangers and sojourners with me" (Lev.
:23)

f) "For he [the Edomite] is your brother" (Deut. 23:7)

g) "She is your mother, etc." (Incest laws; Lev. 18:7-
)

h) "For he would be taking a life in pledge" (Deut. 24:

i) "For that is an abomination to the Lord your God"
eut. 17:1; 18:10-12; 22:5; 23:18 (Eng.); 24:1-4; 25:13-16;
v. 18:22; cf. 18:23; 19:5-8; variant: "which the Lord your
d hates" Deut. 16:22)

j) "For that is his only covering, it is his mantle for
s body; in what else shall he sleep?" (Exod. 22:26-27 [Eng.])

k) "For he is the first issue of his strength" (Deut. 21:
-17)

l) "For the blood is the life" (Deut. 12:23; Lev. 17:10-
)

m) "For, are the trees in the field men that they should
besieged by you?" (Deut. 20:19)

n) "For a bribe blinds the officials, and subverts the
use of those who are in the right" (Exod. 23:8; Deut. 16:
)

o) "For at half the cost of a hired servant he has
rved you six years" (Deut. 15:18)

Reason and good will are appealed to regularly in these
auses which allude to the present. The assumption that those
dressed desire to please God may be detected in a couple of
aces. The types of appeals which are made may be classified
 follows:

1. Calculated responses: In this group reason plays an obvious role. There is only one motive which we are probably justified in calling an appeal to pure self-interest, but it is itself already mitigated by its context. In Deut. 15:12-18 two reasons for letting one's Hebrew slave go at the end of his allotted time are given: "You shall remember that you were a slave in the land of Egypt", the type of clause already discussed, but then, as if that were not enough, "It shall not seem hard to you, when you let him go free from you; for at half the cost of a hired servant he has served you six years" (o). This level of reasoning is unusual in Old Testament law.

Awareness of the value of preserving the social and natural order is a reasonable motive which may be appealed to even when the instincts pull in another direction, and this occurs quite often. Here may be placed the references to preservation of kinship structures which are central to the Israelite social order (g, k), to the maintenance of the cult (a, b), to the proper functioning of the judicial system (n), and to the protection of nature from undue harm (m).

2. Humanitarianism: A small group of clauses strikes us as appealing to something higher than elementary or calculated responses--in that self-interest is not necessarily involved at all--and so they may be called "humanitarian" in their appeal. These have to do with taking a mill stone or one's mantel in pledge (h, j), with the reminder that such treatment of the poor will have dire effects upon them.

3. Religious commitment: Finally, there are appeals which would have force only to those who have a deep religious commitment. One group says, in effect, "we should behave this way because God has made it so". In Lev. 25 the limitation of slavery is based on "for they are my slaves, whom I brought out of the land of Egypt" (c); and Deuteronomy twice justifies a law with "for you are a people holy to the Lord your God, and the Lord has chosen you to be a people for his own possession" (d). Perhaps "for I the Lord your God am holy", which appears so often in the Holiness Code, is also a motive clause; if so it may belong in this group.

Other clauses appeal to the desire to please, or at least avoid displeasing God. The identification of certain acts as an abomination to the Lord fits here (i).[10]

3. *References to the Future:* These clauses describe a result rather than a condition or past act or self-evident truth. There are twenty groups with motives of this type and unlike

the previous types only a few exceptional cases are introduced
by *kī*. Five groups (a-e) use *lᵉma'an*, five groups (f-j) use
the simple future, four groups (k-n) use the future with the
negative particle, one (o) uses the infinitive construct, two
(p, q) use the dissuasive particle *pen*, one group (r) uses a
mixture of four of the above constructions, and one (s) takes
the form of a divine threat.

a) "That you may learn to fear the Lord your God always"
(Deut. 14:22-23; 17:12-13; 19:15-20; 21:18-21)

b) "That the Lord your God may bless you in all the work
of your hands that you do" (Deut. 14:28-29; 15:7-11, 12-18;
16:13-15; 23:19-20 [Eng.]; 24:19)

c) "That all may go well with you and with your children
after you" (Deut. 12:25, 28; 22:6-7; cf. 19:11-13)

d) "That you may live and inherit the land which the
Lord your God gives you" (Deut. 16:20; 22:6-7; 25:13-16; variant: "So that he [the king] may continue long in his kingdom,
he and his children, in Israel" Deut. 17:14-20)

e) "That your generations may know that I made the people
of Israel dwell in booths when I brought them out of the land
of Egypt" (Lev. 23:42-43)

f) "And it shall be righteousness to you before the Lord
your God" (Deut. 24:10-13)

g) "And it be sin in you" (Deut. 15:7-11; 23:21 [Eng.];
24:14-15; variants: "Lest you bear sin because of him" Lev.
19:17; "And so to sin against the Lord your God" Deut. 20:
16-18)

h) "And so cause them to bear iniquity and guilt, by
eating their holy things" (Lev. 22:15-16)

i) "So you shall purge the evil from the midst of you"
(Deut. 13:1-5; 17:2-7, 12; 19:11-13, 15-20; 21:1-9, 18-21;
22:13-21, 22, 23-24; 24:7)

j) "To be happy with his wife whom he has taken" (Deut.
24:5)

k) "That there may be no wickedness among you" (Lev. 20:
14)

l) "Lest innocent blood be shed in your land which the

Lord your God gives you for an inheritance, and so the guilt of bloodshed be upon you" (Deut. 19:8-10). Compare: "So you shall purge the guilt of innocent blood from your midst" (Deut 19:11-13; 21:1-9); "You shall not defile your land which the Lord your God gives you for an inheritance" (Deut. 21:22-23); "That you may not bring the guilt of blood upon your house, if anyone fall from it" (Deut. 22:8); "And you shall not bring guilt upon the land which the Lord your God gives you for an inheritance" (Deut. 24:1-4)

m)   "That his name may not be blotted out of Israel" (Deut. 25:5-10)

n)   "That the land where I am bringing you to dwell may not vomit you out" (Lev. 20:22)

o)   "That they may yield more richly" (Lev. 19:23-25)

p)   "Lest...your brother be degraded in your sight" (Deut. 25:3)

q)   "Lest the avenger of blood pursue the manslayer... and wound him mortally, though he did not deserve to die, etc." (Deut. 19:4-7)

r)   "And so profane the name of your God" (Lev. 18:21; 19:12; 20:2-5; 21:6; 22:2; variant: "Because he has profaned a holy thing of the Lord" Lev. 19:5-8)

s)   "If you do afflict them and they cry to me I will surely hear their cry; and my wrath will burn, and I will kill you with the sword, and your wives shall become widows and your children fatherless" (Exod. 22:22-24 [Eng.]; cf. 22:26-27 and 23:7)

When these references to the future--projections of expected results--are compared with the previous group--types of present conditions which are appealed to in order to motivate compliance with the law--it will be seen that several similar motives appear and that some new ones may be added.

1. Calculated responses: The importance of maintaining the family no doubt is the basis for the law exempting the newly-wed from military service for a year and the reason is attached, "to be happy with his wife whom he has taken" (j), in addition to the law of levirate marriage, with its reason, "that his name may not be blotted out of Israel" (m). The description of the value of certain punishments as deterrants to future disobedience (a) may also correspond to the desire to

preserve the social order. Note, for example, the formulation
in Deut. 17:13: "And all the people shall hear and fear and
not act presumptuously again."

A new grouping may be described as reflecting a rather
strong concern for protection from certain destructive, supernatural or irrational forces. This comes through especially
strongly in the promises that by keeping the law the evil may
be purged from their midst and blood guilt may be avoided (i,
1). Other references to sin, iniquity and guilt, and the
promise "that the land...may not vomit you out" seem to belong here as well (g, h, k, n). These are laws which might be
called "protective" in intent. The words referring to sin,
guilt and evil may at first seem to us to be strongly judgmen-
tal and thus to be related to that single divine threat of
punishment in Exod. 22:22-24, to be discussed shortly. But
there is an impersonal quality about most of this group which
suggests another interpretation. It is true that Deut. 20:
16-18 brings God into the picture: "and so to sin against the
Lord your God", but that is exceptional, because the other
four references to sin are impersonal: "and it be sin in you"
(Deut. 15:7-11; 23:21 [Eng.]; 24:14f) or "lest you bear sin
because of him" (Lev. 19:17). Related to the last of these
are two other motives in H: "and cause them to bear iniquity
of guilt" (Lev. 22:15f) and "that there may be no wickedness
among you" (Lev. 20:14). This sin, guilt or wickedness is
something which may be in or among them, which they may have
to bear.

Nine times we find evil referred to in a similar way:
"and you shall purge the evil from your midst"; attached in
each case (with one possible exception) to the death penalty
(Deut. 13:2-6; 17:2-7, 12f; 19:15-20; 21:18-21; 22:13-21, 22,
23f; 24:7). The same verb, $bi'ar$, is used in two other texts
with "innocent blood" rather than evil as its object (19:11-
13; 21:1-9). Those passages are surely related to two others:
"and blood-guilt will be upon you" (Deut. 19:8-10), and "That
you may not bring blood-guilt upon your house" (Deut. 22:8).
Finally, there are references to something almost physical
which may affect the land, against which the law provides protection, in "you shall not defile your land" (Deut. 21:22-23),
"you shall not cause your land to sin" (Deut. 24:1-4) and
"that the land...may not vomit you out" (Lev. 20:22). Passages such as these have been best explained by G. von Rad,
following K. Koch and others, in this way:

> The evil deed was only one side of the mat-
> ter, for through it an evil had been set in
> motion which sooner or later would inevit-

> ably turn against the sinner or the com-
> munity to which he belonged. On this
> view, the 'recompense' which catches up
> with evil is certainly no subsequent fo-
> rensic event which the sin evokes in a
> completely different sphere--that is,
> with God. It is the radiation of the
> evil which now continues on....[11]

Despite the sweeping nature of von Rad's statement, the Old
Testament elsewhere does display a very strong tendency to
bring God into the picture as one who is personally affronted
by disobedience of the law,[12] but this group of texts does
speak as von Rad described it. They do not condemn Israel for
its sin, but are protective of the individual, society and nature by providing ways in which the malignant forces introduced into the world by certain acts may be nullified. In
this respect they correspond to the general tendency of the
motive clauses to be positive (pointing toward blessing)
rather than negative (threatening with curses).

   2. Humanitarianism: Something higher than a calculated
response is surely appealed to in the law which limits the number of stripes which may be inflicted in flogging, with the
reason being to avoid an undesirable result: "lest...your
brother be degraded in your sight" (p).

   3. Religious commitment: Certain laws which are said to
have as their aim, "that you may learn to fear the Lord" (a)
have been alluded to in connection with the desire to preserve
the social order, but surely the motive clauses have force only
among a people who are already convinced that it is essential
to maintain a healthy relationship between God and his people.
This commitment would also lend force to the laws designed to
prevent Israel from profaning the name of God (r).

   4. Rewards and punishments (or blessings and curses):
These are all of the result type, obviously, and so they have
not appeared in the earlier groupings. All but one are promises of blessing (b, c, d, f, o). The only exception is the
divine threat to kill those who afflict the widow and the
orphan in Exod. 22:21-23 (s). This is surely a matter of some
importance, for the Israelite knew how to formulate threats
quite effectively when he wished, and threats do appear elsewhere, very prominently in the curses at the ends of Leviticus
and Deuteronomy, but the motive clauses almost exclusively prefer the carrot to the stick. In this light the sentence quoted
earlier from *TDNT*, "For this reason there is reference to punishment for violation but not to any special reward for ful-

filment", seems rather strange.

WHY DOES OLD TESTAMENT LAW INCLUDE MOTIVE CLAUSES?

The preceding paragraphs have commented on how the law-giver attempted to motivate Israelites to be obedient to the divine will; in conclusion some reflections will be offered on why motive clauses are used so often. Gemser and others have concluded that the *Sitz im Leben* of these forms of law is the cult, but Gemser also went on to discuss similarities between some of the motive clauses and proverbial sayings. When this is coupled with the rather personal tone of many of these clauses one is led to speculate that a rather more informal setting than what most of us would conceive of as "cultic recitation" may have been responsible for the motive clauses. A recent article by P. J. Budd, on Priestly Instruction, suggests that "It is possible that the motive clauses within the priestly laws point to a genuine teaching role for the priests in so far as they are aimed at fostering particular beliefs and attitudes",[13] and the consideration of motive clauses in this paper tends to reinforce that suggestion.

Most of these motives are very familiar to all of us who have attempted any type of moral teaching, as parents or pastors, or who have been on the receiving end as children and students. We note in passing that certain motives which are well-known from Christian teaching and also from philosophical ethics are not present in any significant way in these clauses. We do not find appeals to a sense of duty, to the need for the preservation of values or to the desire to build character or cultivate the higher virtues. None of that surprises us greatly, for such motives have grown out of an ethical tradition rather different from that of ancient Israel. Our own extensive experience with the threat as a motive, both in daily life and in customary interpretations of the Bible, does make the relative unimportance of threats as motivating clauses, directly attached to Old Testament laws, a matter of considerable interest, however.

But why should these clauses, consisting as they do mostly of reminders and assurances, motivate an Israelite to obey the law? They seem to be based on the conviction that Israel presently lives in a condition of wholeness established by Yahweh and to be concerned to preserve and protect that condition from the damaging effects of certain kinds of human behavior. The concern of law to preserve the status quo is, of course, not unusual but the normal thing. Neither is it unusual for a society to consider its own order to have divine legitimation. One of the special features of Israelite law, however, is its insistence on remembering that its society was created out of a band of slaves who were freed from foreign masters and given their own land, and on drawing moral consequences from that. The character of Israelite society was defined by the God who freed slaves, has mercy on aliens and gives land to the landless. It was an order of life having that quality which he established in Canaan and the wholeness of life in that land is destroyed when that order is violated.

Hence Israelite law is not addressed to the lower classes to define their duties to their betters.[14] It speaks to the powerful, to define their obligations. The just order does not have to be established, by revolution or legislation; it exists as a creation of God. It can only be preserved by those who have power. Of course, anyone may have the power to introduce destructive forces, by murdering, for example; hence much of the law applies to all, but the motive clauses are especially directed toward those who have power enough to be able to decide whether to benefit themselves at the expense of others, or to work to preserve the wholeness of God's order.

Those to whom people who have power are specifically obligated are: widows, orphans and aliens, priests, Levites, the poor, Edomites and Egyptians, one's children, trees and birds, slaves, debtors, manslayers, one's deceased and childless brother, and one being punished by flogging. Obligations toward equals involve customers and neighbors. The only superior who is mentioned in a motive clause is God. Where the land sits in this hierarchy I shall leave to others to decide.

Israelite law assumes, then, that justice may be found in the present order by everyone who lives in it. The positions of some within the order are precarious, however, and so a moral obligation is set upon all others to be sure that justice is preserved. Although not all are equal in every respect, the special quality of Israelite society, as composed of former slaves living in a land not originally their own, was biased against any rigid class structure. The very existence in a law code of motive clauses, which have no legal function whatever, is based on the assumption that the Israelite lived in the "fear of the Lord", i.e. a relationship of loving, willing obedience to a God whom he understood to be his father (Deut. 14:1) and the source of all blessing; and also on the assumption that he was a reasonable person, capable of understanding what is best for the society in which he lives and of deciding to live in accordance with that aim.

Would that it were so!

Within the legal corpus of the Old Testament itself, then, already appears a recognition of the limits of what law in its narrow sense can accomplish in human society and an effort to go beyond that by means of appeals to motives which might lead the Israelite to behave in ways which could never be coerced by the legal process. When that fails, as it always does, the groundwork is laid for the deeper considerations of the human predicament which appear in Old Testament wisdom and in the prophets.

The legal materials of the Old Testament show an awareness that "law" as a set of do's and don'ts is an insufficient basis for peace and justice, for it adds admonitions and promises to its laws. This brief consideration of such motive clauses may have helped us to appreciate the humanitarian concerns of Old Testament law and the depth of its appreciation of the human condition, but we recognize that these measures also are inadequate, for they appeal to the reasonable person whose heart is in the right place. The prophets and the wise men learned that the law preached is still inadequate (as Paul would later affirm) not because there is something wrong with the law but because something in human beings, which no motive clause can ever touch, needs to be made right.

NOTES

1. D. L. Sayers, *Busman's Honeymoon* (Harper & Row, 1937; quotation from Avon Books edition, 1968), p. 187.

2. G. von Rad, *Studies in Deuteronomy* (*SBT* 9; SCM Press, 1953), chapters I & II.

3. H. Cazelles, *Etudes sur le code de l'alliance* (Paris: Letouzey et Anê, 1946); A. Cholewinski, *Heiligkeitsgesetz und Deuteronomium. Eine vergleichende Studie* (*Analecta Biblica* 66; 1976); H. W. Gilmer, *The If-You Form in Israelite Law* (*SBL Dissertation Series*, 15; 1975); R. Kilian, *Literarkritische und Formgeschichtliche Untersuchung des Heiligkeitsgesetzes* (*BBB* 19; 1963); W. Kornfeld, *Studien zum Heiligkeitsgesetz (Lev 17-26)* (Wien: Verlag Herder, 1952); G. Liedke, *Gestalt und Bezeichnung alttestamentlicher Rechtssätze: Eine formge-schichtlich-terminologische Studie* (*WMANT* 39; 1971); R. P. Merendino, *Das deuteronomische Gesetz; eine literarkritische, gattungs- und überlieferungsgeschichtliche Untersuchung zu Dt 12-26* (*BBB* 31; 1969); S. M. Paul, *Studies in the Book of the Covenant in the Light of Cuneiform and Biblical Law* (*VTS* 18; 1970); H. Graf Reventlow, *Das Heiligkeitsgesetz, formgeschicht-lich untersucht* (*WMANT* 6, 1961); J. Van der Ploeg, "Studies in Hebrew Law" *CBQ* 12 (1950) 248-259, 416-427, *CBQ* 13 (1951) 28-43, 164-171, 296-307.

4. This paper makes no attempt to be a complete study of motive clauses. It is confined to the three major law codes, which provide a large enough sampling to reveal some of the main concerns expressed in such material. The comments focus on a few of those concerns and do not attempt to discuss all the clauses quoted.

5. W. Gutbrod, "*nomos*, The Law in the Old Testament" *TDNT* 4 (Eerdmans, 1967; German original published 1942), pp. 1036-1047.

6. B. Gemser, "The Importance of the Motive Clause in Old Testament Law" *VTS* 1 (Brill, 1953) 50-66.

7. Points 1 & 2 appear on pp. 52-53; points 3, 4 & 5 on pp. 62-64.

8. Also, W. Beyerlin, "Die Paränese im Bundesbuch und ihre Herkunft" in *Gottes Wort und Gottes Land*, Festschrift für H.-W. Hertzberg (Göttingen, 1965), pp. 9-29. The tendency

in recent form-critical studies is to consider motive-clauses
to be redactional, however; probably because of a bias in
favor of pure legal forms.

9. Cf. P. J. Budd, "Priestly Instruction in Pre-exilic
Israel" *VT* 23 (1973) 1-14; D. Patrick, "I and Thou in the
Covenant Code" *SBL 1978 Seminar Papers*, Vol. I (Scholars
Press, 1978), p. 75.

10. Gemser concluded the motive force of "it is an abomination to Yahweh" is not in abhorrence or fear of legal penalty but in the nature and will of God; p. 58. Cf. J. L'Hour,
"Les interdits *To'ēbā* dans le Deutéronome" *RB* 71 (1964) 481-
503; P. Humbert, "Le substantif *to'ēbā* et le verbe *t'b* dans
l'Ancien Testament" *ZAW* 72 (1960) 217-237.

11. G. von Rad, *Old Testament Theology* (Harper & Row,
1962), Vol. I, p. 265.

12. J. G. Gammie, "Theology of Retribution in Deuteronomy"
CBQ 32 (1970) 1-12.

13. Budd, p. 6.

14. Patrick, p. 75.

8

THE FUNCTION OF ST. NICHOLAS IN CHRISTENDOM

Alfred M. Johnson, Jr.

Our subject is especially timely, considering the present state of the world, which cries out for "a little Christmas" at the moment, and the fact that 1979 was declared by the United Nations as "The Year of the Child". Moreover, this is the age of J. R. R. Tolkien and C. S. Lewis, when fiction seems to have come closer than usual to predicting the future.[1] Hence we have decided to consider the subject of the function of St. Nicholas in Christendom.

Although numerous great Christian scholars through the ages have written on the subject of Christmas from the viewpoint of the theological significance of the incarnation of God in Jesus of Nazareth,[2] very little has been written about the theological and social significance of the patron saint of little children, sailors, Christian scholars!, and merchants, St. Nicholas of Myra, and his relationship to the Christmas festival. Indeed with the notable exception of a few Roman Catholic and Greek Orthodox priests writing about St. Nicholas, primarily in defense of the sites and relics in their care,[3] Christian scholarship has been notably mute about him. And what is written about this almost taboo and forbidden (yet unquestionably religious) subject is almost invariably negative. Indeed the rites, legends, cults, and customs which vary from country to country and are still an integral part of Christmas, i.e. the gift giving, Christmas trees, visits to and from St. Nicholas (or Father Christmas, Kris Kringle, Santa Clause, etc.) are almost always interpreted by serious scholars as relics, survivals, and vestiges of a pre-Christian pagan past which it would be better to abandon and forget.

Thus it would seem to be important to attempt to shed some new light on the Christmas rituals we perform, apparently in order to celebrate the birth of the Christ child. What we are suggesting therefore is a new look at these alleged "pagan survivals" in order to demonstrate hopefully that they are really not as "pagan" as is claimed, but rather that they perform a necessary and perhaps even profoundly human and Christian function.

As one of the guides to this new view, we propose to use one of the very few articles specifically on a religious subject written by the reknown anthropologist Claude Lévi-Strauss.[4] It is not surprising that a Jewish guide should be used to help us understand our Christian religious practices, as such have been the best guides from the beginning. In sum, what we propose to show is that the present-day Christmas cults and practices which are associated with St. Nicholas, especially as they are performed in the U.S., are really logical extensions of some of the basic tenets of Christianity, and especially Protestant Christianity. But perhaps one of the most fascinating aspects of St. Nicholas is the ecumenism which he symbolizes, having great appeal in virtually all the major divisions of Christendom, i.e. among Protestants, Roman Catholics, and the Greek, Russian, and Eastern Orthodox. And as will be seen, he also served as a bridge of trust between Christians and Jews.

Before beginning however, it should be made clear that *there is relatively little concern here with the question of whether or not St. Nicholas of Myra actually existed.* And it should also be added that *a distinction will not be drawn between the historical St. Nicholas of Myra and the St. Nicholas now connected with Christmas.* As was stated at the beginning, we are speaking in the spirit of J. R. R. Tolkien and C. S. Lewis,[5] in which it is the symbols and meanings which count, although some reference will be made to the historical St. Nicholas of Myra. As C. S. Lewis so brilliantly foresaw and attempted to accomplish with his acclaimed *Chronicles of Narnia*, even the most secular individuals and institutions can be penetrated with the Christian gospel when it is delivered in the form of fiction for children.[6] This knowledge was also unwittingly received by the Hebrew scholar, Dr. Clement Clarke Moore, when he wrote a short poem about St. Nicholas for his daughter, who was appropriately enough named "Charity".[7]

But the story of St. Nicholas or Père Noël, as Lévi-Strauss calls him, is neither a myth nor a legend.[8] Rather what we are dealing with is an unusual phenomenon in Christianity which is perhaps without precedent. St. Nicholas and the stories which surround him are something unique, and it is this uniqueness which we propose to investigate. Perhaps it is significant to recall in this post-Nietzschean ("God-is-dead") theological age that in the Russian church St. Nicholas was often equated with God himself and given equality to Jesus and his mother, Mary,[9] and later it was sometimes said that St. Nicholas would become God when God became too old for the task.[10]

As further support for the appropriateness of this sub-

ect, an incident in the life of Jesus should be recalled,
which in our view has been misinterpreted by some as a reference to infant baptism. It may be recalled that Jesus often
refers to children, and almost invariably he cites them as
examples of Christian perfection (Mt. 7:11; 18:3-6; Mk. 7:27;
Lk. 1:17; 11:13; 13:34; Jn. 1:12; 11:52, 13:33; 21:5). But
there is one story in particular which seems to be especially appropriate for the subject at hand and which appears in
all three Synoptics. In Mt. 19:13-15; Mk. 10:13-16; and Lk.
18:15-17 children are brought to Jesus *against the protests
of the disciples*. The disciples are rebuked, and Jesus states
that the Kingdom of God must be received like little children
or the disciples will not enter it. This does *not* mean we are
arguing, as some do now, in favor of a simplified Christianity
which might be appropriate to appeal to a six year old child.
And it is significant that it is precisely C. S. Lewis who has
spoken out most forcefully against such a conception.[11] Rather we think the key to understanding this passage is to be
found in the First Letter of John, where the people of God
are addressed more often than in any other book of the Bible
as "little children" (1 Jn. 2:1, 12, 13, 18, 28; 2:1, 2, 7,
10, 18; 4:4; 5:2, 21). The writer of that book seems to appeal to a faith with righteousness and innocence, which is also aware of the anti-Christ, but its author asserts that he
can be overcome with love for one another and faith in Jesus
Christ. Thus we see no conflict here with St. Paul's assertion that Christians must be mature in their understanding
(1 Cor. 13:11).

So with these caveats we continue. Despite the complicated wickedness in the world, we must have an innocent faith
that God lives and that Jesus died for us and more importantly
lives with us now. For adults there would appear to be no
better example of this kind of faith than the faith that a
little child has that St. Nicholas will remember him or her
on Christmas day. And if our interpretation of Mt. 19:13-15
and par. is correct, it is that kind of faith that best serves
as an example for us to emulate. Is it perhaps the little
children who teach this innocent faith to their parents without their even knowing it? In any case, the Christian clergy,
like the original disciples of Jesus, seems unable to perceive
this. And it is this blindness which we think explains their
attacks upon something they do not understand as mere survivals
of ancient paganism.

Moreover, it is not only the clergy who have this problem.
Turning to secular scholars and sources, it is again said that
the Christmas festival, as we know it today, is merely a remnant of the ancient Roman Saturnalia celebrated December 17-24.
The choice of December 25, which significantly enough lies out-

side these dates, is explained as the birthday of Mithra, the
Iranian god of light.[12] But the very same source reveals the
weakness of that argument when May Day celebrations in Social-
ist countries are explained as survivals of the spring fertility festivals once celebrated in the Magna Mater Hellenistic
mystery religions.[13] Are we really expected to believe that
just because two dates for two different festivals, which are
separated by vast historical and cultural differences, coin-
cide that they have the same function? In short, are the
Socialists worshipping the Magna Mater on May Day? The foolishness of this argument is apparent when it is realized that
so many different festivals in so many different cultures have
occurred, and no doubt still occur, on the same or approximate
dates, that it is probably possible to pick any date of the
year out of the possible 365 and find several festivals exactly coincident.[14]

So the proper question, we believe, is to ask what *function* (or functions) St. Nicholas and the Christmas festival
fills for the Christian community. It is only an answer to
that question which will give us the true significance of the
relationship between St. Nicholas, Christmas, and Christianity
And it must always be recalled, in the words of M. Ebon, that
"The church has always had difficulties with dramatic elements
that are strongly rooted in folklore."[15]

St. Nicholas of Myra

In Acts 27 the story begins of the last sea voyage of St.
Paul to his trial in Rome. And we read in Acts 27:5-6 as follows: "And when we had sailed over the sea of Cilicia and Pam-
phylia, we came to *Myra*, a city of Lycia. And there the cen-
turion [i.e. Julius, cf. 27:1] found a ship of Alexandria
sailing into Italy; and he put us therein." (A.V., italics
ours.) This is perhaps the only N.T. reference to our subject,[16] and it refers only to a place, Myra.[17] Nevertheless,
it will be seen that even this brief reference says more than
is at first apparent.

For centuries St. Nicholas, bishop of Myra, has been many
things to many people, but he has always been held in special
esteem by children (primarily in the western church), in addition to being the patron saint of *sailors* (primarily in the
eastern church), *merchants*, unmarried and childless young
women, the falsely accused, endangered travelers, *perfumers*
(for a special reason),[18] and even *pawnbrokers* among others.[19]
Actually as M. Ebon notes, the commercialism of present day
Christmases is not far removed from medieval church fairs,[20]

nd this collection of special interests is one of the keys
or unlocking the true function of St. Nicholas.

Written sources concerning the so-called "historical"
t. Nicholas, bishop of Myra, are very late and filled with
egend, the earliest perhaps being the sixth century Greek
ork *Praxis de Stratilatis* (ca. 527-565, during the reign of
ustinian), the *Vita Per Metaphrasten*, the *Vita Per Michaelem*,
nd the *Vita Compilata*.[21] Of all the folktales surrounding
im, perhaps the most famous is the story of his dowry gifts
o three destitute young daughters whose father was contem-
lating selling them into prostitution in order to make ends
eet. As for biographical information, according to these
ources St. Nicholas was born in Patara (sometimes spelled
anthera; cf. Acts 21:1!) ca. 280 A.D. According to the *Vita
ompilata* his parents were wealthy but gave large alms to the
oor. The stories concerning his birth are very similar to
hose about Samuel in the O.T. (e.g. 1 Sam. 1:11; 2:26). His
ather's name was Epiphanius, his mother's Nonna. He had an
ncle, also named Nicholas, who was also a bishop and had
uilt a monastery named "New Zion" by the time St. Nicholas
as ordained at the age of 19. There are several stories
bout St. Nicholas making sea voyages to Palestine and Egypt
n Egyptian boats (cf. Acts 27:6). En route during one of
hem, St. Nicholas foresaw an approaching storm. He warned
he sailors but also reassured them, "Do not be afraid. Trust
n God because he will protect you from death" (cf. Acts 27:9-
0, 21-25ff.). During the storm a man was killed but revived
y St. Nicholas' prayers to God.[22] Still other tales of the
historical" St. Nicholas assert that he was constantly in
attle with the Greek goddess Artemis (cf. Acts 19:24-35).[23]
ence we can see a possible transfer of the traditions con-
erning St. Paul to the later folktales about St. Nicholas.
It is significant that these similarities have apparently
een ignored by most Christian scholars.

Perhaps the most interesting, although it is evidently
historically worthless, is that of his participation in the
First Council of Nicaea (325 A.D.).[24] In 1896 an Athenian
monk Damaskinos wrote that while the other bishops at the
council silently listened to Arius present his views, St.
Nicholas became so enraged that he walked up to Arius and
slapped him on the face.[25]

Although all these stories are questionable, these facts
are known. His feastday is December 6. Nicholas of Clairvaux
preached a sermon in which he argued that St. Nicholas should
be the patron saint of Christian scholars because he had been
an extremely diligent scholar. His shrine was well-known in
Myra. However, on May 9, 1087 A.D. his relics were moved to

Bari, Italy where they were enshrined in the basilica of S. Nicola in the presence of Pope Urban II.[26] Thousands of churches in both the East and West are dedicated to him, one as early as 560 A.D. built by Justinian I at Constantinople (Procopius, *De aedificiis* 1,6). And appropriately enough, on Dec. 5, 1972 some of his relics were moved from Bari to the Greek Orthodox Cathedral in New York City and the Shrine of St. Nicholas in Flushing, N.Y.

The St. Nicholas cult seems to have reached a climax in the twelfth century, and icons and stained glass windows of him appear in many of the most famous churches of Christendom, e.g. North Moreton (Berkshire), the Jerusalem Chamber, Westminster, Great Malvery (Hereford and Worcester), Hillesden (Bucks), S. Maria Antiqua (Rome), S. Sophia (Istanbul), St. Mark's (Venice), Monreale (Sicily), and the cathedrals at Le Mans, Tours, and Chartres. Among the many Christian scholars who have composed prayers to him were Anselm and Godric. Hence any thought or plan of erasing all traces of St. Nicholas of Myra from Christendom would simply be impractical, as well as inconceivable. Yet that is what should be done, were we to follow the views of the majority of the Christian clergy today.

The Function of Father Christmas or St. Nicholas

It is at this point that a short study of Claude Lévi-Strauss, published in 1952 is most relevant.[27] Perhaps, as we hope to demonstrate, the real problem is that the Christian clergy does not understand the true function of St. Nicholas in the Church. Perhaps, as has been implied, the so-called "over-commercialization" of Christmas is not accidental! And Protestant clergy in particular should beware of condemning the commercialization of Christmas, considering the many scholars, such as Max Weber, who have demonstrated the symbiotic relationship between Protestantism and Capitalism![28]

In his 29 page article, Lévi-Strauss commented on an uproar concerning Father Christmas (or St. Nicholas) which arose during Christmas 1951. It seems that a large number of the Roman Catholic church authorities had arrived at the conclusion that the figure of Father Christmas represented, "an alarming 'paganization' of the Feast of the Nativity",[29] which diverted Christians from the so-called true spirit of Christmas. Moreover, French protestant ministers agreed with them. Inevitably events escalated to the point that Father Christmas was hanged and burned in effigy in the parvis of the Cathedral of Dijon.[30]

In a scene somewhat reminiscent of Christ's own crucifixion by the Jerusalem religious authorities, Father Christmas was hung in the afternoon on the iron gates of the cathedral and then burned in the parvis. Father Christmas was condemned orally as a usurper and heretic, *especially since he
had been introduced into the public schools, where the crèche
was expressly forbidden*. This act divided the citizens of
Dijon, and as usual the local politicians refused to join
sides! The opposition, however, planned a "resurrection" of
Father Christmas whereby he would reappear that same night and
circulate among the children of the town as was customary.[30]

As Lévi-Strauss noted, this event was especially interesting to him because the clergy was attacking a religious
figure, and the so-called pagans were defending him. But he
felt the important question to be answered, and it is the one
which we are seeking to answer here, is why Christian adults
had invented Père Noël or Father Christmas, *Weihnachtsmann,*
St. Nicholas, Kris Kringle (from the German *Christ-Kindlein*
or Christ child), Sinta Claes or Santa Claus, etc., in the
first place?[31]

As has been noted, the St. Nicholas cult has for the most
part been explained as a relic of the past. And indeed, Lévi-
Strauss noted that the great interest in Father Christmas in
France had primarily developed in the post-World War II era,
which might be explained as a cultural remnant left by the
occupation of France by American soldiers during the war. In
any case, he saw in this incident at Dijon a great paradox.
Father Christmas had become a "symbol of irreligion". It was
the churchmen, who he considers to be "guardians of supersti-
tions" who had become the rationalists and vice versa.[32] In
short, "This apparent inversion of roles is enough to suggest
that this simple affair goes back to deeper realities."[33]

The fact that this phenomenon was contemporary with himself and his culture was seen by Lévi-Strauss as both advan-
tageous and disadvantageous:

> For it is easier and at the same time more
> difficult to argue about some acts which
> are unfolded under our eyes and of which
> our own society is the theater. It is
> easier, since the continuity of the ex-
> perience is protected, with all its mo-
> ments and each of its nuances. It is al-
> so more difficult because it is on such

rare occasions that the extreme and even
the finest complexities of social trans-
formations are perceived. *Because the
apparent reasons that we give to the
events in which we are the actors are
very different from the real causes
which assign us a role.*[34]

But he went on to discard an explanation based solely
upon the simple diffusion or borrowing of Father Christmas
from American movies, magazines, novels, newspapers, etc.
Rather Lévi-Strauss interpreted the Father Christmas phenomenon as an excellent example of Kroeber's concept of "diffusion by stimulation" (*stimulus diffusion*).[35] In other words,
instead of a new custom merely being borrowed and assimilated
by one culture from another, the new custom stimulates *"the
appearance of an analogous custom which was already present
in a potential state in the secondary milieu".*[36]

Lévi-Strauss went on to assert that "Christmas is essentially a modern festival".[37] However, this is not the case,
despite the arguments which he makes concerning the lateness
of Yule logs, Christmas trees,[38] mistletoe, holly, etc. Lévi-
Strauss simply fails to consider the early Christian sources.

Although the early history of Christmas is still clouded,
it is certain that Christmas was celebrated at least as early
as the fourth century (and thus as early as St. Nicholas of
Myra himself!), and perhaps as early as the second! We know
this because the celebration of Christmas on "the twenty-fifth
of the ninth month" is referred to in the so-called *Constitutions of the Holy Apostles* in two passages. These purport to
give the Feasts of the Lord which are to be kept. They read
as follows:

> Brethren, observe the festival days; and
> first of all the birthday which you are
> to celebrate on the twenty-fifth of the
> ninth month; after which let the Epiphany
> be to you the most honoured, in which the
> Lord made to you a display of His own God-
> head, and let it take place on the sixth
> of the tenth month.... (*Constitutions* V,
> iii,13).[39]

And concerning the days upon which Christians are not to work:

> Let them rest on the festival of His birth,

because on it the unexpected favour was
granted to men, that Jesus Christ, the
Logos of God, should be born of the Vir-
gin Mary, for the salvation of the world.
(*ibid*, VIII,iv,33).[40]

Despite this minor correction, we think that Lévi-Strauss
is correct when he explains Father Christmas as "the product
of a phenomenon of convergence and not an ancient prototype",[41]
and also that Christmas has had a varied history of popularity.
But most importantly, we entirely agree with Lévi-Strauss when
he states, *"It is necessary, confronting problems of this kind,
to distrust too simple explanations by an automatic appeal to
'vestiges' and 'survivals'."*[42]

Although there is no doubt that the modern Christmas celebration, as we know it, is a phenomenon in which many disparate
elements from many different times and cultures have been syn-
cretized together, that still does not explain why these elements have, like wandering satellites, decided to attach themselves to Christmas and not to other secular or religious festivals.

Let us see if we can begin to understand at least why St.
Nicholas has become attached to Christmas, especially since
his feast day is December 6 and not December 25. As Lévi-
Strauss notes, there are some signs from the manner of his
dress and appearance. He is dressed in fur-lined scarlet,
which clearly evokes royalty,[43] although this has not always
been the case.[44] He is an *old* man, and thus he seems to represent an aged, benevolent monarch.[43] He also has certain
supernatural powers, such as omniscience, and he is "wor-
shipped" by children who send him letters and prayers in December. He theoretically dispenses justice to them, rewarding
good children and punishing bad ones by deprivation. Above
all, *he is believed in only by children.* Indeed, as Lévi-
Strauss notes, *the only difference between St. Nicholas and
the deity is that Christian adults do not believe in him, although they encourage their children to do so,* by going to
great lengths to protect this belief by what he calls "mysti-
fications".[45]

Thus St. Nicholas expresses *a difference in status* between
little children on the one hand, and adolescents and adults on
the other. As an ethnologist, Lévi-Strauss is quite familiar
with this phenomenon, which is almost universal in all societies, namely a means of initiating children, who are excluded
from the adult mysteries, into adolescence by some rites of
passage. And it is significant to add that in many societies

adult women are also excluded from these mysteries (feminists will add that this has not changed in modern societies!). In any case, the similarity of the status of women to that of little children (both of them are non-initiates) is especially significant with regard to the St. Nicholas cult.[46]

St. Nicholas and the Pueblo Katchina

Taking a synchronic viewpoint, Lévi-Strauss notes that the Pueblo Indians have figures known as *katchina* which play essentially the same role as St. Nicholas in modern Christmas celebrations. Among the Pueblos these katchina are masked and disguised parents who incarnate the tribal gods and ancestors. Periodically they enter the villages to reward good children with gifts. It is precisely because there is virtually no possibility of the katchina having been created by diffusion from St. Nicholas, and vice versa, that a study of them can give us the true function of St. Nicholas.[47]

It becomes evident from our knowledge of both of them (i.e. the katchina and St. Nicholas) that they perform a practical and necessary function in society. Both are tools or weapons used by parents and other elders to restrain or keep the little children on their good behavior. Hence throughout the year children are reminded, especially when they misbehave, that the katchina and St. Nicholas know and see "who's naughty and who's nice".[48] The gifts St. Nicholas and the katchina bring are an especially interesting form of restraint. They may be seen as a *transaction* by which wealth is transferred from the older (the "haves") to the younger (the "have-nots") members of the society. In other words, to a certain degree it imposes an obligation on the older members of the society towards the younger members; and at the same time bestows the weaker and younger members of society with certain rights and privileges they do not ordinarily possess, except at this particular time of the year.[49]

In sum, there is a transaction between two different classes of society, which is confirmed by the great charity drives that are undertaken by virtually all Christian communities at Christmas. In fact, as Lévi-Strauss notes, in 18th century England it was customary for *the women* to go "a gooding" from house to house on Christmas eve. That is, they would take up collections for the poor in exchange for which the donors would receive green branches in return. In addition, sometimes children would be dressed *as women* to make collections for St. Nicholas. In other words, the children (and sometimes the women) were "non-initiates", but at the same time "super-initiates".[50]

From the Pueblo myths about the katchina, we are told that the katchina represent the souls of some children of their ancestors who were drown during their primordial migrations. Originally, according to the myths, when the Pueblos adopted a sedentary life the katchina would come each year to visit and then depart, taking away the children like the Pied Piper of fairy tale fame. To prevent this and keep the katchina in the otherworld, the parents agreed to represent the katchina by disguising themselves to fool their children.[51]

But Lévi-Strauss adds:

> If the children are excluded from the mystery of the katchina, it is not therefore, at first nor especially, in order to intimidate them. I would say readily that it is for the opposite reason: it is because they [i.e. the children] *are* the katchina. They are considered to be outside the mystification because they represent the reality with which the mystification constitutes a sort of compromise. *Their place is elsewhere: not with the masqueraders and the living, but with the gods and the dead. It is the gods who are the dead and the children are the dead.*[52]

This he thinks is true of all initiation rites or rites of passage. In other words, underneath the opposition between non-initiates and initiates there lies the deeper opposition between the dead and the living or death and life. And he adds that this same opposition also lies beneath the rituals connected with St. Nicholas.[53]

Hence from Lévi-Strauss' synchronic analysis it becomes clear that the St. Nicholas phenomenon in Christendom is more profound than has previously been believed. Indeed it touches upon the very question of life and death that lies at the heart of the Christian gospel.[54] And it should be added that the synoptics also make allusions in their birth narratives to this same opposition which Jesus has come to destroy.[55] And the same thing is true of the opposition between the haves and the have-nots which Christians go to great lengths to eliminate *primarily at Christmas*.

The Saturnalia and Medieval Christmases

No doubt much syncretism of religious and secular traditions has occurred in the present day Christmas festival. But "survival" or "vestige" explanations are not enough to explain Christmas today. As Lévi-Strauss notes, "The survival explanations are always incomplete; because customs neither disappear nor survive without reason. When they continue, the cause is to be found less in historical viscosity than in the permanence of a function that present-day analysts must reveal."[56] Hence, "The Saturnalia and the medieval celebrations of Christmas do not contain the final reason for a ritual which is otherwise inexplicable and devoid of signification."[57] However, it is possible that a study of the earlier celebrations of the Saturnalia and medieval Christmases can help us understand better some of the reasons why Christmas is now celebrated as it is.

It can be noted, for example, that in medieval Christmases the rigid class distinctions between serfs and nobles were temporarily abolished. Servants and serfs were even seated at their masters' tables and served by their masters. Men and women even exchanged their clothing! Sometimes children were allowed to elect a ruler, a boy bishop; for example, in Scotland he was known as the "Abbot of Unreason", who kept "order" (if that can be said) over a wide variety of anti-social behavior, i.e. blasphemy, thievery, rape, and occasionally even murder. An Abbot of Liesse, a similar figure, was also enthroned by the clergy in France. His duty was also to contain such excesses within certain limits. Clearly such customs were abandoned as society became more law abiding. Hence these figures became transformed in some way. The *young* ruler of misconduct became an *old* ruler who encouraged good behavior.[58] Or, according to Lévi-Strauss:

> A real person became a mythical personage;
> an emanation of youth, symbolizing his
> antagonism towards adults, is changed in-
> to a symbol of old age in which he trans-
> lates benevolent dispositions towards
> young people. The apostle of misconduct
> is entrusted with encouraging good con-
> duct. For adolescents openly aggressive
> towards their parents, parents secretly
> acting under a false beard to satisfy
> their children are substituted.[59]

Despite this transformation, however, the "foolishness" that once occurred at Christmas still continues to some ex-

ent. As Lévi-Strauss notes, such "foolishness" reaches its
pogee today primarily only on New Year's Eve in Times Square,
ew York and a few other places.⁶⁰ Such misbehavior apparent-
y functions as an outlet for pent up frustrations, as it were,
o that they can be vented and the differences within a soci-
ty balanced and redressed without too much real damage being
one. Hence ascetics among us who would like to see such
ites eliminated are obligated to supply some acceptable sub-
titute or risk the destruction of society as a whole.⁶¹

In this respect, it is interesting to note that Halloween
lso exists as another outlet for the frustrations and hostil-
y of children towards adults. In 18th century Scotland a
imilar ritual occurred *during Christmas*, when children would
o from house to house collecting fruits and sweets while sing-
g this song:

> Rise up, good wife, and be no'swier
>   [i.e. lazy],
> To deal your bread as long's you're here;
> The time will come when you'll be dead,
> And neither want nor meal nor bread.⁶²

Again, with Lévi-Strauss, we note the reference to death.
hus from Halloween (the Eve of All Saints' Day) to Christmas
The Christ Masse) a seasonal and theological progression can
e seen from the beginning of Autumn until the Winter Solstice,
hich again symbolizes clearly death and life. According to
évi-Strauss, it is a "dialectical process" with four major
hases: "the return of the dead", "their menacing and perse-
ating conduct", "the establishment of a *modus vivendi* with
he living, made in an exchange for services and presents",
nd "finally the triumph of life when, at Christmas, the dead
aden with gifts depart from the living to leave them in peace
ntil next Autumn".⁶³

he Theological Significance of St. Nicholas

But in our view the theological importance of Christmas
nd a visit from St. Nicholas is that by encouraging little
hildren to believe in St. Nicholas (who as has been noted
as many of the attributes and thus can somewhat be considered
o be a surrogate for God Himself) and by rewarding their be-
ief, *our own children help us to believe in life.*⁶⁴ *And that
or us is the reality of the incarnation of God in His Son Je-
us Christ.* That would not be possible without St. Nicholas.
t comes at a price, however, and that is perhaps the problem,

i.e. the anthropomorphization of the deity. As we know that
is a problem which goes back to the very origins of the O.T.

With respect, however, to the accusation that Christmas
has been exploited by greedy merchants and others to the det-
riment of the celebration of the Nativity, we would respond by
noting the inherent self-righteousness implicit in singling
out the mercantile class for such blame. Indeed there are
perhaps many of the clergy professing to live a life of as-
cetic poverty, while in reality their most basic material
needs are much more secure than those they so self-righteously
criticize. In short, there are very few who live like Sister
Mother Teresa in the slums of India "feeding the sheep".[65]
Moreover, we have noted throughout this paper that St. Nicholas is indeed the patron saint of the mercantile class, and
thus what has occurred was to be expected. After all was not
Matthew a tax collector and St. Paul a tent merchant?

For this reason, it should be no surprise that the U.S.,
the bastion of capitalism, was the place where, through the
pens of Washington Irving and especially Dr. Clement Clarke
Moore, the role of St. Nicholas was carried to its logical
conclusion. And, as we noted, the relationship which has
existed between Protestantism and Capitalism *from their simultaneous beginnings* only adds additional support to these conclusions.[66]

But what of the Christian significance of St. Nicholas
and his sleigh full of toys? On this point history is clear.
The St. Nicholas legends have been a very powerful means for
the propagation of the Christian gospel. His appeal to children of many different cultures has been virtually irresist-
ible. Who are we then to take it upon ourselves to rid ourselves of him? And who or what would we put in his place,
especially now that we know some of his functions? In a sense
he serves as a perfect mediator between the most profane and
the most sacred things in our culture, as well as representing
the opposition of life and death which the Christian gospel
proclaims has been overcome only in Jesus Christ.

But in addition to children, we have noted a relationship
between St. Nicholas and women. In France, for example, he is
often prayed to by marriageable young girls for husbands. So
at the Fécamp Sein-Intérieure young girls throw small pebbles
at St. Nicholas' statue, just as in fiction three coins are
tossed into fountains and young boys throw stones against a
girl friend's windowpane to gain her attention. Likewise in
the Dept. of Seine-et-Marne, young girls jiggle the lock of the
St. Nicholas chapel and chant this verse: *"Patron des filles,
saint Nicholas: mariez-nous, ne tardez pas"*, which may be

ranslated, "St. Nicholas, patron of girls: get me married
rithout delay!" Childless couples have similar verses re-
questing children. But perhaps one of the most interesting
of all is used in Normandy: *"Saint Nicholas, marie les filles
avec les garrons"*, i.e. "Saint Nicholas, marry the girls to
the boys."[67]

Two Stories about St. Nicholas

We conclude this brief study with two stories about St.
Nicholas. The first appears in four scenes on the stained-
glass windows of the magnificent Chartres Cathedral. It is a
story of a Jew who was vindicated by St. Nicholas after having
been victimized by a Christian friend.[68] A Christian had borrowed some money from a Jewish friend and swore by St. Nicholas that he would repay the debt when due. The day for pay-
ment arrived and the Christian refused to pay, although he
could. Moreover, as a further act of cruelty the Christian
took his Jewish friend to court, no doubt relying on anti-
Semitism to relieve him of the debt. As a ruthless trick the
Christian concealed the promised sum in his cane, which he
duped his Jewish friend into holding for him during the trial,
so that he could "truthfully" swear the debt had been paid.
The Christian won his case, but St. Nicholas was not to be
tricked. En route home the Christian lay down to sleep on the
road where a horse and wagon ran over him, crushing him in a
painful death. In addition, his walking stick was broken,
spilling the money. His former Jewish friend was called to
the scene and all discovered what happened, i.e. St. Nicholas
had settled the account. But the Jew refused to accept the
money with his friend lying dead on the road. He stated that
if St. Nicholas were powerful enough to take a life, he should
be able to restore it. Scarcely had it been said than the
Christian was miraculously revived. As a result of the miracle the Jewish friend and his family became Christians.[69]

But there is one defense of St. Nicholas (or in this
case, Santa Claus) which has become a classic in newspaper
journalism. It was written by Francis Pharcellus Church, the
son of a Baptist minister. Virtually unknown beyond his circle of friends, "He specialized in writing editorials on con-
troversial theological subjects".[70] We are repeating it here
in full because it is sometimes hard to find and it is the de-
finitive statement, as far as we are concerned, on our subject.
It first appeared in a New York newspaper named *The Sun* on
Sept. 21, 1897 as a letter to the editor from a little girl
named Virginia O'Hanlon. She wrote:

Dear Editor, Some of my little friends say there is no Santa Claus. Papa says 'If you see it in the *Sun* it's so.' Please tell me the truth, is there a Santa Claus?

After a short introduction, Francis Church responded:

Virginia, your little friends are wrong. They have been affected by the skepticism of a skeptical age. They do not believe except they see. They think that nothing can be which is not comprehensible to their little minds.

All minds, Virginia, whether they be men's or children's, are little. In this great universe of ours man is a mere insect, an ant, in his intellect, as compared with the boundless world about him, as measured by the intelligence capable of grasping the whole of truth and knowledge.

Yes, Virginia, there is a Santa Claus. He exists as certainly as love and generosity and devotion exist, and you know that they abound and give to your life its highest beauty and joy. Alas! How dreary would be the world if there were no Santa Claus! It would be as dreary as if there were no Virginias.

There would be no childlike faith then, no poetry, no romance to make tolerable this existence. We should have no enjoyment except in sense and sight. The eternal light with which childhood fills the world would be extinguished.

Not believe in Santa Claus! You might as well not believe in fairies! You might get your papa to hire men to watch in all the Chimneys on Christmas Eve to catch Santa Claus, but even if they did not see Santa Claus coming down, what would that prove?

Nobody sees Santa Claus, but that is no sign that there is no Santa Claus. The most real things in the world are those that neither children nor men can see. Did you ever see fairies dancing on the lawn? Of course not, but that's no proof

that they are not there. Nobody can conceive or imagine all the wonders there are
unseen and unseeable in the world.

You tear apart a baby's rattle and
see what makes the noise inside, but there
is a veil covering the unseen world which
not the strongest man, nor even the united
strength of all the strongest men that ever
lived could tear apart.

Only faith, fancy, poetry, love, romance, can push aside that curtain and view
and picture the supernatural beauty and
glory beyond. Is it all real? Ah, Virginia, in all this world there is nothing
else real and abiding.

No Santa Claus! Thank God he lives,
and he lives forever. A thousand years
from now, Virginia, nay, ten times ten
thousand years from now, he will continue
to make glad the heart of childhood.

And thus we have arrived at the meaning of one of the verses
we cited at the beginning: "Verily I say unto you, Whosoever
shall not receive the kingdom of God as a little child shall
in no wise enter therein" (Lk. 18:17 A.V.).

NOTES

1. This is a paraphrase of a comment made by Walter Cronkite on the CBS evening news with respect to the nuclear accident at Three Mile Island, Pennsylvania.

2. Perhaps one of the most interesting was written by Friedrich Schleiermacher entitled *Weihnachtsfeier*. See also Richard R. Niebuhr's *Schleiermacher on Christ and Religion*, New York: Scribner, 1964, which discusses this work in great detail.

3. We apologize to these priests for being unable to include some materials from their studies. The reason for this is simply the unavailability of the sources in our region. In the Dominican order the St. Nicholas expert seems to be Father Damiano Bova.

4. C. Lévi-Strauss, "Le Père Noël supplicié", *Les Temps modernes* 7 (1952), 1572-1590. Although he was a professor of religion for a time, we are aware of only the following additional works by him on religious subjects: *idem*, "A Confrontation [over myths with Paul Ricoeur et al.]", *New Left Review* 62 (1970), 57-74 = "Réponses à quelques questions", *Esprit* 31 (1963), 628-653 (with some changes); *idem*, "Le dualisme dans l'organisation sociale et les représentations religieuses", *Annuaire de l'Ecole Pratique des Hautes Etudes* (Sciences religieuses), 1958-59 (listed by several biographical sources, but a bibliographical inquiry concerning this work was sent to the Library of Congress and returned stating it did not exist); *idem*, "Gott-gibt et den eiberhaudt? Ein Gespräch zwischen Christian Chabanis und Claude Lévi-Strauss über Religions-philosophie, Metaphysik und Wissenschaftstheorie", *Linguistica Biblica* 32 (1974), 38-55; *idem*, "Le syncrétisme religieux d'un village mog du territoire de Chittagong", *Revue de l'histoire des religions* 141 (1952), 202-237; *idem*, *Totemism*, trans. R. Needham, Boston: Beacon Press, 1963 = *Le Totémisme aujourd'hui*, Paris: P.U.F., 1962; *idem*. "Witch Doctors and Psychoanalysis", *UNESCO Courier* 9 (1956), 8-10.

5. It is significant that these two were friends.

6. C. S. Lewis's *Chronicles of Narnia* have already been partially shown on television, as has Tolkien's *Lord of the Rings*. Both have also recently been bestselling books.

7. We are referring of course to his poem, "A Visit from
t. Nicholas", which was first composed and read to his chil-
ren on Dec. 23, 1822. The poem was intended for family con-
umption only, but a daughter of Rev. David Butler copied it
nd had it published in 1823 in *The Sentinel* newspaper, Troy,
ew York. Dr. Moore concealed his authorship of it for sever-
l years, until he published an anthology of his poems in 1844.
or a discussion of its composition see, S. W. Patterson, *The
oet of Christmas Eve: A Life of Clement Clarke Moore, 1779-
863*, New York, 1956, and especially the most recent we could
ind, Martin Ebon, *Saint Nicholas: Life and Legend*, New York:
arper & Row, 1975, esp. pp. 97-99. Clement Clarke Moore was
 leading Hebrew scholar of his day and one of the founders
f the General Theological Seminary (*ibid*, 92).

8. C. Lévi-Strauss, "Le Père Noël supplicié", 1579. He
rites: "He is not a mythical being, because there is no myth
hich gives an account of his origin and functions. And he is
ot a legendary character, since no semi-historical narrative
s attached to him." The latter statement may be disputed
onsidering the semi-historical narratives or "legends" about
t. Nicholas of Myra. But it should be added that these leg-
nds, which are briefly discussed below, are very different
rom the present conception of St. Nicholas as one who lives
t the North Pole, has reindeer, etc. Likewise, although
here are myths about the Nordic god Odin (or Othin, Woden,
odan, etc.), which it is claimed are very similar to the
resent St. Nicholas traditions, it should be noted that St.
icholas was apparently not very well known in the Scandinav-
an countries until very recently (see M. Ebon, *St. Nicholas*,
. 88).

9. This was particularly true in Russia, *ibid*, 2.

10. In Russia he was considered to be "the heir of Mikou-
a, the god of harvest, 'who will replace God, when God becomes
oo old'" (J. Coulson [ed.], *The Saints: A Concise Biographi-
al Dictionary*, New York: Hawthorn Books, 1958, 337).

11. C. S. Lewis, *Mere Christianity*, New York: Macmillan,
960, 46-47:

> *It is no good asking for a simple re-*
> *ligion. After all real things are not sim-*
> *ple. They look simple, but they are not.*
> The table I am sitting at looks simple:
> but ask a scientist to tell you what it is
> really made of--all about the atoms and
> how the light waves rebound from them and

hit my eye and what they do to the optic nerve and what it does to my brain--and, of course, you find that what we call "seeing a table" lands you in mysteries and complications which you can hardly get to the end of. A child saying a child's prayer looks simple. And if you are content to stop there, well and good. But if you are not--and the modern world usually is not-- if you want to go on and ask what is really happening--then you must be prepared for something difficult. *If we ask for something more than simplicity, it is silly then to complain that the something more is not simple.*

Very often, however, this silly procedure is adopted by people who are not silly, but who, consciously or unconsciously, want to destroy Christianity. Such people put up a version of Christianity suitable for a child of six and make that the object of their attack. When you try to explain the Christian doctrine as it is really held by an instructed adult, then they complain that you are making their heads turn round and that it is all too complicated and that if there really were a God He would have made 'religion' simple, because simplicity is so beautiful, etc. You must be on your guard against those people for they will change their ground every minute and only waste your time. *Notice, too, their idea of God 'making religion simple': as if 'religion' were something God invented, and not His statement to us of certain quite unalterable facts about His own nature.*

12. See the presentation of this viewpoint by Linwood Fredericksen, "Feast and Festival", *The New Encyclopaedia Britannica*, Chicago: Encyclopaedia Britannica, 1975, VII, 202; anon. "Saturn", *ibid.*, VIII, 916, where it is stated: "The influence of the Saturnalia upon the celebrations of Christmas and the New Year has been direct." See also the detailed discussion of the relationship between the Saturnalia and Christmas in Lévi-Strauss, "Le Père Noël supplicié", 1583ff.

13. So Fredericksen, "Feast and Festival", 202.

14. Actually, if the arguments used for Christmas and the aturnalia, etc. are accepted, the possibilities are even reater, since that means one would have to accept a direct elationship between any two festivals merely falling within he same month!

15. M. Ebon, *St. Nicholas*, 58.

16. There is a Nicolaus (Νικόλαος) referred to in Acts :5, who was a member of the seven "deacons" of the Jerusalem hurch. There are some very interesting traditions connecting im with the Nicolaitians in Revelation (Rev. 2:6, 15), which e have discussed before (see A. M. Johnson, Jr., "The Cultur- l Context of the Gospel of John--A Structural Approach", Ann rbor: University Microfilms, 1979, 188, 284 n. 98). See al- o K. G. Kuhn, "προσήλυτος", *TDNT*, VI, 742-743. In brief, the icolaitians (Rev. 2:6, 15) are said by some early church athers to have appealed to Nicolaus as the founder of their ect.

17. On Myra (Μύρα), which was one of the sixth largest ities in the Lycian confederation situated on the Andracus iver 2.5 miles from sea with a seaport named Andriaca, see . V. Filson, "Myra", *IDB*, III, 478. Codex D adds "and Myra" fter "Patara" in Acts 21:1. Patara, as will be seen, was the lleged birthplace of St. Nicholas! The apocryphal "Acts of aul and Thecla" tell of St. Paul preaching in Myra (see W. chneemelcher, "Acts of Paul", *New Testament Apocrypha*, eds. . Hennecke and W. Schneemelcher, trans. R. McL. Wilson, Phil- delphia: Westminster, 1965, II, 322ff.).

18. It is intriguing to us that one of the most favored ifts to give on Christmas today is a bottle of perfume. How- ver, St. Nicholas of Myra is associated with perfume because is shrine at Bari, Italy is said (even today) to produce a manna" or "myrrh" with healing properties (see J. Coulson, *he Saints*, 337; David Hugh Farmer, *The Oxford Dictionary of aints*, Oxford: Clarendon Press, 1978, 292).

19. There are several other special interest groups who ave also chosen him as their patron, e.g. apothecaries, haritable fraternities and guilds (even thieves, see Shake- speare, *Henry IV*, part I, act 2, scene 1), the cities of Fri- ourg, Switzerland and Moscow, the regions Apulia and Lor- aine, and the countries of Russia and Greece. It is primar- ly the eastern church which has shown the most interest in im, ranking him next to the great fathers of the church (see . H. Worman, "St. Nicholas of Myra", *Cyclopaedia of Biblical, heological and Ecclesiastical Literature*, eds. J. Strong and

J. M'Clintock, New York: Harper & Brothers, 1877, VII, 60-61).
Apparently the western church only began to take notice of him
in the tenth and twelfth centuries. In this respect, in Greek
portraits he appears as a Greek bishop. He has no mitre with
the cross in place of the crosier and the Trinity embroidered
on his cope. While in the west he appears dressed as a bishop
with a mitre and very elaborate cope, the crosier and gloves
with jewels on them. It is in the west that *three balls are
associated with him, which pawnbrokers claim is the source of
their symbol.* They may either represent the three purses of
money he used to save the three destitute daughters from prostitution (briefly discussed below), three loaves of bread for
feeding the poor, or perhaps the trinity (see on this J. H.
Worman, "St. Nicholas of Myra", 62).

20. M. Ebon, *St. Nicholas*, 3.

21. Most of these Greek primary sources are available in
G. Anrich (ed.), *Hagios Nikolaos*, 2 vols., Leipzig, 1913-17.
Other references to him are found in *Leonis imperat. orat. gr.
prod.* (Tolos, 1644); *Andreae Cretensis inter ejusdem orationes
Lat.*, ed. Combefis; *Vita et Metaphraste*, et aliis collecta a
Leonardo Justiniano, tom. I, ap. Lipom et ap. Surium, 6 Dec.;
Nicolai Studitae in tom. II, *Auctar. novi*, ed. Combefis. N.
C. Falconius, *Sancti Nocolae Acta Primigenia* (1751); Nitti di
Vito, *La leggenda della translazione di S. Nicola da Mira a
Bari* (1937); K. Meisen, *Nikolauskult und Nikolausbrauch in
Abendlande* (1931).

22. As J. Coulson notes, a large number of small chapels
built on cliffs facing the sea near seaports were dedicated to
St. Nicolaus (J. Coulson, *The Saints*, 338). For some of the
seafaring stories (trans. into English) concerning St. Nicholas, see J. H. Worman, "St. Nicholas of Myra", 61 as well as
M. Ebon, *St. Nicholas*, 12ff.

23. So M. Ebon, *St. Nicholas*, 35-36.

24. His presence at Nicaea, although it is chronologically possible (his alleged death date is 345 or 352 A.D.), is
questionable because his name does not occur as one of the
signers of the decrees, and he is not mentioned by any of the
other church fathers said to be present, esp. St. Athanasius,
nor by any of the historians. But in spite of this almost
every scholar is confident that he lived and was the bishop
of Myra (Demre) sometime during the era in question (see J.
H. Worman, "St. Nicholas of Myra", 61).

25. See M. Ebon, *St. Nicholas*, 34f.

26. With the attack on the church holding St. Nicholas'
tomb by Achmet, commander of the fleet of Harūn Al Raschid in
807 A.D., the western church was prodded into action. Although most agree that the merchants and sailors from Bari
actually obtained his body, the Venetians dispute this claiming they have the real remains of St. Nicholas, which, according to them, were rescued by Venetian merchants in 1100 A.D.
(see J. H. Worman, "St. Nicholas of Myra", 62). Not to be
outdone, the Medici of Florence chose the symbol of St. Nicholas for their heraldic sign.

27. See note 4 above.

28. Max Weber, *The Protestant Ethic and the Spirit of
Capitalism*, trans. Talcott Parsons, New York: Charles Scribners' Sons, 1958.

29. C. Lévi-Strauss, "Le Père Noël supplicié", 1572. All
the quotes from this article to follow will be our translations.

30. *Ibid*, 1572-1574. Lévi-Strauss draws his description
of the events from an account in the journal *France-Soir*.

31. *Ibid*, 1574. We are attempting to give all the various names for the "Christmas" St. Nicholas at this point.

32. *Ibid*, 1574-1575.

33. *Ibid*, 1575.

34. *Ibid*, 1576.

35. *Ibid*, 1576-1577.

36. *Ibid*, 1577.

37. *Ibid*.

38. The Christmas tree may be the most "Christian" symbol
of Christmas, if we agree with the argument by Mircea Eliade
in his *Images & Symbols: Studies in Religious Symbolism*,
trans. P. Mairet, New York: Search Books, 1969, 44ff. and
61ff. Although other religions have used trees as religious
symbols, he writes, "Christianity has utilized, interpreted
and amplified this symbol. The Cross, made of the wood of the
tree of good and evil, appears in the place of this Cosmic
Tree; the Christ himself is described as a Tree (by Origen)."
Moreover, Pseudo-Chrysostom refers to the Cross as "a tree

which 'rises from the earth to the heavens. A plant immortal, it stands at the centre of heaven and of earth; strong pillar of the universe, bond of all things, support of all the inhabited earth; cosmic interlacement, comprising in itself the whole medley of human nature...'" (*ibid*, 161-162). Eliade goes on to refer to Byzantine liturgies which refer to the Cross as "a tree of life planted on Calvary". Moreover, these images are even present in the O.T. where in Prov. 3:18 Wisdom (who was frequently equated with Christ in the early church) is described as "a tree of life to those who lay hold of her"; cf. also Dan. 4:7-15 (*ibid*). See also Lévi-Strauss' discussion of the magical tree of light in *Les Romans de la Table Ronde* (C. Lévi-Strauss, "Le Père Noël supplicié", 1578-79).

39. *The Ante-Nicene Fathers*, ed. and trans. A. Roberts and J. Donaldson, Grand Rapids: Wm. B. Eerdmans, 1970, 443.

40. *Ibid*, 495.

41. C. Lévi-Strauss, "Le Père Noël supplicié", 1578.

42. *Ibid*.

43. *Ibid*, 1579.

44. The appearance and dress of St. Nicholas has varied greatly through the centuries from the garb of a Greek or Roman bishop discussed earlier (see note 19) to his present appearance, which has been strongly influenced by a series of paintings begun in the 1920's made for the Coca Cola company by Haddon Sundblom.

45. C. Lévi-Strauss, "Le Père Noël supplicié", 1580-1581.

46. *Ibid*, 1580-1581.

47. *Ibid*, 1580ff.

48. In Bari, Italy, St. Nicholas' role as "Santa Claus" is removed (no doubt because his shrine is located there) and taken over by a good witch named "Befana" (apparently a corruption of the word "Epiphany"), "Who knows who's naughty or nice". It is said there that she missed seeing the Three Magi, and as a result she is condemned to search for them forever. Like the katchina and our St. Nicholas she is often used to frighten children into good behavior so that she will give them something on Jan. 6, the eve of Epiphany (see M. Ebon, *St. Nicholas*, 78).

49. C. Lévi-Strauss, "Le Père Noël supplicié", 1581.

50.   *Ibid*, 1580, 1583.   This may also help explain the
ason why St. Nicholas is the patron saint not only of chil-
en but also unmarried women (see p. 142 below).

51.   *Ibid*, 1582.

52.   *Ibid*.

53.   *Ibid*, 1582-83.   Lévi-Strauss writes: "the katchina
e therefore, at the same time, evidence of death and of life
er death" (p. 1582).   And further, "They [the beliefs con-
ted to Father Christmas] put into evidence, behind the op-
ition between children and adults, a much deeper opposition
ween the dead and the living" (p. 1583).

54.   The N.T. gospels may be explained as an exposition of
it is possible for God (an immortal being) to die in order
t Man (a mortal being) might become immortal.

55.   We are simply referring here to the death motifs
sent in the birth narratives of Matthew and Luke which are
l-known to N.T. scholars, i.e. the myrrh (Mt. 2:11; cf. Mk.
23), the flight into Egypt to escape the slaughter of the
born by Herod, etc.

56.   C. Lévi-Strauss, "Le Père Noël supplicié", 1584.

57.   *Ibid*.

58.   *Ibid*, 1585-1586.

59.   *Ibid*, 1586.

60.   *Ibid*.

61.   It should be recalled that the primary function of
tivals appears to be to supply the possibility for "psycho-
ical, cathartic, and therapeutic outlets", but most impor-
tly to create a *greater cohesiveness* in a particular group
society.   The effect of Christmas on the strengthening of
nuclear family is well-known in this regard.   (See Linwood
dericksen, "Feast and Festival", 202.)

62.   C. Lévi-Strauss, "Le Père Noël supplicié", 1587.

63.   *Ibid*.

64.   As Lévi-Strauss himself concludes, *ibid*, 1588.

65.   We are making an allusion here to Jn. 21:15-19.

66. See n. 28 above.

67. M. Ebon, *St. Nicholas*, 54.

68. St. Nicholas seems to have played a very important role during the Middle Ages in the relationship between Christians and Jews. In addition to this tale, there is another about a Jew of Calabria who possessed an icon of St. Nicholas (see J. H. Worman, "St. Nicholas of Myra", 61).

69. M. Ebon, *St. Nicholas*, 68-69.

70. *Ibid,* 107.

CONTINUAL INVOCATIONS OF SAINT AUGUSTINE: REINHOLD NIEBUHR IN AMERICAN THEOLOGY

Paul Lehmann

I

Epistolary Pre-amble

Dear Markus,

It is a joy and a privilege to greet you upon the occasion of your sixty-fifth birthday, and to thank you for your friendship and your scholarship across the years. As your friendship has been evocative, enriching, and enlivening, your life and work--devoted to the *recte praedicatio verbum Dei*--have been perceptive, probing, and provocative. Whether in concurrence or in dissent--be it the state of Christian discipleship or the state of Israel--I have been a too often silent beneficiary of your creativity. Thus, this occasion for breaking the silence and telling you so, is more than a little welcome to me.

When was it we first met? It must have been about twenty-five years ago, at the very beginning of your American odyssey. You had just come to Dubuque, where Rosemarie and you received me with a cordiality and encouragement more heartening than either of you had any way of knowing. As it turned out, you were on a journey which took you via Chicago and Pittsburgh to Basel. Two decades earlier, you had become an hypostatic name to me during the semester spent in Bonn in 1933, where for the first time I met your father in person. His troubles with the "Third Reich" were beginning to intensify, since "the Fuehrer" had come to power at the end of January. Could it have been that you were lurking somewhere in the wings, during one or another of those weekly evenings when we students were cordially received at Siebengebirgstrasse 18, for what, for some of us at least, was an initiation into the delicate and dangerous reciprocity between theology and politics, with its excitement and its risks, its promise and its ambiguity, but in any case, with its inevitability? Or, were you away at school, preparing for your imminent and irrevocable commitment to theology?

In retrospect, at any rate, it seems to me that our friendship, though occasioned by your father's formative presence in our lives, has been rooted in and nurtured by a double kinship. We have shared the passionate conviction that theology is the passion *par excellence*--at once liberating and fulfilling--for the human living of human life. The corollary is that theology, so understood and pursued, especially requires--sooner or later, soon and late, and from time to time because always between the times--the risk of non-conformity. No! I did not "refuse to be confirmed", or tend "to be involved with communist groups".[1] Nor did I ever earn the knowledgeable competence: first, to establish the sacramental inviolability of infant baptism, and then, to challenge its sacramental appropriateness altogether.[2] More tardily and timidly, I managed to be uncomfortable about the pastoral habit of arranging ordinations of sons by fathers as a dubious replication of apostolic succession; and to keep as far away as possible from the anti-communist hysteria in the United States, which must have astonished you upon your arrival in Dubuque in 1953.

When last we were together for a conversation--*unter sechs Augen*--were Rosemarie and you on your way to Basel, or were we at a meeting in Toronto of the Karl Barth Society of North America? In any event, our talk concerned your painstaking and all but successful attempts to bring *Carolus Magnus* to a liberating revision of his discussion of man and woman against every trace of conventional and unconventional chauvinism. How close he came, and how far you really did go, makes the relevant passages of the KD worth a further and more careful look.[3] After all, has it not been written that Rosemarie is one of "three...distinguished daughters-in-law, each of (whom) gives me all sorts of things to think about..."[4]; and are you not one of the three sons to whom KD, IV/1, is dedicated, named according to the pentateuchal order of blessing?

It is your passion for theology and your practice of theology in non-conformity that I should like to underline in joining fellow-contributors to this volume, and in joining with your many friends in thankful acknowledgement of who you are and have been to us and for us, and to and for the times through which we have lived together. Theology understood and pursued with passion and practiced in non-conformity is theology at once self-critical and critical of the times in which and against which theology is called to undertake its critical reflections upon the church's language about God. *Dei providentia et hominum confusione*, it happens that my own copy of KD, IV/1, wears on its title page, below the author's signature, and the date, 7 July 1955, a memorable inscription which has prompted the pre-occupation of these pages in tribute to you. The inscription cites J. A. Bengel, as follows: *In regno Dei non valet neutralitas*.

Although KD, IV/1, had been published in 1953, I had not acquired it for myself until 1955. From Strasbourg, where I was on sabbatical leave, I came to Basel in early June for a visit with your father. Your mother and he graciously invited me to lunch. As on similar previous occasions, a lively conversation ensued. This time, however, there were two differences. The first was that the conversation continued unabated on the veranda overlooking the idyllic garden behind the house at Pilgerstrasse 25. The second difference was that on the veranda, the conversation suddenly turned, upon your father's initiative, to Reinhold Niebuhr.

I had not come to discuss Niebuhr but rather Dogmatics with the Aquinas of the twentieth century. For some reason which still eludes me (perhaps you know), *Carolus Magnus* could not be diverted from that topic. For nearly three hours, I found myself under intense interrogation concerning Niebuhr during which, in various ways, I tried to state the thesis that a major misfortune of our "theological existence today" was that two of its most formidable theologians continued to talk past each other rather than to talk with each other. I can still see the intense, sharp eyes penetrating to the core of every facet of the Barth-Niebuhr relation, as well as to the core of the hapless receiver of one question after another, one puff of pipe smoke after another, in accelerating tempo. When courtesy finally required my departure, I made my way back to Strasbourg under a strong sense of having failed to carry my point at any point. Since the bookshops in Basel were momentarily out of stock of IV/1, I also returned with Karl Barth's cordial consent to sign the copy which a student friend had agreed to purchase for me, bring round to Pilgerstrasse 25, and send on to me. About three weeks later, the volume, duly inscribed, reached me in Strasbourg.

In regno Dei non valet neutralitas! So *that* was what the conversation about Reinhold Niebuhr had *really* been about! With ill-concealed fury, I sat down immediately and wrote of my dismay, and asked whether I had not learned above all from him, resolutely to avoid every form of "theologische Schulmeisterei"? By return mail came a characteristic and unforgettable reply. It said, in substance: "I knew I should not have written that! Lolo told me that I should not have written it! Es war aber schon geschrieben! You have my full permission to apply ink remover to the offending inscription!"

You will understand that J. A. Bengal, in Karl Barth's

own hand, continues to look up at me from the title page of
my autographed copy of KD, IV/1. It could be, of course, that
the *neutralitas - question* is now being disposed of in the
church triumphant, perhaps even to the accompaniment of *"Ta-
mino mein, o welch ein Glueck...!"*[5] *There*, the unique master
of "the art of playing" which "pre-supposes a child-like knowing about the center of all things"[6] could already have effected the reconciliation of the irreconcilable. If so, an
assist from the church militant could be all the more appropriate; and if not, it could be all the more urgent. *Here*,
"the clever Basilio and the tender Cherubino; Don Juan, the
nobleman, and Leporello, the rascal; the gentle Pamina and the
wild Queen of the Night;...the wise Sarastro and the foolish
Papageno" still give utterance to "an authentic and undampened
vox humana along the whole scale of its possibilities".[7]

Perhaps, then, dear Markus, among the celebrative dimensions of your sixty-fifth birthday, this one also may be included: *hic et nunc!* to attest to "that unconcealed and un-
constricted conversation"[8] which *illic et tunc!* is already
under way. After all, it is a matter of record, that in the
matter of baptism, an ageing father had to allow himself to be
told, on the basis of sheer evidence assembled by his son,
that, as regards the father's own treatise on Baptism (1943),
"not one stone could be left upon another".[9] Accordingly, you
will understand that I should find it more than congruent with
your self-critical and non-conformist practice of theology,
that the corrections effected in the matter of Baptism might
be extended--*ubi et quando visum est Deo*--to the Baptized,
especially to those who could only be set free for each other
by gathering them under the umbrella of Mozartian freedom.

Towards such an undertaking, I venture to send you an
aide-mémoire concerning Reinhold Niebuhr. The paragraphs that
follow come to you "in hope...believed against hope" (Romans
4:18), that the word of the prophet will be fulfilled yet
again: "He will reconcile fathers to sons and sons to fathers, lest I come and put the land under a band to destroy it"
(Malachi 4:6).[10]

With ongoing respect and gratitude, friendship and affec-
tion,

Paul

New York
In the First Octave of Epiphany,
1980

II

Reinhold Niebuhr in the Context of American Theology[11]

In the memorable chronicle of his reflections upon his observations of *Democracy in America*, Alexis de Tocqueville remarks that "in the United States there was an alliance between the spirit of religion and the spirit of liberty....For my own part," he concludes, "I doubt whether man can support at the same time complete religious independence and entire public freedom. And I am inclined to think, that if faith be wanting in him, he must serve, and if he be free, he must believe."[12]

"If faith be wanting in (man), he must serve, and if he be free, he must believe"! If there be any focal and succinct formulations of American theology as the context of the life and thought of Reinhold Niebuhr, these words of de Tocqueville express it. Although Niebuhr himself does not cite this passage, he does quote a similar observation. This remark pertains to what Niebuhr calls "this remarkable prescient prophecy about both America and Russia".[13] Writing in 1835, de Tocqueville notes:

> There are at the present time two great nations in the world, which started from different points, but seem to tend towards the same end. I allude to the Russians and the Americans....All other nations seem to have nearly reached their natural limits, and they have only to maintain their power; but these are still in the act of growth....The American struggles against the obstacles that nature opposes to him; the adversaries of the Russians are men....The Anglo-American relies upon personal interest to accomplish his ends and gives free scope to the unguided strength and common sense of the people; the Russian centers all authority of society in a single arm. *The principal interest of the former is freedom; of the latter servitude.* Their starting point is different and their courses are not the same; yet each of them seems marked out by the will of Heaven to sway the destinies of half the globe.[14]

Plainly, to a careful observer of the beginnings of democracy in America, a unique relationship between religious independence and public freedom, between faith and emancipation from servitude, characterized "the American Commonwealth" as James Bryce entitled his account of the people, places, happenings, and institutions which had come under de Tocqueville observant scrutiny.[15] The major themes of the American sage seem, indeed, to have been: "a religiously oriented sense of mission, an abundant land, a noble hero, and a favoring Providence". So Sydney Ahlstrom summarizes them,[16] and goes on to note the introductory words of George Bancroft:

> It is the object of the present work to explain how the change in the conditions of our land has been brought about; and, as the fortunes of a nation are not under the control of blind destiny, to follow the steps by which a favoring Providence, calling our institutions into being, has conducted the country to its present happiness and glory.[17]

The formative core of this story, and the secret hidden in the link between religious independence and public freedom as de Tocqueville has put it; or between the commitment to freedom and the abhorrence of servitude, emphasized in the passage cited by Reinhold Niebuhr, was "the Puritan Spirit".[1] Contrary to a still widely prevalent and misleading stereotype, Puritanism "was something more than an austere exodus from the flesh-pots of Egypt or a resurgence of experimental piety. It was a vigorous effort to bring God's discipline to this world, its people, and, pre-eminently, to God's Church.. Detesting those who were

> 'at ease in Zion', determined to have a church whose holiness was visible, the Puritan turned to Holy Scripture, where he found a witness to the Creator that inspired him to be a fruitful part of God's order as a citizen and in his vocation....
>
> With regard to personal life, the Puritan demanded of himself--and of others--a reformation of character, the rejection of idle recreations and vain display, and sober, obedient godliness....

> In the public realm the Puritan sought,
> in Governor John Winthrop's words, 'a due
> form of government both civill and ecclesi-
> astical'....Because of his concern for duti-
> ful living, the Puritan was usually more
> orderly than disruptive so long as govern-
> ments did not obstruct or harass those who
> sought to obey God's Law. When free to
> speculate or encouraged to innovate, how-
> ever, the more thoroughgoing Puritans moved
> towards modern democratic ideas.[19]

The operational principle of Puritanism was the idea of
the covenant. The roots of this idea lie, as is well known,
in the Scriptures. Its most catechetical expression is in the
Heidelberg Catechism of 1563; its most elaborate dogmatic formulation was given by the Dutch theologian, Johannes Cocceius
(1603-69). As Calvin and Bullinger had given forceful clarity
to the notion of a covenant of grace, which forcefully echoes
in the Heidelberg Catechism,[20] so Cocceius, from his professorship in Leyden, found colleagues among the New England Puritans
in the pursuit of a covenantal theology. Both Cocceius and the
Puritans in New England had found their mentor in William Ames
(1576-1633). Ames had had to give up his university appoint-
ments in England in 1610 because of his refusal to wear the
surplice, and had fled to Holland. There he taught theology
at the University of Franeker from 1622-32, and thus, became
the teacher of Cocceius.[21]

Although the covenant theology was not to be expounded
and applied without its share of doctrinal rigidities--culmin-
ating on the Continent in the Synod of Dort (1618-19), and in
the "Holy Commonwealths of New England"[22]--the covenant theology must, nevertheless, be understood as mainly an attempt
to humanize the stricter Calvinist predestinarianism. Divine
election was as a frame-work within which an "irreducible personal faith" could be nurtured and combined with a lively
sense of responsibility for the world. It was not to be interpreted as "a vast impersonal and mechanical scheme". This
shift of emphasis provided a link between the personal and the
public responsibilities for life in this world. It also ele-
vated *conversion* disproportionately, even to the extent of
making it a requirement for church membership. This problem-
atical correlation is still part of theology and church life
in the United States. Its formative influence was not lost on
Reinhold Niebuhr; and this, not least, because it facilitated
an accommodation with the purposes and passions of the great
and not so great awakenings that combined with Puritanism to
make America "a Protestant Republic".[23] To advert briefly to

de Tocqueville,

> 'I do not know', he wrote, 'whether all
> Americans have a sincere faith in their
> religion, for who can search the human
> heart? But I am certain that they hold
> it to be indispensable to the maintenance
> of republican institutions. This opinion
> is not peculiar to a class of citizen or
> to a party, but it belongs to the whole
> nation, and to every rank of society.'[24]

A month before Niebuhr began his remarkable professorship
and ministry in Union Theological Seminary, New York, he declared himself to be "not...a Methodist (but) a Lutheran".[25]
This self-identification arises from a concern of Niebuhr's
with the importance of decision in the Christian life. Important as his own tradition, with its stress upon confirmation,
was, he felt that it did tend to overestimate the effectiveness
of Christian family nurture in furthering a genuine and life-
changing commitment. "We don't expect people to come into the
Christian life", he declared, "by a critical decision....We are
confirmed without being confronted with a decision and may have
lost a certain uniqueness that they have achieved who came into the Christian life by a critical experience."[26] One need
not regard this declaration of denominational affiliation as a
subliminal hint of a Niebuhrian preference for Methodism. It
is rather a sign of the easy concourse between the Puritan
ethos of "America", as de Tocqueville keeps referring to us,
with the pietistical evangelicalism which informed a quarter
of the population of St. Louis and Southern Illinois in the
middle of the nineteenth century.[27]

It was in this context that Reinhold Niebuhr's formation
happened. The beginnings seem to have been made on 15 October
1840, under the leadership of Pastor Louis Nollau in Gravois
Settlement, now Mehlville, Missouri. By 1848, a foundational
statement was available which acknowledged "the symbolic books
of the Lutheran and the Reformed Church, the most important being: the Augsburg Confession, Luther's and the Heidelberg Catechisms, in so far as they agree; but where they disagree the
German Evangelical Church Society of the West adheres strictly
to the passages of Holy Scriptures bearing on the subject and
avails itself of the liberty of conscience prevailing in the
Evangelical Church".[28] A year earlier, 1847, this same Society had adopted its own Catechism, a composite of the Lutheran
and the Heidelberg Catechisms, and this Catechism was the
basis of an extended commentary by Professor Andreas Irion
(1823-67). Irion was "a fervent mystical product of Wuerttem-

berg pietism with strong philosophical interests, whose early death robbed the Church of an original 'Union Theologian'".[29] Thus, it would seem that instead of *one* "original 'Union Theologian'", the Evangelical Church Union of the West--which in 1866, became the Evangelical Synod of North America--was to be granted *two* original theologians, who bore the names of Reinhold and Helmut Richard Niebuhr.

American Theology which provided the context of Reinhold Niebuhr's formation was a compound of Puritanism, Pietism, and Evangelicalism. Its principal accents are: a lively awareness of the sovereignty of God in and over the world; an inner, individual, conviction of sin; a trustful assurance of salvation, *Christo pro nobis*;[30] and a commitment to the proclamation of the Gospel attested in Scripture, together with a firm persuasion that the Scriptures are "the Word of God, the only rule of faith and obedience".[31]

It is, perhaps, too soon to assess the lasting ways in which Reinhold Niebuhr drew upon his own formation, and moved beyond it, towards a formative impact upon the present and future of theology in America. Nevertheless, there are certain focal accents in his writings which may be underlined as indicative of a boundary between retrospect and prospect. In retrospect, these reflections *come* forward, and in prospect, *point* forward; and they may be regarded as intrinsic to and decisive for the ongoing story of theology in the United States.

III

Reinhold Niebuhr: Retrospect and Prospect

It is, of course, an historical truism that boundaries between retrospect and prospect are difficult to draw. The relativity and the complexity of happenings in the human story combine with the diversity and the precariousness of historical judgments to render dubious the fixing of times and seasons, turning points and epochs, that make the difference between looking back and looking ahead. As regards Reinhold Niebuhr, it may be suggested that we are in better case than historical prudence would lead us to expect. And in any case, a boundary between retrospect and prospect is significant as a convenient orientation rather than as an irrevocable finding.

In his instructive, vivid, and charming biography of Martin Luther, Roland Bainton has noted that: "one might take the date 25 June 1530, the day when the Augsburg Confession was publicly read, as the death day of the Holy Roman Empire".[32] Similarly, Bainton's colleague at Yale, Sydney Ahlstrom speaks of "the decade of the sixties" which "seems in many ways to have marked a new stage in the long development of American religious history....It may even have ended a distinct quadricentennium--a unified four hundred year period--in the Anglo-American experience". Ahlstrom writes further:

> A Great Puritan Epoch can be seen as beginning in 1558 with the death of Mary Tudor, the last monarch to rule over an officially Roman Catholic England, and as ending with the election of John Fitzgerald Kennedy, the first Roman Catholic President of the United States. To underline the same point, one might note that the age of the Counter-Reformation began in 1563 with the Council of Trent and ended in 1965 with the closing of the Second Vatican Council. Histories of the rise of organized Puritanism begin their accounts with the decisive first decade in the reign of Queen Elizabeth; and the terms 'post-Puritan' and 'post-Protestant' are first popularly applied to America in the 1960's.[33]

Thus, the context of American theology, compounded of Puritanism, Pietism, and Evangelicalism, which shaped America as "a Protestant Republic", and which shaped Reinhold Niebuhr for the future of theology in America, crosses a kind of rubicon in "the turbulent sixties", as Ahlstrom has called them.[34] According to Ahlstrom,

> They seem to involve a deep shift in the pre-suppositional substructures of the American mind. One can designate them as metaphysical, moral, and social:
>
> 1. A growing commitment to a naturalism or 'secularism' and corresponding doubts about the supernatural and the sacral
>
> 2. A creeping (or galloping) awareness of vast contradictions in American life between profession and performance, the ideal and the actual

3. Increasing doubt as to the capacity
    of present-day ecclesiastical, po-
    litical, social, and educational in-
    stitutions to rectify the country's
    deep-seated woes.[35]

The boundary thus drawn between retrospect and prospect
finds Reinhold Niebuhr, although in relative retirement, at
the "eye of the storm". To those of us who knew him at the
height of his powers and in the heyday of his influence; and
who were shaped by his age of maturity for our own "age of
anxiety", his early writings seem startlingly surprising.
They are at once quaint in their simplistic echoes of a simplistic tradition *and* anticipatory of what has been called
"the Protestant search for political realism".[36] They also
offer more than a hint of the self-critical perception of human ambiguity, both personal and public. Indeed, these echoes,
in retrospect, *come* forward, and in prospect, *point* forward,
to the truth and relevance of Christian faith for the human
living of human life on the other side of any rubicon, the
contemporary American one included.

One is tempted to cite at length from William Chrystal's
fascinating compilation. A few random indications, however,
must suffice; as indeed, they well may, since the rest is
available.[37] The earliest of Niebuhr's writings was an
article published in February 1911, in *The Keryx*, the student
periodical of Eden Theological Seminary. It bore the title:
*The Attitude of the Church Towards Present Moral Evils. Inter
alia*, the article declares:

> Morality,...as a unit force in society is
> born of religion and is related to it as
> effect is to cause....*To make mere men
> Christians and all Christians truer would
> then be the only correct method by which
> we could achieve the aim of our day and
> start the fastly declining and degenerat-
> ing morals on the ascent.* Unfortunately
> other methods are being used at the ex-
> pense of this one in fighting present
> evils.
>
> Again we come to the truth that real
> morality can not come from without,
> but must come from within, from *entire-
> ly changed hearts* and ideals, the gos-
> pel of Jesus Christ.[38]

The theme of the relation of religion and morality to personal and social change occurs without variation, in an address more than a decade later:

> 'I believe', says Niebuhr, 'we can change human nature with all its brutal and selfish instincts, first by religion, second by education. Because it has unlimited resources, it can be developed into something much finer than our imagination can conceive....Religion can change us.... Nothing else can make man more than a beast, religion can make him a child of God. *Uncompromising sacramentalism is the only religion that can bring these about.* But we have not learned yet what it means to be spiritual beings. Many do not know what it is to be spiritual themselves, a son of God. And many do not know how to treat the other man as a son of God.'[39]

In an open forum, the question was raised: "What would you consider the most effective process of establishing a new Christian morality?" Niebuhr replied:

> Not only one way; but rather two things must go together. First, increasing spirituality, secondly, through more honest and intelligent application of Christian principles to specific problems.

> Our final end is to win men to Christ with the distinct aim to follow Him, to form a Christ-like character.[40]

In retrospect, the "Reinie" that many of us knew and that all of us remember, sounds in these passages like a committed Evangelical Leaguer, or a Christian Endeavorer; indeed, all but a Crusader for Christ. The tonalities take us by surprise; and one is tempted to remark: "No wonder he won the prize of the 'First Honor Thesis' in the Lincoln Lyceum Thesis Contest!" The thesis topic, chosen by Niebuhr's most influential teacher, and increasingly close and admired friend, Professor Samuel D. Press of Eden Seminary, was: *Religion: Revival and Education.*[41]

In retrospect, however, there were also other tonalities, resonant with accents destined for the prospect, in those days still more than half a century in the future. To begin with the Prize Essay itself, we read that a distinction must be made between "religious revival and religious education". The essay then continues:

> the revival appeals to the emotions and education to the reason of man both with the purpose thereby of influencing his will. This distinction is, however, only a general one....History, however, has proven the general distinction to be a correct one, notwithstanding the vigorous protest of many champions of the revival against the same.[42]

Similarly, the address on "Winning the World", in which the firm declaration is made "to win men to Christ", "to form a Christ-like character", also asserts:

> All organizations are dangerous at times. ...The more we succeed in our Brotherhood, the more we let it go at that....We want a Brotherhood that serves the congregation, and also the denomination. We are still hectic and frantic, trying to win over the congregation to the denomination, and as soon as we effect this the denomination cannot be anything, because it does not win more people to Christianity....*To a certain extent it may be possible to transcend the world in which you live, but it is not altogether possible....You cannot build a Christ-like character without having a Christ-like world.*[43]

In these two passages, there are advance echoes of Reinhold Niebuhr's first book: *Does Civilization Need Religion?*[44]

Again, the address before the Tenth National Convention of the Evangelical League, already referred to, tells us:

> I do not want to make any unqualified statement about the Christian Church, for I belong to it as you do. I have helped build it as it is with all its faults and short-

comings. All I ask is: How can I be a
Christian without being a hypocrite? Or
rather: How can I be a Christian without
being too much a hypocrite?[45]

From "Winning the World", already referred to, we hear:

I do not mean that you are going to overcome evil by smiling at it; the gospel according to 'St. Polly Anna' sickens me.
You are not going to overcome evil by
walking genially through life. Psychologically, a person is only the sublima-
tion of the brute in us. If we now kill
by machine guns instead of scratching
their eyes out as formerly, we are not
better.[46]

It is apparent from these two random passages that the celebrated diary from Niebuhr's years in Detroit was already in
the making. Niebuhr came to Bethel Evangelical Church, Detroit on 8 August 1915. A decade later, the extent to which
pietistic simplicity bordering on optimism was being chastened
by the hard realities of power and human ambiguity in a society undergoing industrialization, is strikingly indicated in
an article called "Tyrants and Servants". The piece is Niebuhr's first writing published in book form. A vivid passage
observes that:

These big cities in which we live and of
which we are so inordinately proud should
be regarded with more suspicion and less
veneration by the men whose servants they
are expected to be....The eight-hour day
is the fruit not of legislation, but of
labor-saving machinery. Our comforts have
certainly been increased by machine indus-
try. But no one seems concerned to note
the price we have paid for these blessings.[47]

Four years later, the tamed cynic was widely read and widely
heralded.[48]

Two further indications of the boundary between retrospect
and prospect in Reinhold Niebuhr's life and work can scarcely
be omitted because they exhibit so clearly the link between the

arliest and the maturest and most memorable writings. The
atter consist of *Moral Man and Immoral Society; An Interpre-
ation of Christian Ethics*; and the celebrated Gifford Lec-
ures on *The Nature and Destiny of Man.*[49] A return to "Ty-
ants and Servants", the article just cited, tells us, nearly
en years before *Moral Man and Immoral Society* that:

> Man has a curious weakness for giving such
> unthinking devotion to the institutions and
> governments which are meant to serve him
> that he tempts them to assume arbitrary
> power over him and to conceive their life
> as an end in itself....Human history is
> filled with evidences of this curious
> perversity.

> Nothing is so good and so useful but that
> it cannot be corrupted by excessive venera-
> tion....Human life is more social than it
> once was; and therefore, the authorities
> which are the by-products of social order
> are more potent; life is more complex, and
> the institutions through which we express
> it have therefore become more difficult to
> control.

> We have permitted civilization to become
> our master through the same weakness which
> raised servants to tyrants in other days.
> To make civilization again the servant of
> man will require a penetrating insight on
> the one hand and a robust faith on the
> other.[50]

On the eve of Niebuhr's move from Detroit to Union Seminary, New York, he addressed the Seventh National Convention
of the Evangelical Brotherhood, in which the themes of his
most important works already emerge. The richness, range,
and depth of Niebuhr's insights and analyses of power and its
limits, of justice and love, of faith, society, and culture,
are on the nearer edge of their fulsome elaboration and formative impact upon theology in America, and indeed, in the ecumenical movement of the churches.[51] The address declares *inter alia*, that:

> The fact is that of all the problems of
> people, *the business of living decently
> with other people is the most difficult*

of all....It has been the rule of old for
the strong man to command the weak and inevitably to exterminate them....We need a
state of society where people are going to
stop this business of exterminating the
weak and establish some kind of society
from chaos. The most interesting thing
is that this strategic application of
*justice is mistaken by a good many
people for Christianity.*

The Gospel definitely pits the idea of
love against the idea of justice....It is
very *hard to be decent to people you don't
know*, particularly when they are different
from what you imagine them to be....Thus
we can see how difficult it is even for
good people to attempt the Christianizing
of international relations--to be not only
just but imaginative and loving. *For love
is finally nothing more than justice plus
imagination.*

One is almost overcome by a sense of despair. There can never be a final peace
until there will be nations, who can in
the moments of crisis, actually *sacrifice
their own rights for the good of the
world*....In all the intricate and complex problems of today, with the ruthless
application to the practical, *nations
must be made to see and to submit themselves to the dominion of the Christ
Spirit of service and sacrifice.*

IV

"Continual Invocations of Saint Augustine"[52]

These retrospective and prospective tonalities exhibit a
movement of Reinhold Niebuhr's conviction and thought from the
piety of faith to the *faith of piety*. As this movement un-
folds--from "Tyrants and Servants" in 1926, to *Faith and Politics* in 1968; from the first of Niebuhr's writings to appear
in book form to the last collection of Niebuhr's writings to

appear in book form[53]--the puritanism, pietism, and evangelicalism in which and by which he was formed, undergo a radicalization. This radicalization is the rubicon between *the piety
of faith* and *the faith of piety*, across which there is no turning back. It carried Niebuhr beyond his own times and into the
very maelstrom of secularism, contradiction, and even terrorism
which the 1960's have bequeathed to the foreseeable future.
The *piety of faith* is characterized by the simplicities, assurances, foundational sources and certainties which nurture
believing communities whose last fortress is the inner stead-
fastness of the individual. The scope of its aspirations,
nurture, and expectations includes orthodox and liberals,
militants and pacifists, literalists and modernists in a
varied and shared commitment to Christian perfection. The
faith of piety is characterized, root and branch, by an embattled struggle between simplicity and complexity, between
believing and doubting, between conviction and criticism, certainty and ambiguity, destiny and despair. The *faith of piety*
nurtures communities of commitment and criticism as steadying
contexts of personal and public self-correction and renewal,
whose ultimate hope and trust are sustained by the disclosure
within history of a fulfillment beyond history. In the light
of this disclosure, all human happenings are signs of the mystery of revelation and hiddenness, of grace and sin, of mercy
and meaning, and of forgiveness and fulfillment *in* human life
of human life in this world and in the world to come.

Referring to H. Richard Niebuhr's *The Kingdom of God in
America*, as "a masterpiece of re-assessment in which the prophetic stance of Puritanism and Jonathan Edwards, as well as
the great evangelical enterprises of the nineteenth century
were appreciatively considered" and "liberalism was then
weighed and found wanting"[54], Sydney Ahlstrom goes on to say
that "nowhere else is the living relationship of Neo-orthodoxy
and Paleo-orthodoxy better illustrated--unless in Reinhold
Niebuhr's *continual invocations of Saint Augustine*".[55] Perhaps these invocations also illuminate, if not explain, an
underlying affinity of insight and spirit between Reinhold
Niebuhr and Perry Miller, each so very different in many ways.
Of the Puritan spirit, Miller writes that it was infused with
"the Augustinian strain of piety".

> I venture to call this piety Augustinian
> ...simply because Augustine is the arch-
> exemplar of a religious frame of mind of
> which Puritanism is only one instance out
> of many in fifteen hundred years of reli-
> gious history....There survive hundreds of
> Puritan diaries and thousands of Puritan

> sermons, but we can read the inward mean-
> ing of them all in the *Confessions*.[56]

I do not know whether there are diaries, or even a diary, kept by Reinhold Niebuhr. But in addition to the *magna opera*, there are Sermons, and unforgettable prayers, a treasury of which, together with certain sermons from the later years of his life, has been selected and recently made available. The occasions were for the most part the daily chapel services and the Sunday services in James Memorial Chapel at Union Theological Seminary.[57] This little volume documents, as nothing else in the corpus of Reinhold Niebuhr's writings does, the integrity, depth, vitality, and range of Reinhold Niebuhr's faith and life.

The phrase, "the faith of piety" is, of course, an Augustinian, not a Niebuhrian phrase. It links the *Confessions* with the *City of God*. With Augustine, as with Niebuhr, the movement from the *piety of faith* to the *faith of piety* is unmistakeably and persuasively under way. And more than merely co-incidentally, the phrase leaps out of a perceptive and penetrating rebuke to Cicero, whose view inversely brings us back to Alexis de Tocqueville. In Augustine's criticism of Cicero, he comes alongside Reinhold Niebuhr, as Reinhold Niebuhr's "continual invocations of Saint Augustine" discover his companionship with the Bishop of Hippo. Concerning man's "stature, virtue, or place in the cosmos" and the contradictions of his freedom therein involved, "when fully analyzed", as the opening pages of the Gifford Lectures tell us,[58] Augustine tells us,

> Cicero chooses to reject the foreknowledge
> of future things, and shuts up the religious
> mind to this alternative, to make choice be-
> tween two things, either that something is
> in our power, or that there is foreknowl-
> edge--both of which cannot be true; but if
> the one is affirmed, the other is thereby
> denied. He therefore, like a truly great
> and wise man, and one who consulted very
> much and very skillfully for the good of
> humanity, of those two chose the freedom
> of the will, to confirm which he denied
> the foreknowledge of future things; and
> thus, *wishing to make men free, he makes
> them sacrilegious. But the religious
> mind chooses both, confesses both, and
> maintains both by the faith of piety.*[59]

Augustine's point, applied to human freedom and destiny in relation to the cosmos, de Tocqueville makes about human freedom and destiny in relation to society and politics. "I doubt", it will be recalled that he wrote, "whether man can support at the same time complete independence and entire public freedom. And I am inclined to think, that if faith be wanting in him, he must serve, and if he be free, he must believe."

In pursuit of Reinhold Niebuhr's "continual invocations of Saint Augustine", one could add to the dialectical relation between the faith of piety and the piety of faith, the further exploration of the dialectical relation between the power to will and the will-to-power; and of the dialectical relation between the justice of love and the love of justice, as among the principal Augustinian themes with which Reinhold Niebuhr was principally concerned.[60] These explorations, however, would carry the present essay beyond its proper limits as a grateful offering in tribute to Markus Barth. Meanwhile, it may be both pertinent and fruitful to keep before us the Augustinian significance of Niebuhr's own account of the purpose to which his life and work were given.

As we all know, Augustine looked back upon a civilization in decay and disarray, its authority and stability collapsed, and barbarian primitivism on the march. Reinhold Niebuhr looked forward to--and beyond--a civilization similarly in decay and disarray, and on a precarious frontier between technological barbarism and a new world order in the making. On that frontier, his legacy to us approximated a tradition in American theology which he steadfastly shaped, and no less steadfastly nurtures. As Niebuhr himself wrote, in the *Preface* to his last published book:

> My...purpose is to explain, or perhaps justify, the contrasting method in two of the major themes of these essays. The one theme is to validate the resources of biblical faith by applying its moral imperatives and its law of love, enjoining responsibility for the neighbor's welfare in a technical age.... The second theme is an explanation of the vitality of religious life in an age which expected the death of religion....The reason for this vitality is that religious faith is an expression of trust in the meaning of human existence, despite all the cross purposes, incongruities, and ills in nature and history.[61]

Pro mundo contra mundum: Athanasius redivivus! Augustinus redivivus! In regno Dei non valet neutralitas; sed valet fraternitas: ad maiorem Dei gloriam!

NOTES

1. Eberhard Busch, *Karl Barth*, translated by John Bowden, Philadelphia, Fortress Press, 1976, pp. 220, 530, note 90.

2. *Ibid.*, p. 369.

3. For example, III/4, 1951, Par. 54,1, pp. 153f., 216f.

4. Eberhard Busch, *op. cit.*, p. 440; adapted.

5. Karl Barth, *Wolfgang Amadeus Mozart - 1756 - 1956*, Zoellikon, Evangelischer Verlag, 1956, p. 7. Translation mine.

6. *Ibid.*, p. 8. Translation mine.

7. *Ibid.*, pp. 45, 44. Translation mine.

8. *Ibid.*, pp. 44, 45. Translation mine.

9. Karl Barth, *Kirchliche Dogmatik, Die Lehre von der Versoehnung, Bd. IV/4, Fragment*, Zuerich, Evangelischer Verlag, 1967, pp. X, XI. Translation mine.

10. *Ibid.*, p. XI. Translation mine.

11. The pages which follow are a revised and adapted form of the first of three lectures on Reinhold Niebuhr, delivered at Eden Theological Seminary, Webster Groves, Missouri, upon the occasion of the annual convocation of the Seminary, 17-19 April 1979. The Convocation was designed as *The Niebuhr Celebration*, honoring Hulda, Reinhold, and H. Richard Niebuhr for their contributions to the formation of "the Niebuhr Tradition in American Theology: Retrospect and Prospect".

12. Alexis de Tocqueville, *Democracy in America*, translated by Henry Reeve, London, 1875, Vol. II, pp. 40-41.

13. Reinhold Niebuhr, *The Self and the Dramas of History*, New York, Charles Scribner's Sons, 1955, p. 210.

14. Alexis de Tocqueville, *op. cit.*, Vol. I, p. 434; cited by Reinhold Niebuhr, *ibid.*, pp. 210-11.

15. James Bryce, *The American Commonwealth*, London and New York, Macmillan, 1891, 2 vols.

16. Sydney E. Ahlstrom, *A Religious History of the American People*, New Haven, Yale University Press, 1972, p. 2.

17. These words, first written in 1834, were substantially left standing in the revised edition of 1876. See George Bancroft, *History of the United States*, 1:3; cited by Ahlstrom, *op. cit.*, p. 2.

18. So Ahlstrom, *ibid.*, chapter 8.

19. *Ibid.*, pp. 128-29.

20. *The Heidelberg Catechism*, especially, QQ. 1, 2, 10-15, 19, 21, 27, 28, 45, 60, 61.

21. Ahlstrom, *op. cit.*, pp. 130-31. Ames' *Medulla Theologiae* (Amsterdam, 1623) was translated in 1642 as *The Marrow of Sacred Divinity*. It became the Puritans' principal theological text. Ames' *De Conscientia* (1632), translated in 1639, as *Cases of Conscience*, became their chief guide in Moral Theology. So Ahlstrom.

22. The phrase is Ahlstrom's. See *op. cit.*, Part II, chapter 9.

23. Ahlstrom, *ibid.*, p. 387.

24. Alexis de Tocqueville, *Democracy in America*, 1835; quoted by Ahlstrom, *op. cit.*, p. 386.

25. In an address given at the Tenth National Convention of the Evangelical League at Milwaukee, Wisconsin, which met 7-12 August 1928. The address in which this remark occurs was entitled: *An Aristocracy of Spiritual and Moral Life*. See William Chrystal, *Young Reinhold Niebuhr: His Early Writings --1911-1931*, St. Louis, Eden Publishing House, 1977, p. 180. A year later, Eden Publishing House suspended business, in consequence of which Bethany Press in St. Louis has taken responsibility for this book. Chrystal has critically edited and introduced these early writings hitherto accessible in the archives of Eden Seminary and the Evangelical Synod of North America. I am greatly indebted to him for making available these documentary materials.

26. See William Chrystal, *op. cit.*, pp. 180-81.

27. The statistics are Ahlstrom's. *Op. cit.*, p. 755.

28. This account of the context of Niebuhr's beginnings is based upon William Chrystal's edition of his early writings

ready referred to. The passage cited here is, *op. cit.*, pp.
-21.

29. So Ahlstrom, *op. cit.*, p. 755.

30. The centrality of this Lutheran core of piety in
inhold Niebuhr's thought has been discussed elsewhere. See
ul Lehmann, "The Christology of Reinhold Niebuhr", in *Rein-
ld Niebuhr: His Religious, Social and Political Thought*,
ited by Charles W. Kegley and Robert W. Bretall, New York,
e Macmillan Co., 1956, chapter 11.

31. So, the *Westminster Confession of Faith*, chapter 1,
r. 9; and the *Westminster Larger Catechism*, Question 3.

32. Roland Bainton, *Here I Stand*, New York, Abingdon-
kesbury Press, 1950, p. 325.

33. Ahlstrom, *op. cit.*, p. 1079.

34. *Ibid.*, chapter 63.

35. *Ibid.*, p. 1087.

36. *Ibid.*, p. 932.

37. William Chrystal, *op. cit.* The pages indicating the
tations follow Chrystal's account. The writing referred to
ll be identified as noted below.

38. *Ibid.*, pp. 42-43. Italics are mine. Niebuhr was 18
ars of age when he wrote this article.

39. *Ibid.*, p. 162. The address was entitled, *Our Educa-
onal Program*, and was delivered at the Fifth National Con-
ntion of the Evangelical Brotherhood in East St. Louis,
linois, from 14-17 September 1924.

40. *Ibid.*, pp. 187, 175. The first passage is from an
dress given at the Tenth National Convention of the Evangeli-
l League, 7-12 August 1928. See note 25 above. The second
cerpt is from an address on: *Winning the World*, delivered
 22 August 1926, in Buffalo, New York, before the Sixth
tional Convention of the Evangelical Brotherhood. Punctua-
on has been added.

41. The Lincoln Lyceum was a literary Society founded in
09, by Eden Seminary's first English language Professor, Dr.
muel D. Press. Niebuhr's prize-winning essay was published

in the June 1913 issue of *The Keryx*. So, Chrystal, *op. cit.*, p. 46.

42. William Chrystal, *ibid.*, p. 47.

43. *Ibid.*, pp. 174-175. Italics mine.

44. Reinhold Niebuhr, *Does Civilization Need Religion?*, New York, The Macmillan Co., 1927, chapter 1, and *passim*.

45. Reinhold Niebuhr, "An Aristocracy of Spiritual and Moral Life", in William Chrystal, *op. cit.*, p. 184.

46. See William Chrystal, *ibid.*, p. 178. Punctuation added. There is an *erratum* here in Chrystal's text. Niebuhr obviously said: "formerly"; not "formally".

47. This little known essay appears in *Preachers and Preaching in Detroit*, edited by Ralph Milton Pierce, Grand Rapids, Fleming H. Revell, 1926. Chrystal points out that: "Niebuhr was so little known at this point that his name appeared throughout the article as 'Neibuhr'." *Op. cit.*, p. 165. The passage cited is on pp. 168-69. The misspelling accompanied Niebuhr all his days. His growing renown reduced it but did not succeed in tutoring the Anglo-Saxon ear to Teutonic phonetics. Similarly, *either* and *neither* are still widely pronounced in the German manner, i.e., as *Nie*buhr, especially in the Middle West.

48. Reinhold Niebuhr, *Leaves from the Notebook of a Tamed Cynic*, New York, Richard R. Smith, Inc., 1930.

49. Reinhold Niebuhr:

> *Moral Man and Immoral Society*, New York, Charles Scribner's Sons, 1934;
>
> *An Interpretation of Christian Ethics*, New York, Harper and Brothers, 1935;
>
> *The Nature and Destiny of Man*, 2 volumes, New York, Charles Scribner's Sons, 1941, 1943.

50. See William Chrystal, *op. cit.*, pp. 165, 166, 171. The third excerpt adumbrates, it seems to me, the thrust and scope of the Gifford Lectures.

51. The address was delivered on 18 September 1928 in Indianapolis, Indiana. The following week, Niebuhr began his teaching in Union Theological Seminary, New York. Chrystal

rightly notes that the address "served as a fitting testament to Niebuhr's maturing thought". *Ibid.*, p. 199. The passages cited from the address are, in order, from pp. 199-200; 201, 203, 207, and 207-08. In each instance, the italics are Niebuhr's.

52. The phrase, which also provides the title of this essay, is Sydney Ahlstrom's. See *op. cit.*, p. 943. I came upon it as a surprise confirmation of the focus and direction of this attempt to indicate Reinhold Niebuhr's central and lasting importance as an interpreter of Christian thought. In the search for an identifying clue, I found myself turning again and again to Augustine. Professor Ahlstrom says it exactly, and I am pleased to acknowledge my indebtedness to him. As will be suggested below, Niebuhr is best understood and remembered in and for the theology of the twentieth century as: *Augustinus Redivivus.*

53. Reinhold Niebuhr, *Faith and Politics*, edited by Ronald H. Stone, New York, George Braziller, 1968.

54. Ahlstrom, *op. cit.*, p. 942.

55. *Ibid.*, p. 943. Italics mine.

56. Perry Miller, *The New England Mind: The Seventeenth Century* p. 3. Quoted by Ahlstrom, *op. cit.*, p. 127.

57. Ursula Niebuhr has painstakingly and movingly edited and published these sermons and prayers, according to the church year, in a posthumous volume entitled, *Reinhold Niebuhr: Justice and Mercy*, New York, Harper and Row, 1974.

58. Reinhold Niebuhr, *The Nature and Destiny of Man*, Vol. I, New York, Charles Scribner's Sons, 1941, pp. 1, and ff.

59. Aurelius Augustine, *The City of God*, translated by Marcus Dods, New York, Random House, The Modern Library Edition, 1950, Book V, chapter 9. Italics mine.

60. Some attempt to do so was undertaken in the second and third Reinhold Niebuhr Lectures at Eden Seminary.

61. Reinhold Niebuhr, *Faith and Politics: A Commentary on Religious, Social and Political Thought in a Technological Age*, edited by Ronald H. Stone, New York, George Braziller, 1968, pp. vii, viii.

10

THE SOCIAL TEACHINGS OF THE PROPHETS

Joseph L. Mihelic

The people of Israel were blessed with an unusual group of spiritual leaders called prophets. Moses, Samuel, Nathan, Elijah, Amos, Hoseah, Micah, Isaiah, Jeremiah, Ezekiel, and others were such leaders. Some of these we know only through the traditional stories that were passed on orally from one generation to another, and finally written down and collected many years later. Others we know through the books that bear their names and contain the messages spoken to their people in their particular times.

In this essay I shall explore briefly the social teachings of some of these prophets. Through our exploration we may see how their messages were called forth by the conditions of their day, and how their messages may speak to the conditions of our day.

There are two misconceptions of prophet and prophecy that must be recognized as we begin our survey.

First, there is the popular notion that a prophet is a crystal-ball gazer, predicting the shape of things to come. It is true that the prophets did a certain amount of predicting, but not in the manner of a fortune-teller. The prophets, living in the midst of the crises of their times, saw in the events of the day the character and the purpose of God. Perceiving the inner essence of a particular situation, they spoke about the ultimate outcome of that situation. In this sense we may say that they were able to *foretell* a coming disaster, or a coming salvation.

The other misconception concerning the prophets is that they were *mere* social reformers and that they were the innovators of advanced religion of Israel. It is true that the prophets denounced the social injustices and corruption of their day with a vehemence seldom if ever equaled, yet their cry for social justice and righteousness and for personal and social morality was deeply rooted in their faith in Yahweh, the God of Israel, and in the tradition about Israel's election and covenant. In order to adequately understand our subject, we must view it against both *the theological traditions* and *historical background*. Because of the brevity of time this must be dealt with in a very sketchy manner. Yet I hope that it will help you in grasping the Social Message of the Prophets.

1. *The Theological Tradition*

One of the basic theological traditions which we meet again and again in the prophetic literature is God's election of Israel for his own people. When Israelites were slaves in Egypt, God *heard* their cry, saw *their* suffering and sent Moses to deliver them out of Egyptian bondage. After many trials, Moses brought them to Mt. Sinai where God made a covenant with Israel to the effect that Yahweh would be *their God* and Israel would be *his people*. Then after some forty years of desert wandering they came to the eastern border of Canaan which they entered and eventually conquered for their own possession.

This tradition became celebrated annually in Canaan at the harvest festival when the individual Israelite would present the priest with a basket of first fruits, and make the following confession of faith:

> 'A wandering Aramean was my father;
> and he went down into Egypt and sojourned
> there, few in number; and there he became
> a nation, great, mighty and populous. And
> the Egyptians treated us harshly, and af-
> flicted us, and laid upon us hard bondage.
> Then we cried to the Lord the God of our
> fathers, and the Lord heard our voice, and
> saw our affliction, our toil, and our op-
> pression; and the Lord brought us out of
> Egypt with a mighty hand and outstretched
> arm, with great terror, with signs and
> wonders; and brought us into this place,
> and gave us this land, a land flowing
> with milk and honey. And behold, now I
> bring the first of the fruit of the
> ground, which thou O Lord, hast given
> me.'

This Credo or Confession of Faith now recorded in Deuteronomy 26:5-10, recapitulates the great saving acts which brought the Israelite community into being. Along with this tradition there went also a conception of Yahweh, the God of Israel, which describes his character as one of *truth* (emeth),

faithfulness (emunah), of *righteousness* (tsedekah), of *jus-
ce* (mishpat), and *steadfast love* (hesed). From the begin-
ng of his choice of Israel as his people, *God's dealings*
th them were always governed by these (social) attributes
his character. On the other hand, the primary obligations
Israel were those of *loyalty* and *obedience*. These were to
expressed (1) in the exclusive worship of this unique God
the nation, (2) in listening to his messengers, and (3) in
ithful embodiment of Yahweh's *ethical* and *moral* standards as
pressed by his divine attributes. In time this whole rela-
onship was summed up in the famous confession of Deuteronomy
4:

>'Hear O Israel: the Lord our God is one
>God, and you shall *love* the Lord your God
>with all your heart, and with all your
>soul, and with all your might....'

When the prophets came on the scene, these attributes of
d's character became the starting point for their messages
their people. Their prophetic function was (1) to be a
okesman for God, declaring his living word, and (2) to be a
tchman (Ezekiel 3:16-21; 33:1-20) whose duty it was to warn
e people about the impending disaster which God would send
on them as a punishment for breaking their covenant obliga-
ons.

The Historical Background

The problem of Israel's religious and communal life began
en she came into the Promised Land. In Canaan the simple region and pastoral life of the Nomadic Israel became changed
dically. "The way-of-life of her desert traditions and of
r religion had to accommodate itself to the new physical con-
tions of a settled land, and to the more developed civiliza-
on of its inhabitants." The transition from mobility to a
rmanent settlement created problems for the unity and integ-
ty of the Israelite society. The conversion from a mainly
storal economy to a predominantly agrarian and commercial
onomy, and from a communal property system to a system of
ivate ownership, gave power to an individual and also created
stratified society. But most notable of all was the incom-
tibility of the ethics and morality of the nomadic Yahweh region with the institutions of the Baalistic religion of Ca-
an. It was this fact that called forth the various prophetic
rsonalities and their social messages which, as we shall see
ter, were the direct result of the teaching of their ances-

tral faith. (Scott, *The Relevance of the Prophets*, p. 161ff.

The prophets' attack upon the existing social order was that it did not maintain the human and social values which were integral to their Yahwistic faith. On the contrary, the new hybrid social order which arose in their community after several generations of living in Canaan, destroyed these values. We note this as early as the time of Samuel, when under the pressure of existing conditions, the people were ready to exchange the old charismatic type of leadership for a military monarchical system, which, while providing them with a measure of physical security in time of a political crisis, deprived them of their freedom and material wealth. The warning of Samuel on this score is a case in point (I Samuel 8:10-18).

According to Hosea and Micah and other prophetic teach-ings the foundations of a social order which include the eco-nomic and political structures, must be built upon ethical, moral and religious precepts. Justice, righteousness, truth, integrity, faithfulness, and love "are the necessary strands in the social bond". Micah similarly states that the divine imperative for man's social and individual living is "justice steadfast love and humility" (Micah 6:8).

In a social order these attributes are the prerequisites for a life of peace, security and well-being which men most desire from their social order (Isa. 32:16, 17). Israel, how-ever, mesmerized by the "glitter of a material civilization and seduced by its passions" went astray and exchanged its spiritual heritage for a mess of Canaanite potage.

Some of the prophets, notably Hosea and Jeremiah, con-sidered the period of Wilderness Wandering as the ideal period of Israel's relationship with God, and of their own ideal com-munal relationship. Hosea looked on that Wilderness period as one which was so wholesome that by returning to it, Israel could solve all of her problems which she created for herself when she came into the cultural life of Canaan. God says through Hosea,

> 'Therefore, behold, I will alure her,
>   and bring her into the wilderness,
>   and speak tenderly to her.
> And there I will give her her vineyards,
>   and make the Valley of Achor a door of
>   hope,
> And there she (Israel) shall answer
>   as in the days of her youth,

                     as at the time when she came
                        out of the land of Egypt.'

                                    (Hosea 2:14-15; Jer. 2:2-3)

Hosea states further that after Israel will be returned to the
wilderness God will establish a new relationship with Israel--
a relationship that will be based on righteousness (Tsedek),
justice (mishpat), steadfast love (hesed), mercy (raham), and
faithfulness (emunah).

                    'And I will betroth you to me forever;
            I will betroth you to me in righteousness
            and in justice, in steadfast love, and
            mercy. I will betroth you to me in faith-
            fulness, and you shall know the Lord.'

                            (Hosea 2:19, 20)

     In like manner Jeremiah regarded the wilderness or the
nomadic period as the time of Israel's complete faithfulness
to God, and as the time when the community of Israel was living in an ideal relationship of peace, freedom and mutual harmony. Again God is speaking.

           'Thus says the Lord,
               I remember the devotion of your youth,
                  Your love as a bride,
               how you followed me in the wilderness,
                  in a land not sown.
               Israel was holy to the Lord,
                  the first fruit of his harvest
               All who ate of it became guilty;
                  evil came upon them, says the Lord.'

                            (Jer. 2:2-3)

3. *The Social Message of Pre-Exilic Prophets*

     The Hebrew prophets are divided into pre-exilic, exilic
and post-exilic prophets. The pre-exilic prophets are usually
further subdivided into (1) pre-literary prophets: Moses,
Samuel, Nathan, Ahijah of Shiloh and Elijah, to mention just
the most important ones, and (2) the literary prophets which
include: Amos, Hosea, Micah, Isaiah, Jeremiah, etc.

From the pre-literary group, I should like to select only three to show how they served as a conscience of the leaders and the people. They conceived their task as the voice of God, denouncing the sins of the powerful and defending the cause of the poor, the weak and all those who were at the mercy of greedy royalty and ambitious nobility. Their fearless courage was rooted in their religious conviction that the particular evils in their society: oppression, violence, debauchery, greed, theft, dishonesty, lust for power, callous inhumanity, faithlessness to trust were utterly abhorrent to a just God and hence an insult to his character. This was especially true when these evils were practiced by the leaders against the members of their own covenant community.

The first of these three prophets is Nathan, the prophet in King David's court. The form of social evil which David committed was adultery with Bathsheba and the premeditated murder of Uriah, the Hittite, the husband of Bathsheba. Though David was a king, this did not excuse him in the eyes of a just God. The prophet Nathan by means of a skillfully told parable had David condemn himself for his crimes. Though the royal sinner had the power to either ignore Nathan's accusing finger, or even spitefully punish the prophet, it is to his credit that he repented his double crime (II Samuel 12:1ff.). This, however, did not mean that he escaped all punishment. As the Biblical record reveals, his sins were visited both on himself and his children (2 Sam. 12:14). By his evil actions David not only broke several of the Ten Commandments, but also weakened the moral fiber of the nation, and gave an excuse for other philanderers to follow the example of their royal master.

The second prophet is the prophet Ahijah of Shiloh. He was sent by God to condemn the grave social evil which King Solomon had perpetrated against Northern Israel. By conscripting the man-power of the northern tribes into forced labor, and by imposing upon them heavy taxation, this power-hungry king assumed the tyrannical role of foreign kings. The God who heard the cry of the oppressed Israel in Egypt, also heard the voice of the suffering Israel at the hands of tyrannical King Solomon and his bureaucratic clique. By means of a picturesque symbolic action, the prophet of Shiloh gave Jereboam the divine blessing to commence a rebellion against the duly anointed King Solomon. Though at a later time God, through the same prophet (I Kgs. 14:7), condemned Jereboam for his faithlessness and idolatry, he was on this occasion God's instrument to liberate the people of northern Israel from an inhuman policy of King Solomon who had forgotten to use the wisdom which God gave him in answer to his prayer at the inception of his reign (I Kgs. 3:9-12; cf. II Chr. 1:10-12).

The third example in this list of social evils from this early period is the prophet Elijah and King Ahab of northern Israel. Here again we have a double crime committed by a royal person, namely *robbing a poor man of his inherited parcel of ground by means of a judicial murder*. While this case appears as solitary, it was probably a typical case which occurred frequently when a powerful and rich landlord coveted the adjoining property of a poor Israelite. Elijah's confrontation of King Ahab as he was enjoying his ill-gotten gain, is not only full of scorn for the royal scoundrel, but also contains the verdict of poetic justice which he and his wife Jezebel will meet in due time.

> 'Thus says the Lord, "Have you killed and
> also taken possession?...In the place where
> dogs licked the blood of Naboth shall dogs
> lick your own blood."'

> (I Kings 21:17-19)

These three social evils, though committed by royal persons, did not put them above the common law of human decency and even less above the covenant law which specifically stated, "you shall not kill; you shall not commit adultery; you shall not steal; you shall not bear false witness and you shall not covet...". The prophets did not accuse these royal criminals with vague generalities but with a merciless candor they stripped from them their royal prerogatives and pretended respectability, and revealed them as adulterers, murderers, tyrants and common thieves. It takes no great imagination to see how contemporary these social evils are.

As we move on to the so-called literary prophets, we will find that those who were selfishly ruining Israel as a covenant people and political nation, were not limited to the royal persons, but included also the members of the secular and the ecclesiastical officialdom. By the time of Amos and other prophets, the unity of political Israel was a thing of the past. Because of Solomon's oppressive policy toward the northern tribes, and the short-sighted policy of his son Rehoboam, Israel became irreparably split into two political states: the Kingdom of Judah ruled by the descendants of David, and the Kingdom of Israel whose throne became a coveted prize for various political and military adventurers.

4. *Literary Prophets and Their Messages*

Great as some of these early preliterary prophets were, others, even greater than they, were to follow them during the eighth, seventh and sixth centuries before Christ. During these centuries the Hebrew prophecy broke through the narrow confines of the Israelite covenant community, and now the prophets' concern extended to all the people of the world. The prophetic conception of Yahweh, the God of Israel, was too profound and too universal to keep him limited to Israel only.

This group of spokesmen for God went beyond their predecessors both in thought and spirit of their messages. However, the source of their inspiration was the same as for the former prophets: the Word of God and the traditions of Israel. The environment of their labor was still Israel, but an Israel that was living in a wholly different political, social and religious atmosphere. For Israel had become a nation and a political power. Although divided into two separate political states, the two were nevertheless ethnically, religiously and linguistically one people, worshipping one God, and speaking the same language. Moreover, by the beginning of the eighth century, both Judah and Israel found themselves living in a world dominated by empire-hungry nations, which threatened their existence as political states.

The world of the Near East had undergone great political changes since the days of David and Solomon. To the northeast of Palestine, Assyria, an old imperial nation that had been quiet for a time, began to reassert herself and started on a military conquest of her neighbors. In 802 B.C. Adad-nirari III (809-782), king of Assyria, conquered Syria or Aram, Israel's neighbor. This gave the Northern Kingdom, Israel which was dominated by Syria up to that time, not only political freedom, but also the opportunity to recover its lost territory and even augment it at the expense of its southern neighbor Judah. Judah, in turn, was reduced to a tribute-paying state (II Kings 13:25 to 14:14). During the reigns of two Northern Israel kings: Joash (801-786) and Jeroboam II (786-746), Israel became a powerful political and military state. This brought to the country a period of peace and prosperity. The people took the military security and economic affluence as signs of God's special favor toward them. Into this materially affluent and morally corrupt society came Amos of Tekoa, thundering forth in the name of God a denunciation of their social injustices and oppression and exploitation of the poor, and predicting a terrible national disaster.

A. *The Prophets of the Northern Kingdom, Israel: Amos (ca. 750-740) and Hosea (ca. 735-725)*

Amos and Hosea were the only literary prophets whose activity took place in the Northern Kingdom. Amos, a Judean from Tekoa, about ten miles south of Jerusalem, was a shepherd and a dresser of sycamore trees. His periodic business trips to Samaria's markets gave him an insight into the religious, social and economic conditions of the people. What he saw there disturbed him deeply. In addition to the highly developed culture, he observed the social and moral corruption of the people, the oppression and exploitation of the poor, the arrogant disregard of the rights of the weak, and the debasing immorality of worship.

When he returned to his wilderness home in Tekoa in the solitude of the rugged Judean hills, Amos could no longer keep silent, because God compelled him to speak:

> 'The lion has roared;
>   who will not fear?
> The Lord God has spoken;
>   who can but prophesy?'

(Amos 3:8)

His little book of only nine chapters contains perhaps only a gist of some of his speeches which he himself or some of his disciples collected and preserved for posterity. The book begins with seven oracles against the surrounding nations of Israel, which are summoned to the judgment bar of Yahweh to answer for their attrocities against the civilian population in war, while Israel is called on to account for her attrocities against the poor and defenseless in time of peace.... While her crimes are no less terrible than the former, they are constant, and hence they are more damnatory than those of foreign nations.

In subsequent chapters Amos condemns the exploitation of the poor and the debauchery of worship. Two sins against the spiritual light which has been given to Israel, and for which she will have to pay dearly. For in chapter 3:2 appears this significant judgment:

> 'You only have I known
>   of all the families of the earth;

> therefore I will punish you
>   for all your iniquities.'

(Amos 3:2)

When one examines the various messages of warning which Amos delivered to the people of Israel at various times, one finds that the social and religious elements were all closely intertwined, and that the bitter fruit of social evils were the products of the breakdown of the covenant religious ideals. In general there are five closely related forms of sin, all of which helped in destroying the spiritual, the social and political foundations of the nation.   These are:

1. *Exploitation of the poor and the oppressed.*   This form of sin was especially abhorrent to God's will and his revealed character.   God hears the cry of the needy and knows the suffering of the oppressed.   There are many references in the Scriptures which show that the poor are under his special protection.   Let me cite only two passages out of many from Amos that deal with this sin.

> 'Hear this, you who trample upon the needy,
>   and bring the poor of the land to an end,
> saying, "when will the new moon be over,
>   that we may sell grain?
> And the sabbath,
>   that we may offer wheat for sale,
> that we may make the ephah small
>   and the shekel great,
> and deal deceitfully with false balances,
>   that we may buy the poor for silver
> and the needy for a pair of sandals,
>   and sell the refuse of the wheat."'

(Amos 8:4-6)

This heartless disregard of human need by the businessmen of the day, which is spawned by an unrestrained greed for profit, that impatiently waits for the sacred season to end so that it may carry on its cheating commerce, is matched by the cruel demands of their insatiable wives.   With a biting sarcasm, Amos addressed them,

> 'Hear this word, you cows of Bashan,
>   who are in the mountain of Samaria,
>   who oppress the poor, who crush the
>   needy,

```
            who say to their husbands,
                "bring that we may drink!"
        The Lord God has sworn by his holiness
            that behold, the days are coming upon
                you,
        when they shall take you away with hooks,
            even the last of you with fishhooks,
        And you shall go out through the breaches,
            every one straight before her;
            and you shall be cast forth into Harmon,
        says the Lord.'
```

(Amos 4:1-3)

2. *Another form of this sin was the lack of equal jus-tice and the venal judges who forgot that justice was the es-ential attribute of God.* Thus the well-being of the commun-ty was poisoned at the very source.

```
            'O you who turn justice to wormwood,
                and cast down righteousness to the
                    earth!

        For I know how many are your
                transgressions,
                and how great are your sins--
        you who afflict the righteous,
            who take a bribe,
        and turn aside the needy in the
                gate....'
```

(Amos 5:7, 12)

3. *The third form is the boastful luxury of the rich and the shameful orgies of debauched men and women who gorged themselves with delicacies, and wasted food, but failed to hear the anguished cry of hungry men, women and children.*

```
            'Woe to those who are at ease in Zion...
                who lie on beds of ivory...
                and eat lambs from the flock...
                who drink wine in bowls...
                    but are not grieved over the ruin
                        of Joseph....'
```

(Amos 6:1-7)

4. *The fourth form is the substitution of ceremonial and magical means to approach God in place of the personal*

*relationship that should prevail between the covenant people
and its God* (Amos 4:4-5; 4:5ff.; 6:3; 8:14). They forgot
that God said, "I am holy, therefore you must be holy" (Lev.
11:44), and that their holiness must be expressed by righteous
personal and communal lives. With biting sarcasm he spoke to
them.

> 'Come to Bethel, and transgress;
>   to Gilgal, and multiply transgressions;
> bring your sacrifices every morning,
>   your tithes every three days;....
>   and proclaim freewill offerings,
>   publish them;
>   for so you love to do, O people
>   of Israel.'
>
> > says your Lord God.
>
> > (Amos 4:4-5)

5. *The fifth form of sin is the spiritual arrogance*
which dares to pride itself upon its unique privilege as the
favorite of God, and believes that no evil will ever come
near it, and fondly prays for the Day of the Lord, believing
that it will be a day of destruction for her enemies (Amos 3:
2; 5:18-20; 6:103), instead of a Day of Punishment for her.

> 'Woe to you who desire the day of the Lord!
>   Why would you have the day of the Lord?
> It is darkness and not light...!'
>
> "I hate, I despise your feasts,
>   and I take no delight in your
>   solemn assemblies....
> But let justice roll down like waters,
>   and righteousness like an over-
>   flowing stream.'
>
> > (Amos 5:18-20; 21, 24)

The various social and religious evils which Amos saw in
the northern Kingdom, and which he condemned with such vehemence, were only the symptoms of a deep sickness, Israel's
estrangement from God and his covenant. Yet there was a
glimmer of hope that through repentance and return to God
and her covenant obligations, Israel might be saved;

> 'Seek good and not evil...
> Hate evil, and love good,

> and establish justice (mishpat)
>> in the gate;
> It may be that the Lord, the God of hosts,
>> will be gratious to the remnant
>>> of Joseph....'

(Amos 5:14-15)

Since the times were comparatively peaceful, and on the surface the nation was prosperous, rich, proud and apparently secure, the harsh and bitter words of Amos shocked the people. Amaziah, the priest of the royal sanctuary at Bethel, became frightened by Amos' words and reported him to King Jeroboam II,

> 'Amos has conspired against you in the
> midst of the house of Israel; the land is not
> able to bear all his words. For thus Amos has
> said,

>> "Jeroboam shall die by the sword,
>>> and Israel must go into exile...."'

(Amos 7:10-11)

and then expelled him from the country. As he was leaving, Amos flung into the face of the royal ecclesiastic some of the most bitter words that are found in the Scriptures (Amos 7:12-13).

After King Jeroboam II died about 747 B.C. the social, moral and religious decay which Amos perceived, completed its work of disintegration. The people became an easy prey for political and military adventurers who turned the country into chaos and anarchy.

Such were the conditions in Israel when Hosea, a young contemporary of Amos and a native of Israel began his ministry. His tragic family life gave Hosea his unique message. He likened the covenant which God made with Israel at Sinai to a wedlock. Yahweh was the husband and Israel his wife. As such he demanded the same fidelity from Israel that a husband expects from his wife. Israel, however, in worshipping the Baalim, the fertility gods of Canaan, committed "adultery" and therefore deserved to be punished and rejected. This part of Hosea's message is found in the first three chapters of the book, and in a sense lays the groundwork upon which the oracles collected in chapters 4-14 are based.

In these chapters (4-14) Hosea's message deals with the chaotic period that followed the death of Jeroboam II, and the resulting struggle of various claimants for the throne. Within a period of 23 years four kings were assassinated and the throne seized by as many usurpers. Hosea saw the same evils as Amos, and looked upon them as signs of a profound evil--the wholesale repudiation of the covenant relationship with Yahweh. This in turn resulted in a national moral confusion which is described for us in chapter 4:1-3,

> '...the Lord has a controversy
>   with the inhabitants of the land.
> There is no faithfulness or kindness,
>   and no knowledge of God in the land;
> there is swearing, lying, killing,
>   stealing, and committing adultery;
>   they break all bounds and murder
>   follows murder,
> Therefore the land mourns,
>   and all who dwell in it languish,
> and also the beasts of the field,
>   and the birds of the air;
>   and even the fish of the sea
>   are taken away....'
>
> (Amos 4:1-3)

It used to be that scholars would question the last part of this verse, and wonder how could irreligion lead to the destruction of nature. Yet today we know, and to our sorrow, that a failure to observe the moral and ethical requirements of our faith leads to a wholesale befouling of the earth.

In his analysis of the causes that produced the social and religious anarchy in his land, Hosea pointed his fingers at three main evils of the nation's history.

First Hosea condemns "entangling foreign alliances" because they placed security in military arms and alliances, rather than in God.

> '...Ephraim went to Assyria,
>   and sent to the great king,
> But he is not able to cure you
>   or heal your wound....'
>
> (Hosea 5:13)

'Ephraim mixes himself with the peoples;
   Ephraim is a cake not turned.
Aliens devour his strength,
   and he knows it not;
gray hairs are sprinkled upon him,
   and he knows it not.
The pride of Israel witnesses against him;
   yet they do not return to the
      Lord their God,
   nor seek him, for all this.'

                 (Hosea 7:8-10)

'Ephraim is like a dove
   silly and without sense,
   calling to Egypt, going to Assyria.'

                 (Hosea 7:11)

Secondly, Hosea is opposed to the institution of monarchy.
He looked upon it as the cause of all the evil that had come
upon his people. The establishment of the monarchy was against
the will of God.

       'Israel has forgotten his Maker,
          and built palaces....'

                 (Hosea 8:14)

       'They made kings but not through me,
          they set up princes, but without
             my knowledge....'

                 (Hosea 8:4)

       'Samaria's king shall perish,
          like a ship on the face
             of the waters....'

                 (Hosea 10:7)

    Hosea was not afraid to criticize severely the existing
government. He saw the tragic consequences of ambitious corrupt leaders who would use assassination to seize the throne
and then would use any means to stay in power. We get "the
sickening picture of the king, holding court attended by
drunken, unscrupulous cut-throats, waiting only for a favorable opportunity to murder their royal master, who himself had
mounted the throne by the use of the assassin's knife" (Sanders

and Kent, *The Message of the Earlier Prophets*, p. 62).

Thirdly, Hosea blames the idolatry as one of the basic causes for its national apostasy which had brought the nation to the brink of its destruction. With an impotent anger he ridicules the bull worship of Samaria which was first introduced by Jeroboam I (I Kings 12:28-30), in order to prevent people from going to Jerusalem to worship.

> 'I have spurned your calf, O Samaria,
>   My anger burns against it...
> A workman made it;
>   it is not God.
> The calf of Samaria
>   shall be broken to pieces.'
>
>   (Hosea 8:5)

As I already mentioned, this crude apostasy was due to the environment when Israel passed from its nomad life to that of the agricultural civilization. Monarchy, as well as hierarchy, developed out of the same environment, and brought with it the conditions which destroyed the old desert covenant relationship. In chapters 4-14 we find a list of social wrongs that indicate the deepest moral depravity and the greatest disregard of the principles of social justice. The decay in family integrity, of which his own domestic tragedy was an example, may be regarded as the source of most of social derelictions that came upon the people of Israel. The ideal of domestic life had given place to infidelity. Untruthfulness, stealing, debauchery, drunkenness, and robbery had overcome the basic virtues of religion. The destruction was inevitable. Yet God was trying to save Israel from its calamity. In one of the most poignant passages of the whole Scriptures, God cries out in bitter anguish:

> 'How can I give you up, O Ephraim!
>   How can I hand you over, O Israel!...
> My heart recoils within me,
>   my compassion grows warm and tender.
> I will not execute my fierce anger,...
> for I am God and not man,
>   the Holy One in your midst,
>   and I will not come to destroy.'
>
>   (Hosea 11:8, 9)

Alas, he could not do it. The corruption had gone too far. In 722 Samaria paid the penalty for her unwise policies

nd her immoral practices (II Kings 17:5-6). Assyria invaded
he country and besieged the city of Samaria for three years.
he city was captured and the people of Israel were carried
nto Assyrian exile where they disappeared.

B. *Prophets of Judah: Isaiah & Micah (750-700 B.C.)*

About the same time that Amos and Hosea were active in
he Northern Kingdom, Isaiah and Micah performed their pro-
hetic ministry in the Southern Kingdom of Judah. While their
ocial and religious messages are in the main very similar to
hose of Amos and Hosea, yet there is a distinct approach to
each of them. The society of Judah was neither as wealthy nor
as socially sophisticated as that of the northern Kingdom.
Nevertheless Judah faced serious social, economic, political
and religious problems during most of her existence. Such
prophets as Isaiah, Micah and others in the eighth century,
and Jeremiah, Ezekiel and others in the seventh and sixth
centuries not only called the attention of the people and
their leaders to these problems, but also proposed basic
solutions for them. In their estimation these various problems arose out of the same situations as those in the northern
kingdom: unfaithfulness to the covenant rules for their religious and social life, and their apostasy from their ancestral
faith. This weakening of their loyalty to the traditional
faith, led to a corresponding weakening of their traditional
values and directions of life. The inevitable result was that
"political forms, economic activities, legal and judicial
practice, social institutions, public morals, culture and re-
ligion--all were deformed" (Scott, *The Relevance of the Prophets*, p. 172), and their effect was felt throughout the society,
with the heaviest burden falling upon those who could least
bear it: the poor and the weak.

One of the clearest expressions of these social evils
which pervaded the Judean society, is found in Isaiah 5:8-24
in a series of "Seven Woes" which the prophet Isaiah declares
against various classes. Each "woe" hints at a retribution
that will be visited upon that particular evil trait. He begins with an attack on the big landowners who in their greed
use unscrupulous means to enlarge their holdings.

> 'Woe to those who join house to house,
>   who add field to field,
> until there is no more room,

> and you are made to dwell alone
> in the midst of the land.'

> (Isaiah 5:8)

In a similar vein, only with greater bitterness, Micah of Moresheth-Gath in southern Judah, attacked the same type of greed for land. It is possible that Micah himself was a victim of such a land-grab.

> 'Woe to those who devise wickedness
>   and work evil upon their beds!
> When the morning dawns, they perform it,
>   because it is in the power of their
>   hand.
> They covet fields, and seize them;
>   and houses, and take them away;
> they oppress a man and his house,
>   a man and his inheritance.'

> (Micah 2:1-2)

In the following "woes" the prophet directs his accusing finger at the drunkards; the scoffers who in their pride ask that God would hasten with his judgment so that they may see it; the expedient in morality who "call evil good, and good evil"; the self-satisfied; the intemperate heroes at drinking; the bribe-taking judges. Another "Woe" which is probably displaced from this group is found now in 10:1-2 and is directed toward the high government officials:

> Woe to those who decree iniquitous decrees,
>   and writers who keep writing oppression,
> to turn aside the needy from justice
>   and to rob the poor of my people
>   of their right,
> that widows may be their spoil,
>   and that they may make the fatherless
>   their prey.

> (Isaiah 10:1-2)

The three main social evils which seem to be characterized by Isaiah are (1) greed for land and its unscrupulous acquisition; (2) the liquor question and (3) corrupt government officials and venal judges, working together to enrich themselves at the expense of the poor, the widows and the orphans. To these three another social evil may be added, one which was

lready condemned by Amos, namely, the extravagant luxury of
ome women (Isa. 3:16).

These and other social sins worked like poison through
he Judean society, eating away at its moral fiber until the
ocial order became totally corrupt, and its end was inevita-
le. Since Jerusalem, as the seat of the secular and spiri-
ual power was regarded as the heart of the people, it was
sually characterized as the symbol for the whole country.
saiah throws light on overall social conditions of Jerusa-
em with a brief but a highly descriptive poem:

> 'How the faithful city
>   has become a harlot,
>   she that was full of justice!
> Righteousness lodged in her,
>   but now murderers.
> Your silver has become dross,
>   your wine mixed with water.
> Your princes are rebels
>   and companions of thieves.
> Everyone loves a bribe
>   and runs after gifts.
> They do not defend the fatherless,
>   and the widow's cause does not
>   come to them.'

> (Isaiah 1:21-23)

But as time went on, the religious ceremonies became more
rnate, and the social morality more degenerate in its prac-
ice. Isaiah likens the leaders and the people to those of
odom and Gomorrah. Their sabbaths, solemn assemblies, their
acrifices and offerings have become an abomination to God,
nd therefore he will not listen to their many prayers. Only
 thorough repentance and the practice of social morality will
ake these people acceptable to him again.

> 'Wash yourselves; make yourselves clean;
>   remove the evil of your doings
>   from before my eyes;
> cease to do evil,
>   learn to do good;
> seek justice,
>   correct oppression;
> defend the fatherless,
>   plead for the widow.'

> (Isaiah 1:16-17)

One of the greatest problems that Isaiah faced was to persuade King Ahaz *not* to appeal to Assyria for military aid during the crisis, precipitated by the invasion of Judah by the combined armies of Israel and Syria (Isa. 7:1-9; II Kings 16:1-20). Isaiah perceived the far-reaching political and religious consequences of such an appeal. Unfortunately King Ahaz did not listen to Isaiah, and the country came under complete Assyrian domination for over a century.

When we turn to Micah and his social message, we find that the list of social wrongs is monotonously the same as that of his contemporaries: Amos, Hosea and Isaiah: oppression and dispossession of the poor (Micah 2:1-3; cf. Isa. 5:8) corrupt administrators who like cannibals devour the sustenanc of the people (Micah 3:1-4); priests, prophets and judges concerned only for material gain (Micah 3:9-11). As one surveys Micah 7:1-6, one is presented with the terrible consequences of this social corruption. Distrust had become universal. Faith among men had ceased to exist. Suspicion pervades the very atmosphere of the home.

> 'Put no trust in a neighbor,
>   have no confidence in a friend,
> guard the doors of your mouth
>   from her who lies in your bosom;
> for the son treats the father with
>   contempt,
>   the daughter rises up against her
>   mother,
> the daughter-in-law against her
>   mother-in-law;
>   a man's enemies are the men
>   of his own house.'
>
>   (Micah 7:5-6)

"No moral teacher ever penetrated deeper into the ultimate consequences of social wrong-doing than has Micah in these last words. Confidence tends to break down under the weight of selfishness and injustice, and the antisocial classes are augmented by these same conditions. When the home becomes antisocial, the basis of social structure is disintegrated, and the organization of society is dissolved" (William B. Bizzell, *The Social Teaching of the Jewish Prophets*. Boston: Sherman, French & Company, 1916, p. 112).

As we can see from the few examples there was nothing theoretical about the prophet and his prophetic ministry. He faced the social problems of his day and exposed them with

utter candor. He pointed his accusing finger at the guilty,
irrespective of their social, political, economic or ecclesiastical position and told it as he perceived it.

The corruption and degradation of the ancient society was
basically the same as that of our day. The greedy merchant,
the cheating loan shark, the lying high pressure salesman,
the shyster lawyer, the money grabbing physician, the dope
peddler, the ghetto apartment owner, the sanctimonious morti-
cian and the holier-than-thou preacher who raves about "those
damnable radicals", yet is unwilling to help the black men and
the migrant laborers to obtain better living conditions and
more equitable pay for their labor. These modern oppressors
and extortionists of the poor and defenseless are not a particle different from those of the days of Amos, Hosea, Micah and
other prophetic personalities who have left us a record of
their work.

The prophets spoke for God, and in the name of God condemned the dastardly behavior of their fellow creatures, many
of whom, under the pretext of religion, plied their greedy and
corrupt trade. Their indecent treatment of their fellowmen was
the profanation of the Holy God. These prophets saw in any
kind of a mistreatment and exploitation of a fellow human being as being equal to defaming God who had created in His own
image both the exploiter and the exploited one.

The prophets believed themselves to have been called by
God to the prophetic service. This service did not mean fore-
telling who and what the Messiah will do, and when he will
come. But rather to expose the religious pretensions of the
rich, the powerful nobility, and the merchant class and the
hypocritical practices of the religious leadership of their
day, who under the guise of serving God, were only serving
themselves and their lust for power and their greed for material possessions.

One of the reasons for prophetic vehemence in their pronouncements against the nefarious practices of their hearers,
was the fact that they truly loved God and their people. They
saw in the misguided behavior and acquisitive attitudes toward
the less fortunate of their people, a supreme tragedy--a tragedy, if not prevented, will inexorably lead to the destruction
of the political state and eventually of the people. To the
prophets the exploitation of their fellow Israelites, was simply incomprehensible. How could a member of the covenant community defraud a fellow member? How could he take advantage
of the misfortune of a fellow Israelite? How could he bring
an offering to the Lord, part of which was the result of
cheating some widow of her meagre possession, or depriving

some orphan of his liberty or a stranger who sought his protection, of his cloak?

The inequities which the prophets saw all around them, could not be ignored or rationalized away as we do so often. To them inequities in the social life were not to be tolerated It was God who made them cognizant of their ability to look beneath the thin veneer of supposed religiosity of the rulers, the nobility, the priesthood and their fellow prophets (Jeremiah 20:7-12). For not all of the prophets were exponents and champions of the rights of the depressed and the deprived. According to the preserved prophetic literature and their ascribed authors and supposed authors, there were only about *fifteen* of them. These, however, are only a remnant of many, whose words were never recorded and whose names have been forgotten. It is quite possible that among the present material there are included the prophetic messages of these unknown and forgotten men of God. Still, when we consider the manner in which these prophetic messages have been preserved and transmitted across centuries of time, we are extremely fortunate to have them. These words speak of the heartfelt concern of one group of men for the welfare and well-being of their less fortunate men, women and children.

Considering the hard and tragic history of mankind, the slow and tedious upward climb of the human race from its primitive stage, the many vicissitudes of life; the suffering caused by natural catastrophies: earthquakes, storms, floods, famine caused by drought or destruction of crops by hail, etc.; these misfortunes were enough to toughen mankind physically and make him the survivor of nature's calamities. However, the hardness of the lot of mankind caused by the harsh nature, is nothing compared to the tragedy of man's inhumanity to man. By comparison, man has caused more misery to his fellow human creatures than nature's calamities have. For nature's catastrophies, in spite of making human life harsh and difficult, toughened mankind to survive in an otherwise hostile environment. Thus they were eventually beneficial. But this cannot be said of man's inhumanity to his fellow creature. We can find no beneficial increment to humanity because of his hostile action toward his kin and the animal kingdom. On the contrary, it only created the spirit of animosity, fear and greed --all of which, when left unchecked produced and created only more misery, until eventually the whole human race may end in cosmic self-destruction. In his long history of upward climb, man may have reached the end of his existence. At the height of his achievements in technological knowledge and "know how", when he is about to conquer the space, man may annihilate himself and turn the "green earth" into a barren cosmic body, and make it like the moonscape.

BIBLIOGRAPHY

The following are a few of the sources consulted and used in preparation of the preceding essay.

The Holy Bible, The Revised Standard Version.

Bizzell, W. B., *The Social Teachings of the Jewish Prophets*, Boston: Sherman, French & Co., 1916.

Bright, John, *A History of Israel*, Philadelphia: Westminster Press, 1949.

_____, "The Prophets Were Protestants," *Interpretation*, April 1947, 153ff.

Eichrodt, Walther, *Theology of the Old Testament*, 2 vols., Philadelphia: Westminster Press, 1961-67.

Gottwald, Norman K., *All the Kingdoms of the Earth*, New York: Harper & Row, 1964.

Heschel, Abraham Joshua, *The Prophets*, New York: The Jewish Publication Society of America, 1962.

Jenni, Ernst, *Die politisches Voraussagen der Propheten*, Zürich: Zwingli Verlag, 1956.

Kraeling, Emil G., *The Prophets*, Chicago: Rand McNally, 1969.

Kraus, Hans-Joachim, "Die prophetische Verkündigung des Rechts in Israel," *Theologische Studien*, Zollikon: Evangelischer Verlag A.G., 1957.

Lindblom, J., *Prophecy in Ancient Israel*, Philadelphia: Fortress Press, 1962.

Paterson, John, *The Goodly Fellowship of the Prophets*, New York: Charles Scribner's Sons, 1948.

Rad, von Gerhard, *Old Testament Theology*, 2 vols., New York: Harper & Row, 1962, 1965.

Sanders, F. K. and Kent, C. F., *The Messages of the Earlier Prophets*, 2nd ed., New York: Scribners, 1899.

Scott, R. B. Y., *The Relevance of the Prophets*, New York: The Macmillan Co., 1944.

Smith, J. M. P., *The Prophets and Their Times*, rev. ed. W. A. Irwin, Chicago: The University of Chicago Press, 1941.

11

PREACHING THE GOSPEL

Donald G. Miller

In spite of repeated cries that the day of preaching is past,[1] the church has almost universally kept its pulpits. We channel a good deal of time, money, energy, and skill into the task of maintaining an intelligent and respectable ministry to fill them. We insist on preaching. But do we insist equally on preaching the *gospel*?

We frequently confront ourselves with Paul's dictum: "Woe to me if I do not preach", but we do not as frequently look Paul's complete thought in the face: "Woe to me if I do not preach the gospel!"[2] If much of our contemporary preaching is the criterion, we seem to think that we are at liberty to revise Paul at this point, and omit the last two words of his aphorism. But if we do that, we are not revising Paul; we are creating a word of our own. For what are three words to us, one of which we may keep and two of which we may omit, were only one word on the lips of Paul. Paul was not suggesting that "gospel" is one possible object of the verb "to preach", whereas others might be added at discretion. "Preaching" and the "gospel" were to him one and the same thing. Paul literally was saying: "Woe to me if I do not *gospelize*!"[3] The burden of this study, then, is that in our thinking about preaching central attention should be given to the substance of preaching rather than its form, and that we ought always to be under judgment when the major content of our preaching is not *gospel*. Hans-Joachim Kraus has recently lamented "how many people there are who think the authority of preaching is demonstrated by the emotional force with which it is delivered. The vital, inner relation to the content is decisive for the message; nothing else is,"[4] he insists. We are conditioned to evaluating sermons by the quality of oratory they display, or the diction used, or the scintillating glow of the illustrations, or the brilliance of the thought, or the effectiveness of the preacher's personality. We would no doubt have been content with Apollos' "eloquence" and would not have been bothered by that which disturbed Priscilla and Aquila who "took him and expounded to him the way of God more accurately".[5] Seldom do we ask of a sermon: Was it gospel? And even

more seldom are we willing to put our own sermons under the
judgment of this question: If it was not gospel, was it
preaching?

I

In exploring this theme, let us first of all remind ourselves what the gospel is. It is not primarily a body of
ideas, nor a philosophy of life, nor a system of ethics, nor
even a formulation of doctrine. It is "good news!" And news
is of things that have happened! "For this reason," says
Gustaf Wingren, "the Bible is a book that relates what God
did, a book that describes events and does not deal in conceptions, a book which describes and depicts, not one that
puzzles things out."[6] In the same vein, Luther asserted:
"The Gospel is, and cannot be other than, the account or
the story of Christ."[7]

But this story of Christ centers in his death and resurrection. If anything is plain from recent New Testament study,
it is that the Gospel record is not the story of Christ in the
biographical sense but in the *kerygmatic* sense. The proportion of the Gospel story is determined neither chronologically
nor psychologically, but theologically. Approximately one-
quarter of the entire story is given directly to the death and
resurrection of Jesus. But more than that, the death and resurrection dominate the entire story indirectly. Luke makes
this plain when he has Jesus steadfastly setting His face to
go to Jerusalem long before geography forces this on him.[8]
In this way, Luke is insisting that all of Jesus' teaching in
the long so-called "Travel Document" is to be interpreted in
the light of His death and resurrection. In a recently published article Paul Achtemeier reaches a similar conclusion
about Mark. He writes: "it is clear that for Mark, there is
no real comprehension of Jesus apart from knowledge of his
final fate on the cross and the subsequent resurrection....
that theme pervades Mark's narrative from the outset, and in
countless ways Mark finds renewed opportunities to drive it
home. Thus the climax of Jesus' career becomes also the key
to understanding that career; and Mark seeks to deny anyone
the possibility of seeing in Jesus primarily a wise teacher,
a compassionate friend, or a worker of miracles....he was the
crucified and risen Lord. For Mark, to ignore as central the
cross of Jesus is to miss the meaning of the revelatory drama
in which Jesus played the central role."[9] Edwin Lewis once
remarked that *nobody* took the trouble to preserve a single
word Jesus said as a teacher, except those who believed in

the cross and resurrection and looked at his teaching in the
light of these.

The story of the Good Samaritan, for example, is not a
mere piece of ethical counsel about neighborliness. It is
rather to be interpreted in the light of the fact that the
One who told it is on the way to Jerusalem to die. The story
of the Prodigal Son is not a mere sentimental description of
human family relations (one occasionally hears psychological
analyses of what was wrong with the father that the son left
home!), nor even of man's relationship to God apart from the
cross. It is rather the description of the way God receives
sinful men solely because of the coming death and resurrection
of Jesus. There is a "hidden Christology" in this story. It
is one of the few authentic sayings attributed to Jesus by the
most skeptical of critics. After eliminating everything that
could be accounted for either by a Jewish or a Gentile background as the product of the church rather than Jesus, extreme
critics usually grant that neither a Jew nor a Gentile would
have thought of God as he is depicted in this story. Jesus,
therefore, it is held, actually told this story. But why
would men be offended to the point of crucifying one for such
lovely and innocent stories? The setting in Luke's Gospel
tells us. Chapter 15 opens: "Now the tax collectors and sinners were all drawing near to hear him. And the Pharisees and
scribes murmured, saying, 'This man receives sinners and eats
with them.'" In the story, Jesus says that *God* receives sinners. Since *he* was receiving sinners, the implication was
that he stood to them in the place of God. It was this implication rather than the story which angered his enemies. Even
the "mighty works" of Jesus are to be interpreted, not as isolated wonders wrought by a thaumaturge to startle and impress,
but in the light of the cross and resurrection. To refer once
more to Wingren, "Christ's death and resurrection is the
stream that flows deep down in every individual passage, the
stream under any particular event described in the Gospels,
for example, the stories of the son of the widow of Nain and
what Jesus did for him, the healing of the lame man and so
on."[10] Even the "temptation was the beginning of Christ's
resurrection",[11] for it was the beginning of the process
whereby Jesus destroyed him who had "the power of death" and,
as Suzanne de Dietrich has pointed out, it may be said that
"the cross stood on the horizon" even "from his infancy, for
both Matthew and Luke give us from the very beginning a pre-
sentiment of which it will be the climax".[12] "In fact the
great and all-embracing New Testament message of Christ's
cross and resurrection is set forth in every single story
in the Gospels."[13]

To pass from the Gospels to the apostolic preaching in

the Acts is to move in the same terrain of the centrality of
Jesus' death and resurrection. "Jesus...you crucified....But
God raised him up"[14] is the central theme of the early apostolic preaching in the Acts. The same is true with Paul,
Peter, the writer to the Hebrews, and the Revelator. The
slain lamb who is alive forevermore *is* the New Testament gospel. To preach the gospel, then, is to make Christ's death
and resurrection the center and focus of all our preaching.
Ethical instruction, or guidance in worship, or attempts to
cast meaning on contemporary events and issues should draw
their life from and point to the cross and resurrection; for
if these efforts are Christian they must be directly related
to Christ. And if they are related to the Christ of the New
Testament, he is the Christ whose total significance grows out
of the fact that he died and was raised from the dead.

II

It is instructive, and somewhat startling, by following
through in a concordance the verbs translated "preach", to
examine the *grammatical objects* which the New Testament writers used to describe the activity of preaching. A variety of
terms is used, but each in its own way is saying pretty much
the same thing. The range of New Testament preaching is
strictly limited in its central emphases. What did the
apostles preach?[15] They preached "Jesus"; "the Lord Jesus";
"good news of Jesus"; "Christ"; "the Christ"; "Jesus as the
Christ"; "him" (meaning God's son); "Jesus Christ as Lord";
"Christ...as raised from the dead"; "Jesus and the resurrection"--and this to a purely pagan gathering in Athens, where
many feel that Paul preached the least distinctively kerygmatic of all his recorded sermons; "the kingdom" and the "kingdom of God", which in the New Testament is never dissociated
from Jesus as its King, and which in one place is described
as "good news about the Kingdom of God and the name of Jesus
Christ"; Jesus as "the Son of God"; "the gospel" or "the gospel of God", which in I Corinthians 15:3ff. is clearly stated
as the fact "that Christ died for our sins in accordance with
the Scriptures, that he was buried, that he was raised on the
third day in accordance with the Scriptures, and that he appeared..."; "the word", or the "word of the Lord", or the
"word of God", which Acts 10:37ff. delineates as the word
about the life, ministry, death and resurrection of Jesus;
"the faith", described as that which Paul once tried to destroy and, as we have just seen, Paul describes the faith for
which he "persecuted the church of God" as that "Christ died
for our sins...that he was raised...and that he appeared";

"the word of faith", which Paul defines as confessing with
the mouth "that Jesus is Lord" and believing in the heart
"that God raised him from the dead"--the faith that "comes by
the preaching of Christ"; "in Jesus the resurrection from the
dead"; "Christ in you, the hope of glory"; "forgiveness of
sins" through the "man" whom "God raised up"; the one who
"rose from the dead" as "the one ordained by God to be judge
of the living and the dead".

If it were not for the gloriousness of the "good news"
around which the apostolic preaching centered, the constant
reiteration of its content would suffer from dull monotony.
When it is all summed up, it may be stated thus: The kingdom
of God anticipated in the Old Testament by the prophets has
come in the man Jesus Christ, who in his lifetime did "mighty
works" manifesting his power over all forms of evil, who died,
who was raised from the dead, who by his resurrection is manifested as Lord of the universe, through whose Lordship redemption is offered to all men and final judgment is to be made.
The early church preached this, then summoned men to respond
in faith and behavior. If, then, the New Testament is to be
the guide of our preaching, it must center in Christ--Christ
crucified, raised, now reigning as Lord, the future final
Judge--the one, therefore, who is Lord of life now, whose will
is to be sought and embodied insofar as is possible for sinful
man in every aspect of life. On this Luther commented:
"Therefore one must preach about Jesus Christ that he died
and rose from the dead, and why He died and rose again, in
order that people may come to faith through such preaching
and be saved through faith. This is what it means to preach
the genuine Gospel. Preaching of another kind is not the Gospel, no matter who does it."[16] He remarked just before this
statement, "God help us, how little preaching of this kind one
finds in all the books, even in those that are said to be the
best,...."

III

But to center preaching in Christ's death, resurrection,
lordship, and final judgment means that it is "good news" about
events--events which involved a struggle and a victory. If our
preaching is gospel, it is the announcement of the decisive
victory of all time, which becomes the pledge of God's final
victory over all evil. An examination of the very word "gospel" conveys this meaning. Friedrich, in Kittel's *Wörterbuch*,
says that the word ἐυαγγέλιον is a *terminus technicus* for *news
of a victory*. It was used by the Greeks--and is so used in the

Septuagint--to describe the announcement of any joyous event, such as the birth of a son; but more particularly it came to be related to the reporting of a victory on the field of battle. A messenger would appear in the distance, his face radiant, the point of his spear decorated with laurel, a laurel wreath around his head, a waving palm branch in his hand. Coming either by boat, on horseback, or on foot, he brought glad tidings of the victory of the army, or the death or capture of the enemy. And in words immortalized in the dramatic arrival of Philippines at Athens after the Battle of Marathon, the messenger would cry out: Χαίρετε νικῶμεν: "Rejoice; we conquer!"[17]

The early church sensed the appropriateness of the word "gospel" as a vehicle of their faith. They believed not in a new religion, but in a victory. "Jesus is Lord",[18] was their earliest creed. He had met every foe of man on the battleground of human history and manifested his lordship, then had invaded the lair of man's "last enemy",[19] death, and conquered it. To preach him, then, was to preach his victory--to announce to all that he had "overcome the world",[20] had conquered sin and death, and graciously offered to men the gift of his victory. To preach Christ is not to propagandize for Christianity as a religion among other religions, nor to persuade men to become more "religious", nor to try to shed philosophic light on life which will clarify the mystery of human existence, nor to persuade men to be good in order to make the world a better place to live in. It is rather to declare that by the mercy of God "we have been born anew to a living hope through the resurrection of Jesus Christ from the dead",[21] that "the sovereignty of the world has passed to our Lord and his Christ, and he shall reign for ever and ever!"[22] The gospel is: "Rejoice, Christ is victor!"

IV

The proclamation nature of Christian preaching is further reinforced by the *verbs* used to describe it. We have already seen that εὐαγγελίζω means "to bring good news", or "to announce glad tidings".[23] The second most frequent verb is κηρύσσω (most frequent if we include the Gospels where it refers to Jesus' preaching), which means "to be a herald", or "to proclaim after the manner of a herald".[24] The third verb in frequency is καταγγέλω, which means "to announce, declare, ...to proclaim publicly, publish".[25] The one word twice in the same incident translated "preach" in the older English versions,[26] but rightly changed to "talk" in the Revised

Standard Version and "address" in the New English Bible, which does not have the innate character of proclamation is διαλέγομαι, which means to "argue", or "discuss" or "dispute".[27] It has been pointed out that the only instance in which Paul is described as doing this in a Christian congregation, a young man went to sleep and fell out of the window! In all other instances save two, διαλέγομαι is used of Paul arguing in Synagogues with Jews and "God-fearers" out of the Old Testament that "it was necessary for the Christ to suffer and to rise from the dead". The argument, therefore, was concerning the right way to interpret the Messianic theme of the Old Testament, and was followed by the proclamation that "Jesus... is the Christ".[28] What discussion there was was set in the framework of proclamation and was carried on with those who already accepted the authority of the Old Testament Scriptures. The two instances where this word is used to describe activities outside a Synagogue were in Athens, where we have already seen that it is associated with the declaration "he preached Jesus and the resurrection",[29] and in Paul's dealing with Felix, where the description that Paul "argued about justice and self-control and future judgment" is placed in a setting in which Felix "sent for Paul and heard him speak upon faith in Christ Jesus".[30] With a consistency that is hardly challengeable, the verbs used in the New Testament to describe the activity of preaching describe it as a declaration, a proclamation, an announcement of "good news" about events that have happened, about God's "mighty acts" in the life, death, resurrection, and exaltation of Jesus Christ "for us men and for our salvation". To preach, then, is to preach "the gospel", to tell what "gospel" means in Anglo-Saxon, the "god-spell" of "God-story".

V

This necessary relation between preaching and the gospel is further reinforced in the light of the *human situation to which preaching is addressed* in the New Testament. The New Testament does not picture the human situation as one where false ideologies are to be corrected, or where men are to be ed from immature to mature behavior by rational persuasion nd the power of logic, or one that is to free men from their nhibitions and repressions and hangups and complexes and comulsions by psychological therapy. It pictures the human situation rather as one of enslavement. Man is not merely mistaken, he is a victim; he is not merely raw material in need f intelligent moulding, he is a prisoner; he is not merely ound by his inherited or acquired psychological disorders, he is a slave to powers outside himself. Man is in thrall, the "spoil" of a strong enemy whose power he is helpless to break. To stand outside the prison and call in advice can do little more than help him while away his imprisonment; or even worse, divert him from his true situation and amuse him until he grows so accustomed to his slavery that he mistakes it for freedom. What man needs is to be set free. And he cannot free himself. He is enslaved by one whom Jesus described as "a strong man, fully armed" who "guards his own palace", and so far as any possible challenge to his power by his victims is concerned, "his goods are in peace".[31] It is only when "one stronger than he assails him and overcomes him" and "takes away his armor in which he trusted"[32] that his spoil is divided and his victims set free. That is what Jesus has done. He is the "stronger" one who has assailed and overcome the "strong man", and set his victims free.

It is in the light of this view of the human situation that the New Testament message becomes vital. Victory in the war against cosmic evil is the deep undertone of the whole Gospel story. God is not the only power in the universe; there is a rival power. The nature miracles of Jesus, for example, are not included in the story merely to manifest Jesus' power to suspend nature's laws, but rather to indicate his power over the demonic forces which have nature in thrall and seek to destroy the creation which came from the hand of God as "good". Paul insists that the created order has been "subjected to futility" and is in "bondage to decay"[33] through the dominion over it of cosmic "principalities" and "powers",[34] but Christ's mastery of them assures us that they are not mighty enough to "separate us from the love of God".[35] Jesus' healing miracles likewise are not included in the Gospels to astound or to coerce faith as though by magic, but to manifest Jesus' lordship over the evil which seeks to destroy men by enslaving their bodies. Jesus described the woman afflicted for eighteen years as "bound" by Satan who, by his healing, was "loosed from this bond".[36] His raisings from the dead are not mere isolated wonders, which as such raise more questions than they answer; but are rather anticipations of his own resurrection where his lordship over evil's final weapon--death, was achieved. Behind every Gospel incident, and running like a golden thread through the Acts and the epistolary literature of the New Testament is the picture of cosmic struggle in which man is victim, but looking always toward the victory of Jesus Christ through which man becomes victor. The gospel is the announcement of this victory, and nothing other than this can strike at the very depths of the human situation and offer hope and redemption.

Is it possible that the loss of this note in contemporary

preaching accounts in large measure for its lack of radical
effectiveness? The element of the demonic has largely been
eliminated or demythologized, transformed from an objective
reality into an existential or psychological dimension. The
gospel is no longer deliverance from an enemy, but deliverance
from the self. But when the self knows that its problem is
the self, and wants to be delivered from the self, but finds
the bonds of self tightening by the very effort at self-de-
liverance, is it believing too much to believe that the self
is in thrall to another, a power above and beyond the self
who has captured, enslaved, and weakened the self?

A few years ago, Edward Langton in a book on the demonic
concluded that in "Christian theology and in sermons until the
modern period such beliefs [as those in Satan and demons] held
place near the center of the picture but now their place is
only on the fringe, as out-of-date conceptions".[37] In a theological climate that would seem to offer almost universal
agreement with this view, there have been a few voices bold
enough to raise the query as to whether this may be at least
partially the root of our ineffectiveness in preaching. If we
abandon the biblical view of the human predicament, then the
biblical "good news" which is the answer to this predicament
may also be abandoned. For the proclamation of freedom from
enthrallment to the devil by Christ's breaking the bonds and
liberating us, we have substituted discussions of self-understanding and authentic existence. In place of joyfully announcing Christ's victory--Rejoice! Christ is victor!--we
advise each other, with sombre and muffled tones, as to how
to carry on the struggle by self-affirmation and self-reali-
zation.

James Stewart has questioned whether it is not a great
loss when "St. Paul's 'principalities and powers' and 'spirit
forms of evil'" are considered to be "mere apocalyptic imagin-
ings", whereas the New Testament gospel "spoke of the irrevocable defeat of the powers of darkness".[38] "Here," he insists, "we are dealing not with some unessential apocalyptic
scaffolding, but with the very substance of the faith." "Were
Paul to come back today," he says, "and look out upon the
tragic conflict of our world, he would still say that 'our
wrestling is not against flesh and blood'; not against any
group of men or nations, Caesarism, Communism, as though the
interests of democracy were synonymous with the righteousness
of God--nothing so naive as that. The real warfare cuts across
all such alignments, and lies deeper down in the invisible
realm where sinister forces stand flaming and fanatic against
the rule of Christ."[39] The gospel is the declaration that
Christ has "disarmed the principalities and powers..., triumph-
ing over them",[40] and has delivered men "who through fear of

death were subject to lifelong bondage".[41]

Not long before he died, William Manson confronted us with the same issue. In his presidential address as president of the Society of New Testament in Britain, he wrote: "From the whole New Testament standpoint, when the Christ bowed his head on the cross, all the powers of darkness, all the demonism of the cosmos, affronted Him and closed with Him in mortal combat. Behind all 'the fearful enmity of the carnal heart of man towards God,'...stood the embattled hosts of the invisible world, hazarding all on a last trial of strength, and Jesus, when he faced and accepted that challenge, was taking upon Himself all that hatred, all that guilt, and all that judgment of God which lay upon it, in order...to complete His work of delivering men from the power of the Enemy and so restoring them to forgiveness and to God."

"But in the worship and preaching of the church today," he asked, "are we allowing sufficiently for this mysterious background to human existence which the Lord recognized and accepted as real when He came and preached...? Is there enough religious realism in the atmosphere of our worship and in the terms of our doctrinal teaching to take a grip on [people's] minds? Or are we speaking to them in the abstract impersonal terms of a purely rational paraenesis, laboring ethical points which have not perhaps a primary relevance to the existential situation of the hearers, and forgetting their fears, their appalling insecurity, and their despair?[42]

Gustaf Wingren reminded us that "the background...to the whole faith of the early Church without exception, is a deep-rooted certainty that the whole world of men lies in the hand of an enemy of humanity....It would be totally impossible," he says, "to revive the message of the Scriptures at all--for any generation in any century--if first of all it was desired to cut away belief in conflict, in demons, and in victory as too 'primitive' and 'superstitious'."[43]

Roland H. Bainton raised this problem graphically in his life of Luther, *Here I Stand*. He writes: "Luther had come into a new view of Christ and a new view of God. He had come to love the suffering Redeemer and the God unveiled on Calvary. But were they after all powerful enough to deliver him from the hosts of hell? The cross had resolved the conflict between the wrath and the mercy of God, and Paul had reconciled for him the inconsistency of the justice and the forgiveness of God, but what of the conflict between God and the Devil? Is God Lord of all, or is he himself impeded by demonic hordes? Such questions a few years ago," he says, "would have seemed to modern man but relics of mediaevalism, and fear of demons was dispelled simply by denying their existence. Today so much of the sinister has engulfed us that we are prone to wonder whether perhaps there may not be malignant forces in the heavenly places....Luther's answer was not scientific but religious. He did not dissipate the demons by turning on an electric light, because for him they had long ago been routed when the veil of the temple was rent and the earth quaked and darkness descended upon the face of the land. Christ in his utter anguish had fused the wrath and the mercy of God, and put to flight all the legions of Satan."[44]

It was Bishop Aulen's judgment that Luther rescued the New Testament dimension at this point from a thousand years of neglect and made it "central in his revitalized evangelical theology".[45] This would seem to be confirmed by Luther's statement in his *Galatians* commentary that "the primary article of Christian teaching" is that in Christ we see "sin, death, God's wrath, hell, the devil, and all evil, overcome and dead".[46] His *Shorter Catechism* likewise says: "Christ has delivered, purchased, and won me, a lost and doomed man, from all sins, from death and from the devil's power."[47] This is in accord with Edwin Lewis' understanding of what Jesus thought of his own work. "For him," wrote Lewis, "the question of evil is much more than a question of making the hearts of men right with God. It is a question of guaranteeing the destruction of the very cause of evil. There is an enemy alike of God and man--*and that enemy is why he was here*.... Calvary was the meeting-place of the elemental powers of existence--and if anyone wants to say the Hosts of Heaven and the Hosts of Hell, he has New Testament warrant for doing so. *The daring language represents metaphysical reality*."[48]

James Kallas, in three books on the demonic element in the New Testament, seems to me to have demonstrated conclusively that both Jesus and Paul believed "in the reality of demonic forces, in their actual existence as external realities, personalities in their own right, not to be confused with existential bad impulses".[49] Modern scholars, he insists, have been forced to grant this, but do it in the "embarrassed manner in which one confesses publicly that one's oldest son is a mongoloid",[50] then immediately reinterpret it in such fashion that its reality is denied. The refusal to accept the demonic seems to be a presupposition of what has been called "a new infallibility, the infallibility of human judgment",[51] which refuses to accept a dualism which will allow for cosmic evil greater than the sum-total of human rebellion against God, which evil enslaves man and uses him often for ends that he himself does not will. In spite of this, however, men today are beset with fears and despairs and defeats which leave them helpless and hopeless. It may be that we have neglected the demonic dimension of the human situation, and have trimmed our gospel accordingly, which becomes good advice to slaves, rather than a gospel of victory over man's enslaver and emancipation from his power.

Whether the demonic is personal or not is a difficult question. Edwin Lewis thought not. He was so sure of the objective reality of the demonic, however, that he wrote, "It were better than one believe tremendously in the Devil, and so keep vivid before one's mind 'the mystery of iniquity', than that one should lightly wave the mystery aside by relegating the Devil to the limbo of exploded myths."[52] Paul Ricoeur has countered belief in a personal Devil by suggesting that the demonic is the exact opposite of personality--it is a total depersonalization.[53] Profound though this may be, I have difficulty with it. Can you depersonalize non-personality? It seems to me that you cannot depersonalize that which has no potential for personality. Can you depersonalize a stone? Perhaps it is only the perversion of personality that is depersonalization. At least the worst forms of the demonic seem to manifest themselves in history in depersonalized persons, such as Hitler and the Rev. Jim Jones. It is only *persons* who can become so disorganized and demonic. No animal, and no blind force, could be that intelligently bad.

The great London missionary leader of a generation ago, William Paton, said that for years he could not believe in a personal Devil. He visited Shanghai in 1937, however, and decided that there must be a personal Devil. He said that if you gathered the greatest intellects of the ages and asked them to use all their ingenuity to plot the worst that they could think of, they would be incapable of producing a situation as bad as Shanghai was at that time.[54]

Dr. Ben Lacy, former president of Union Seminary in Virginia, once observed that he had found reinforcement for his belief in the personality of the demonic during his years in the pastorate. He said that if he tried to lead a man to Christ, just about the time the decision seemed imminent, a dozen things would arise to block the decision and impede the man from accepting Christ. Why? Dr. Lacy could not account for this on the basis of anything that either he, or the person involved, or his loved ones and friends did. There was something mysterious about it. And it happened too often to be happenstance. He could only conclude that there was a demonic intelligence who became active in opposing anyone who was about to close with the offer of grace.

To paraphrase Paul in his address before Agrippa, "Why

is it thought incredible" that there should be such things as what A. M. Hunter has called "discarnate intelligences"?[55] If it is possible for men who are intelligent personalities to resist God and impede his will or respond to his will, why should there not be other personal intelligences in the universe who can either further or resist the will of God as men do?

A recent book written by a man whose first name is Robert carries an interesting statement: "Call me Bob. That's short for Beelzebob. For I am well acquainted with the devil--the real devil. I shave him every morning....I have met the devil, and he is me."[56] There is truth in this, but is it the whole truth? When Jesus said to Peter, "Get thee behind me, Satan," was he calling Peter Satan? I very much doubt it. He was rather saying that he heard in the voice of his most intimate follower the voice he had heard at the Temptation. And that was the voice of Another than Peter, unless at the Temptation we are willing to say that the voice of Satan was Jesus' own evil nature rising up within him, which my belief in his sinlessness forbids.

When the story of William Paton's coming to belief in a personal Devil was told in the hearing of Dr. William Logan, who was one of two Southern Presbyterian missionaries through whose ministry Kagawa became a believer in Christ, he immediately replied: "I did not have to go to Shanghai in 1937 to believe in a personal Devil. All I have to do is to go to a meeting of Presbytery!" After the laughter had died down, he explained that he was serious. Said he: "Once in a while, in a meeting of Presbytery, someone proposes a really good idea. Immediately, twelve men are on their feet opposing it. Why? Not because they are bad men," said Dr. Logan, "but because Satan uses them, unbeknown to them, as his instruments in opposing the good."

The late Professor Kenneth Foreman who studied under B. B. Warfield at Princeton told me that once in class Professor Warfield asked a student if he believed in a personal Devil. The boy replied, "Yes." "On what grounds?" asked the professor. "On the grounds that I have had personal dealings with him," replied the student. "Do you mean to suggest," asked the professor, "that you have had direct dealings with the Devil himself?" "Yes," replied the student. "Well," said Professor Warfield, "personally, I think he is out after bigger game!" If the professor sensed a bit of undue pride in the student's view, what about the view that "I have met the devil, and he is me"? It may be a bit of spiritual arrogance to give one's self such a position of centrality and importance in the moral universe, even on its destructive and dis-creative side![57] Cosmic evil is greater than we are!

Whether the Devil is personal or not we cannot, of course, determine with finality. We may be sure, however, that the New Testament presents the reality of some kind of supra-human dimension of the demonic with which Jesus did battle on Calvary. When he sweat great drops of blood, and when he bowed his head in that piercing cry of dereliction which no sinful man has the capacity to fathom, it is difficult to believe that he was dealing only with my sin against him, or with the demonic elements inherent in modern corporations, or our technological woes or ecological hazards, or our political isms embodied in political or military organizations or persons. He was rather doing battle with him whom the Fourth Gospel calls "the ruler of this world",[58] and Paul calls "the prince of the power of the air".[59] He grappled with the cause of all this human evil and triumphed over it.[60]

VI

The victory of which we are speaking is, of course, a hidden victory. It is a victory in defeat. It is the victory of the cross. This victory cannot be seen save by the eyes of faith. A glance at the morning newspaper would not convince one that Jesus Christ is lord of the world. When Christ and Caesar confront each other, all the visible evidence places the odds on Caesar. The salvation we proclaim is a scandal.

The late Lucien Rimbault, dean of the Protestant Seminary in Montpellier, France, was captured at the Maginot Line in the early days of the Second World War and spent five years in a prison camp. He told me many interesting things about that camp. Among other things, in the latter months of the war, the prisoners were able to have smuggled in sufficient parts to set up a small radio receiving set. The German captors suspected this. When the pressure got hot, the prisoners would dismantle the set and bury the parts in various places around the camp. Then, when the pressure eased, they would re-assemble the parts into an operating radio set. By this means, they had news of allied victories which not even their captors knew. Imagine now that with this news, one of the prisoners should have confronted his guard and said, "By the way, did you know that our side was winning?" One can well imagine what would have happened. At the point of a bayonet, he would have been herded back to his cell, still the victim of a power he could not overcome. The fact remains, however, that it was true that the allies were winning. The prisoners

re soon to be rescued by a power outside themselves. The
ctimized had news of victories unknown to those who made
em victims, and of victories to which they themselves were
t contributing.

Christians are like these prisoners in a concentration
mp. They have news of a victory unknown to the world--the
ctory of Jesus Christ at the resurrection, a victory wrought
him for them to which they have contributed nothing. In
is victory they hope and by it they live, even in defeat.
is the news of this hidden victory that we are committed
proclaim. And it may be, contrary to all our natural ways
thinking, that the more hidden the victory the more genu-
e, and that outward signs of defeat may be the harbingers of
pe. Paul Minear speaks of a "little-observed but important
iom in biblical thought: Awareness of rebellion is an occa-
on not for despair but for hope (Romans 8:18-20). What
ems to outsiders to be morbid obsession with the pervasive-
ss of evil becomes for insiders the ground of confidence and
y."61

VII

If we retain the biblical view of the human situation--
at man is bound, enslaved, imprisoned--that his true situa-
on is expressed by Paul: "I can will what is right, but I
nnot do it. For I do not do the good I want, but the evil
do not want is what I do"62--then this situation demands
at preaching be a *gospel*, a proclamation of Christ's victory
d man's deliverance: "thanks be to God who gives us the
ctory through our Lord Jesus Christ."63

Has our preaching had that note? Has it been *gospel*?
s it been a proclamation of victory? Sometimes the hymn
iters grasp the gospel better than we who are commissioned
preach it. One of them has phrased it thus:

> The strife is o'er, the battle done;
> The victory of life is won;
> The song of triumph has begun. Alleluia!
>
> The powers of death have done their worst,
> But Christ their legions hath dispersed:
> Let shouts of holy joy outburst. Alleluia!

He closed the yawning gates of hell;
The bars from heaven's high portals fell:
Let hymns of praise His triumphs tell.
                                    Alleluia![64]

Does the tone of our worship and the content of our preaching offer men this sense of glad triumph?

NOTES

1. These, strangely, often involve preaching against preaching! Dr. George Buttrick once told of a woman who addressed a group in his congregation for an hour, decrying preaching and insisting that the future of the church lay in religious drama. In the discussion that followed, the speaker finally asked Dr. Buttrick for a comment. He simply said: "You did not put on a drama to tell us that the church's future lay in religious drama. You *preached* it to us!"

2. I Corinthians 9:16c.

3. ἐυαγγελίσωμαι

4. *The Threat and the Power* (Richmond: John Knox Press, 1971), pp. 76f.

5. Acts 18:26b.

6. *The Living Word*, translated by Victor C. Pogue from the Swedish (Philadelphia: Muhlenberg Press, 1960), p. 77.

7. Quoted by Wingren, *op. cit.*, p. 64.

8. See Luke 9:51.

9. "Mark as Interpreter of the Jesus Traditions," *Interpretation* (October, 1978), pp. 351f.

10. *Op. cit.*, p. 68.

11. *Ibid.*, pp. 87f.

12. *The Gospel of Matthew* (*Layman's Bible Commentary*) (Richmond: John Knox Press, 1961), p. 7.

13. Wingren, *op. cit.*, footnote, p. 67.

14. Acts 2:23f.

15. To list references to all the specific passages where the objects of the verbs translated "to preach" occur would be too cumbersome here. They may be identified by using any standard New Testament Concordance.

16. *Luther's Works*, edited by Jaroslav Pelikan (Saint Louis: Concordia Publishing House, 1968), Volume 30, p. 10.

17. *en loc.* Cf. English translation, *Theological Dictionary of the New Testament* (Grand Rapids: Wm. B. Eerdmans Publishing Co., 1964), Volume II, p. 722.

18. Romans 10:9, *et al.*

19. I Corinthians 15:26.

20. John 16:33.

21. I Peter 1:3b.

22. Revelation 11:15b, *The New English Bible* translation.

23. J. H. Thayer, *A Greek-English Lexicon of the New Testament, en loc.*

24. *Ibid., en loc.*

25. *Ibid., en loc.*

26. Acts 20:7, 9.

27. Thayer, *op. cit., en loc.*

28. Acts 17:2f.

29. Acts 17:18b.

30. Acts 24:24f.

31. Luke 11:21.

32. Luke 11:22.

33. Romans 8:20f.

34. Romans 8:38.

35. Romans 8:39.

36. Luke 13:16. Karl Barth comments on this passage: "It is certainly not an exhaustive description of what is envisaged in the passages which deal with exorcisms to explain that they deal only with what we now call mental or psychological ailments..., and that their healing is simply by what we realise, or think we realise, to be the appropriate psychi-

co-physical treatment....we must not think that what the Gospel passages have in mind in relation to these sufferers, and
especially to the action of Jesus, can be exhaustively described, let alone grasped in its decisive spiritual and theological meaning and character, in this explanation....we may
well ask whether, even if the narrators had had our more enlightened knowledge of spiritual sickness and its treatment
and eventual cure, they would have expressed themselves in
essentially different terms from those actually used." *Church
Dogmatics* IV, 2, p. 228.

37. O. S. Rankin, in a review of Langton's *Essentials of
Demonology* in *The Scottish Journal of Theology* (Volume 3,
1950), p. 218. Paul Minear reminds us of another modern biblical scholar, typical of a large segment of contemporary
opinion, who "has dismissed biblical demonology with this
verdict: 'Though full of quaint interest from the point of
view of folk-lore, the subject is not an edifying one.'"
Minear comments: "Early Christians would agree neither on
the quaintness nor on the absence of edifying value. They
assumed the existence and sway of demons as implicitly as
Oesterley rejects them. Struggle with 'the principalities
and the powers' was integral to their whole perspective.
Apart from this presupposition, they would have found little
meaning in the grace of God, in the coming of his kingdom, in
salvation through his Anointed....No interpretation of the
Bible is adequate that does not do justice to the experiential
realities which were expressed in such terms as sin, idolatry,
death, and Satan." *Eyes of Faith* (Saint Louis, The Bethany
Press, 1966), pp. 110f.

38. "On a Neglected Emphasis in New Testament Theology,"
Scottish Journal of Theology (Volume IV, 1951), pp. 292, 294.

39. *Ibid.*, pp. 300f.

40. Colossians 2:15.

41. Hebrews 2:15.

42. "Principalities and Powers," *Studiorum Novi Testamentum Societas* (Bulletin III, 1952), pp. 14, 16.

43. *Op. cit.*, p. 165. Paul Minear adduces a striking quotation from David Friedrich Strauss on this subject: "The
whole idea of the Messiah and his kingdom is as impossible
without the counterpart of a kingdom of demons with a personal
ruler at its head as the north pole of the magnet is impossible
without the south pole. If Christ has come to destroy the
works of the Devil, there would be no need for him to come if

there were no devil." *Op. cit.*, p. 103.

44. (New York and Nashville: Abingdon-Cokesbury Press, 1950), pp. 65f.

45. Quoted by Edwin Lewis, *A Philosophy of the Christian Revelation* (New York: Harper and Brothers, 1940), p. 298.

46. *Ibid.*

47. *Ibid.*

48. *Ibid.*, p. 302.

49. *Jesus and the Power of Satan* (Philadelphia: The Westminster Press, 1968), p. 203. See also *The Significance of the Synoptic Miracles* (London: S.P.C.K., 1961); *The Satan-ward View: A Study in Pauline Theology* (Philadelphia: The Westminster Press, 1966); *Revelation: God & Satan in the Apocalypse* (Minneapolis: Augsburg Publishing House, 1973).

50. *Ibid.*, p. 206.

51. Lewis, *op. cit.*, p. 131.

52. *Ibid.*, p. 125.

53. In informal discussion with a faculty group at Union Theological Seminary in Richmond, Virginia.

54. I have searched in vain for the reference to this which I read perhaps 30 years ago, but am sure of its authenticity.

55. *The Gospel According to St. Paul* (London: SCM Press Ltd., 1966), p. 30. Hunter attributes the phrase to Thomas Hardy.

56. Because of the critical view of this expressed later, the work shall remain nameless.

57. Karl Barth speaks to this: "The devil is that being which we can define only as independent non-being. Of course, when man sets himself up in the image of this non-being, he cannot make himself a devil; he cannot change his nature into that of this non-being; he cannot make for himself this awful independence; he can deny but he cannot dissolve his nature as proceeding from God and open to God. But it is not man himself who prevents it. And it cannot be denied that when he chooses to set himself up in this way he sells himself and

'goes to the devil'." *Church Dogmatics*, IV, 1, p. 422.

58.   12:31, 14:30, 16:11.

59.   Ephesians 2:2.

60.   Karl Barth speaks of this: Jesus "saw and experienced what there was actually to be seen and experienced: an abyss of darkness which was not merely supposed or imagined or invented or projected into the sphere of being but was actual and concrete; the presence and action of nothingness, of the evil in the background and foreground of human existence.... Far beyond the sin and guilt of man, but also far beyond his need and tragedy, even beyond death itself, the activity of Jesus invaded at this point the sphere of that power which was introduced into the cosmos by the sin and guilt of man and works itself out in his need and tragedy, enslaving all creatures. It penetrated to the poisonous source whose effluents reach out to the whole cosmos and characterise its form as that of 'this present evil aeon' (Gal. 1[4])." *Church Dogmatics*, IV, 2, p. 230.

61.   *Op. cit.*, p. 109.

62.   Romans 7:18b, 19.

63.   I Corinthians 15:57.

64.   A Latin hymn, translated by the Rev. Francis Pott in 1861.

12

TO ASK AND TO RECEIVE:
SOME CLUES TO JOHANNINE ONTOLOGY

Paul S. Minear

There is a saying of Jesus that has long hypnotized my
imagination. In this tiny capsule a direct command is supported by a brief promise: "Ask and you will receive" (Jn.
16:24). The command is so unqualified, the promise so inclusive, that any reader with an atom of sceptical inclination is
bound to respond with disbelief. For some readers, however,
this incredulity generates curiosity. How is it that a teacher, any teacher, could be induced to sponsor such a fantasy?
Was he aware of the odds against its acceptance? In making
this promise was he entirely sane?

Although a similar saying appears in the Synoptic Gospels
(Matthew 7:7; Mark 11:24; Luke 11:9), the teacher's wisdom is
perhaps most at stake in the Fourth Gospel where, within the
space of three chapters, the promise recurs no less than four
times (14:12-15; 15:5-8, 16-18; 16:22-27).[1] In these chapters
the statement is not easily detached, but is woven so tightly
into the fabric of thought as to threaten everything if the
truth of this saying should be rejected. In fact, confidence
in the Evangelist becomes dependent on explaining in a plausible fashion how and why he could indulge in so extreme a fantasy. In my case, then, the curiosity generated by incredulity has in turn generated an inquiry into the basic thought-
patterns of this author.

Those who are acquainted with ancient literature, biblical
and non-biblical alike, will recognize that a similar promise
appears in many, widely scattered writings. Numerous fables
encourage children to believe in the miraculous fulfillment of
an impossible dream. Every culture has a Cinderella legend
which nourishes the hope that ugliness will be transformed into beauty or rags into riches. At the end of the rainbow there
can be found a pot of gold. Such legends invite, of course,
aphorisms that express an opposite cynicism: "If wishes were
horses, beggars might ride." Yet the incredible legends live
on as poignant tributes to the stubbornness of human optimism.
In these legends the power of each ruler is gauged by his
ability to keep such promises; his generosity is measured by

his readiness to do so. An example is King Herod's promise t
an expert dancer who had pleased him (Mark 6:14-29) (cf. Mark
Twain, *A Connecticut Yankee in King Arthur's Court*). But why
should so extreme a promise become a central feature in Chris
tian thinking? Is this an example of exploiting the readines
of a gullible public to accept the big lie?

We may suppose that the author of the Fourth Gospel, whom
we call John, was fully aware of the widespread currency of
this teaching and of its rootage in universal human hungers.
He must also have recognized the futility of many of the
dreams it had nourished. Why then did he rely on it so fully
This is the objective before us: by examining the structure
of his thought-patterns to grasp the contribution of this
teaching to that structure and to assess its ontological
weight. We have divided the project into four stages. Because all primary versions of the saying appear within the
Farewell Discourses we will analyze that *literary setting* to
learn the Evangelist's intentions. Because the teaching is
lodged within an extensive constellation of idioms and images
we will explore its interrelations with those *conceptual patterns* as a whole. Because the Evangelist was a church leader
concerned to discharge his duties toward a specific Christian
audience, we will try to recapture a picture of the *social
situation* that audience faced.[2] Because the ultimate issues
in church decisions stemmed from competing world-views, we
will assess the *ontological implications* of the teaching.

Before going further, however, let me seal a bargain with
my readers. For my part, I will try to avoid any hidden agen-
da. I will not try to win readers over to my own theological
or ethical position nor will I covertly identify myself with
any of the participants in the ancient dialogue: John's enemies, his readers, himself, the first disciples of Jesus, Jesus....Only after I succeed in making John's thought-patterns
intelligible will I be in a position to decide whether to accept or reject them. And I ask readers also to postpone that
same decision. John was not writing with us in mind, but for
readers who were residents in a world far different from ours
For us to force our attitudes to conform to theirs might destroy both their integrity and ours; it might guarantee a distortion in the Gospel itself. When we have completed exploration of those alien thought-patterns we may, of course, find
unsuspected linkages to our own position; but until that time
arrives it is better not to confuse the two perspectives by
premature belief or doubt. Let us hold ourselves ready to
learn from the results, whether positive or negative. That
bargain made, we can proceed.

Literary Setting

There is little doubt that John intended these five chapters (13-17) to form a unit and to serve as a major pivot in his narrative. They mark the point of transition from Jesus' ministry to his Passion. He has completed his public work to and among "the Jews" and now engages in intimate conversations around the table with his "friends". At this table he clearly acts as their host. Later Christian readers could hardly read these chapters without hearing overtones of the Eucharistic and baptismal liturgies.[3] In that day, Jewish Christians as surely recalled the full range of their memories of the Passover preparations. The Evangelist himself probably had in mind the scriptural traditions of Moses' farewell to the twelve tribes immediately before his death (Deuteronomy 29-33).[4] So the time and place of this occasion evoked vast horizons of meaning for the Evangelist and his readers, most of all perhaps because at this time and place their own invisible relationships to the Father and the Son were so vividly expressed (cf. especially chapter 17).[5]

I have spoken of this place as if it could be easily located on the usual map: the Holy Land, Judea, Jerusalem, the Upper Room....That is quite true. For John and his readers, however, another kind of map was even more important, a map that reduced to scale a theological geography. For one thing, this map located Jesus' position with regard to a subtle distance from his enemies: "He departed and hid himself from them" (12:36). He was now embarked on a journey where they could not come. In this place he encountered a personal representative of the devil, Judas; and the story took pains to show how out of place that man was. For another thing, this map marked the place where Jesus departed from the world and returned to the Father, in contrast to the disciples who remained "in the world". The promises were given by one who had come from God and was going to God, a prophet who could therefore speak simultaneously from both vantage points. By his very presence Jesus linked the immediate locale of the Upper Room to a wider if less specific locale. He referred to that second locale with the words "Where I am going".[6] The disciples also were related to both spaces, but in a different way: "You cannot come [there] now...later on you will come" (13:33). So this literary setting made it clear that the promise "whatever you ask..." was issued by a prophet who was at home in both places. Its wide band of overtones emanated from the conjunction of these two spatial magnitudes. Addressed to disciples[7] in the world by a leader who was leaving that world for the Father's house, the promise continued to bind them to him, so that henceforth their habitat would also include both places; asking "in the world", they would receive from the Father.

As modern readers we may more easily visualize that double locale if we think of a technical device often used in television. Telecasters employ a split screen to show simultaneously things that are happening in different places. Baseball fans will recall how helpful it is to see on half of the screen a pitcher poised for a throw to the plate and to see on the other half a runner at first base, poised for a streak to second. Symphony orchestra addicts are now accustomed to simultaneous views of cellists and drummers, photographed from different angles by different cameras. So in these chapters of John we must be prepared to understand some of Jesus' statements as spoken from the Upper Room and others from the place where he was about to go. This may confuse us if we insist on only one map. But John's readers found it quite natural to fuse prospect and retrospect in the same conversation, in part because they had not themselves known Jesus in the first location but only in the second. Viewing the double stage, they could see the reciprocal relation of those two *wheres*: the Upper Room helped to make more specific the meanings of the second *where*; the latter location gave a dimension of universality and omnipresence to those conversations.[8]

Some characteristic references to these two spaces may help us discern the split screen:

he had come from God

> he was going to God (13:3)

I came from the Father and have come into the world

> I am leaving the world and going to the Father
> > (16:28)

I am (or was) with you

> I go to prepare a place for you (13:33)
> I am going to him who sent me (15:4; 17:12)

a little while and you will see me no more

> a little while and you will see me (16:16)

I glorified you on earth

> glorify me in your own presence (17:4)

But what is most important here is not a visualization of two
maps but the way of thinking that perceives two places, one
visible and the other invisible. Both of these places represent ways of expressing important relationships: Jesus' relation to God, to "the world", and to his disciples. One set of
relationships obtains in the world;[9] another obtains in the
presence of God. All of these relationships, even that to the
world, are person-to-person and not person-to-things. And all
are ways of describing movements of coming and going, from
origin to goal, movements that find their orientation-center
in God, in "his house", in the glory of his presence which is
seen as both primal and final reality.[10] John's readers, like
John himself, were acutely sensitive to the conjunction of
these two spaces and these two movements.

We must of course admit that the analogy of the split TV
screen is not entirely applicable, since in John's thought
different times as well as different spaces are involved. To
be sure, there is a spatial coordinate in the saying: "I came
from the Father and have come into the world....I am leaving
the world and going to the Father" (16:28), but the different
spaces are linked to two or three successive time-zones. "A
little while...a little while...a little while." These zones
take account of the time before and the time after Jesus'
death, and such contrasts can hardly be pictured simultaneously on the TV screen. Yet what is impossible on television is
entirely possible in biographical narratives, as many recent
novelists have shown. John took full advantage of this possibility, for in these chapters he referred to several time-
zones in the lives of the disciples.

First of all, he pictures the chief features in the position of the disciples before Jesus' glorification, when their
incapacity took many forms. They did not, and in fact could
not, at first understand his action in washing their feet (13:
7); they were unable to understand his remarks about where he
was going (13:33) or about his role as the way, the truth and
the life (14:5). Peter represented the others in his self-
deception and denial (13:38). Their involvement in both
space and time was indicated by their scattering at the on-
set of crises (16:31). Their habitat and their hour were different from that of Jesus, who loved them to the end in spite
of their incapacity and treachery (13:1; 15:9). Implicitly
John was entirely confident that God would give Jesus whatever
he asked (17:1-5); but he also recognized that during this
period before his glorification the disciples were quite un-
prepared to ask.[11]

The next time-frame was inaugurated by that glorification,
because after that event the same men were able to believe that

"I am he" (13:19; 14:29). Their sorrow was then replaced by joy, turmoil by peace, fear by courage. Seeing Jesus they were enabled to see and to know the Father and to recognize the way to his truth and life (14:1-7). In an important sense the Father and the Son had come to them to make their home with them (14:3). Their memories could now recall what he had taught them and what they had at first failed to understand. They could now distinguish their earlier subjection to "the prince of this world" from Jesus' triumph over that prince. This period in their lives was fully reflected in the perspective of the Upper Room.

The glorification of Jesus also inaugurated the period in which they would fulfill their vocation as his messengers (13:20). They would continue to do his works (14:12), to produce fruit as branches of the vine (15:1f.), giving their witness *in* the world *to* that world. It was in that time that they would wash one another's feet (13:14f.) and obey his commandment to love one another (13:34f.). They would then live as those who had been cleansed by his logos (15:3)[12] and would come to share in his knowledge of the Father (14:28) and in his joy (15:11). As an essential resource in this vocation they would receive from Jesus the Counselor-Paraclete (14:15-17, 25f.; 16:7). In fact, the central concern of Jesus during the whole of his conversation with them was "to keep them from falling away" (16:1) during that later, most difficult time.

The command to ask was assigned to this very time-frame and was designed to provide the help which they would need during that period. Having been sent on assignment, on the mission which Jesus had begun, they would be wholly dependent on help to be received from God, his Son and the Paraclete. The teaching articulated that dependence.

Still another time-frame should be mentioned; the time when they would complete their mission. The conversation clearly anticipated the time when Peter would fulfill his pledge to lay down his life for Jesus (13:37; 21:18). An hour would come when they would take the same way to the Father as Jesus had taken (13:36), the hour when their enemies would fully exploit their power (16:3). When disciples were marytred his promise would reach its intended goal: "I will take you to myself." "Where I am there will you be" (14:3). That would be the hour when the command to ask anything in his name would become especially relevant (16:23-26).[13]

From the standpoint of the Evangelist as he was writing the Gospel, all of these periods, even the last, had been adumbrated in the Farewell Discourses, for he himself looked back on the death of the last survivor (21:23, 24). To the modern

historian the confusion of these time-frames in a single conversation creates huge difficulties, for he considers his
task one of separating that initial event from the anachronistic distortions due to later developments. Actually, the
human memory, whether individual or communal, consists at any
given moment of a fusion of consecutive time-frames into a
single cumulative retrospect. Although hindsight often distorts the mirror, it also can give true insights into the
meanings of earlier events. But whether we prefer the perspective of the historian or that of the Evangelist, we cannot deny that this particular command/promise was in fact
oriented toward the vocation of the disciples during the
period after Jesus' death. In his role as prophet Jesus here
inaugurated their later work as his prophetic spokesmen, as
they would relay to their community and to the world their
knowledge of the Father and the Son.[14]

Parenthetically, we may note that this fusion of several
time-zones in John 13-17 does not appear in the Johannine
Epistles where a leader addresses his fellows in his own name
and uses much the same language and substance (I John 3:21-
23; 5:14, 15). However, the teaching as it appears in the
Epistle has lost much of the rich resonance that it received
in the Gospel from the direct linkage to Jesus and to his Passion. We turn now to the second stage in the inquiry.

Conceptual Patterns

The teaching with which we are concerned always appears
within a complex constellation of motifs. To recover its affiliations to those motifs we should examine closely the following passages, recognizing that in separating them from
their larger contexts we disrupt longer trains of thought.[15]

Context 1

> ...he who believes in me will also do the
> works that I do, and greater works than
> these will he do, because I go to the
> Father. Whatever you ask in my name, I
> will do it, that the Father may be glori-
> fied in the Son; if you ask anything in
> my name, I will do it. If you love me
> you will keep my commandments....
>
> 14:12ff.

Context 2

> ...If a man does not abide in me, he is
> cast forth as a branch and withers....If
> you abide in me, and my words abide in
> you, ask whatever you will, and it shall
> be done for you. By this my Father is
> glorified, that you bear much fruit, and
> so prove to be my disciples....
>
> 15:5ff.

Context 3

> ...You did not choose me, but I chose you
> and appointed you that you should go and
> bear fruit and that your fruit should
> abide; so that whatever you ask the Fath-
> er in my name, he may give it to you.
> This I command you, to love one another.
> If the world hates you, know that it has
> hated me before it hated you....
>
> 15:16ff.

Context 4

> ...So you have sorrow now, but I will see
> you again and your hearts will rejoice,
> and no one will take your joy from you.
> In that day you will ask nothing of me....
> If you ask anything of the Father he will
> give it to you in my name. Hitherto you
> have asked nothing in my name; ask and
> you will receive, that your joy may be
> full. I have said this to you in fig-
> ures; the hour is coming when I shall no
> longer speak to you in figures but tell
> you plainly of the Father. In that day
> you will ask in my name; and I do not
> say that I shall pray the Father for you;
> for the Father himself loves you, because
> you have loved me and have believed that
> I came from the Father....
>
> 16:22-27

An examination of these contexts supports many of the observations already made. In every case the author of the command/promise is Jesus, speaking in the role of one who has been sent from the Father. In every case the audience is the initial group of disciples (Judas excepted). In every case the time-zone anticipated by the teaching is the period after his death and before their own. In that period, the act of asking will be qualified by at least five factors.[16]

In the first place, such action will be taken in the name of Jesus (Contexts 1, 3, 4). The frequency of this phrase, as well as its strategic placing, indicates the importance of this factor to John (*onoma* appears in the Gospel 24 times). The name of Jesus carries the authority and power of God, which Jesus conveys to the disciples. Wherever this name is used, there he will be present with his ability to perform the works of God. So the command represents simultaneously both his separateness from the disciplic community and his union with it.[17]

Second, obedience to this command is closely affiliated with the works (*erga*) which they will do in his name (Context 1) (*erga* appears 25 times in the Gospel). These works appear to be synonymous with the fruit which they will bear as branches of the vine (Context 2, 3). Both works and fruit are typical Johannine images that presuppose direct continuity between Jesus' assignment and theirs. In fact their works are seen to be his own works, which have been empowered by the event of his going to the Father (Context 1). These works become a form of asking, and asking a form of working. The two actions have the same degree of credibility, of authenticity, of reliability. Each action discloses a degree of separation, disciples from master, and also a degree of interdependence, since he will be present in their works (Context 3).[18]

A third coordinate of asking is believing; in fact they are almost equivalent terms: to believe is to ask, and vice versa. This affiliation conditions the force of both terms: to the term *believing* it conveys a strong sense of trusting Jesus to do what he has promised; to the term *asking* it conveys a strong sense of personal response to the direct appeal of one who has been sent to them from God. Asking and believing reflect the fact that disciples have now entered the same realm, the same psychic space, where they are enclosed by the same communal boundaries and have begun to share the same field of force (Contexts 1, 2, 3). In this connection it is essential to recall that this field spans any conceivable distance between the two spaces: the disciples "in the world" and their master who has gone to the Father. (In this and other respects, this teaching becomes a Johannine parallel to the Matthean promise of the keys. Mt. 16:19; 18:18-20.)

The character of this psychic space is also indicated by
the affiliation of asking to loving. Loving the master takes
many forms: keeping his commandments, holding firm to his
logos (14:15), doing his works, bearing his fruit and asking
in his name. By the same token, this love entails hatred by
the world, for after his death the world would hate them as it
had hated him before his death. Just as his love is co-exten-
sive with his sovereignty, so this hatred would be co-exten-
sive with the sovereignty of the prince of this world. This
love and this hatred mark out the psychic boundaries within
which disciples could abide with him, within which he could
transfer his authority and power to them, whenever they asked.

The character of those boundaries is perhaps best indicated by the term *abiding*. Their asking and his promising
take place within this space. The Greek verb (*menein*) is
used some 33 times in the Gospel, and in many contexts it refers to an important reciprocal relationship.[19] They abide in
him; he abides in them. This bond between this lord and "his
own" embraces the other affiliations we have mentioned: the
name, the works and fruit, the believing, the loving, and the
asking. Perhaps the best epitome of this complex constellation is provided by the allegory of the vine. The act of asking on the part of the branches reflects the fact that they
have been cleansed by his *logos* and are producing his fruit.
When they ask they accept the role of branch; when he fulfills
his promise, he produces the fruit.[20]

Thus far we have focused attention upon the conceptual
affiliations of John's idea of asking; we now turn to similar
affiliations of his idea of the promise: "I will do it." The
first affiliation is that of glory and glorification, as reflected in the words "that the Father may be glorified in the
Son" (Contexts 1, 2). A basic criterion of this glory had,
of course, been made real in the Son's Passion (13:1f.; 17:1-
5). It is highly significant that this same glory was to be
realized in the works of the disciples, inasmuch as their
"greater works" would become in fact works done by the ascended Son. Here the Evangelist took care to link the promise of fulfilled requests not to the gratification of the disciples, but to the glorification of the Father. In biblical
thought, of course, this concept of glory carried major ontological implications, far surpassing psychic experience or
social prestige. It represented nothing less than the basic
purpose of God in his work of creation.[21]

We have already noted that all asking was to be done in
the name of the Son. Now we observe that the fulfillment of

e promise was to be accomplished by God in the same name
6:23). This fact emphasized the pivotal importance of that
me; its authority was recognized by the Son's Father as well
 by his friends. The reciprocal power of that name was an-
her way of expressing the mutual abiding of the Father and
e disciples in the Son. This is why there was no real dif-
rence between the fulfillment of their requests by the Son
ontext 1) and the fulfillment by the Father (Contexts 3, 4).

The idea of fulfillment was also closely affiliated with
e idea of sending. In his prayer in chapter 17, Jesus' con-
dence that his own requests would be granted was based on
e truth that God had sent Him for this very purpose. None
 those persons whom God had given him would be lost. The
ccess of his work validated God's commissioning. So, too,
e fruit of his disciples' work, which constituted the inner
bstance of their asking, would validate their commissioning.
e chain of askings and the chain of fulfillments were thus
separable from the chain of sendings,[22] clear evidence of
d's involvement in their existence. Their sonship, in fact,
nstituted a major form of his creative activity.

Similar evidence was provided by those gifts which con-
ituted God's granting of their requests. The gift of peace
s one example of this; so, too, the gift of joy (Context 4).
e gift of love, in particular, illustrated how tightly inte-
ated was the Evangelist's conception of asking and receiving.
king was an action expressive of the community's love for
d; fulfilling the request was an action expressive of God's
ve for this community (Contexts 1, 3, 4). Moreover, these
o actions could not be disjoined. None of the separate con-
pts, such as asking, could be understood apart from the con-
ellation as a whole; that constellation, in turn, pointed
yond the realm of ideas to a realm of personal and communal
lations. Moreover, we cannot fully grasp the nature of that
alm without considering the social and historical situation
ich provoked the writing of the Gospel. To that problem we
w turn.

Social Situation

What specific challenges were facing John and his readers
ring the time when the Gospel was being written? In answer-
g that question as briefly as possible, we will move from a
neral description to a more specific one.

The general picture in early Palestinian Christianity has

been well described by Gerd Theissen as being composed of the interaction of three roles:

> The internal structure of the Jesus
> movement was determined by the interaction
> of three roles: the wandering charismatics,
> their sympathizers in the local communities,
> and the bearer of revelation.[23]

Although Theissen did not relate those three roles to the Fourth Gospel, we may do so here.

Not often in the Gospel do we detect explicit references to the second of these three groups, those who sympathized with the wandering charismatics. They appear only in the margin of the Farewell Discourses, since the presumed center of concern in those chapters was the original band of disciples (e.g. 13:20). Those sympathizers were indicated in Jesus' prayer as those who would come to believe in him through the word of the first disciples (17:20). They were possibly referred to as the fruit produced by the branches of the vine (15:4, 16). The chief thrust of these discourses concerned the other two groups: the relation of the "wandering charismatics" to "the bearer of revelation". Theissen characterize their interaction in these words:

> Their relation to him was character-
> ized by reciprocal expectations. The
> various christologies express the atti-
> tudes of expectation directed toward the
> bearer of revelation, the ethical and re-
> ligious commandments formulated what he
> expected of believers. Mutually deter-
> mined roles are assigned to both.[24]

That summary admirably fits the situation in John.

We are now especially concerned with the mission of these charismatics in the world after the death of the bearer of revelation. Their assignment from him entailed the full acceptance of homelessness and the surrender of family ties, along with the abandonment of possessions and of the normal forms of self-protection. In these respects they recognized that a close congruity pertained between their roles and his. "A servant is not greater than his master" (15:20).

> The role of the Son of man as an out-
> sider corresponds both positively and nega-
> tively to the role of Christians. To take
> the positive side first: like the Son of
> man, his disciples transcended the norms
> of their environment....[Negatively] the
> Son of man is not alone in being homeless
> and vulnerable....The wandering charismat-
> ics, too, have forsaken everything.[25]

These more general pictures take on a harsh immediacy
when we look closely at two statements that are strategically
located near the center of the Farewell Discourse. First of
all, this statement: "I have said *all this* to you to keep you
from falling away" (16:1). We can be confident that "all this"
refers to the surrounding conversation as a whole. We can be
equally confident that the statement envisions the situation
anticipated after Jesus' death when these followers would be
particularly vulnerable to "falling away" as a consequence of
their work in his name. That image of falling is a rather in-
nocuous equivalent for the Greek verb (*skandalidzein*) that
pictures a pedestrian being caused to stumble and to fall.
Someone has waylaid a pilgrim pursuing his chosen way, has
set a trap for him that prevents him from continuing. So, in
New Testament thought, the death of Jesus had been a stone set
by God which had made men stumble (I Peter 2:4-8). The idea
in John is similar. When they faced death for their faith,
Jesus' disciples would be tempted to fall away and surrender
their share in Jesus' victory over the world.

That such death was a lively prospect is proved by the
second statement.

> 'They will put you out of the syna-
> gogues; indeed the hour is coming when
> whoever kills you will think he is offer-
> ing service to God.'

> John 16:2

No statement in the Gospel is more valuable in defining the
orientation of the Evangelist as he edited these discourses.

"They"...by implication this pronoun stands over against
its antithesis "We". *They* are members of the synagogues who
have enough popular support and enough authority to exclude
these wandering charismatics from their previous membership.
Popularity, prestige, scriptural legitimacy, the aura of tradition belong to *them*.

"put you out"...this tells us that these charismatics have
been insiders, attempting to carry out a mission in, through
and to their neighbors in the synagogues. They have now become, in a real sense, orphaned from their native religious
habitat.

"the synagogues"...this penalty would be painful to the
degree that those excluded had been at home in the synagogues,
had received their training there, had invested their loyal-
ties there, and there had accepted God's covenants with Israel.
Exclusion would represent deep personal anguish as well as
severe strain to their new faith and vocation, a strain so
great that at least some of them would "fall away".

"the hour"...Because these same discourses spoke so frequently of Jesus' hour, this term linked the completion of the
disciples' task to the completion of his. "He came to his own
and his own received him not" (1:11). To be sure, their time
of testing would come later than his, but this phrase suggested
that in a real sense they shared the same hour.[26]

"whoever kills you"...Now we see the radical cleavage between these two groups of insiders, those willing to kill and
those willing to be killed. The psychic boundary between the
two groups was even greater than any institutional boundary.
To fall away would reestablish the bond with the majority
group; to remain faithful to Jesus would be to recognize the
external breach as permanent. The depth of this breach was
measured by martyrdom.[27] This verse forces us to realize that
by the term "world" John was not indulging in nebulous general-
izations. His term "hatred" was no rhetorical exaggeration.

"offering service to God"...These authorized representatives of the synagogues could claim with Paul: "as to zeal a
persecutor of the church, as to righteousness under the Law
blameless" (Philippians 3:6). So, too, these wandering charismatics faced with Paul brutal treatment and even death at
the hands of their own kinfolk (II Corinthians 11:22-27).
Here we see that the boundary between "us" and "them" is
grounded in contradicting conceptions of what the God of
Israel demands of Israel. To accept *their* conception would
induce a person to fall away. To defend *"our"* conception
would be to hold fast to Jesus' *logos*. Every decision by the
"wandering charismatics" would in effect be an answer to the
question: which bearer of revelation do we trust? These five
chapters were shaped in such a way as to help them answer that
question.

If this be accepted as a cogent description of the issues, we should be alive to the intensely personal character

of the situation. We should be capable of genuine empathy with the leaders of the synagogue who hated Jesus' disciples. John himself stresses their loyalty to God and their willingness to make sacrifices in his service. Every Sabbath found them worshipping the God of Israel; every festival found them rejoicing in the traditions inherited from the fathers. Devoted to Moses and the Torah, they awaited the fulfillment of God's promises to Abraham. It was in good faith and in response to a good conscience that they took such vigorous action against these ostensible enemies of God's people. By the change of pronouns only, Paul's statements would have expressed their self-image:

> We are Israelites, and to us belong
> the sonship, the glory, the covenants,
> the giving of the Law, the worship, and
> the promises; to us belong the patri-
> archs....

Romans 9:4f.

Our empathy with this majority position of the synagogues is desirable for reasons other than that of maintaining scholarly objectivity and neutrality. It is needed before we can fully appreciate the position of the minority. Empathy with the opponents of the Jesus' movement allows us to sense how attractive would be the option of "falling away". To members of this majority, Judas was more a loyalist than a traitor! Only when we realize how attractive was this option can we assess the strength of the inner, communal cohesion that could prevent loyal Jews from choosing that option. In fact we need an empathy with both sides to comprehend the intensity of feeling that permeates the Farewell Discourses and especially the prayer of Jesus. We can be sure that the new boundary separating insiders from outsiders would have cut through many families, would have turned many close friends into bitter enemies. The recurrent stress in John on the treachery of Judas surely reflects the fact that he had many successors in the church, successors whose treachery John could also attribute to the foreknowledge of Jesus and to the intervention of the devil (13:2). So, too, the story of the denial of Peter and the scattering of the band of Jesus' disciples would have been all too relevant to their later "waffling".[28] The intensity of this personal conflict was indicated in the identification of their ultimate enemy as "the ruler of this world". Therein lay an ironic use of the term *world*, since in this context it referred to a devoted religious community for whom separation from the pagan and corrupt *world* had been a major motive. At the same time, this identification assigned ultimate guilt not to the hostile kinfolk and friends themselves but to the "father of lies" who had deceived them. John used the farewell of Jesus as an appropriate occasion for showing that his ultimate enemy (14:30) remained the ultimate enemy of his disciples after his death (16:11; 17:15).[29]

This discussion may be sufficient to indicate the social situation at the time the Gospel was written, to underscore the depth of the civil war within Israel and the nature of the options facing John's readers. These chapters of John were anything but pleasant devotional readings to be used on an afternoon stroll with Jesus in the rose-garden. They were weapons being used in a tense nip-and-tuck struggle for the ultimate allegiance of men and women who were about to enter their own Gethsemanes, often feeling that they were engaged in a futile struggle with overwhelming power.

Ontological Implications

In the verses at the beginning of Chapter 16 there is still another statement that formulates the issues in the briefest possible way. Speaking of those who would kill his followers as a way of making an offering to God, Jesus said:

> 'They will do this because they have
> not known the Father nor me'
>
> (16:3; also 16:21)

Here John forces us to visualize two opposing groups, a group of murderers and a group of martyrs.[30] Any complete picture of the two groups would, of course, disclose a broader spectrum of attitudes. Not all members of the majority would have fully approved the murders; not all members of the minority would have readily accepted martyrdom. Even so, the existence of the extremes discloses what was at stake in the conflict. Moreover, the issue could not be resolved in terms of a simple human judgement concerning which set of prejudices was in fact right. By their actions both murderers and martyrs were obeying what they presumed to be divine orders. Their actions demonstrated the incompatibility of two theologies, in spite of the fact that both groups were Jews, pledged to obey the god of Israel. Each group thought of itself as chosen to be sons of that god, and thought of its enemies (fellow-Jews) as sons of the devil. The greater the loyalty, the more acute the mutual hostility. In a civil war like this no third party

ould serve as mediator, for the point at issue was the divine
will, and neither side would entrust to a third party the
right to reveal that will or to define the proper mode of
obedience. To John's readers the basic error of opponents
was formulated by Jesus: "they have not known the Father or
me" (16:3, 21). Apart from knowing Jesus as the Son sent by
the Father they could not know God as the Father who had sent
him and who had been glorified in his martyrdom. The ultimate
issue for both groups was one of theology: through whom does
the true God reveal himself? Through whom the devil? Which
object of loyalty is truly the God of Abraham? And because
both sides were convinced that the God of Abraham was the God
of all creation, the theological issue was nothing less than
the ultimate ontological issue: which God was the creator of
all things? Which *logos* was in the beginning with God? When
we focus attention on this issue, each aspect of the conceptual pattern which we have studied assumes decisive signifi-
ance.

For example, we can better grasp the importance of John's
emphasis on the name. It was in the *name* of God that the synagogues opposed the messianic claims for Jesus, but it was in
the *name* of the Son that Jesus' movement came to their knowledge of the Father. The ontological dimension of this issue
comes through clearly when we recall that to the rabbis the
name of the Messiah was one of the seven things that were in
existence with God before the foundation of the world. The
acuteness of this issue helps to explain the emphasis in the
Fourth Gospel on the "I am" claims of Jesus (the Bread of
Life, the Good Shepherd, etc.). To Jesus' followers the command to ask had been uttered by this martyr on the night before his martyrdom; consequently his promise to fulfill their
requests carried the full authority of his name. When other
martyrs asked in his name, they could be assured of God's fulfillment in his name. When the members of the second generation asked, the name transcended the two generations which
separated them from Jesus. This name designated a psychic
and an ontic space within which God's sovereignty prevailed
and which separated them from the space ruled by the prince
of the world.

So, too, the situation of martyrdom adds ontological
resonance to the concept of works. We have seen how all asking had been correlated with the idea of working. The basic
Johannine definition of works, whether those of God or of
Jesus, focused upon the action of giving life to the dead
(5:21). It had in fact been this action on the part of Jesus
that had prompted "the Jews" to seek to kill Jesus (5:18).
Here probably lies the climactic importance in the Johannine
scenario of the raising of Lazarus from the dead, an act which

demonstrated Jesus' role as the resurrection and the life but which for adversaries was the final blasphemy. Jesus promised those who followed him on the way of martyrdom that they would do greater works. By raising the question of the efficacy of this promise, the death of those martyrs became in fact a mode of asking in Jesus' name. Their request would contain petitions not only for their own resurrection but also for forgiveness and life for their opponents. Thus the command/promise of the martyred Jesus served to set the continuing works of his followers within the context of ultimate horizons. Those who believed in the *logos* of the apostles (17:20) entered the realm of eternal life which linked them to primal beginnings (1:1f.) and to final mercies (1:14f.).

To keep in mind the human issues posed by the actualities of martyrdom also serves to sharpen sensitivity to the Johannine concept of believing. To believe in Jesus, when the cost was excommunication and even death, was to believe that God (and not the devil) had sent him. From this standpoint one can grasp the truth that to see and to know this prophet as the Son was to see and to know God as his Father. To obey Jesus' commands (including the command to ask) was to trust him as sharing God's power to fulfill all requests. Such obedience, such trust, must have become most difficult in times of their persecution by accredited and respected religious leaders; this very difficulty would serve to define what was involved in the act of believing. How can a person believe when his witness has provoked intense hostility, when his love for his people has released their hatred, when his assigned task has become futile? In that situation John was aware that a person could not trust in Jesus without hearing this command and promise; nor could he believe in Jesus without obeying. This very situation conferred on the command to ask an aura of mystery and miracle. That aura pervades the prayer of Jesus in John 17, which is in itself an epitome of what it means for a prophet facing martyrdom to ask and to receive.

If we now return to one of our initial questions we may discern some possible answers. Why should so fantastic and incredible a promise have become so central a feature in Johannine thought? The high degree of incredibility is an honest recognition of the paradoxical contrast between the humiliation and weakness implicit in martyrdom and the glory and power which this Father conferred on the martyrs. Jesus was not the only prophet whose death coincided with being lifted up in the glory of the Father. The incredibility of this command/promise was used to show the relation between one ontic space and another, both their distance from and their nearness to each other. One space was the realm of light, that primal light which on the very first day of creation had disclosed, in response to God's word, the opposing realm of darkness (Genesis 1:1ff.; John 1:1-5).

Finally, the religious civil war in which Jesus' followers were engaged helps to explain the ontological dimensions in the concepts of reciprocal love, glorification, and abiding. All of these concepts are reciprocal in that the same actions spring from activity shared by God and the band of servants.

"I am in the Father, and you in me, and I in you" (14:20). The reference here is to a very extensive realm, whose ontological weight is indicated by the concepts of life and glory, and whose unity and integrity is indicated by the concept of love. Asking and receiving are actions that reflect the interdependence of all residents of that realm, an interdependence that becomes most visible and audible in the active witness of martyrs. At every point that activity finds its antithesis in the community that is ruled by the Devil. Those who "have not known the Father or me" constitute the world; their hostility is the manifestation of the sovereignty of its ruler. Those who have known the Father and the Son constitute another realm. John uses many images to help the members of that realm understand their continuing relation to God, to Jesus and to the Spirit-Paraclete. Not the least of those images is expressed in this assurance:

> 'If you abide in me, and my words
> abide in you, ask whatever you will,
> and it shall be done for you. By this
> is my Father glorified....'

(15:6)

Ultimately the very audacity of this promise reflects the truth that the Evangelist believed it to be grounded in ontic reality, in the glory of God that is both primal and final. Is this the truth? Or is it an illusion? That is precisely the question that John forced his readers to answer.

NOTES

1. I have analyzed this saying with primary focus on the Synoptic versions in *Commands of Christ*, Nashville, Abingdon Press, 1972, pp. 113-131.

2. For John's original audience, cf. my essay "The Audience of the Fourth Gospel," *Interpretation*, 31 (1977), pp. 339-354.

3. For sacramental associations, cf. C. H. Dodd, *The Interpretation of the Fourth Gospel*, Cambridge, University Press, 1953, pp. 401f., 411ff.

4. Cf. R. E. Brown, *The Gospel of John* I, p. 492. Also my essay "The Beloved Disciple," *Novum Testamentum*, 19 (1977), pp. 105-123.

5. Cf. R. Bultmann, *The Gospel of John*, Philadelphia, Westminster, 1971, pp. 457ff.

6. Cf. "We don't know where...," *Interpretation*, 30 (1976), pp. 125-140.

7. It is altogether too easy to identify the Johannine term *disciples* with all subsequent followers of Jesus in all generations. That identification has become habitual with virtually all readers and commentators. It is therefore highly important to recover the perspective of John in which a distinction is drawn between *mathetai* as the initial group of disciples who were present with Jesus in the Upper Room and those who later would believe in Jesus through their *logos* (17:20).

8. Cf. G. Vann, *The Eagle's Word*, London, Collins, 1961, p. 12: "The prophetic vision is many-levelled, mingling past or present with future, the temporal and the eternal, the literal with the metaphorical, history with symbol...in the fourth gospel there are no parables because the whole gospel is a parable."

9. One must be careful not to impart into Johannine thought the customary inclusive quantitative concept of the world. As we will see, John linked *kosmos* directly to the source of Israel's hostility to God as proved by her rejection of Jesus as emissary from God. Cf. "Evangelism, Ecumenism and John 17," *Theology Today*, 35 (1978), pp. 7ff.

10. "There is no transfiguration story in John because the whole gospel is a showing of the glory, and at the same time a showing of how man is transfigured." G. Vann, *op. cit.*, p. 25.

11. In this picture of the disciples before the Passion John shares the same perspectives as the Synoptic Evangelists. Again it is important to recognize a distinction between the original band of disciples and the later generations of believers, although of course this distinction does not rule out a basic continuity.

12. Readers must be careful not to telescope all the rich meanings of the Johannine term *word* to its minimum denotation. It connotes "not merely the teaching of Jesus nor the works of Jesus, but the very person of Jesus as the manifestation of the Father. Jesus' manifestation of the Father is not complete until he lays down his life for men, fully revealing God as life-giving love." J. F. Forestell, *The Word of the Cross*, Rome, Biblical Institute, 1974, p. 192.

13. These sayings would have had special potency for readers who had heard of the martyrdom of the first band of apostles and who had been tempted to doubt by the obvious futility of their witness. Could they continue to believe that the martyrs' cries had been answered, petitions not only for their own souls but also for the unshaken faith of their converts, and the salvation of the world?

14. Much Johannine research has underestimated the extent to which this Gospel reflects the prophetic character of the early Christian movement as a whole. John pictures both Jesus and his messengers as prophetic successors to Moses, as martyred witnesses to the truth, and consequently as those who through the Spirit could "see" the conjunction of different times and spaces.

15. In what follows I have chosen to ignore varied scholarly efforts to rearrange the discourses into a more logical sequence, as well as current schemes to separate the different stages in the development of the Johannine tradition, from the earliest sources to the latest redaction. Such efforts and such schemes do not, I think, basically affect the conceptual patterns.

16. It is significant that John shows no interest in, and in fact makes no mention of, the *things* for which disciples should ask. What bulks large in most discussions of *asking* bulks very small in his discussion. For him the sole

concern appears to be attached to the inner relationships of *askers* and *givers*.

17.   "*onoma* expresses the concrete connection between God and man, the personal relationship which declares itself in a specific approach of God and which demands a specific approach from man." As suggested by John 12:28, "three words, father, glorify, name are so closely connected that they have to be expounded together". H. Bietenhard in Kittel, *TWNT* V, p. 272f.

18.   These statements about *works* and *fruit* carried a rich resonance to John's readers who probably viewed themselves as being the works and the fruit of the original disciples (15: 5, 15; 17:20).

19.   Cf. R. E. Brown, *op. cit.*, I, p. 510ff.

20.   Again the connotations of the term fruit depend in part on John's readers' readiness to identify themselves with the fruit produced by these branches, the initial company of Jesus' apostles. When we examine all the matters included within the "psychic boundaries", it becomes inadequate to speak of John's thought as a form of mysticism.

21.   Cf. Jonathan Edwards, "Concerning the End for Which God Created the World," *The Works of J. Edwards*, New York, Carter, 1864, II, Chapter 2.

22.   From the standpoint of John's readers this chain already had three links: The commissioning of Jesus by God, of the apostles by Jesus, and of the Christian readers by the apostles. This chain of sendings is an essential presupposition of the promise "whatever you ask I will do it".

23.   G. Theissen, *Sociology of Early Palestinian Christianity*, Philadelphia, Fortress Press, 1977, p. 7.

24.   *Ibid.*

25.   G. Theissen, *op. cit.*, p. 26.

26.   R. E. Brown, *op. cit.*, I, p. 517f.

27.   Account should be taken of the fact that some of the best exegetes have reconstructed several distinct stages in the history of church-synagogue relations, all of which are reflected within the present gospel. One aspect of their reconstruction is a tendency to trace 16:1-3 to a later stage in that history, as a culmination of periods of relative tolerance and gradual alienation. I have not yet been con-

vinced by these reconstructions. Cf. J. L. Martyn, "Glimpses
into the History of the Johannine Community," *Ephemerides
Theologicae Lovaniensis*, 1977, pp. 149-175; R. E. Brown, *Interpretation*, 31 (1977), pp. 379-393.

28. Although the Gospel appears to stress a black-and-
white distinction between loyalty and betrayal, it actually
reflects a rather broad range in the degrees of loyalty to
Christ and in the degrees of alienation from the synagogue
authorities. (Examine the symbolic roles of Judas, Peter and
the beloved disciple.) It also recognizes different stages in
the movement of some of the actors in their movement from synagogue to church (e.g. Nicodemus, Joseph of Arimathaea).

29. Much has been made of the anti-Semitism of John.
Without denying the evidence for that reading of the Gospel,
we believe too little has been made of the probability that
within this document we are in touch with a bitter civil war
within Israel, that *all* of the major participants were Jews,
that the original *audience* of the Gospel was composed of Jewish Christians, and that they were everywhere visualized as
being sent from God *to* Israel, in spite of active hostility.
In view of these features, the charge of anti-Semitism becomes an example of anachronistic revisionism that distorts
the original situation, where followers of Jesus were a
powerless minority and their adversaries a powerful majority.

30. It is significant that in John 13-17 all instances
of the command to ask are expressed in the plural, that is,
they are addressed to the entire company of disciples and
anticipate a group response that will articulate the inner
axis of reality between Israel and God. It is a measure of
modern individualism that we visualize an address to individuals and their response as individuals. In consequence, we
lose a sense of the sharp contrast between two hostile communities and their respective "worlds". When we visualize
those two communities, we may detect a congruence between
communal asking in the Gospel and in Revelation 6:9-11, and
a congruence between the communal promises in the Gospel and
in Revelation 7:13-17.

13

SOCIAL JUSTICE AND THE PURITAN 'DUAL ETHIC'

Robert S. Paul

The Puritans of the seventeenth century reveal an intriguing paradox in ethics. According to their ecclesiological principles and New Testament restorationism,[1] we would
have expected the Puritans and Separatists of the 1640s to
have been committed to a thoroughgoing withdrawal from the
sins and ambiguities of this world, yet they fought and won
a bitter civil war, governed the maverick nations of the
British Isles, helped forge the political concepts of parliamentary democracy, and established the successful transatlan-
tic colonies from which the American phenomenon was to emerge.

Some years ago, in the course of examining the relationship of politics to religion in the life of Oliver Cromwell,
I hit upon a Puritan principle that might help to explain the
paradox--the 'dual ethic'.[2] Perhaps the time has come to look
at it again for the light it may possibly throw on the way
Puritanism contributed to later Anglo-Saxon secularity.

The thesis starts from the belief that the Puritans and
Separatists who took part in England's Great Civil War were
convinced that the Bible was the ultimate authority for what
they did in every sphere of life, but they were embroiled in
a situation where they did not have the luxury of being able
to reflect quietly on social and political matters of great
moment, but where they had to 'think on their feet'. This
may have involved them in some inconsistency, but if we are
to understand them fairly I suggest we should expect to find
them meeting new ethical challenges on the basis of that
biblical authority. To put my thesis in its simplest terms,
I submit that as militant Puritans encountered the problem of
their appropriate action within a hostile, secular society
they discovered a 'dual ethic'[3] in the Bible: they therefore
turned to the Old Testament as defining the highest possible
christian conduct in civil society, just as they relied on the
New Testament to define the optimum christian standard of action in the community of grace, the Church.

There were refinements to this, as we shall see, and it
is clear that Puritans saw the Old Testament pointing to the

time when the Kingdom of God would reveal the whole of society as the proper sphere of grace, but that belonged to God's providence in the future. For the time in which they were involved, I suggest that Puritan attitudes are more fairly to be described in terms of a biblical 'dual ethic' than in terms of a principle of 'segregation' in which the secular and the sacred were totally unrelated.

I

'The Principle of Segregation'

Perhaps the best way to introduce the 'dual ethic' is to begin with the publication on August 3rd, 1643, of Edmund Calamy's little compilation called, *The Souldiers Pocket Bible*--or to give it the full treatment of its title page:

> The *Souldiers Pocket Bible:* Containing most (if not all) those places contained in holy Scripture, which does show the qualifications of his inner man, that is a fit souldier to fight the Lords Battels, both before he fight, in the fight, and after the fight; Which Scriptures are reduced to several heads, and fitly applied to the Souldiers severall occasions, and so may supply the want of the whole Bible; which a Souldier cannot conveniently carry about him: And may be also usefull for any Christian to meditate upon, now in this miserable time of Warre.

This appeared about a year after the outbreak of the Puritan Great Rebellion, the bitterest civil war in English history.

C. H. Firth reminds us that there is no evidence that *The Souldiers Pocket Bible* enjoyed general circulation among the parliamentary troops during the English Civil War, but the number of copies suggests that it was popular. The work shows the way in which the Puritan automatically turned to the Old Testament to help him in the circumstances of war, for although the anonymous editor of an 1895 reprint is in error when he says that the quotations "with two exceptions only, are taken from the Old Testament",[4] the overwhelming preponderance of citations certainly comes from that source.

At this point we must try to understand the dilemma in which the exponents of the 'gathered churches' found themselves in the struggle with the Stuarts, which was to some extent shared by all the Reformed. The medieval church recognized a double standard of Christian morality--the ethical standard of Christian perfection which was attempted by comparatively few (the clergy and the 'religious' who lived essentially apart from this world and its standards), and the lower standard of morality to which the rest of the Church conformed and which could be lived out in secular life.[5] To guide the layman in the moral conflicts and ambiguities of life in this world, the medieval Church had developed the whole science of moral theology with the special expertise of casuists to determine the particular problems of special cases. Puritanism was in the process of developing its own 'moral theology' in the voluminous 'Cases of Conscience' and producing its own kind of casuist in ministers, such as Richard Baxter in England and Thomas Hooker in America, who were specially known and gifted in the art of offering spiritual counsel.[6]

Meanwhile there was the problem of a struggle with the crown to be undertaken at the basic level of secular politics and eventually in a civil war; and all this had to be undertaken on a theological basis that denied any double standard of conduct between specially 'religious' people and the rest of the membership, because all God's people are 'called to be saints'. In other words, the ecclesiology of both the Puritans and the Separatists engaged in the fight with Charles refused to concede any fundamental difference between the moral standards required of clergy and laity--all Christians were expected to strive towards achieving the Christian *ethic*--the Christian optimum--for that alone was the standard of behaviour appropriate to 'sainthood'.

Their problem was how to apply this standard. The ideal seemed clear and simple enough when it was being lived out in the exiled congregations in Holland or America, or even within separated but persecuted conventicles in England, but it became immeasurably more complicated in the turmoil of the Civil War. When 'the Lord's gracious outcastes' returned from exile, they found themselves engaged in the secular affairs of civil government, having to deal with people who scoffed at 'visible saints', and (after the King's defeat) having to take responsibility in government and in parishes for citizens for whom their forms of churchmanship held little attraction. Was the Christian ethic of love, which they recognized as the rule among Christian brethren, to be applied in precisely the same way to enemies on the battlefield, to political opponents in Parliament or even to the mass of apathetic or profane people whose interests were basically secular? The ethic of love did not seem to be appropriate when one was face to face with Rupert's cavalry; but if Christians were called to an *ethic*, to conduct befitting 'saints', how was the dilemma to be resolved?

Because Puritanism undoubtedly helped to produce our own secular world, the most obvious answer for historians gifted with twentieth century hindsight is to say that the Puritans simply employed their theology to cover up for attitudes and objectives that became increasingly secular. "The Puritan," observed A. S. P. Woodhouse, "turned to the theological aspects of a question as naturally as the modern man turns to the economic; and his first instinct was to seek guidance within the covers of his Bible," but then he paused significantly to ask the question, "or was it rather to seek there justification for a policy already determined, on political and economic, grounds?"[7]

Let it be admitted that Puritans, like religious idealists in any age, could often deceive themselves, convincing themselves that they were acting on clear Biblical principles when they were actually motivated by far more mundane considerations; let it be admitted that the modern secular world *was* rapidly emerging, and was to appear even more rapidly after the movement went into its sudden decline after 1660; let us also admit with Woodhouse that in the rise of the Leveller Party and Agitators in the Army we see the beginning of the first political party in the modern sense, and that its representation in the Army Council was "predominantly democratic in tendency, and ultimately secular in aim, though it...at times adopts the language of religious enthusiasm".[8] With all these caveats, I suggest, we must look for the answer to the *Puritan* dilemma not in terms of the secularism that arose out of the demise of Puritanism, but within the Puritans' own distinctive patterns of thought. Woodhouse himself may have recognized this when he claimed that if one ignores those theological categories, "the Puritan mind has eluded you",[9] and he reminds us that "the Puritan viewed the world as a twofold system, a scheme of *nature* and of *grace*".[10] However, from this seeming dichotomy in Puritanism, Woodhouse discerned a 'principle of segregation' that, he suggested, cuts across the normal tendency of the Puritan to carry his dogma into secular life. "This principle thoroughly applied," he observed, "imposes severe limits on the intrusion of dogma into secular life. In other words it completely secularizes one division of existence."[11]

This goes too far too quickly for my purpose. First, I would freely admit that secularization did eventually take place, but only as the religious reality behind Puritan theology became ineffective and as its ecclesiastical discipline eroded. This process may have been already far advanced among the Levellers and some of the political radicals in the New Model Army, but I would insist that until internal erosion in Puritan theology and ecclesiology took place, the Puritan would insist on an essentially theological interrelationship between the spheres of 'nature' and 'grace' even while accepting their distinctiveness: both nature and grace were under the Kingship of Christ.

There is an intermediate stage that is missing before that 'principle of segregation' was able to force the complete separation of the individual's life in the church from his life in this world, and hence before it could slide into secularism. There is, I suggest, during the English Civil War a period when Puritan thinking on this issue could have developed in two different directions, when the issues were being hotly debated in the Army Councils of 1647.

II

The 'Dual Ethic'

The fulcrum on which this balanced was 'the dual ethic'. Woodhouse quite rightly reminds us that the Puritan's "first instinct was to seek guidance within the covers of his Bible"; but if this insight is given its full value, the Puritan would almost automatically apply the Old Testament (the Old Law) to the scheme of nature and the New Testament to the scheme of grace.

If this is true then the Puritans solved their ethical problem not by becoming 'secular' in their dealings outside the covenant of grace, nor by conceding that nature and grace demand double (i.e., 'lower' and 'higher') standards of conduct for christian action, but by insisting that each of these spheres had its own proper christian autonomy and that it therefore had its own proper 'ethic' expressed in the two Testaments. We must emphasize, that each of these standards, both those of the Old Testament and the New, would be seen as absolute and therefore 'christian' for the sphere it governed. The morality of the Old Testament would not be read as a lower standard that simply contrasts with the higher ethic of the New Testament, but as an optimum standard of conduct for the people of God as citizens of the nation acting within the secular company of nations.[12]

I am not suggesting that this 'dual ethic' was consciously

adopted, or (as we shall see) that it remained or could remain as simplistic as we have stated it, but on the basis of seventeenth century Puritan Biblicism it would be the much more logical way to approach their dilemma; and it would help to explain why, despite the Puritans' insistence that all christians are 'called to be saints', historians have always discerned a cleavage between the way they acted as members of the church and as members of secular society. If this 'dual ethic' is seen in the light of their fundamental beliefs, rather than in terms of our own twentieth-century secularity,[13] then we can appreciate that such a 'dualism' potentially represented the beginnings of a Puritan 'moral theology' in which both Testaments would be equally authoritative within their respective spheres: it would be an appeal, in matters concerning a secular society not yet under grace, to the Law which operated before the Kingdom of Grace, not because the gospel had ceased to exercize its claims on the Christian within secular society, but because those were the only standards that an unregenerate world could recognize.

The 'dual ethic' was never clearly distinguished as such by the Puritans themselves. They continued to read their Old Testament always in the light of the New, and therefore Puritans inevitably moved either in the direction of the secularism illustrated by the Levellers or in that of the 'christian realism' that I find illustrated by Cromwell. But the original point of departure is represented in the appearance in 1643 of Edmund Calamy's *Souldiers Pocket Bible* with its almost exclusive reliance on Old Testament texts, and in the sermons that were preached before Parliament during the Civil War.

In his detailed study of these sermons, John F. Wilson has noted that of the two hundred and seventeen sermons preached, "the Old Testament especially was mined thoroughly: one hundred and sixty-two sermons were based upon it"[14] as against fifty-five from the New Testament. He added the comment:

> The readiness of the preachers to
> select texts from the broad range of the
> Old Testament in preference to the New
> Testament is evident. Thus the distri-
> bution of texts among the biblical books
> is interesting confirmation that the
> puritans, while reading their Old Testa-
> ment in the light of the New Covenant,
> yet were drawn back toward the earlier
> and richer materials in elaborating
> their conceptions of political and so-

cial life. It also provides specific evidence that the puritans construed ancient Israel's library as a source of 'authoritative words.' With the abundance of its teachings the Old Testament legitimated their many and various convictions.[15]

...e offers this significant quotation from the 1643 *An Apologie of the Churches in New England*, which indicates a similar approach on the part of the Puritans in the New World:

Whatsoever Ordinance of the Old Testament is not repealed in the New Testament, as peculiar to the Jewish Paedogogie, but was of morall and perpetually equitie, the same bindes us in these dayes, and is to be counted the revealed will of God in all ages, though it be not particularly and expressly mentioned in the writings of the New Testament....The Scriptures of the New Testament doe speake little in these cases; onely the Scriptures of the Old Testament doe give direction, and light about them.[16]

Admittedly when we speak of a 'dual ethic' we are in one of those grey areas of history where we have to look to the preferred or natural ways in which Puritans thought rather than being able to point to a deliberate or consciously recognized policy. The evidence has to be seen in hints and impressions, but an expert in the field of American Puritanism seems to have recognized the principle when he suggested that "both Pilgrim and Puritan met the problem of the allocation and exercize of authority on the basis of what I have called 'two polar points of view simultaneously believed.' From the divine viewpoint, the world is monarchically ruled by God in the person of Christ; from the temporal viewpoint, the perfect society is (in the words of Samuel Stone) 'a silent democracy in the face of a speaking aristocracy.'"[17]

It is the biblical basis of such duality that is suggested in the dual ethic; and although this might imply a clear dichotomy to the modern reader, it was a dichotomy that the Puritan would not have conceded or even understood, since for believers the sacred and the secular were equally under the Kingship of Christ.

III

The Army Debates of 1647: Providence and Justice

With the fall of Charles I's war-time capital, Oxford, in
June 1646, the First Civil War came to an end; but this un-
leashed a struggle for power that found the parliamentary supporters hopelessly divided and the government of England in
complete disarray. Parliament--or at least the Presbyerian
majority in control at Westminster--was openly suspicious of
the New Model Army and actively trying to undermine the power
of the military Frankenstein it had created. It was abetted
by financial interests in the City of London that feared the
egalitarian principles appearing in the army, and by the Scots,
who would have been ready enough to turn their forces against
Fairfax and Cromwell if Charles had been willing to guarantee
the Covenant and Presbyterian uniformity.

All parties made tracks to Charles and tried to win his
support for a settlement of the nation that would guarantee
the things they regarded as central in the struggle. Although
the king was under guard and defeated militarily, he seemed to
hold all the political cards in his hand because none could
conceive a national settlement without him: he thought himself to be in the enviable position of being able to play all
the parties against each other, and it was a game in which he
considered himself supremely adept and into which he was
pushed by Stuart vanity no less than by the fickle fortunes
of war.

Oliver Cromwell and Henry Ireton negotiated with the king
on behalf of the Army, their main concern being to win some
guarantees for a generous religious toleration. They were entirely frustrated, and by 1647 they were also embarrassed by
the appearance on their left wing of the Levellers and Agitators (i.e., Agents) of the rank-and-file who stirred up the
soldiery in the name of social justice to demand a much more
radical political settlement. The Agitators became extremely
suspicious of the negotiations conducted by Cromwell and Ireton, and royalist agents, like Sir Lewis Dives [Dyve], had a
field-day fomenting these suspicions with John Lilburne and
other radicals whenever they had the opportunity.[18] The insistence of the General Officers on being faithful to the
Army's previous 'engagements' did nothing to lessen those
suspicions, for the radicals were more than ready to believe
that the Army had probably been 'engaged' much further than
the ordinary soldier was aware.

. The Responsibility of Those 'Who Carry the Sword'

This is the political background against which we should
see the concern for social justice that permeates the army debates of 1647.[19] All the participants accepted a viewpoint
that was Biblically literal, and if our contention about a
dual ethic is correct, the governing ideas of both groups
in the Army Council with respect to society were basically
those of the Old Testament: justice had a retributive aspect
in the sense that the Old Testament speaks of a retributive
justice against God's enemies, but it had a more positive social aspect in the sense that the Mosaic Law or the words of
Amos were addressed not to a church but to a particular *nation*
and its problems.

Modern theologians find the meaning of the Old Testament
to be a good deal more complex, but we must remember that for
all who shared the Puritan presuppositions, the meaning of
scripture was essentially simple, straightforward and literal.
The members of the Puritan army were serious about justice because they were serious about the Bible, and that was remarkable enough in the midst of a revolution and the almost total
breakdown of regular government.[20] By 1647 both legal forms
of national authority were impotent--the king was in custody,
and Parliament, when not running scared of the Scots or of its
own army, was at the mercy of the city mob. On July 26th,
1647, a mob of rioters had broken into the chamber and, holding
the Speaker in his chair, had forced the members to vote the
recall of Charles to his capital city.[21] Obviously, if they
were not to lose everything they had won in the war, the soldiers had to act.

The Army, headed by Sir Thomas Fairfax and Oliver Cromwell, was the one stable element in the situation that could
keep civil order, and if it was not to see everything disappear
into mob rule, it had to intervene. So it received the Independent members of both Houses who had fled from Westminster,
and entered the city on August 6th.[22] The issue was no longer
whether the nation was to be ruled by legally constituted authorities or by the arbitrary power of the military; there
were no legally constituted authorities with the effective
power to keep any semblance of order. As Edward Sexby, the
agitator, complained, whatever concessions the soldiers had
managed to win from Parliament up to that point had been
granted "rather out of feare then love",[23] and Major Francis
White put the issue bluntly when he observed that there was
"no superintendent authority in this kingdom but what is exercised by the power and force of the sword".[24] In the mind of
Cromwell that force was to be used only in the last extremity--
"I do not know what force is to be used except we cannot get

what is good for the kingdom without force"[25]--but it was undoubtedly the final reality if everything else failed.

2. *The Testimonies of Providence*

In these circumstances--with an untrustworthy and ineffective king, a turbulent capital city, and a parliament that
had become completely unrepresentative of the nation--it is
hardly to be wondered that the Army began to see itself as
more truly representative of the English people than any of
the *de jure* authorities. Furthermore, although the Leveller
Agitators were undoubtedly more secular in their approach to
political theory than the main body of Puritans, they enthusi-
astically accepted the view of Providence held by almost everyone at that time, that regarded success on the battle field as
a sign of divine favour. No modern Marxist has had a more de-
terministic view of history or a stronger belief in the material goals to which history points than had the revolutionary
soldiers of the New Model Army. As Edward Sexby declared to
the Council of Officers at Putney on 28th October, 1647, "We
have been by Providence put upon strange things, such as the
ancientest here doth scarce remember. The Army acting to
these ends, Providence hath been with us."[26] But Sexby went
on to contrast the success they had had in the field, when
they had been sure of their task and singleminded in their
aim, with their recent lack of success in diplomacy, and he
bluntly blamed this failure on Cromwell and Ireton's attempts
to reach a settlement with the king.

They had all 'gone to Egypt for help'[27]--possibly a reference to Parliament's alliance with the Scots--whereas to
Sexby and his Leveller friends it was clear that "the kingdom's cause required expedition" along the radical lines suggested in their paper, *The Case of the Army Stated*, which was
later recast as *The Agreement of the People*.[28] The basic issue throughout these debates in the Army Council was whether
the soldiers were free to impose their radical Constitution
on the nation, or whether they were obligated to work through
the traditional English forms by the promises they had published. From the point of view of the General Officers and
their supporters, the crucial question was how far the Agitators' proposals contravened the statements that the Army had
published earlier in its attempts to secure public trust; but
from the point of view of the Agitators, their proposals were
demanded by common justice, and if there was a question of
'previous engagements', whose were they--the soldiers', or
private engagements with 'that man of blood', Charles Stuart
undertaken by Cromwell and Ireton for their own ends?

There was no doubt in the mind of any in the Army Council,
from Cromwell to the newest Agitator, that they were to be instruments in the hand of God to bring about a more just order
in England, and that purpose would be thwarted only if they
themselves were deflected from the task or if they proved
themselves to be unworthy exponents of God's righteous will.
Whether he was radical or conservative, the Puritan believed
that his own integrity as an exponent and exemplar of biblical
justice was a basic guarantee that Providence would bless his
efforts to bring in the Kingdom of God. That put the edge in
Sexby's speeches, and the agony in Lt.-Col. William Goffe's
self-doubt. Goffe feared that God had been withdrawing himself from their councils and urged that they should hold a
prayer meeting to discover how they had offended the Lord.
When Cromwell threatened to resign his commission rather than
hinder unanimity, Goffe entered this remarkable plea:

> If we would continue to be instruments in
> his hand, let us seriously set ourselves
> before the Lord, and see him and wait upon
> him for conviction of spirits. It is not
> enough for us to say, 'If we have offended
> we will leave the world, we will go and
> confess to the Lord what we have done
> amiss, but we will do no more so.' Aaron
> went up to Hor and died; and Moses was
> favoured to see the land of Canaan--*he*
> did not voluntarily lay himself aside.
> I hope our strayings from God are not so
> great but that a conversion and true hu-
> miliation may recover us again; and I de-
> sire that we may be serious in this, and
> not despise any other instruments that
> God will use. God will have his work
> done: it may be, we think we are the
> only instruments that God hath in his
> hands....[29]

3. *Types of Justice: Retribution*

The philosophical definition of Justice hardly entered
into the head of Puritans, who were still in the euphoria that
came from being able to read the Bible in their own language.
They were convinced that what they read was God's word to
them. Nor were they concerned to make the distinction between
'justice' and 'righteousness', or to recognize scriptural am-

biguities. For the Puritan radicals of the seventeenth century, the divine meaning of justice was self-evident in a scripture that was to be interpreted literally and exactly, and a great deal of the anti-clericalism that one encounters in the sects of the period is to be explained in part as lay reaction to ministerial professionals: exegetical hair-splittings threatened to rob simple christians of the Bible that the Reformation had bequeathed them as a birthright. So justice might be interpreted in terms of God's righteousness, or in terms of the Mosaic Law, but the Puritan did not recognize any essential difference between these interpretations: the second was simply a codification of the first, and they assumed a unity of interpretation had been maintained by all the biblical writers.

Many of the problems that the Protectorate encountered later in the Nominated Parliament or with the Fifth Monarchists was due to the radicals' attempts to sweep away the Common Law, which was ancient and cumbersome but recognized by Englishmen as part of their heritage, and to put the Mosaic Law in its place. It was assumed that the justice about which the Bible speaks is clear, simple and unalterable--as clear and unambiguous as Amos's plumbline (Amos 7:7-9). When the prophet Micah declared, "He hath shewed thee, O man, what is good; and what doth the Lord require of thee, but to do justly, and to love mercy, and to walk humbly with thy god?" (Micah 6:8, K.J.V.) the Puritan (and, I suspect, all later scriptural literalists) had a very clear idea of what 'doing justly' implied, which was drawn from a unified conception of Old Testament ethics. It was clear-cut, even-handed, impartial and in their view absolutely unequivocal, and to lesser mortals it could be very frightening.

Taking the Old Testament scriptures literally, the soldiers in the Army Council had a view of justice that acknowledged a retributive aspect, as when, on receiving the news that a second civil war had broken out, "with tears in their eyes, the officers answered this challenge with a resolution to subdue the kingdom once more and, that accomplished, to bring the King to account for the blood that he had caused to be shed".[30] It was a resolution from which they could not draw back, for this was the direction they believed, in which Providence had pointed them, and their integrity as God's instruments of justice was caught up in the justification of what they were doing. It was later made explicit when the Army's supporters in the House of Commons called for a committee to be appointed "to consider how to proceed in a way of Justice against the King and other Capital offenders".[31] God's justice, even if unpalatable, could not be denied, because it took the nature of a 'call' that must be obeyed.[32]

e can infer from this, however, that when the Puritan spoke
bout justice, he was not likely to confuse it with mere
egality in respect to the law of the land: the trial and
xecution of Charles I was totally illegal, although most of
he soldiers in the New Model Army would have insisted that
t was entirely just. The outbreak of the Second Civil War
n May 1648 unified all elements in the Army on that.

Types of Justice: A Just Social Order

Puritans were also generally agreed that Biblical justice
mplied a more righteous society; but this is where differ-
nces began to appear between the radical Levellers and the
enior officers. Sir Thomas Fairfax took no part in the de-
ates with the soldiers, and left these matters in the hands
f his Lieutenant-General, Oliver Cromwell, and the Commis-
ary-General, Henry Ireton. They represent the more conserva-
ive position that wanted to retain as much as possible the
raditional shape and institutions of English society. On the
ther side, the Levellers had developed a complete social and
olitical program for a new English social order, and they
ere convinced that since justice could not be done for the
ommon people of the land except by the establishment of such
a program, the Army should forthwith sweep away anything that
tood in its way.

The senior officers were also concerned to see a more
just society in England, but they were not committed to any
articular political program, and they were primarily con-
erned with acting justly towards the great body of parliamen-
ary support which expected a certain amount of continuity in
government. Such supporters had certainly not expected to see
all the familiar landmarks torn down. It was this concern
which lay behind Cromwell and Ireton's insistence that the
army must act in a way that was consistent with its previously published promises, and therefore they argued strongly to
retain property qualifications in the right to vote.

The Puritan officers would not have admitted any fundamental difference from the radicals about the ultimate goal,
for, after all, their final objective was the Kingdom of God,
but there *was* a fundamental difference in the way they proposed to pursue that objective. Later historians, with the
advantage of hindsight, have usually endorsed the justice of
the Leveller's demands because it carried within it the claims
of the future, for despite their use of Puritan theology, the
Levellers wished to push English society headlong into the
modern secular world of 'one man, one vote'. They reached
this position by forcing a distinction between the spheres

of Nature and Grace with which the true Puritan could never
feel comfortable or--within his own unified view of society
under God--ultimately concede. Perhaps the Leveller's view
of society owned a similar unity under God, but for *him* it
was the order of Nature (i.e. Creation) that was primary and
determined the pattern of human societies. To that extent
the Levellers could not help but be more 'secular' than Puritans like Cromwell who would reverse that priority. There is,
for example, a contemporary ring in Major William Rainsborough's speeches:

> I do hear nothing at all that can con-
> vince me, why any man that is born in Eng-
> land ought not to have his voice in elec-
> tion of burgesses. It is said that if a
> man have not a permanent interest, he can
> have no claim; and [that] we must be no
> freer than the laws will let us be, and
> that there is no [law in any] chronicle
> will let us be freer than that we [now]
> enjoy.[33]

Then in commenting upon an earlier contribution, he related
rational justice (as a Law of Nature) to his understanding of
Biblical justice (the Law of God):

> I do think that the main cause why
> Almighty God gave men reason, it was that
> they should make use of that reason, and
> that they should improve it for that end
> and purpose that God gave them. And
> truly, I think that half a loaf is better
> than none if a man be anhungry....And
> therefore I say, that either it must be
> the Law of God or the law of man that
> must prohibit the meanest man in the
> kingdom to have this benefit as well as
> the greatest. I do not find anything in
> the Law of God, that a lord shall choose
> twenty burgesses, and a gentleman but two,
> or a poor man shall choose none: I find
> no such thing in the Law of Nature, nor
> in the Law of Nations. But I do find
> that all Englishmen must be subject to
> English laws, and I do verily believe
> that there is no man but will say that
> the foundation of all law lies in the
> people....

> ...And therefore I do [think], and am
> still of the same opinion, that every
> man born in England cannot, ought not,
> neither by the Law of God nor the Law
> of Nature, to be exempted from the
> choice of those who are to make laws
> for him to live under, and for him,
> for aught I know, to lose his life
> under.[34]

At one point in the debate Ireton had argued that God himself
had instituted property, and hence, presumably, the property
qualification for voting. Rainsborough responded and insisted
that he and his colleagues were not seeking to bring about
anarchy, but he refused to budge from his original position.[35]

Edward Sexby put the issue of political justice about as
plainly as it could be stated for the troopers who had borne
the brunt of the warfare:

> ...There are many thousands of us soldiers
> that have ventured our lives; we have had
> little propriety in the kingdom as to our
> estates, yet we have had a birthright.
> But it seems now, except a man hath a
> fixed estate in this kingdom, he hath no
> right in this kingdom. I wonder we were
> so much deceived. If we had not a right
> to the kingdom, we were mere mercenary
> soldiers....
>   I shall tell you in a word my reso-
> lution. I am resolved to give my birth-
> right to none.[36]

To whatever extent the Levellers gave lip-service to
Puritan theology, here they were not putting forward their
claims as church members but as citizen-soldiers. They maintained as much as their senior officers that there was no
contradiction between the Law of God and the Law of Nature,
but if there was any apparent conflict then they insisted
that the Law of Nature provided the basis for exegeting the
Law of God: they point the way in which the seventeenth century world of the National Covenant would eventually become
the eighteenth century world of the *Contrat Social*.

By modern standards, the position taken by Cromwell and
Ireton appears far less consistent, but it was no less concerned with justice. The issue was between those who were

ready to employ any means (even methods regarded by some as
unjust) to secure a more egalitarian society immediately, and
those who were anxious to act justly towards those who had supported their cause, even if it meant tolerating an imperfect
society indefinitely. It was expressed very simply by Ireton,
who declared that if Providence saw fit to sweep away all the
traditional forms of society, he hoped he would recognize the
hand of God in it and be prepared to submit to it, but he
hoped that God "will so lead this Army, that they may not incur sin, or bring scandal on the name of God, and the name of
the people of God",[37] and for that reason he urged that they
should consider the engagements they had undertaken and published to the nation.

This represented Cromwell's position, and the debate in
the Army Council was a classic example of the perennial conflict between the radical revolutionary and the conservative
reformer. The positions were often irreconcilable, but that
is not because one side was exclusively concerned with justice
while the other was involved only with injustice; both were
concerned with social and political justice, and both were
involved in injustice, but at different points.

Cromwell himself stated the dilemma in a later debate
when he observed:

> Truly we have heard many speaking to us;
> and I cannot but think that in many of
> those things God hath spoke to us. I
> cannot but think that in most that have
> spoke there hath been something of God
> laid forth to us; and yet there have
> been several contradictions in what
> hath been spoken. But certainly God
> is not the author of contradictions.
> The contradictions are not so much in
> the end as in the way. I cannot see
> but that we all speak to the same end,
> and the mistakes are only in the way.
> The end is to deliver this nation from
> oppression and slavery, to accomplish
> that work that God hath carried us on
> in, to establish our hopes of an end
> of justice and righteousness in it.
> We agree thus far.[38]

Cromwell faced a basic problem that appeared in Puritan-
ism--if the Bible spoke with such clear unanimity on these issues, why was it that sincere Christians, as most of these men

appeared to be, could arrive at such fundamentally different answers? It was precisely the same dilemma that Independent and Presbyterian Puritans were facing as they debated the church polity in the Westminster Assembly and which Winthrop had faced with the Antinomians in New England: if the Bible offered a unified, unambiguous and essentially clear answer to all the fundamental questions, how could Christians differ? There had been "several contradictions in what had been spoken. But certainly God is not the author of contradictions." Cromwell minimized the differences by suggesting that they were concerned with method rather than with substance, but still the questions remained, why did the differences arise and how were they to be resolved? The existence of this dilemma in a movement that from the first had claimed a 'plain sense' for scripture and a consensus of biblical unanimity,[39] forced men like Cromwell to search for more sophisticated answers in their theology.

Early in the debates Henry Ireton had admitted that there were many things in the Levellers' proposals that he would like to see incorporated into the national settlement,[40] but the matters at issue between them were those of proper timing, of practicality, and of their own political integrity before the nation. The Leveller, John Wildman argued that the sole criterion as to whether the Army's earlier promises should be honoured or not was to be decided by the inherent justice of those documents--by which he meant, of course, the extent to which they supported the Levellers' proposals. Then Ireton had laid down the basis of the conservative case when he affirmed that society itself was based on the general law that a contract was to be honoured, and he went on:

> Covenants freely made, freely entered into,
> must be kept one with another. Take away
> that, I do not know what ground there is
> of anything you can call any man's right.
> I would very fain know what you gentlemen,
> or any other, do account the right you have
> to anything in England--anything of estate,
> land or goods, that you have, what ground,
> what right you have to it. What right hath
> any man to anything if you lay not [down]
> that principle, that we are to keep cove-
> nant? If you resort only to the Law of
> Nature, by the Law of Nature you have no
> more right to this land, or anything else,
> than I have. I have as much right to take
> hold of anything that is for my sustenance,
> [to] take hold of anything that I have a

> desire to for my satisfaction, as you.
> But here comes the foundation of all
> right that I understand to be betwixt
> men...we are under a contract, we are
> under an agreement....[41]

Ireton could not give primacy to the Law of Nature. For
him, the natural state of humanity was far closer to the continual state of warfare depicted later in Thomas Hobbes's
Leviathan than it was to the freedom and innocence presupposed
in Rousseau's *Contrat Social*. For the Puritan Ireton, human
laws were grounded not in a *jus naturale* but in the Law of God,
and because of that, the civil magistrate had a proper place
in God's plan: although abstract justice or the just society
was not to be equated with human laws, one could not assume
that justice would be done by simply discarding them.

At the heart of his position there was the sacredness of
the biblical idea of covenant: this was the reason for the
Scots' insistence on a 'Solemn League and Covenant' with England in 1643[42] and their persistent demand that Presbyterian
uniformity should be established in England under its terms,
just as in the Army debates it was the basis of Ireton's plea
that the Army could not simply ignore its previously published
statements.

Only a biblical principle that was more immediate and imperative could abrogate this biblical principle--only when
Providence revealed its will (justice) through events in a
more immediate way would these men feel themselves justified
in acting without regard for earlier declarations. Such a moment came in May 1648 when the Duke of Hamilton's army invaded England, and through his complicity in this renewed outbreak of civil war the King seemed to have forfeited all further consideration.[43]

IV

Towards a More Developed Political Ethic

The difference of approach between the radicals and the
conservatives in the New Model Army's debates was real, and
this suggests that in the development of political ethics
Puritanism could move in two directions. What we may call
'rationalistic puritanism' (or a society that had been influenced but not altogether committed to Puritan theology) would

end to move like the Levellers in an essentially secular, rationalist direction. On the other hand, Puritanism proper always had to deal with the primacy of revealed truth, not only in its understanding of the Church but also in its understanding of society. It would necessarily be committed to an ongoing principle of exegeting that revelation in relationship to human institutions.

However, what we see at the time of the Army debates is that the participants were poised. Whether they belong to the right wing or the left wing of the movement, they tended to apply Old Testament standards of Justice uncritically, and made little distinction between the righteousness of God and the justice demanded of Israel in civil matters. Indeed, the soldiers of the New Model Army were deeply suspicious of those clerical gentlemen who from their London pulpits and in the Westminster Assembly seemed to be trying to undercut the revolution by tricks of linguistic and exegetical expertise.[44]

It may even have been a major reason why they were becoming suspicious of the better-educated officers.[45] They must have sensed in Cromwell and Ireton a more sophisticated approach to the problems of political ethics than they were prepared to recognize. This more sophisticated approach may have been due to the ambiguity in which the officers sensed themselves to be as they tried to reconcile their Puritan faith and revolutionary hopes to the practical possibilities in England at that time.

Christian 'Realism'

Although the Levellers drew more heavily on purely rational arguments than the more religiously oriented officers like Colonel Goffe, the General Officers demonstrate a less doctrinaire and, at one level, a more pragmatic attitude to political questions than the radicals. For Cromwell, justice involved not only what was ideally 'just' but also what was politically viable, and this was possible because he had an overwhelming sense that he was but an instrument in the hands of a Providence that was revealing his will in the situation: God was revealing *in events* what he wanted English society to be.

This pragmatism, which is certainly not to be dismissed as simply rationalistic, is illustrated in a remarkable speech by Oliver Cromwell at the time when the Levellers' 'paper' had first been submitted. He feared that if constitutional theorizing became widespread, it could lead to social chaos and the division of the country into mutually independent and hostile districts--indeed, to the kind of localized nationalism which the 'United Kingdom' has witnessed in recent years:

> I ask you whether it be not fit for every
> honest man seriously to lay that upon his
> heart? And if so, what would that produce
> but an absolute desolation--an absolute
> desolation to the nation--and we in the
> meantime tell the nation: 'It is for
> your liberty; 'tis for your privilege;
> 'tis for your good.' (Pray God it prove,
> so whatsoever course we run.) But truly,
> I think we are not only to consider what
> the consequences are if there were noth-
> ing else but this paper, but we are to
> consider the probability of the ways and
> means to accomplish [the thing proposed]:
> that is to say, whether, according to
> reason and judgment, the spirits and
> temper of the people of this nation are
> prepared to receive and to go on along
> with it, and [whether] those great dif-
> ficulties [that] lie in our way [are] in
> a likelihood to be either overcome or re-
> moved. Truly, to anything that's good,
> there's no doubt on it, objections may
> be made and framed; but let every honest
> man consider whether or no there be not
> very real objections [to this] in point
> of difficulty.[46]

But the word 'reason' was, of course, a 'trigger word' to seventeenth century Puritans. Was the Lieutenant-General of the Puritan Army suggesting that *reason* should take prior- ity over *faith*? Cromwell's digression on the relationship be- tween the exercise of reason and the guidance of the Holy Spirit may seem to have very little to do with the constitu- tional and political questions at issue, but it was extremely germane to the way in which these men thought. His plea that they should decide matters with 'reason and judgment' would otherwise have been immediately seized upon by his opponents. No seventeenth century Puritan could concede that reason was to have precedence over faith, and could not Edward Sexby, John Wildman and their friends claim faith and the guidance of the Holy Spirit with as much justification as Cromwell him- self? Oliver would have to do better than that if he was to get a little less heat and more light into the discussion. So he ploughed into this lengthy digression:

I know a man may answer all difficulties
with faith, and faith will answer all difficulties really where it is, but we are
very apt, all of us, to call that faith,
that perhaps may be but carnal imagination, and carnal reasonings. Give me
leave to say this. There will be very
great mountains in the way of this, if
this were the thing in present consideration; and, therefore, we ought to consider the consequences, and God hath
given us our reason that we may do this.
It is not enough to propose things that
are good in the end, but suppose this
model were an excellent model, and fit
for England and the kingdom to receive,
it is our duty as Christians and men to
consider consequences, and to consider
the way.[47]

Then he brought himself back to the point at issue:

It is not enough for us to insist
upon good things. That every one would
do. There is not [one in] forty of us
but could prescribe many things exceeding
plausible--and hardly anything worse than
our present condition, take it with all
the troubles that are upon us. It is not
enough for us to propose good things, but
it behoves honest men and Christians (that
really will approve themselves so before
God and men) to see whether or not they
be in a condition--whether, taking all
things into consideration, they may
honestly endeavour and attempt that
that is fairly and plausibly proposed.[48]

A new element was entering the picture. It was no longer the
'dual ethic' and the unadorned application of Old Testament
concepts of justice in the search for a just society. They
were required to act in a reasonable and responsible way, but
this did not simply arise from rationalism, for they were to
act 'as Christians and men to consider consequences'.

2. *'Christian' Realism*

To Cromwell this was much more than secular pragmatism. They were to act as 'honest men and Christian (that really will approve themselves so before God and men)': their profession of Christian faith implied certain public standards of conduct that should be obvious to everyone, so that when justice was done it would be recognized as the justice of God's people. The Old Testament might still provide the basic standard of justice in society, but the reasonable way in which it was to be applied was to be characteristically and recognizably Christian.

Later in the debate, when Ireton found it necessary to defend his actions as a negotiator, he made the point explicit. Ireton declared that he didn't care much one way or the other about the Army's earlier pronouncements in themselves, "but I look upon this Army as having carried with it hitherto the name of God, and having carried with it hitherto the interest of the people of God, and the interest which is God's interest, the honour of his name, the good and freedom and safety and happiness of his people".[49] God had appeared for them in their military successes, and "...we have carried the name of God (and I hope not in show, but in reality), professing to act, and to work, as we have thought, in our judgments and consciences, God to lead us; professing to act to those ends that we have thought to be answerable and suitable to the mind of God, so far as it hath been known to us".[50]

Since that was so, he continued, it obviously behooved them not to act in a way that would bring scandal either on God's name or on the name of his people. Where they had seen God's leading they had been obedient to him, even when it seemed contrary to their own reason.

Implicit within all of Ireton's words was the claim that God would not lead them into policies that would be sinful or dishonourable, and his words also possibly contain the warning that God would certainly not justify them if they adopted unjust policies. In a passage cited earlier which we should now quote more fully, Ireton protested against the suspicion that he and Cromwell were for their own private reasons committed to maintaining the traditional constitution of King, Lords and Commons:

> For whatever I find the work of God tending to, I should desire quietly to submit to. If God saw it good to destroy, not only King and Lords, but all distinctions

of degrees—nay if it go further, to destroy all property, that there's no such
thing left, that there be nothing at all
of civil constitution left in the kingdom—if I see the hand of God in it I
hope I shall with quietness acquiesce,
and submit to it, and not resist it.
But still I think that God certainly
will so lead those that are his, and I
hope too he will so lead this Army, that
they may not incur sin, or bring scandal
upon the name of God, and the name of
the people of God, that are both so
nearly concerned in what this Army does.
And [therefore] it is my wish, upon
those grounds that I before declared,
which made the consideration of this
Army dear and tender to me, [that] we
may take heed, [that] we may consider
first engagements, so far as they are
engagements publicly of the Army. I
do not speak of particular [i.e. private engagements]; I would not have
them considered, if there be any. And
secondly, I would have us consider of
this: that our ways and workings and
actings, and the acting of the Army, so
far as the counsels of those prevail in
it who have anything of the spirit of
Jesus Christ, may appear suitable to
that spirit. And [as] I would [not]
have this Army...incur the scandal of
neglecting engagements, and laying
aside all consideration of engagements,
and [the scandal] of juggling, and deceiving, and deluding the world, making them believe things in times of
extremity which they never meant; so
I would [not] have us give the world
occasion to think that we are the dis-
turbers of the peace of mankind.[51]

There are several things that might be worthy of comment
i this lengthy extract—we might, for example, point to the
ntrast between revolutionary principles based upon natural
ghts and those based upon providential leading that Ireton
presses here; but the main point for our purpose is that in
is passage Ireton was approaching again the problem of Puri-
n social ethics. In Ireton's view, it was not enough that

the Army should regard itself as the instrument of God's purpose, or even that their successes seem to confirm this sense
of vocation, but the Army's actions had to be intrinsically
and christianly ethical. It was the issue of credibility:
the sense of vocation and of being providentially led must
ultimately be authenticated by evidence of the Spirit in those
called--"our ways and workings and actings" ought to appear
suitable to "the spirit of Jesus Christ".

This does not mean that Ireton had switched to the Sermon
on the Mount as his ethic for public affairs, since in dealing
with enemies on the field of battle it is doubtful if he would
have gone beyond the equity of the Mosaic Law, but apparently
he would have maintained that when this Law is applied by
Christians, it must be held within the context of the gospel.

Later in the debate (in a speech quoted earlier[52]) Cromwell stated the same position.

In that speech Cromwell had attempted a summary of the
points at issue between himself and the radicals, and had made
the comment that he believed that all those present were coming to a common mind about the danger they apprehended from
the power of the King and the Lords. He went on to say, "I
do to my best observation find unanimity amongst us all that
we would set up neither. Thus far I find us to be agreed, I
think it is of God."[53] But he wanted to be absolutely sure
he was reading God's will for England correctly, because although he admitted he was a person who awaited 'some extra-
ordinary dispensations' to reveal God's will in accordance
with prophecies concerning the latter days in which they were
living, yet he was extremely wary of promiscuous 'prophesy-
ing', and he reminded his hearers that the more sure word of
prophecy was to be found in scripture.

In the early part of the speech I feel Cromwell is cir-
cling around the problem of how the Army was to act christianly. In some of his earlier speeches he had seemed to
appeal to pragmatism or to reason, but as a good Calvinist he
could hardly be satisfied with that as his final answer. As
in so many of his other speeches, the solution seems to have
become clearer to him in the course of his speaking:

> ...And this to me seems to be very clear,
> how we are to judge of the apprehension of
> men [as] to particular cases, whether it
> be of God or no. When it doth not carry
> its evidence with it, of the power of God
> to convince us clearly, our best way is to

> judge the conformity or disformity of [it
> with] the law written within us, which is
> the law of the Spirit of God, the mind of
> God, the mind of Christ.[54]

He then turned appreciatively to the earlier comments of
Lt. Colonel John Jubbes, who had reminded them all that the
only authority they had came from Jesus Christ and was to be
recognized in the Christian virtues. But this also presented
a problem to Cromwell, because after all, they had had to
fight hard for their liberties and they had to act in a situation that was obviously secular. So he commented on that:

> On the other hand, I think that he that
> would decline the doing of justice where
> there is no place for mercy, and the
> exercise of the ways of force, for the
> safety of the kingdom, where there is
> no other way to save it, and would de-
> cline these out of the apprehensions of
> danger and difficulties in it, he that
> leads that way, on the other hand, doth
> [also] truly lead us from that which is
> the law of the Spirit of Life, the law
> written in our hearts.

Here is an extension of the 'dual ethic', on one side based
upon justice in relation to secular society in general and
to the situation of civil war in particular, and on the other
based upon mercy as the rule for a Christian community; yet
insofar as both were governed by 'the law written in our
hearts', both of these, in Cromwell's view, were to be accepted as conformable to God's will and therefore Christian.

Cromwell's statement of the extent to which the Army
council was agreed upon the next steps to be taken in the
settlement of the nation prepares us in some measure for a
radical change in his attitude to Charles I, but in the concluding paragraphs of this same speech he reveals not only his
conviction that the King would be destroyed but also the grim
forecast that this would be achieved in a way that would leave
the Army with a clear conscience. The passage indicates the
importance that these men placed on their own personal integrity before God as the authentication of the justice they were
trying to establish in society:

> I do wish that they[55] will take heed of
> that which some men are apt to be carried

away be, [namely] apprehensions that God
will destroy these persons or that power;
for that they may mistake in. And though
[I] myself do concur with them, and perhaps concur with them upon some ground
that God will do so, yet let us [not]
make those things to be our rule which
we cannot so clearly know to be the mind
of God. I mean in particular things let
us not make those our rules: that 'this
[is] to be done; [this] is the mind of
God; we must work to it.' But at least
[let] those to whom this is not made
clear, though they do think it probable
that God will destroy them, yet let them
make this [a] rule to themselves:
'Though God have a purpose to destroy
them, and though I should find a desire
to destroy them--though a Christian
spirit can hardly find it for itself--
yet God can do it without necessitating
us to do a thing which is scandalous, or
sin, or which would bring a dishonour to
his name.' And therefore those that are
of that mind, let them wait upon God for
such a way when the thing may be done
without sin, and without scandal too.
Surely what God would have us do, he
does not desire we should step out of
the way for it. This is the caution,
on the one hand, that we do no wrong to
one or other, and that we abstain from
all appearance of wrong, and for that
purpose avoid the bringing of a scandal
to the name of God, and to his people
upon whom his name is bestowed.[56]

Although this is not the clearest of Cromwell's public
utterances, its meaning is not in much doubt. The downfall of
the King was foreseen not with any personal malice, but in
terms of what the speaker believed would be the intervention
of Providence. The members of the Puritan Army must not pre-
sume to anticipate that event or directly hasten it, for it
would be accomplished by God himself, and Charles in the mean-
time must be allowed to heap upon himself divine judgment.
One cannot escape the grim detachment that runs through the
passage, and it clearly demonstrates that Cromwell expected
Charles's ruin some time before there is any evidence that he
had any hand in it himself, for he was stating here not what

he meant to do, but what he felt had been decreed and would be accomplished by Providence. Whatever the soldiers' views about that, he was sure that they should act scrupulously in accordance with their previous published statements, for, he said, "if we do act according to that mind and that spirit and that law which I have before spoken of[57]...God will lead us to what shall be his way, as many of us as he shall incline their minds to, and the rest in their way in due time".[58]

Several years later, when his military prowess had brought him to the pinnacle of power, Cromwell tried to divest himself of responsibility for governing by putting the civil authority into the hands of the Nominated Parliament; but on July 4th, 1653 he initiated the new government by delivering to the members of Parliament a remarkable speech[58] which, I have suggested elsewhere, has all the characteristics of an Ordination Charge.[59] This speech is particularly germane to our present subject because it illustrates the way in which Cromwell was trying to relate the Old and New Testaments in determining the conduct appropriate to a Christian magistrate. His initial appeal was to the Old Testament--to Hosea 11:12[60] and II Samuel 23:3,[61] but then he finds himself beginning to address them as Christian magistrates and at once he begins to expound James 3:17, 18 and at once he is calling on them to do no more than is required of them *as Christians*:

> Truly the judgment of truth will teach you to be as just towards an unbeliever as towards a believer; and it is our duty to do so. I confess I have often said, foolishly, I had rather miscarry to a believer than to an unbeliever. This may seem a paradox:--but let's take heed of doing that which is evil to either! If God fill your hearts with such a spirit as Moses had, and as Paul had, which was not a spirit for believers only, but for the whole people! Moses, he could die for them; wish himself blotted out of God's book: Paul could wish himself accursed for his countrymen after the flesh, so full of affection were their spirits unto all. And truly this would help you to execute the judgment of truth, and of mercy also.[62]

The whole of this speech might be interpreted by the way in which the 'dual ethic' had been transmuted in the mind of

Cromwell into a new understanding of the way in which social ethics should be interpreted by the Christian magistrate. Through his somewhat involved and always tortuous phrases it shows him using the Spirit of the New Testament to interpret the Old Testament ethic of justice within a civil society. And that is not very different from the Christian Realism that has been developed by theologians in our own twentieth century.[63]

Cromwell and his associates faced unprecedented responsibilities in a situation to which they were firmly convinced they had been brought by God. In the deep wrestling they had with their own consciences during the course of these events, it appears that a new political ethic was beginning to take shape; it may have begun with a view of justice extrapolated literally from the pages of the Old Testament, but they came to see that it was a concept of justice that had to be applied by Christians in a 'Christian' way, in accordance with 'a Christian spirit' and the law that is 'written in our hearts'. Because of this, it was not sufficient to apply the strict justice of the Old Testament literally, for the righteousness that God's people sought to establish in the kingdom had to be a righteousness that would redound to God's honour and appear obvious to all: it demanded actions and policies that would themselves be finally justified before God by the credibility of those who were God's chosen instruments. That is where the Puritans and most modern revolutionaries part company.

NOTES

1. For ecclesiological restorationism, see Robert S. Paul, *The Church in Search of Its Self*, Grand Rapids, 1972, chapter IV.

2. *The Lord Protector: Religion and Politics in the Life of Oliver Cromwell*, London, 1955.

3. In this study the word 'ethic' is not used as a synonymn for 'morals', but rather in line with the distinction which Kenneth Kirk made between 'christian ethics' and 'christian morals', i.e., employing the former to designate the optimum standard of christian behaviour, and the latter to indicate the minimum standard. Cf. K. E. Kirk (ed.), *The Study of Theology*, London, 1939, pp. 363f.

4. Cf. *The Lord Protector*, p. 60, note 4.

5. *Ibid.* p. 61, note 3.

6. It is clear that English Puritan theologians gained considerable reputation in Europe for their interest in practical theology, and their theologians devoted a great deal of attention to the relationship between sound doctrine and right action. Cf. Keith L. Sprunger, *The Learned Doctor Ames* (Urbana, University of Illinois, 1972) for the influence of William Ames on the mainland of Europe. Puritan 'Cases of Concience', such as Richard Baxter's *A Christian Directory* (London, 1673), have yet to receive the scholarly critical examination they deserve.

7. A. S. P. Woodhouse, *Puritanism and Liberty: Being the Army Debates (1647-9) with Supplementary Documents*, London, 1938, Introduction [p. 39]: I agree with most of Woodhouse's insights, but in applying his 'principle of segregation' too widely, I think we might assume that the Puritans became secularized too quickly. The process of secularization could not really develop until the doctrine of the church and church discipline had eroded in the Puritan communities. But during the time of the Army Debates, there is no indication of any such erosion of faith or ecclesiology, except among the more politically-minded Levellers.

8. *Ibid.* [p. 18]. Square brackets around the pagination of this work indicate that it is from Woodhouse's Introduction.

9. *Ibid.* [p. 39].

10. *Ibid.* I would emphasize, however, that if we are speaking of the Puritans--as distinct from some of the sectarian radicals--this two-fold system of nature and grace does not imply 'natural' system which is secular and one system of grace that is secular. Both systems to them would be regarded as biblically founded and under the immediate sovereignty of God.

11. *Ibid.* [p. 58]. Cf. [pp. 57-60]. See also my notes 7 and 10 above.

12. It has been suggested that to speak of 'nature' and 'grace' as autonomous spheres with their own absolute standards of ethics sounds hyper-Lutheran, and the Puritans were not Lutherans. This may be so, because I do not think it impossible that going to the same biblical source as Luther, they may have unknowingly come away with similar answers on this issue. But to me the Puritans seem to be far closer to Calvin's teaching about the two kingdoms in man, "a temporal and a spiritual jurisdiction" [*iurisdictio spiritualis et temporalis*], for Calvin observed that "there are in man, so to speak, two worlds, over which different kings and different laws have authority" (*Institutes* III. xix. 15), and although he is speaking about the individual, it is clear from the remainder of this section that he intended his thought here to be carried over into what he would say later on civil government. Calvin, *The Institutes of the Christian Religion* [The Library of Christian Classics, Vol. XX], Philadelphia, 1960, edited by John T. McNeill, and translated by Ford Lewis Battles.

13. This is not to deny that the dichotomy represented in Woodhouse's 'principle of segregation' would not become more pronounced and accelerate a very rapid descent into secularism during Puritanism's decline after 1660. After the Restoration of the monarchy Puritan churches were in no position to assert themselves and their discipline became largely ineffective. Furthermore, Deism in the Church and cynicism in society provided a fertile soil in which the later secularism could grow.

14. John F. Wilson, *Pulpit in Parliament*, Princeton, N. J., 1969, p. 148.

15. *Ibid.* p. 149.

16. *Ibid.* p. 143, quoting *An Apologie of the Church of New England*, 1643, p. 8.

17.   Harold Field Worthley, in a letter to the present writer.

18.   The suspicions and anger of John Lilburne, the ideological leader of the Levellers, were deliberately inflamed by Sir Lewis Dives, a fellow-prisoner with Lilburne in the Tower, by constantly feeding him with hints of an accommodation with Charles I by Cromwell and Ireton for their own personal gain, because Dives "judged it for the King's service to divide Cromwell and the Army". Sir John Berkeley's *Memoirs*, 1699, p. 41. See also Sir Lewis Dives Correspondence with Charles I during this period, in 'The Tower of London Letter-Book of Sir Lewis Dyve, 1646-47', edited by H. G. Tibbutt, *The Publications of the Bedfordshire Historical Record Society*, Vol. XXXVIII, 1958, pp. 49-96.

19.   The Army Debates were first transcribed and edited by Sir Charles Firth in *The Clarke Papers*, 1891-1901. This contains a good deal more contemporary material than Woodhouse's *Puritanism and Liberty*, but Woodhouse's book represents the most available and best research on the debates themselves.

20.   We are reminded of the secular immigrants who had accompanied the Pilgrims in the Mayflower. The Mayflower Compact was "occasioned partly by the discontented and mutinous speeches that some of the strangers amongst them had let fall from them in the ship--That when they came a shore they would use their owe libertie; for none had power to command them, the patent they had being for Virginia, and not for New-england, which belonged to another Government, with which the Virginia Company had nothing to doe." William Bradford, *History of Plymouth Plantation*, edited by William T. Davis, 1908, p. 106. The Army debates of 1647-9 were, in a sense, similar to the attempt of the godly people on the Mayflower to provide a new basis for civil order.

21.   See Sir Lewis Dives's letters to Charles I, July 26th and 31st, 1647, in 'The Tower of London Letter-Book of Sir Lewis Dyve, 1646-47', *The Publications of the Beds. Hist. Soc.* XXXVIII, 1958, p. 72.

22.   Cf. *ibid.* pp. 74ff.

23.   Sir Charles Firth (ed.), *The Clarke Papers* (1891-1901), I, p. 206.

24.   *A Copie of a Letter...by Francis White*, 1647. This was a little too blunt for even the Army Council, and White was expelled for making this statement.

25. *Puritanism and Liberty*, p. 418; cf. W. C. Abbott, *The Writings and Speeches of Oliver Cromwell*, Cambridge, Mass., 1937-1947, I, p. 483.

26. *Puritanism and Liberty*, p. 1.

27. Cf. Isaiah 31:1 (cf. 36:6, 9; 2 Kings 18:21, 28). I think this was an oblique reference in Sexby's speech to the alliance with the Scots, for at that time the Scots were trying to block everything the Levellers wanted.

28. Cf. Stuart E. Prall (ed.), *The Puritan Revolution*, Garden City, N. Y., 1968, pp. 225-238; S. R. Gardiner (ed.), *Constitutional Documents of the Puritan Revolution*, Oxford, 1906, pp. 333ff.

29. *Puritanism and Liberty*, p. 20.

30. May 1648, Abbott, *Writings and Speeches of O. C.*, I, p. 599.

31. Quoted from the *Journals of the House of Commons*, VI, 102, by W. C. Abbott in *Writings and Speeches of O. C.*, I, p. 716.

32. Note Cromwell's attitude at the time of the King's execution, *The Lord Protector*, pp. 181-195.

33. *Puritanism and Liberty*, p. 55. Square brackets are employed by Woodhouse to make the sense clear where the text is defective.

34. *Ibid.* pp. 55-6.

35. *Ibid.* p. 59.

36. *Ibid.* p. 69.

37. *Ibid.* p. 50.

38. *Ibid.* p. 104.

39. In *The Art of Prophecying*, William Perkins, who had probably been the greatest single influence on the men who were to become the Puritan leaders during the early Stuart period, had maintained that in expounding the Bible, "There is one onely sense, and the same is the literall", and he had maintained that "The supreame and absolute meane of interpretation is the Scripture it selfe." *The Workes of that Famovs and Worthie Minister of Christ in the Universitie of Cambridge,*

M. W. Perkins, London, 1608-9, II, 737.

40. *Puritanism and Liberty*, p. 10f.

41. *Ibid.* p. 26.

42. Robert Baillie in his account of the debate in the Scottish General Assembly on the proposed alliance with England in 1643, wrote, "The English were for a civill League, we were for a religious Covenant." *The Letters and Journals of Robert Baillie, A.M.*, 1841, II, 90.

43. Cf. *The Lord Protector*, pp. 151-163.

44. See Richard Baxter's account of what he found among the troops of the New Model Army, *Reliquiae Baxterianae*, 1696, I, 50ff.

45. Cromwell and Ireton had both been at universities and then studied law in the London Inns of Court--Cromwell at Sidney Sussex College, Cambridge, and then at Lincoln's Inn; Ireton at Trinity College, Oxford, and then at the Middle Temple. Cromwell did not hesitate to correct what he regarded as Sexby's faulty exegesis; *Puritanism and Liberty*, p. 103.

46. *Ibid.* p. 8.

47. *Ibid.*

48. *Ibid.* pp. 8-9.

49. *Ibid.* p. 49.

50. *Ibid.*

51. *Ibid.* pp. 50f.

52. Cf. *supra* p. 266 and note 38.   The whole speech is in *Puritanism and Liberty*, pp. 103-7.

53. *Ibid.* p. 104.

54. *Ibid.* p. 105.

55. I.e., The radicals, who were already determined to get rid of monarchy and the nobility.

56. *Ibid.* p. 106f.

57. "The law written within us, which is the law of the

Spirit of God, the mind of God, the mind of Christ." *Ibid.* p. 105.

58. *Ibid.* p. 107.

59. *The Lord Protector*, pp. 276-280. Cf. Abbott, *op. cit.*, III, 52-66.

60. "Judah yet ruleth with God, and is faithful with the saints" (KJV).

61. "He that ruleth over men must be just, ruling in the fear of God." Abbott, apparently following the faulty reference given by Carlyle, erroneously cites this as II Sam. *21*:3. Cf. Abbott, *op. cit.*, III, 61, note 34, and Mrs. S. C. Lomas's edition of Carlyle's *The Letters and Speeches of Oliver Cromwell*, New York, 1904, II, 291.

62. Abbott, *op. cit.*, III, 61f.

63. E.g. Emil Brunner, *Justice and the Social Order*, London, 1945, pp. 22-28.

14

HISTORICAL DEVELOPMENT AND IMPLICATIONS
OF THE FILIOQUE CONTROVERSY

Dietrich Ritschl

The church in the West, in a long and by no means clearly planned theological development, has added the word 'filioque' to the phrase 'the Holy Spirit...who proceeds from the Father' in the Nicene-Constantinopolitan Creed, the only truly ecumenical creed in Christianity. The thesis is that the Spirit proceeds from the Father *and* from the Son. This reference to the procession of the Holy Spirit would be completely misunderstood if it were taken to be something other than a reference to an inner-trinitarian process. 'Within' the triune God, within the 'immanent Trinity', the Holy Spirit is to be understood as experiencing an eternal *processio* from both the Father and the Son. To understand the controversy over this issue,[1] one must try to let one's thoughts sink into the classical trinitarian modes of argumentation. The theologian will then discover-- perhaps much to his surprise--that the issue is of enormous relevance to our contemporary understanding of the church, of ethics, of authoritative teaching and--last but not least--of the various forms of the charismatic movements in our time. It could be argued, of course, that it is daring to move such subtle issues of inner-trinitarian speculations to the center of attention, especially at a time when many of us find it difficult to justify any God-talk at all. However, it could well be the case that the very study of this subtle issue will show that Western theology has suffered for a long time from a tendency to speak of God "in general", i.e. not of God as the triune God. Such modalistic tendency (the reduction of Father, Son and Spirit to three aspects of the Godhead, as it were) would indeed create difficulties for 'God-talk'.

Behind the controversy lies a conception of the Trinity which is different in the Eastern and the Western parts of the early Church. The controversy itself, however, had at its center at all times the unilateral decision of the West to add an important trinitarian clause to the ecumenical creed. It is difficult throughout the history of the controversy to draw dividing lines between theological and political thoughts and sentiments. The early Western theologians' incomplete understanding of the intricacies of Eastern theology, and the Eastern theologians' difficulties in appreciating Western church historical developments, as well as their criticism of Roman papal authority, added much to the complexity of the controversy. The situation is further burdened by the fact that Western theology did not display any convincing consistency in defending the Filioque theologically. Medieval theologians, notably Anselm and Thomas Aquinas, advanced justifications which were quite different from the traditional 'double procession' as taught by Augustine or in the 'Athanasianum'.

The Western Church's addition of the Filioque to the NC-Creed[2] has been refuted by theologians of the Orthodox Churches at different stages of the history of the controversy[3] for at least three reasons. The addition is said to be: a) non-canonical, i.e. not based upon ecumenical council decisions, b) not grounded in the NT and in early tradition, and c) dogmatically untrue and of dangerous consequences. Orthodoxy today can look back to an impressive array of defenders of the original text of the NC-Creed, reaching from John of Damascus to Patriarch Anthimos' reply to Pope Leo XIII in 1894.

The problem of dealing with this controversy today presents itself on two levels:

1. Is the Filioque merely an addition to the text of the NC-Creed--an addition which contemporary orthodox theologians could perhaps tolerate or explain historically as a typical expression of Ambrosian-Augustinian trinitarian thoughts? Or, is the Filioque the symptom of a deep difference in the Eastern and Western understanding of the Trinity, and, in consequence, of piety and worship, of the dogmatic understanding of the meaning of the presence of Christ as well as of the Holy Spirit's contact with the church and with mankind?

2. The Filioque is considered in the East and in the West in quite different ways and an entirely different degree of importance is assigned to it in the two parts of the church. This is so not because of different historical analyses, but primarily because of the fact that the West assigns at least as much dignity to the Apostles' Creed as it does to the NC-Creed. Moreover, the importance of fixed credal formulations is seen differently in East and West. (One will also have to pay attention to the different evaluations of credal formulations within the Western tradition, i.e. between the Roman Catholic Church, the Anglican community and the different Protestant denominations. Example: the writer of this paper is free to favor the orthodox critique of the Filioque without getting into difficulties with the church which ordained him.)

These two levels of the problem will have to be kept in mind by those who search for a possible consensus on the Filioque question. A promising analysis of the issue depends upon a proper distinction between the historical and the systematic aspects of the question. In the following account of the history of the controversy and of its implications, we will proceed from a brief summary of the external church-historical developments to a discussion of the theological issues from the point of view of history of doctrine and conclude by briefly describing the more recent stages of the dispute. Parts II and III will pay special attention to the systematic-theological aspects of the question.

I. *A Brief Account of the External Evidence of the Controversy*

The bare facts and years of the history of the controversy provide an exceptionally incomplete picture of the issue in question. This is surprising only if one considers the controversy a matter of conciliar decisions. It is, however, much more than that. The councils of Toledo[4] and the synods of Gentilly, Frankfurt, Friuli and Aachen promulgated decisions which by no means represented the official teaching of the pope in Rome, although the concept of the Filioque unquestionably did represent a theological tendency in Latin theology if not a necessary corollary of the generally accepted trinitarian concepts of Tertullian,[5] Novatian,[6] Ambrose[7] and Augustine.[8] Moreover, the official decisions of the church in the East, especially at Constantinople, must be seen in the context of problems connected with the Latin church's missionary strategy and activity among the Slavs (Bulgaria in particular) and other tensions with Rome,[9] not to speak of the fact that the Latin West had at best understood half of what the Cappadocian fathers had been teaching about the Trinity. The classical Eastern Orthodox concepts concerning the Trinity and the Holy Spirit were known to the West (and to Augustine in particular) only in the form of summarized end-results. The background of these results was not understood.[10] Nor did the Eastern theologians, at the crucial time of the controversy, understand the difficult situation of the church in Spain in relation to new forms of Arianism, or the peculiar interests of the Frankish church at the time of Charlemagne. In other words: the problem of the addition of the Filioque is imbedded in church-historical and in gradually developed theological positions, and the possibilities for a consensus faded away with the increasing lack of understanding of the other church's tradition and current problems.

The following list of events and dates, representing a selection of interesting steps in the history of the controversy, is, therefore, no more than an external manifestation of a very broad problem.

The West: Events and Texts	*The East:*
Early 5th cent.: Filioque in liturgical use in Spain (against Priscillianism?) Toledo (446/47)	
Athanasianum[11] ("Spiritus s. a Patre et Filio...procedens", 22)	
589 3rd council of Toledo[12]	
633 4th council of Toledo[13]	
	after 742: John of Damascus, *Expos. fid. orth.* I, 8, 12, advances the first Eastern refutation of the Filioque
767 Synod of Gentilly	
794 Synod of Frankfurt	
796 Synod of Friuli: Paulinus of Aquileia (d. 802) defended the Filioque (*Migne PL* 99, 9-683)	
808 Leo III writes Charlemagne that he believes the Filioque to be correct but does not want it included in the Creed	Struggle between Frankish and Eastern monks at St. Sabas monastery in Jerusalem over the former's use of the Filioque
809 Charlemagne asks Theodulf of Orléans (d. 821) to write his *De Spiritu Sancto*[14]	
Synod of Aachen, Filioque included in the Creed	

The West: Events and Texts	*The East:*
810 Synod in Rome: Leo III declares the Filioque orthodox but does not want it included in the Creed; two silver plaques with the text of the unaltered NC-Creed exposed at St. Peter's in Rome	
Alcuin's *De processione Spiritus s.*	
	858 Photius replaces Ignatius as patriarch
863 pope Nicholas I confirms Ignatius as patriarch	Emperor Michael III persuades the pope to re-open the matter
The Latin church claims Bulgaria	
	867 Photius (patriarch) condemns missionary activity of Rome in Bulgaria and rejects the Filioque
	Council of Constantinople excommunicates pope Nicholas
	Also 867: Ignatius re-instated
869 Rome anathematizes Photius	869 Council of Constantinople confirms Rome's condemnation of Photius
870 Rome condemns Ignatius' claim on Bulgaria	

The West: Events and Texts	*The East:*
	877 Ignatius dies; Photius again patriarch
papal legates to Constantinople sign the Creed without Filioque and confirm Photius' re-installation (so F. Dvornik against older research)	879/80 Council of Constantinople recalls decision of 869
	886 Emperor Leo VI deposes Photius
Rome excommunicates Photius? (F. Dvornik thinks this a later forgery)	Cf. Photius' *Liber de Spiritus S. mystagogia*[15]
1009 Pope Sergius IV includes the Filioque in his statement of faith addressed to Constantinople	Pope Sergius' namesake patriarch Sergius omit the pope's name from the official diptychs (such has happened before by mistake)
1014 Pope Benedict VIII[16] officially adds the Filioque to the NC-Creed (pressured by Emperor Heinrich II) as part of the Roman mass	
1274 Council of Lyons,[17] re-union attempted	Emperor Michael VIII (1259-82) re-approache Rome in need of help against the Turks
Eastern delegates accept the Filioque (and papal supremacy)	Eastern churches recall the agreement of the delegates to Lyons
1438/39 Council of Florence, the patriarch and all orthodox delegates (except Mark of Ephesus) signed the Filioque as well as other points of Roman doctrine	no official proclamation of the decision in Byzantium until 1452

The West: Events and Texts	*The East:*
	29th May 1453: destruction of Constantinople (after combined Orthodox and Roman service at Hagia Sophia early on May 29th)

It may be helpful at this point to interrupt the mere listing of external events by adding some comments and summary statements. The actual 'Filioque-controversy', as it is treated in history books, is connected with the name of Patriarch Photius, a learned theologian and a problematic personality. His doctrine--procession 'from the Father alone'--was theologically grounded and politically defended. But since Photius had no Western counter-part to match his theological and philosophical learning, the West resorted to almost exclusively political manoeuvring in combatting his position. This attitude remained typical of the Western church until and including Pope Benedict's official addition of the Filioque to the text of the creed. Benedict VIII himself was certainly more interested in the wars against Saracens and Greeks than in theology. A potentially serious theological controversy was pitifully reduced to political power struggles. The lucidity of Augustine's trinitarian thoughts and the helpful attempts of explaining the differences between East and West by Maximus the Confessor in the seventh century, seemed to have disappeared from the memory of the participants of the struggle. The councils of Lyons and of Florence, with their attempts to superimpose the Filioque upon the Eastern church, brought no solution and created much bitterness on the part of the Eastern Christians. The final mass, sung by Greeks and Latins together on the morning of May 29th, 1453, the day of the destruction of Constantinople--fourteen years after the humiliating council of Florence--is like a funeral song to a constructive theological exchange between East and West.

The thin contacts between the churches of the Reformation and Eastern Orthodoxy did not lead to a re-examination of the Filioque question. The confession books of the Reformation maintained the Filioque, partly because of the relatively high esteem for the Athanasianum. And one of the few experts on Western theology in the East, Cyril Lukaris (murdered in 1638), did not reopen the discussion either. But Peter Mogila, who also knew Western thought very well, attacked the Filioque in his *Orthodox Confession* together with papal primacy.

The development since the 17th century can again be listed according to significant events, whereby the theological positions of the Anglican and the Old Catholic churches become increasingly relevant to the Filioque question.

The West: Events and Texts	*The East:*
17th cent.: Various theological writers in England reconsider the Filioque in the interest of contact with Eastern Orthodoxy	In Peter Mogila's *Orthodox Confession* (1642/3) the Filioque (and papal primacy) are called separating issues
1742 Pope Benedict XIV considers the Filioque not as conditio sine qua non for union with the orthodox church[18]	
19th cent.: Several English theologians advocate the deletion of the Filioque from the NC-Creed	
1874/5 Consultations between Old Catholic and Orthodox Churches in Bonn, with Anglican representation, Old Catholics begin to delete the Filioque	
1894 Pope Leo XIII appeals to orthodox churches to unite with Rome	Patriarch Anthimos of Constantinople replies that union is acceptable if Rome can demonstrate full consensus in doctrine until 9th cent., including proof that the Filioque has been taught by the early Eastern fathers

The West: Events and Texts	*The East:*
1912 Anglican-Orthodox consulta- tions in St. Petersburg,	
1931 continued by 'Joint Doctrinal Commission'[19] which met again	
1973 in Oxford and	
1976 in Moscow	
1978 Lambeth Conference recommends the deletion of the Filioque- clause[20]	

This very brief survey requires some preliminary comments. It is obvious from the outset that the actual development of the controversy was interwoven with political interests and conflicts. But to observe this does not permit the conclusion that the issue as such was a political one. It was not. The issue is a trinitarian question, *viz.* an entirely different development of concepts and expectations concerning trinitarian theology in East and West. More helpful than the reference to political and church political interests would be the observation that East and West operated with "irreducibly diverse forms of thought", as Avery Dulles puts it in quoting W. Kasper.[21] But even after having insisted on this way of approaching the famous controversy one will have to proceed to an investigation on a deeper level. Nor will it suffice to list the passages in the few Greek fathers who openly teach a filioque-concept,[22] or the statements of some more recent orthodox theologians who seem to tolerate or belittle the importance of the Filioque.[23] These references are of no real significance.

The tension which erupted in the Filioque controversy has its roots in the different trinitarian concepts in the Latin and Greek churches. These differences, in turn, are part of different forms of piety and of expectations regarding the accessibility of God or of God the Holy Spirit by the believers. Without being able to go into a full investigation of these important areas, it will be necessary to list at least some of the basic trinitarian concepts which are at the roots of these other differences between the two parts of the church.

II. *The Theological Issues Behind the Controversy*

The decision is arbitrary where to begin in describing the development of patristic trinitarian thought. If one is interested in the philosophical and systematic conditions available to the early fathers for articulating trinitarian concepts, one might best look at the details of aristotelian influence upon Greek theology in the fourth century, especially the second half of it, and--with regard to Latin theology-- one would have to be interested in Ambrose's and Augustine's peculiar ways of appropriating Plotinus' philosophy (merged with aristotelian and stoic cosmology). If, however, one focuses on the history of theology in the narrower sense, the proper starting point in the East would be Athanasius[24] and the fuller development of his thoughts in the Cappadocians[25] and in Didymus the Blind and Evagrius; in the West it would undoubtedly be Tertullian.[26] With regard to the roots of the Filioque-problem one would have to look also at early concil- iar decisions, i.e. the synod of Alexandria in 362 which was expressly confirmed in Constantinople in 381. Moreover, one will have to bear in mind that the whole conceptuality--in the East and in the West--would not have been possible without Plotinus' philosophical categories. These analyses cannot, of course, be carried out here. The purpose of the following ob- servations is merely to provide some material for the under- standing of the fact that the theology of the church in the East could not possibly have produced the Filioque concept whereas the church in the West could perhaps not have been done without it.

A. *Athanasius and the Cappadocians*

Theology in the East only gradually learnt to distinguish sharply between *ousia* and *energeia* and between *ousia* and *hypo- stasis*, or *hypostasis* and *prosopon*. It is clear, however, that, after the work of the Cappadocians had been done, the distinction between *ousia* and the *energeiai* had become abso- lutely essential for Greek theology. Although the "energies" in God cannot be separated from his *ousia*, it is impossible for the believers to reach God in his very own *ousia* which transcends all beings, names and concepts. Any being has its being only in the *energeiai* of (or within) God and it is in participating in God's energies that the believers can enter into communion with God. This view, the heart of orthodox theology, fully developed by Gregory Palamas, is basically present in Athanasius. The terms, of course, were not clear in Athanasius, and it is not surprising that the Western church was able to claim Athanasius as well. But the substance of later theology in the East was already present in Athanasius and the claim by the Cappadocians that they legitimately continued Athanasius' approach is mostly justified. (However, modern research has shown that there were other theologians too who influenced the Cappadocians, but their importance was surpressed because of lack of orthodoxy in certain points; one such example is Apollinaris of Laodicea[27] whom Harnack calls the "great teacher of the Cappadocians".[28])

Athanasius teaches in *C. Arianos* and later in *Ad Serapionem* that Father, Son and Holy Spirit dwell in one another, that the Spirit is not to be thought on a lower level than the Son, and that the believers' participation in God is a participation of the Spirit.[29] The word is the bridge in this participation. Since the word is in the Father, and since the word and the Spirit participate fully in the Father, and since the word is with the believers (and in them), so the believers are *in* God *in the Spirit*. In this construction of both the Trinity and the believers' participation in God, the phrase "through the Son" is quite appropriate. In fact, the *dia tou hyiou* was (and is) a proper theological formula in Eastern Orthodoxy, although its similarity with the Western "from the Son" resulted over the centuries in a distrust of Eastern theologians for the originally proper concept. Athanasius still teaches clearly that God is "over all" and also "through all and in all", that the Son is "through all" and the Spirit "in all". This is the basis for speaking of the vicarious work of the Spirit on behalf of those who are "in the Spirit". There is a communion of the Spirit with the believers which is grounded in the communion of the Son who is in the Spirit and the Spirit who is in the Son. The incarnation of the Word is, in turn, the ground for the believers' reception of the Spirit. However, the Spirit so fully participates in both, the Father and the *logos*, and this for reasons of a total unity of God's being and activity (*energeia*), that there are some reasons for questioning the later Eastern orthodox theologians' claim that Athanasius too is a crown witness of the distinction between the *ousia* and *energeiai* in the triune God. It could be argued that Athanasius' concept of God making himself present *through* the Word and *in* the Spirit tends to identify God's "being in himself" with the way the believers recognize him. This ultimate abolition of the distinction between the immanent and the economic Trinity is, of course, dear to Western theology. (It is, e.g., *the* basic theological-epistemological thesis in Karl Barth's dogmatics.) It could be argued further that in this point the West has understood Athanasius better than has later Byzantine theology. Since our interest here is not in Athanasius' theology as such but in the Eastern trinitarian concepts which necessitated a denial of the Filioque, we can leave undecided the problem just mentioned. It is a fact that the Cappadocians, and with them all of later Eastern tradition, thought they were truly and legitimately continuing the theological interest of the great Athanasius.

The Cappadocians' interest is characterized by their emphasis on the oneness of the three persons in the Trinity (against Neo-Arians) as well as on the differentiation of the three *hypostaseis* within the unity of the three (against the charge that they taught "two sons"). Whereas Basil is the first to re-think the term *hypostasis*, although without clearly defining the Spirit's eternal procession, Gregor Nazianzen introduced the notion of *ekporeusis*, while Gregor Nyssa reflected upon the continuation of this thought by speaking of the "through the son"-concept. All three of them, of course, accepted the *homoousia* of the Spirit. The reasons they give for this always are connected with the insight that the believers' knowledge of God would be incomplete or impossible if the Spirit were a *ktisma*. Thus the soteriological argument and the direct reference to the liturgy in worship are part of the whole theological reflection from the outset.

Basil faces honestly the problem of the Spirit's neither being a *genneton* nor *genneton* being a *ktisis*,[30] and in *De spiritu s.* he seems to teach the procession of the Spirit from the Son, although Holl denies[31] that he means to do that: rather, Basil referring here to the inner *taxis* within the Trinity, actually distinguishes between an inner order and the outer appearances of the *prosopa*.

With regard to the recognizable *prosopa* the order is--as it was in Athanasius--*from* the Father *through* the Son *in* the Spirit. With regard to the inner-trinitarian relations, however, Basil does not have available a concept for the Holy Spirit equivalent to the *gennesia* of the Son.

The situation is somewhat different in Gregory Nazianzen in that--despite fundamental agreement with his teacher Basil-- he places much emphasis on the origination of the Spirit. A basic text for him is John 15:26. The notion of *exporeusis* permits him to define the *idiotes* of the Spirit, a notion parallel to the *gennesis* of the Son. Gregory's trinitarian interest is, as it was for Basil, intimately connected with the spiritual condition of the believers whose *psyche* he distinguishes from the *nous*. It is the *nous* that is to reach similarity with God (*teleiosis*). This construction operates with the notion of *aggenesia, gennesis* and *ekporeusis*. This Gregory considers sufficient proof against the charge that he teaches *dyo hyioi* in God. It is important to note that Gregory Nazianzen does not use the phrase *ekporeusis dia tou hyiou* or some-

ing like it. Thus Gregory goes beyond Basil in providing a
ear and helpful terminology, but it cannot really be said
at his five theological *Orations* provide complete clarity on
e question of the origination of the Spirit.

Gregory of Nyssa, of course, also bases his thoughts on
e trinitarian thoughts of Basil but he adds a complex of
oughts concerning absolute goodness, evil and the original
ate of man. The influence of Origen and in general of Neo-
atonism is more noticeable than in Basil and Gregory Nazian-
n. An interest in a kind of history of salvation, i.e. of
e soul's gradual approach toward God, is closely connected
th his concept of the Trinity. Gregory's teaching presup-
ses an immanent concept: God is *he zoopoios dynamis*. This
namis operates *immanently* in a threefold way: *pege men*
nameos estin ho pater, dynamis de tou patros ho hyios, dy-
meos de pneuma to pneuma hagion.[32] This immanent trinity
rks toward the outside, but in such a fashion that it is
ways clear that the Father is the *pege*, the source, that the
ergeia is with the Son and the *teleiosis* with the Spirit.
e Father is *agennetos*, the Son is *monogenes*. Again: there
only *one* Son in the Trinity. It could be argued that Greg-
y Nyssa places all emphasis on the economic concept of the
inity. It is more plausible, however, to say that this is
t so. The Father is *aition*, the Son and the Spirit are *ek*
u *aitiou*. It follows clearly: no Filioque concept is being
ught. The *aitia* of the Spirit is in the Father, but the Son
diates in the works of the Trinity *ad extra*. The Holy Spirit
dia tou hyiou and not *from* the Son. This distinction be-
een eternal origination and "salvation-economic" mediation
of great importance. The Cappadocians, like all orthodox
eologians of the East, leave no doubt that the inner or im-
nent Trinity is a mystery into which human thought cannot
netrate.[33] All the more important is the work of the Spirit,
e theological understanding of which Gregory of Nyssa trans-
ted into mystical-ascetic thoughts which, in turn, influenced
. Dionysios Areopagita and, through him, most of Eastern tration. This combination of practical piety and worship with
e most complicated trinitarian thoughts is the most charac-
ristic feature of Eastern Orthodoxy. From the point of view
our interest in the Filioque, the most important dogmatic
sertion of classical Eastern theology is the insight that
d the Father is the *pege*, the source, and *riza*, the root, of
e Godhead with its dynamic energies which reach and transform
r transfigurate) the believers in the Spirit who, in turn, is
the Son as the Son is in him. It is, therefore, correct to
y that the Spirit reaches the believers *dia tou hyiou*, but
is meaningless to say that the Holy Spirit eternally origi-
tes from the Father *and from* the Son, as though there were
o sources or two roots.

The difference between East and West on the Filioque-addition to the NC-Creed is an expression of the differences concerning the epistemological relation between the economic and an immanent concept of the Trinity.

B. *Early Western Concepts of the Trinity*

Although a synod in Rome in 382 accepted the trinitarian dogma of Constantinople of 381, it cannot be said that the West had fully understood the Eastern trinitarian theology. Nor has Augustine--whose conception of the Trinity became the Western concept--fully apprehended the decision of the second ecumenical council in 381 and of the Cappadocians' teaching on the Trinity. There were language barriers--and more than that. Augustine stood deeply in the tradition of Tertullian and of Ambrose and, as Harnack judges[34]--perhaps overdoing the point--Augustine would never have thought of the Trinity had he not felt himself bound to the tradition in which he stood.

Ambrose, with his interest in the Cappadocians and his admiration for Athanasius, emphasized the unity and oneness of God along with the unsearchable mystery of the Trinity, and was tending toward a practical identification of the Holy Spirit with the Father. This is historically quite understandable, but it certainly is not a valid representation of Athanasius and his followers in the East. Athanasius may have been truly presented, however, in Ambrose's and Augustine's unwillingness to make much of a differentiation between the immanent and the economic Trinity. Ambrose's doctrine of the Trinity shows the same aporetic difficulties which we find in Augustine, the difficulty of harmonizing the two concepts: one in three and three in one. If this *conceptual* paradox is the mystery of the Trinity, surely the Western church celebrates another mystery than does the church in the East.

The work of Marcellus of Ancyra[35] is to be mentioned here, partly because it influenced Rufinus whose concepts of the Trinity (indebted to Cyril of Jerusalem) and of the procession of the Spirit influenced later Western theology. Marcellus had taught a "salvation-economic" modalism, i.e. the Son and the Spirit appeared only in order to perform certain functions. It is noteworthy that Marcellus' orthodoxy was accepted at Rome in 340 and at Sardica in 343.

J. Pelikan[36] maintains (against A. Schindler) that Augustine in his trinitarian thoughts was deeply influenced by Hilary of Poitiers' caution not to allow a differentiation between the economic and the immanent concept of the Trinity.

Hilary implicitly taught the Filioque. If this is the case, and also the influence of Marcellus and Rufinus on later Western concepts, one would have reasons to suspect that the Filioque of later Western theology grew out of the Western theological unwillingness to distinguish between the economic and the immanent Trinity. And if this conclusion is correct, it would also follow that Tertullian is not really a witness for later Filioquism. This can briefly be demonstrated in the following way.

Tertullian's *Adv. Praxean* was occasioned by the ideas of the Monarchian Praxeas whose concern was not the Spirit at all but the relation between the monarchy of God and the life of Jesus. Nor was Tertullian's concept of the Trinity shaped by a special interest in the Spirit, an interest one might suspect because of Tertullian's relation to Montanism. His concern was rather the understanding of the economic *distributio* and *distinctio* of the three *personae* within the one *substantia, potestas, virtus* of God, a *differentia per distinctionem* which on the one hand guarantees the unity of the divine substance, on the other the fact that God is not *unicus et singularis*. This he could have only at the price of declaring the Son and the Spirit *portiones* of the divine substance, but fully part of that substance nevertheless. In choosing between a three-partition of God and an inferiority of the Son and the Spirit in relation to the Father, Tertullian, as is well known, chose the latter. This subordinationism, however, is not our concern here. Interesting is the concept of procession from the Father alone. Tertullian teaches in *Adv. Prax.* (4) that Son and Spirit proceed merely for the purpose of creation and revelation and that both proceed *ex unitate patri* (19). In this basic assertion Tertullian does not differ from later Greek concepts, although, of course, his understanding of the reasons for the procession are entirely different from, e.g., the concept of the Cappadocians. The Spirit, who proceeds *a patre per filium*, occupies a 'third grade' within the majesty of God: the Son *'interim acceptum a Patre munus effudit Spiritum S., tertium nomen divinitatis et tertium gradum majestatis...'* (30,5). However, this still amounts to the assertion that the Spirit proceeds from the *Father*. Tertullian teaches the mediatorship of the Son in the procession of the Spirit from the Father, which is to say that he distinguished between origination and procession. *'Tertius enim est Spiritus a Deo et Filio sicut tertius a radice fructus ex fructice et tertius a fonte rivus ex flumine et tertius a sole apex ex radio'* (8,7). The Spirit, like the Son, is (only) a *portio* of the divine substance, although he receives it directly, whereas the Spirit receives it indirectly from the Father. Such reception, it must be noted, occurred before creation, for it was in creation that the Spirit co-operated as the third person of the Trinity (cf. 12,3). For these reasons it does not amount to much to claim Tertullian as a crown witness for the classical Western understanding of the Filioque, as has often been done. A crown witness he is, to be sure, for Western tendencies toward modalism.

The important innovation in Augustine is the (philosophical) decision to think the Trinity not by beginning, as it were, with the Father, but with just that--the Trinity. The *relationes* of the three persons condition each of them in dependence of the others, so much so, that Augustine teaches the Son's active participation in his own sending (i.e. his incarnation). The combination of the neoplatonic idea of simplicity with the biblical concept of the personhood of God, is the main thesis. All three persons of the Trinity share in these qualities which together amount to one *principium*. Augustine *must*, therefore, teach the Filioque. The reasons he gives for this in *De Trinitate* and in the *Homilies* on *John* are elaborate and convincing--provided one shares his quasi modalistic understanding of the innertrinitarian *relationes*. Unsolved, however, remains the problem why the Son should not be thought of as having proceeded from the Spirit, unless one interprets 'conceived by the Holy Spirit' in just this way. In other words: as soon as historical references are made to Israel, to the coming of Jesus, to the church (i.e. to 'economic' dimensions), Augustine's innertrinitarian concept does not seem to be relevant.[37] The Trinity almost becomes a perfect triangle which 'in its work' *ad extra*, as it were, seems reducible to a single point. In Augustine's teaching it is merely the impact of the content of the Bible which prevents the logically possible conclusion that the Father and Son proceed from the Spirit. And it is this impact too that persuades Augustine to teach that, although the Spirit is the symmetrical bond of love (*vinculum caritatis*) between Father and Son and proceeds from both, the Spirit proceeds *principaliter* from the Father (*De trin.* 15,17,29). Thus Augustine's doctrine of the 'double procession', which became typical of later theology including the *Athanasiuanum*, was somewhat balanced by this assertion. This led at a later stage of theology (e.d. the Council of Lyons) to the idea of a single breathing, *spiratio*, by which the Spirit is said to proceed from the two sources as from one single source.

III. *Implications of More Recent Stages of the Controversy*

After this survey of the development of those aspects of patristic trinitarian thought that have a bearing on the later

Filioque controversy, it is safe to conclude that the important trinitarian decisions on the Filioque-issue were made long before the controversy began. This is why the controversy itself is more of church historical than of theological significance.

With reference to Eastern theology, it must be said of course that Photius' insistence on the procession from the 'Father alone' ('Photism'), further developed by Gregory the Cypriot and by Gregory Palamas (who re-visited the 'through the Son-concept' by speculating on a difference between procession and manifestation), did present some new theological concepts.[38] Several Eastern authors drew attention to the shortcomings of the traditional Western identification between the economic and the immanent Trinity, e.g. the Bulgarian archbishop Theophylact of Achrida in the 11th century. Here lie indeed the roots of the whole controversy.[39] But decisively new theological thoughts on the Trinity and on the procession of the Spirit have not been produced by later Eastern Orthodoxy; besides, such innovating ideas would not be in harmony with Eastern Orthodoxy's self-understanding. The emphasis on the philosophical *concepts* introduced by the Cappadocian Fathers in order to point at the mystery of the Trinity has remained typical of all later Eastern theology. The question of the relation between the Son and the Spirit has remained basically unsolved.

With reference to Western theology, on the other hand, it must be admitted that Anselm's and Thomas Aquinas' justifications of the Filioque do seem to have introduced new elements to the discussion. Alasdair Heron[40] makes much of the difference between Augustine's and Anselm's points of view on the matter. He draws attention to the fact that Augustine's allowance for a procession of the spirit *principaliter* from the Father is in Anselm[41] and Thomas Aquinas[42] given up in favor of a completely triangular concept of the Trinity. Anselm is vulnerable to V. Lossky's criticisms, Heron maintains, whereas Augustine—who seems to Heron to be closer to a 'through-the-son-concept'—is not. Here is not the place to argue this interpretative problem. It seems that good reasons could be advanced to show that Augustine too is vulnerable to Lossky's harsh critique of implicit Western modalism. Be this as it may, the Councils of Lyons and of Florence show the clear influence of both Augustinian and of Anselm's and Thomas' trinitarian thought. And later stages in the history of theology, for example at the time of the Reformation, do not give evidence of any new thoughts on the matter. It amounts to little to ask the question whether Luther in his opposition to A. Karlstadt and Thomas Müntzer consciously made use of Filioquism in combatting the enthusiasts' claim

that the Holy Spirit may also blow 'outside' the realm of the
written Word (if Word stands for the second person of the
Trinity, 'outside' the mission of the Son). *De facto* this is
what he *did* teach and the position taken was well in line with
classical Western anti-Montanist thought. The emphasis in the
Roman church on papal primacy and on the institution of the
church has its perfect parallel in the Reformation churches'
insistence on the primacy of the written word in its function
of a criterion with which to judge the movements of the Spirit
--a parallel at least with regard to the ecclesiological util-
ization of trinitarian thought. Moreover, the protestant authors in England who concerned themselves with the Filioque,
e.g. William Sherlock (1690), John Pearson and E. Stilling-
fleet (1664), either did not understand the gravity of the
issue (as in the case of Sherlock), or ultimately reached a
position close to Filioquism. The learned 19th century author
and hymn-writer J. M. Neale came closest to refuting the Filioque. But new thoughts were not added. At best there was a
recollection of the importance of distinguishing between the
'eternal procession' and the 'temporal mission' of the Holy
Spirit, a distinction without which much unnecessary misunderstanding occurs.

If Eastern theology has failed to provide a satisfactory
explanation of the relation between the Son and the Spirit,
and if Western theology is right in suspecting in Eastern Orthodoxy an undue emphasis on the Father's *monarchia* as well as
an overemphasis on (aristotelian) philosophical concepts with
which to approach the mystery of the Trinity, Western theology
surely has shown its shortcomings in its undue tendency to
blend together Father, Son and Spirit into a monotheistically
conceived 'godhead' and by prematurely identifying economic
with immanent trinitarian structures. Nikos Nissiotis[43] would
then be right in saying that neither East nor West have produced an adequate theology of the Holy Spirit and that Western 'christomonism' and Filioquism cannot be an economic sub-
stitute for an innertrinatarian structure.

Karl Barth[44] has provided one of the most extensive de-
fenses of the Filioque in 20th century theology. It is
Heron's judgement that Barth follows completely the lines of
Anselm's trinitarian thought. This may indeed be the case.
More important almost is the obvious tendency in Barth to see
the safeguard against a free-floating spiritualism, which he
rightly desires to have with regard to the 'economic' dimension, anchored in the immanent Trinity. While with regard to
the *relationes* in the Trinity, Barth argues deductively, with
respect to the ultimate defense of the Filioque he proceeds
inductively: the economic desirability of making clear at
all times that the Spirit of God is Christ's Spirit, is seen

o be rooted in the immanent Trinity. The expression of this esirability is quite understandable, the question remains, owever, whether perhaps the price paid is too high, *viz.* the endency to modalism, and hence, the lack of a dynamic doc- rine of the Spirit. George Hendry[45] criticizes Barth's and ltimately Augustine's defense of the Filioque. He does not rovide, however, an alternative which could be acceptable to estern and also to Eastern theology. And to find such alter- atives is very important indeed. The decisions of the Old atholics to delete the Filioque from the NC-Creed and the ore recent Anglican recommendations have been accompanied nd supported by many learned historical studies, but new *heological* thoughts have not really grown out of these en- eavours, unless one would call the partially improved con- acts with Eastern Orthodoxy a new theological result. The eeper issue, however, the solution of which alone would be cumenically promising, is a new way of getting at the much elaboured relation between the economic and the immanent Trin- ty, i.e., a new way of trinitarian articulation. The old ways an altogether be intellectually analyzed, all intricacies can e understood,[46] provided one invests sufficient time and pa- ience, but these analyses as such do not produce what is eeded today.

In approaching the question of the Trinity, it is impor- ant to remember that any reference to the Trinity is original- y doxological in nature. This is important in our time when od-talk is so severely challenged and trinitarian thinking so bviously neglected. Doxological affirmations are not primar- ly definitions or descriptions, rather ascriptive lines of hought, speech and action which are offered to God himself. rinitarian thought in the early church originated within dox- logical contexts and it is only within such contexts that we an speak of the 'inner life' of the triune God. But, as the arly Eastern fathers made clear, all such doxological refer- nces to that inner life must be checked by reference back to he biblical message concerning God's activity and presence ith his people. Such reference will show that the Spirit is onfessed to have been instrumental in the coming of Christ 'conceived by the Holy Spirit'), and to have been the life- iving power of God in his resurrection. Jesus during his min- stry promised the sending of the Spirit, and the earliest hristians understood Pentecost as the fulfillment of that romise. Thus the Spirit precedes the coming of Christ, is ctive throughout his life, and is also sent by him to the be- ievers. This chain of observations suggests that it would be nsufficient and perhaps illegitimate to 'read back' into the rinity only those New Testament passages which refer to the ending of the Spirit by Jesus.

A restructuring of trinitarian articulation will have to pay equal attention to the actual experience of the early Christians and of our Christian existence today, to the 'synthetic' thoughts--mostly in doxological dress--concerning God' presence in Israel, in the coming of Jesus and in the church, as they were expressed by the earliest witnesses of trinitarian thought, and surely also to the logical and linguistic conditions of our time. One must not forget that from its beginnings in the second and third centuries, the doctrine of the Trinity was intended to be a help for Christian believers, not an obstacle nor an abstract intellectual superimposition upon the 'simple faith'. For it was in simple faith that the early Christians experienced the presence of the triune God. They did not deduce their theological conclusions from a preconceived trinitarian concept. So too in our reconsideration of trinitarian concepts, it is desirable that we, in following the cognitive process of the early Church, take ecclesiology as the appropriate theological starting point for re-examining the function of trinitarian thought in the church's faith, lif and work.

NOTES

1. Cf. my briefer account of this controversy in *Concilium*, 128:3-14.

2. Western theology had the Filioque long before the whole Western church had it. The council decisions of Toledo in 446/7 and in 589 (the Filioque-phrase in the council of 400 is most likely a later addition) are only part of the story. Not until the early 11th century was the Filioque officially sung in the Western mass.

3. Cf. the classic history by H. B. Swete, *On the History of the Doctrine of the Procession of the Holy Spirit from the Apostolic Age to the Death of Charlemagne*, 1876; also M. Jugie, "Origine de la controverse sur l'addition du Filioque au symbole" in *Revue des Sciences Philosophiques et Théologique*, 28, 1939, pp. 369ff., also François Dvornik, *Le schisme de Photius, histoire et légende*, Paris, 1950.

4. The many councils of Toledo (from 400 until the 16th century, cf. *Migne PL* 84, 327-562) reflect the special problems of the church in Spain: Arianism (Priscillianism), the Muslim occupation, the re-conquest, the replacing of the Mozarabic rite, etc.

5. *Adv. Praxean* (after 213).

6. *De trinitate* (before 250).

7. The three books *De Spiritu sancto*.

8. *De trinitate* (399-419) and *ep*. 11 and 120.

9. Cf. François Dvornik, *Byzance et la primauté Romaine*, Paris, 1964.

10. Cf. B. Altaner's summary of his investigation into the question of the Western reception of Eastern theology in *Rev. Bén.* 62 (1952), pp. 201ff.

11. Cf. J. N. D. Kelly, *The Athanasian Creed*, New York, 1964, esp. pp. 86-90.

12. Texts in A. Hahn, *Bibliothek d. Symbole u. Glaubensregeln*, Breslau, 1897 (3rd ed.), pp. 232ff.

13. Hahn, pp. 235ff.

14. *Migne PL* 105, 187ff.

15. *Migne PG* 102; cf. in addition to Dvornik the older article "Photius" by F. Kattenbusch, in *RE* (3rd ed., 1904), pp. 374-393.

16. *Migne PL* 142, 1060f.

17. *Denz.* 460-63.

18. Cf., however, the *professio fidei Orientalibus (Maronitis) praescripta,* Denz. 1459-1473.

19. See *Anglo-Russian Theological Conference*, ed. H. M. Waddams, London, 1958, also H. A. Hodges, *Anglicanism and Orthodoxy*, London, 1955, and the essays by N. Zernov and G. Florovsky in *A History of the Ecumenical Movement*, ed. R. Rouse and S. C. Neill, London, 1954.

20. See *Report of the Lambeth Conference 1978*, pp. 51f., also *Anglican-Orthodox Dialogue. The Moscow Statement...Joint Doctrinal Commission 1976*, ed. K. Ware and C. Davey, pp. 97ff., with a history of the dialogue, pp. 4-37.

21. Avery Dulles, S. J., *The Survival of Dogma*, Garden City, 1973, p. 167.

22. One passage in Cyril of Alex. (*Thesaurus de...trinitate* 34), one in Epiphanius, also Ephraem Syrus, and others.

23. Moderate: the Russian theologian V. Bolotov; radical: Pavel Svetlov.

24. Cf. D. Ritschl, *Athanasius*, Zürich, 1964; T. F. Torrance, "Athanasius: A Study in the Foundations of Classical Theology" in *Theology in Reconciliation*, London, 1975, pp. 215-266, and Theodore C. Campbell, "The Doctrine of the Holy Spirit in the Theology of Athanasius" in *Scott. Journ. of Theol.*, 27, Nov. 1974, pp. 408-440.

25. Still important Karl Holl, *Amphilochius v. Ikonium in seinem Verhältnis zu den grossen Kappadoziern*, Tübingen, 1904.

26. Cf. John Burleigh, "The Doctrine of the Holy Spirit in the Latin Fathers", in *Scott. J. of Th.*, June, 1954, pp. 113-132.

27. Cf. E. Mühlenberg, *Apollinaris von Laodicea*, Göttingen, 1969, and T. F. Torrance, "The Mind of Christ in Worship:

The Problem of Apollinarianism in Worship", in *Theol. in Rec-onc.*, pp. 139-214.

28. A. v. Harnack, *DC* (4th ed.), II, p. 295.

29. D. Ritschl, "Die Einheit mit Christus im Denken der griechischen Väter", in *Konzepte*, Ges. Aufsätze Bd. I, Bern, 1976, pp. 78-101 and ch. II in *Memory and Hope, An Inquiry Concerning the Presence of Christ*, New York, 1967.

30. *Contra Eunom.* III, *Migne PG* 29, 668B.

31. Holl, *op. cit.*, p. 141.

32. *Migne PG* 45, 1317 (*adv. Maced.*).

33. Cf. Vladimir Lossky, *The Vision of God*, London, 1963 (German tr. *Schau Gottes*, Zürich, 1963), also his *The Mystical Theology of the Eastern Church*, London, 1957, with his empha-sis on the difference of Eastern and Western spirituality in relation to the single procession of the Holy Spirit, a con-cept which alone permits the transfiguration or deification of the believer in Christ.

34. A. v. Harnack, *Grundriss der Dogmengeschichte*, 7th ed., Tübingen, 1931, p. 237.

35. Cf. T. Evan Pollard, 'Marcellus of Ancyra, A Neg-lected Father', in *Epektasis* (for Jean Daniélou), Paris, 1972, pp. 187-196.

36. J. Pelikan, 'Hilary on Filioque', in his *Development of Christian Doctrine*, Yale Univ. Press, 1969, pp. 120-141.

37. Cf. my discussion of this critical interpretation of Augustine's implicit modalism in *Konzepte I* (see above Note 29), pp. 102ff. and 123-140.

38. Cf. O. Clément, 'Grégoire de Chypre, De l'ekporèse du Saint Eprit', in *Istina*, 1972, No. 3-4, pp. 443-456.

39. Cf. V. Lossky, 'The Procession of the Holy Spirit in Orthodox Triadology', *Eastern Church Quarterly*, 7, 1948, pp. 31ff. See also U. Küry, 'Die Bedeutung des Filioque-Streites für den Gottesdienst der abendländischen und der morgenland-ischen Kirche', *IKZ* 33, 1943, pp. 1ff.

40. A. I. C. Heron, 'Who Proceedeth from the Father and the Son', *Scott. Journ. of Theol.*, 4, 1971, pp. 149ff., as

well as some of Dr. Heron's study papers for the second Kling-
enthal Conference of the Filioque-Consultation, May 1979.

41. *De processione Spiritus* S., e.g. 9.

42. *Summa theologiae*, I, q. 36, Art. 2-4.

43. N. A. Nissiotis, *Die Theologie der Ostkirche im
ökumenischen Dialog*, Stuttgart, 1968, p. 26. Cf. also J. N.
Karmiris, 'Abriss der dogmatischen Lehre der orth. kath.
Kirche' in P. Bratsiotis (ed.), *Die Orthodoxe Kirche in
griechischer Sicht*, I, Stuttgart, 1959, pp. 15-120, esp.
30-34.

44. K. Barth, *Church Dogmatics*, I/1, Paragraph 12 (German, pp. 496-514).

45. George S. Hendry, *The Holy Spirit in Christian The-
ology*, Philadelphia, 1956 (London, 1965), pp. 30-52.--See also
Donald L. Berry, 'Filioque and the Church', *Journ. of Ecum.
Studies*, Summer 1968, pp. 535-554.

46. See e.g. the issue of *Istina*, No. 3-4, 1972, devoted
to this task (pp. 257-467). Cf. also Paul Henry, S. J.,
'Contre le "Filioque"', in *Irénikon*, Vol. XLVIII, 1975, pp.
170-177.

15

ZUM AUFBAU VON LUKAS 1 UND 2

Eduard Schweizer

Markus Barth hat wie kaum ein anderer immer wieder daran erinnert, dass Jesus Sohn und Retter Israels ist, und dass man ihn nicht verstehen kann, ohne diese seine Verwurzelung in und seine Bedeutung für Israel zu sehen,[1] ohne also auch das Gesetz, Israels heilige Schrift, die es als Geschenk Gottes freudig übernimmt,[2] ernst zu nehmen. Mindestens vom Thema her dürfte es ihn also freuen, wenn ich versuche, ein paar Randbemerkungen zu den Eingangskapiteln des dritten Evangeliums zu schreiben, in denen die Freude an Tempel und Gesetz so stark hervortritt und in denen Jesus mit dem Täufer und beide zusammen mit den Vätern und Müttern Israels in engste Verbindung gebracht werden.[3] Vielleicht stellt er auch mit einigem Vergnügen fest, dass ich nicht stur bei dem bleiben mag, was sich als traditionsgeschichtliche Methode eingebürgert hat, sondern gerne von denen lerne, die uns daran erinnern, dass der Text zuerst einmal als ganzer ernst genommen werden und auf seinen Aufbau hin untersucht werden sollte. Ich verstehe das freilich als zusätzliche Hilfe für eine, auch die Traditionsgeschichte ernst nehmende Exegese. Das Nachdenken über die Struktur des Textes bleibt also in sehr bescheidenem Umfang; doch versuche ich, mir darüber klar zu werden, wie seine Bewegung verläuft, um vielleicht hie und da noch etwas deutlicher zu erkennen, was als grössere oder kleinere Einheit zusammengehört, wo über- und wo untergeordnete Aussagen stehen und in welche Richtung der Fortgang des Textes weist. Ich meine dabei nicht, dass sich die Verfasser des Aufbaus bewusst waren, den ich zu sehen versuche, oder ihn gar mit Absicht so geschaffen hätten. Ich bin auch überzeugt, dass man manches anders und auch besser ordnen kann, als es mir gelingt. Dennoch scheint mir da und dort die Gedankenbewegung dieser Kapitel noch stärker hervorzutreten, wenn man auf ihren Aufbau achtet. Dass hinter der rein exegetischen Bemühung gewichtige theologische Fragen auftauchen, die mich brennend interessieren, wird hoffentlich sichtbar werden.

1. *1,5 - 2,52: Beginn des Evangeliums*

Nach der Widmung des Gesamtwerkes an Theophilus in 1,1-4
folgt, was man als bekennendes und Gott lobendes Präludium
bezeichnen kann.[4] Eindeutig ist die Parallele zwischen der
Ankündigung der Geburt des Johannes und derjenigen Jesu (1,5-
25/26-38), sachlich auch die zwischen den jeweiligen Erzählungen über Geburt, Beschneidung und Namengebung (1,57-66/2,1-21).
In beiden Fällen überbietet das von Jesus Berichtete das den
Täufer Betreffende. Alles übrige ist umstritten.

Man kann mit H. Schürmann den Aufbau so sehen, dass auf
je eine Johannesgeschichte zwei Jesuserzählungen folgen, also
auf die Ankündigung des Täufers (1,5-23 + 24f.) die Jesu und
die Begegnung der beiden Mütter (1,26-38 und 39-56), auf Geburt und Beschneidung des Täufers (1,57-66 + 67-79) die Jesu
und seine Darstellung im Tempel (2,1-21 und 22-39).[5] "Magnificat" und "Nunc dimittis" stehen dann je am Ende, der Tempel
am Anfang und am Schluss des Ganzen. Die Geschichte vom Zwölfjährigen, die ja noch betonter im Tempel lokalisiert ist (2,
41-52), bleibt dabei freilich ausser Betracht. Das Loblied
des Zacharias (Benedictus) stünde dann, etwas ungeschickt, als
Parallele zur Notiz vom Beginn der Schwangerschaft bei Elisabet (1,24f), und die ganz parallelen Verse vom Heranwachsen
des Täufers (1,80) und Jesu (2,40) wären dann nicht diesem
entscheidenden Parallelismus eingeordnet, sondern erschienen
innerhalb des zweiten Blocks, freilich je am Ende der Johannes-
und der zweiten Jesuserzählung, beidemal nach dem hymnischen
Gotteslob. Ob man die Begegnung der Mütter so eindeutig als
Jesusgeschichte werten darf - Johannes regt sich ja nach 1,41
zum ersten Mal -, wäre auch noch zu fragen.

Noch fraglicher ist die Einteilung W. Grundmanns, der die
eindeutige Parallele der beiden Ankündigungen und die von Geburt und Beschneidung beider Kinder samt den anschliessenden
Hymnen (Benedictus und Nunc dimittis) betont, dann aber die
Zwischenperikope 1,39-56, die "sich über zwei Pfeilern schlies-
sende Pforte", als Parallele zur Erzählung von der Jordantaufe
Jesu (3,21f) auffasst, weil dabei wiederum die Geschichte des
Täufers (3,1-20) mit der Jesu (ab 4,1) verbunden wird.[6] Das
erscheint doch problematisch; denn in 1,5 - 2,39 werden ja vor
und nach dem Verbindungsstück 1,39-56 je eine Johannes- und
eine Jesuserzählung parallelisiert, während in 3,1-20 nur vom
Täufer, in 4,1ff nur von Jesus die Rede ist. Auch sind die
Parallelformulierungen 1,80 und 2,40 dabei nicht berücksichtigt, und ob man wirklich den Parallelaufbau über den deut-
lichen Neuansatz in 3,1 hinüber verfolgen soll, bleibt fraglich. Ausserdem ist auch dabei die Geschichte vom Zwölfjährigen nicht eingeordnet.

W. Wilkens findet durch das ganze Evangelium hindurch ein Dreiheitsprinzip wirken, dessen erste Triade von je drei Unterabschnitten ebenfalls die Grenze von 3,1 übergreift: (1) 1,5-25/26-38/39-56; (2) 1,57-80/2,1-40/41-52; (3) 3,1-20/3,21-4, 13/4,14-44.[7] Ob man 2,1-40, vor allem aber 3,21-4,13 und 4, 14-44 als je einen einzigen Unterabschnitt zusammenfassen kann, ist doch zu fragen, umso mehr als im weiteren Verlauf der Analyse andere Aufteilungen in je drei Einheiten öfters gewaltsam erscheinen.

Ich nehme die Ergebnisse dieser (und vieler anderer) Versuche auf und sehe - in gewisser Anlehnung an die ersten beiden Dreiheiten bei Wilkens - folgenden Aufbau:

A 1,5-25: Ankündigung des Johannes

A'1,26-38: Ankündigung Jesu

        X 1,39-56 (Verbindungsabschnitt zum Folgenden): Begegnung der Mütter, erstes Lebenszeichen des Johannes (+ Magnificat)

B 1,57-80: Geburt, Beschneidung, Namengebung: Johannes

    a 1,57f: Geburt

    b 1,59-66: Beschneidung und Namengebung

    c 1,67-79: Benedictus

    d 1,80: Heranwachsen

B'2,1-40: Geburt, Beschneidung, Namengebung: Jesus

    a 2,(1-5.)6f.(8-20): Geburt

    b 2,21: Beschneidung und Namengebung

    c 2,22-39: (Darstellung) Nunc dimittis (Prophetie Hannas)

    d 2,40: Heranwachsen

    X'2,41-52 (Verbindungsabschnitt zum Folgenden): der Zwölfjährige, Sohn seiner Eltern und Sohn Gottes.

Bevor wir diese Gesamtschau näher untersuchen, betrachten wir die einzelnen Parallelen.

2. *1,5-25/26-38: Ankündigung*

Die Parallelität dieser beiden Erzählungen ist schon längst aufgefallen; sie wird aber deutlicher, wenn man beide neben einanderstellt:[8]

A 5-7:   allgemeine Situation:
         Zeit, Ort, Personen: Notlage

B 8-11: spezielle Situation: Zeit, Ort,
         Personen: Auftreten des Engels   :26-28

C 12.13a: Reaktion des Menschen, Zuspruch
         des Engels   :29.30a[9]

D 13b-17: Verheissung der Geburt und ihrer
         Bedeutung für viele (Rolle des   :30b-33[10]
         heiligen Geistes)

C'18-20: Reaktion der Menschen, Zeichenzu-
         sage des Engels (Rolle des heili-   :34-37[11]
         gen Geistes)

B'21f: Verstummen/Bekenntnis des Menschen   :38

A'23-25: Erfüllung: Aufhebung der Notlage

Sofort fällt das Fehlen der Abschnitte A und A'[12] in der Mariaerzählung auf. Dadurch rückt hier der Engel, der auch gleich schon als Gabriel bezeichnet wird (nicht erst unter C' wie in 1,19), an die erste Stelle; er wird zum eigentlichen Subjekt des Berichtes. Das wird noch dadurch unterstrichen, dass er auch innerhalb von B vorgezogen wird; die menschliche Person wird erst nachher und nicht als Subjekt (wie in 1,9) eingeführt. Durch den Wegfall von A fehlt auch jegliche Hervorhebung der besonderen (priesterlichen) Position, Gerechtigkeit und Frömmigkeit der vom Engel besuchten Person. Dem entspricht der Unterschied bei B'; während das Verstummen des Zacharias selbst das Zeichen für die Wahrheit der Engelbotschaft ist, erfolgt das gläubige Ja der "Magd des Herrn" schon, bevor sie das zugesagte Zeichen erkennt (V.39f), und von der Erfüllung (A'), dem feststellbaren Eintreten der Schwangerschaft wird überhaupt nichts berichtet. Ebenso wird schon im Aufbau sichtbar, dass der heilige Geist nicht im Mittelstück D, sondern unter C' erscheint. Das hängt damit zusammen, dass er bei Maria eine andere Rolle spielt. Er wird nicht nur dem bald im Mutterleibe lebenden Kind verheissen, damit dieses

einst "in Geist und Kraft Elias" wirken möge (V.15.17); er ist
jetzt nicht mehr der prophetische, er ist der Schöpfer-Geist,
der die "creatio ex nihilo" vollzieht.[13] Der Unterschied
zeigt sich schon in der Sprache von V.32f, wo davidisch-mes-
sianische Kategorien verwendet werden (vgl.V.27), nicht mehr
nur die des charismatischen Propheten wie Elia. Doch wird in
V.35 das Wiedes Vorgangs der verheissenen Schwangerschaft und
Geburt erläutert und damit noch vor V.31-33 zurückgegriffen.
Die Geschichte ist schon in V.27-31 völlig auf Maria ausgerichtet; sie soll ja sogar den Namen geben.[14] Hinter der Formulierung von V.35 stehen gewiss hellenistische Vorstellungen
von einer Jungfrauengeburt; nur muss man sehen, dass sie schon
längst ins Judentum aufgenommen worden sind. Dies gilt sicher
für die philonischen Stellen, die Gottes Wunder an den Patriarchenfrauen in solche Terminologie kleiden.[15] Dazu kommen
jetzt aber die Qumranfunde, die nicht nur die Ausdrücke "Sohn
Gottes" und "Sohn des Höchsten" belegen, sondern auch die Vorstellungen von einer Schwängerung durch Engel, vielleicht
sogar Zengung des Messias durch Gott; selbst die Formulierung,
dass "sich (ein weibliches Subjekt wie z.B. "Geist") auf dich
niederlässt", findet sich dort.[16] So fällt der Milieu- und
Tonunterschied zwischen V.32f und V.35 weithin weg; da man
auch V.35 kaum, abgesehen von Einzelformulierungen, auf Lukas
zurückführen kann, der ja später nirgends die Jungfrauengeburt
Jesu hervorhebt, auch nicht in den Zusammenfassungen der Reden
der Apostelgeschichte. Da ausserdem die Ueberbietung der Ankündigung der Geburt des Johannes ausgesprochen sein muss,
wird man daran zweifeln, dass V.35 gegenüber V.32f traditionsgeschichtlich sekundär sein muss. Vermutlich ist der Vers von
dem formuliert worden, der die ganze Perikope in Anlehnung an
und Ueberbietung von V.5-25 schrieb.

Was der Aufbau verrät, wird durch die Erzählung selbst
und ihre Details bestätigt. Anders als in der ersten Geschichte ist es eine Frau, die die Verheissung empfängt und
- erstaunlicherweise - dem Kind den Namen geben wird. Dass
eine Frau gebären wird, ist selbstverständlich; aber Maria
gebiert das Kind nicht "ihm", dem Josef, wie Elisabet ihren
Sohn dem Zacharias ("dir" V.13) gebären wird. Sie, die Frau,
bewährt sich als Glaubende, als alles Gott überlassende Magd,
während der Mann Zacharias seine Zweifel hegt (1,18.38).

3. *1,57-80/2,1-40: Geburt, Beschneidung, Namengebung*

a) *Die Erzählung als ganze*

Auch hier sollen beide Komplexe zunächst nebeneinander-
gestellt werden:[17]

1,57-80		*2,1-40*	
A 57f: Geburt		6f: Geburt	
B a 59: Beschneidung u. Namengebung	a	21a: Beschneidung und Namengebung	
b 60-63: aufgrund der Engelbotschaft	b	21b: aufgrund der Engelbotschaft	
C (67): Wirken des heiligen Geistes		25d-27a: Wirken des heiligen Geistes	
D 64: als Gotteslob		27b.28: als Gotteslob	
E (68-79): im Hymnus		29-32: im Hymnus	
F 65f: Reaktion der Menschen		33: Reaktion der Menschen	
G 80: Wachsen des Kindes		40: Wachsen des Kindes	

Dass auf der rechten Seite weder die Verse 1-5 und 8-20
noch später V.22-25c und 34-39 berücksichtigt sind, und dass
auf der linken Seite C und E tatsächlich in der Textfolge erst
nach F erscheinen, zeigt schon die bestehenden Unterschiede.
Was sie traditionsgeschichtlich und sachlich bedeuten, muss
bei der Einzelbesprechung gefragt werden.

b) *1,57f/2,1-20: die Geburt*

Schon lange ist vermutet worden, dass die gegenüber der
Täufererzählung überschiessenden Verse 2,1-5, also die aus-
führliche Verbindung der Geburt Jesu mit der Weltgeschichte
vielle icht erst durch Lukas unter Verarbeitung älteren Materials selbst eingefügt worden ist, was der Vergleich mit
3,1 als möglich erscheinen lässt. Ebenso hat man schon lange
in der Hirtenepisode 2,8-20 eine in sich geschlossene Tradition gesehen. Das scheint sich zu bestätigen, wenn man diese
einmal für sich betrachtet:

A	a 8:	Lagern der Hirten	A'b 15a:	Weggang der Engel
	b 9a:	Kommen des Engels	a 15b:	Aufbruch der Hirten

B	a 9b:	Erschrecken der Zeugen	B'c 16:	die Krippe als Zeichen
	b 10f:	Heilsverkündigung des Engels	b 17:	Heilsverkündigung der Hirten
	c 12:	die Krippe als Zeichen	a 18:	Erstaunen der Zeugen

C	13f:	Gotteslob der Engel	C' 20:	Gotteslob der Hirten

In das (passive) Verweilen der Hirten hinein tritt der Engel (A a-b), der Weggang der Engel hingegen bewirkt den (aktiven) Aufbruch der Hirten (A'b-a). Die die Menschen erschreckende Erscheinung des Engels führt zur Verkündigung des Zeichens Gottes, der Krippe (B a-b-c); die Entdeckung des Zeichens Gottes, der Krippe, löst die Verkündigung der Hirten aus, die die Menschen zum Staunen bringt (B'c-b-a). So gründet im Gotteslob der Engel (C) das der Menschen (C'). Zusätzlich wird in V.19 auf Maria hingewiesen, die alles Geschehene in ihrem Herzen bewegt. Sie soll offenbar (in diesem sprachlich deutlich von Lukas geformten Vers) besonders herausgehoben werden als die nicht über Gott Verfügende, ihn auch nicht einfach voll Verstehende, aber für all sein Tun hörend Offene.

Was ist die Funktion dieser über die Parallelerzählung hinausgehenden Abschnitte? V.1-5 ist nicht nur eine Zeitangabe wie 3,1f; der Bericht vom Zensus verknüpft ausdrücklich die Weltgeschichte mit der sich in Betlehem abspielenden Geschichte. Beide laufen nicht nur gleichzeitig neben einander her, sondern die in Rom gefällte Entscheidung bewirkt den Beginn dessen, was in Betlehem geschehen soll. Gottes Geschichte mit Jesus vollzieht sich nicht einfach in einem Winkel ohne Zusammenhang mit dem, was sonst in der Welt vor sich geht. Gottes auf das Ziel der Geburt in Betlehem gerichtetes Handeln beginnt schon in Rom. Heilsgeschichte ist also nicht ein vom übrigen Weltgeschehen einfach geschiedenes, wunderhaftes Geschehen.

Die Hirtengeschichte hingegen zeigt die besondere Dimension auf, die dem Ereignis in Betlehem zukommt. Man könnte zunächst vermuten, ihre Funktion bestehe einfach darin, die Ueberbietung der Geburt des Johannes zu signalisieren. Das stimmt gewiss und spricht auch dafür, dass schon der Vorgänger des Lukas, der die beiden Geschichtsstränge miteinander ver-

316

bunden hat, die ursprünglich selbständige Hirtenerzählung zu
diesem Zweck aufgenommen hat. Aber damit ist ihre Rolle noch
nicht genügend erkannt. In der Johannestradition wird ja die
Geburt selbst nur sehr knapp geschildert, freilich hervorgehoben durch die Mitfreude der Nachbarn; doch charakterisieren
erst die Ereignisse bei Beschneidung und Namengebung ihre
eigentliche Bedeutung. An sich wäre also eine Ueberbietung
nicht bei der Geburt Jesu zu erwarten, sondern dort, wo sie
auch tatsächlich erscheint, in 2,21-39. Das bestätigt noch
einmal die ursprüngliche Selbständigkeit der Hirtenepisode.
Welche Rolle spielt sie aber theologisch im jetzigen Kontext?
Schon der Aufbau zeigt deutlich die Bewegung, die durch den
Einbruch der himmlischen Boten mit ihrer Verkündigung und
ihrem Gotteslob in die Welt der Menschen ausgelöst wird. Ihr
Kommen setzt die Hirten in Bewegung, ihre Verkündigung setzt
sich in der menschlichen Verkündigung auf Erden, ihr Lobpreis
im Lobpreis der Menschen fort. Diese Bewegung gliedert sich
jetzt ein in den Ablauf der Geschichte, die vom Zentrum der
Weltgeschichte her nach Betlehem hin zielt und von dort durch
die Verkündigung zunächst an die paar Leute um die Krippe
herum, dann an ganz Israel und schliesslich an alle Völker
wieder in die ganze Welt hinein zurückflutet und im ungehin-
derten Predigen des Paulus in Rom ihr vorläufiges Ziel erreicht (Apg. 28,31). Das "Zeichen" Gottes für dieses Geschehen ist die Krippe, die schon V.7 genannt und in V.12 und 16
aufgenommen ist. Verständlich wird dieses Zeichen, wie die
Erzählung von den Hirten anschaulich macht, nur durch die Offenbarung Gottes selbst, die vom "Himmel" her kommend sich in
der Verkündigung der Menschen auf Erden vollzieht. Ohne sie
bleibt die Geschichte stumm.

c) *1,67-80: Benedictus*

Wir haben oben schon auf die Umstellung der Abschnitte
C - F hingewiesen. Gewiss kommen chiastische Anordnung und
gewisse Verschränkungen öfters vor; doch handelt es sich hier
ja nicht um einen solchen Fall. Vermutlich ist die Umstellung
einfach dadurch bedingt, dass, wie schon oft vermutet wurde,
der Hymnus (V.68-79) mitsamt seiner Einleitung in V.67 schon
existiert hat, als die Erzählung von Geburt und Beschneidung
des Täufers damit zusammengestellt wurde. Tatsächlich müsste
das Loblied in V.64 eingefügt werden, also gerade dort, wo es
auch dem Schema entsprechend zu erwarten wäre. Die Erwähnung
des heiligen Geistes wäre vor 64 oder 64b, der Hymnus zwischen
64 und 65 einzuordnen, wie es die Buchstaben in der obigen
Zusammenstellung von 1,57-80 und 2,1-40 andeuten.

Der Hymnus des Zacharias ist durch A. Vanhoye[18] und in

seinem Gefolge durch P. Auffret[19] erneut auf seine Struktur hin
untersucht worden. Beide haben eine erstaunliche Wortfolge
nachgewiesen, die sich um V.72b/73a (Bund und Schwur Gottes)
als Zentrum gruppiert. Es folgen sich nämlich: (a) Volk
(68b) - (b) Heil (69) - (c) Profeten (70) - (d) Feinde (71) -
(e) Hand (71) - (f) unsere Väter (72); dann umgekehrt: (f')
unser Vater (73) - (e') Hand (74) - (d') Feinde (74) - (c')
Profeten (76) - (b') Heil (77a) - (a') Volk (77a).[20] Das
scheint zu zeigen, dass der ganze Hymnus, mindestens bis und
mit V.77a, in sich einheitlich konzipiert ist. Freilich hat
Auffret noch eine zweite Wortfolge in chiastischer Ordnung auf-
gezeigt, die die andere durchkreuzt und von V.72 bis V.78a
reicht. Sie umkreist die Aussage vom "Profeten" in V.76a als
ihre Mitte: (a) Barmherzigkeit (72) - (b) geben (74) - (c)
vor ihm (75); darauf chiastisch: (c') vor dem Herrn (76b) -
(b') geben (77) - (a') Barmherzigkeit (78). Auch diese Gruppe
scheint gegen eine Aufteilung des Hymnus in zwei sprachlich
und sachlich unterschiedene Teile (68-75/76-79) zu sprechen,
da sie gerade das Ende der ersten und den ersten Teil der
zweiten angenommenen Strophe zusammenschliesst. Allerdings
bleiben auch hier die für die christliche Interpretation besonders zentralen Aussagen V.78b und 79 ausserhalb des Schemas.
Sollte man etwa gar trotz dem deutlich anderen Charakter der
auf den konkreten Fall zugespitzten und im Futurum gehaltenen
Verse 76-78a (79b) diese schon einem ursprünglichen Täuferlied
zurechnen, in dem mit dem "Herrn" dann wie in 1,15-17 Gott
gemeint gewesen wäre, sodass dann nur V.78b.79(a) christliche
Zufügung wären?

Doch scheint mir hier die Grenze des vom Aufbau her Ein-
sichtigen erreicht zu sein. Notwendig ist ein solcher Schluss
nicht. Zunächst erscheint ja "Heil" noch einmal auch in V.71.
Man könnte hier also auch eine Redefigur b-c-b (Heil - Profet -
Heil) finden. Auf sie folgte dann in V.71-74 die Figur d-e-f/
f'-e'-d', die sich faktisch auf einen einfachen Chiasmus reduziert, weil "Hand der Feinde" eigentlich nur *ein* Ausdruck
ist. Hätte ein Späterer die Verse 76-79 hinzugedichtet, hätte
er die wichtigen Begriffe "vor ihm (dem Herrn)", "geben" und
"Barmherzigkeit" in chiastischer Folge aufgenommen und ausserdem in V.77 vom "Heil" für das "Volk" gesprochen, wie er es in
V.68b.69a las. Diachronisch liesse sich also auch die Entste-
hung des Hymnus in zwei Gängen erklären, und die Schwierigkeit
des Ineinanders der beiden Schemata bei der synchronen Betrach-
tung Auffrets zeigt ja auf alle Fälle, dass die Lösung nicht
ganz einfach ist. Formal erscheinen ab V.76 Futura statt
Praeterita und ist V.75 typische Schlussformel in Ps 16,11;
18,51; 28,9; 29,10. Löst man sich von der Feststellung des
Vorkommens gleicher Vokabeln und betrachtet man die Verse 68-
75 in ihrer stärker vom Inhalt her bestimmten Ordnung, dann
lässt sich, meine ich, ihr Ablauf auch in sich (ohne V.76-79)

gut verstehen:[21]

    68a: Lob Gottes:

A (Begründungssatz mit "weil" und Verbum im Aorist): Gottes
Tat an seinem Volk

  a 68b.69 Parallelismus membrorum: Besuch *Gottes*/Horn des
         Heils für *David*

  b 71 (unabhängiges Objekt) Ergebnis: (1) *Heil* (2) vor den
      Feinden (3) aus der *Hand* der Hasser

B (Finalsatz im Infinitiv): Gottes Absicht

  a 72 Parallelismus membrorum: Erbarmen an *unseren Vätern*/
      Gedenken des *Bundes*

  b 73 (unabhängiges Objekt): Schwur an Abraham, *unseren*
      Vater

A'(Finalsatz in determiniertem Infinitiv): Gottes Ziel für
das Volk

  b' 74 Voraussetzung: (3') aus der *Hand* (2') der *Feinde* (1')
      gerettet

  a' 75 *Gottes*dienst vor ihm für immer.

V.70 ist nicht berücksichtigt; er ist abgesehen von Umstellun-
gen wörtlich = Apg 3,21 und vermutlich lukanischer Einschub.
A und B verlaufen weithin parallel; a besteht beidemal aus
zwei parallelen Sätzen; der "Bund" (V.72) ist wohl der mit dem
"Haus Davids" (V.69) wie in Ps 89,4.29.35; ferner wiederholt b
je ein Stichwort aus a ("Heil" in A, "unser Vater" in B);
formal besteht b aus einem mehr oder weniger unabhängigen
Objekt. A' hingegen nimmt die Struktur von A chiastisch
wieder auf ("Gott" in a entspricht "ihm" in a'; b' repetiert
b in der Reihenfolge 3-2-1 und beschreibt inhaltlich die Voraussetzung für die endgültige Ruhe, die in A b als Ergebnis
des Handelns Gottes geschildert war.

    So verläuft die Bewegung des Hymnus deutlich von der Be-
gründung des Gotteslobes im Besuch Gottes (A) zur Absicht
Gottes (B), die wiederum zum Ziel des Handelns Gottes für
sein Volk (A') hinführt. Der Haupt-Satz in V.68a, der Gott
lobt, wird also durch eine Begründung gestützt, von der ein
finaler Infinitiv abhängt, der wiederum zu einem weiteren
Finalsatz führt. Bemerkt man weiterhin, dass sich in den
Versen 68-75 die Wörter häufen, die auch im Magnificat erscheinen,[22] während sie von V.76 an, abgesehen von Repetition-
en aus dem ersten Teil, fehlen, dass weiterhin die Verse 68-75
wie 46-55 eine Reihe von alttestamentlichen Wendungen enthal-

ten, während die Verse 76-79 wie auch der Hymnus 2,29-32 nur solche alttestamentlichen Formulierungen übernehmen, die schon christlich (oder sogar lukanisch) adaptiert worden sind,[23] dann wird es doch sehr wahrscheinlich, dass ein schon existierender jüdischer (täuferischer?) Psalm durch einen Judenchristen in V.76-79 ergänzt und damit deutlich auf den kommenden Jesus hin ausgerichtet worden ist. Dieser ist als "Aufgang aus der Höhe", der "den in Finsternis und Schatten des Todes Sitzenden erscheint", doch sehr deutlich vom "Profeten des Höchsten" unterschieden.[24] Mit grosser Selbstverständlichkeit werden dabei die "wir", die im ursprünglichen Psalm das Israel der davidisch-messianischen Befreiung bezeichnen, identifiziert mit denen, die der christliche Redaktor repräsentiert.[25]

d) 2,21-40: Beschneidung, Namengebung, Darstellung

Schon in der Täufergeschichte wird die Beschneidung nur kurz erwähnt, während die Namengebung erzählerisch ausgestaltet ist und auf das Engelgebot bei der Ankündigung zurückweist. In 2,21 erscheint die Beschneidung Jesu nur als Zeitangabe für die Namengebung, die hier ausdrücklich mit dem Engelwort von 1,31 verknüpft wird. Das Folgende weist wieder einige Abschnitte auf, die die Parallele zur Johannestradition sprengen. Zunächst ist der ganze anschliessende Abschnitt gerahmt durch den Gang der Eltern Jesu nach Jerusalem und ihre Rückkehr von dort (22.39). Darin spiegelt sich die wichtige Rolle Jerusalems als der Stadt des Heilsgeschehens, die sich auch im ganzen Werk des Lukas findet. Die Verse 22-24 dienen hauptsächlich dazu, die Gesetzestreue der Eltern Jesu dem Leser einzuschärfen. Dass dies in der Tat beabsichtigt ist, zeigt die eingefügte Bemerkung am Ende von V.27. Das läuft dem Parallel, was 1,6 von den Eltern des Täufers aussagte. Wir haben aber schon festgestellt, dass Aehnliches von Maria gerade nicht gesagt ist (1,26f). Die gleiche Charakterisierung der Eltern Jesu findet sich in 2,41f wieder, und wiederum erscheint Maria in jener Perikope anders (V.51b, s. unten unter 3.). Vielleicht darf man sogar zufügen, dass auch der Gehorsam gegenüber dem staatlichen Gesetz in 2,4f bei Josef festgestellt wird, während Maria in 2,19 wie in 2,51b beschrieben wird. Derjenige, der die Ankündigung an Maria formuliert und darin ihre Begnadigung durch Gottes überraschende Initiative unterstrichen hat, ist also nicht derselbe, der in unserem Abschnitt in Anlehnung an die Schilderung der Eltern des Johannes den Ton auf die genaue Befolgung des Gesetzes legt. Beides braucht sich nicht zu widersprechen; gerade M. Barth hat ja immer wieder auf die Gesetzes*freude* Israels hingewiesen. Dennoch

ist der Unterschied in der Betonung dieser oder jener Seite
unübersehbar.

Neu eingeführt werden ferner die beiden profetischen
Gestalten (V.25 und 36-38). Dass neben den Mann die Frau
tritt, ist wieder bemerkenswert. Freilich wird ise nicht sie
Maria als die eigentlich wichtige dem Mann gegenüber überhöht.
Beide werden als "Gerechte" im Sinne der israelitischen Tempelfrömmigkeit gezeichnet, beide aber zusätzlich als auf "den
Trost Israels" und "die Erlösung Jerusalems"[26] Wartende. Dabei wird bei Hanna sogar ein ganzer Kreis solcher Hoffender
sichtbar, dem sie vermutlich angehört.

Noch wichtiger erscheint mir die zusätzliche Weissagung
in V.34f. Nachdem von den Eltern Jesu nur gesagt war, dass
sie über die Worte Simeons "staunten" (V.33), wird in diesen
Versen wiederum Maria herausgehoben. Ihr wird die entscheidende Weissagung zuteil, dass nämlich das jetzt dargestellte
Kind "zum Fall und Aufstehen vieler in Israel und zum Zeichen
des Widerspruchs" werden soll. Die wichtigste exegetische
Schwierigkeit besteht in der Deutung des Doppelausdrucks vom
"Fallen und Aufstehen". Ist er so zu verstehen, dass die
einen fallen, während andere sich erheben?[27] Dafür könnte die
frühchristliche Verwendung des Bildes vom Stein sprechen, der
für die einen zum "Stein des Anstossens", für die andern zum
"Fundament" werden kann,[28] aber auch Parallelen in Qumran.[29]
Dennoch zweifel ich, ob man so interpretieren darf. Alttesta-
mentlich wird das Fallen und (Nicht-)Wiederaufstehen, wenn ich
recht sehe, immer von demselben Subjekt ausgesagt, wenn beide
Ausdrücke zusammen vorkommen. Negativ finden sich: Jes.24,20:
"(Die Erde) fällt, um nie wieder aufzustehen"; Am.5,2: "Gefallen ist, nicht steht wieder auf die Jungfrau Israel"; 8,14:
"Sie werden fallen und nicht wieder aufstehen". Positiv ge-
wendet sind: Pred.4,10: "Wenn der eine fällt, hilft der andere seinem Gesellen auf"; Spr.24,16: "Siebenmal fällt der
Fromme und steht wieder auf"; Mi.7,8: "(Ich harre auf den
Gott meines Heils:...) Wenn ich falle, ich stehe wieder auf;
wenn ich in Finsternis sitze, Jahwe ist mein Licht". Die
letzte Stelle ist nicht nur Heilsansage, die auch das Bild
vom Licht enthält; sie schliesst in V.12 vielleicht sogar
eine Hoffnung für die Völker ein. So ist vermutlich mit dem
ersten Aüsdruck doch die positiv Verheissung gemeint, dass
Jesus "viele" in Israel durch den Fall hindurch zum Aufstehen
führen wird. Das entspricht in gewisser Weise auch der Weissagung, die Maria persönlich gilt, dass sie ihren Weg zur Er-
kenntnis der Rolle Jesu nur so finden wird, dass zuerst ein
Schwert durch ihre Seele dringen wird (V.35a).[30] Allerdings
soll damit nicht geleugnet werden, dass auch von einer Scheidung in Israel die Rede ist. Jesus dient nicht nur vielen zum
Fall und Aufstehen; er ist für andere auch das Zeichen des Wi-

derspruchs. Darin zeichnet sich schon das Programm ab, das
Lukas dann in seinem zweiten Buch aufzeigt: Jesus ist zunächst
das Heil Israels, wie ja selbst Paulus sich deutlich als Apostel Israels versteht. Massenbekehrungen von gesetzestreuen
Juden geschehen: dreitausend, fünftausend, zehntausende (2,4;
4,4; 5,16; 6,1.7; 9,42; 12,24; 13,43; 14,1; 17,11f; 21,20).
Erst wenn Israel sich positiv und negativ entschieden hat,
wird auch den Heiden das Heil verkündet. Sie kommen hinzu,
weil die bisher hindernden Schranken der Beschneidung durch
das Eingreifen des Geistes gefallen sind. Wie die Zwölf als
Repräsentanten des Zwölfstämmevolkes den Anfang der Kirche
prägen, so Paulus, pharisäisch gebildet, gesetzeskündig und
bibelgläubig, als Lehrer Israels auch Israels Hoffnung auf die
Auferstehung ernst nehmend, deren Fortgang. Endgültig geht
die Verkündigung erst an die Heiden, nachdem auch in Rom sich
ein Teil der Judenschaft für, ein anderer Teil gegen das Evangelium erklärt hat (28,24.28).[31] Im Lukasevangelium ist es
ausgerechnet ein die Gesetzestreue stark hervorhebender Abschnitt, in dem die Verheissung für die Heiden zum ersten Mal
auftaucht. Beides widerspricht sich nicht, sondern gehört für
den Verfasser dieser Geschichte wie für Lukas selbst zusammen.

4. *1,39-56/2,41-52: Begegnung der Mütter; der Zwölfjährige
   im Tempel*

Die Erzählung von der Begegnung Marias mit Elisabet ist
ein deutliches Verbindungsstück, das beide Linien zusammenschliesst und sie zugleich auf das weitere Geschehen hin aus-
richtet. Die Begrüssung durch Elisabet hebt Maria aus allen
andern Menschen heraus. Noch stärker ist dies im anschliessenden Hymnus der Fall, der gegenüber dem Parallel-abschnitt
in 2,41-52 überschiessend ist. Sollte er ursprünglich von
Elisabet handeln, wäre die Heraushebung der Maria durch den,
der das Magnificat hier eingefügt hat, noch deutlicher. Insbesondere gilt dies für den Vers 48b ("Denn siehe, von nun an
werden mich seligpreisen alle Geschlechter"), in dem man freilich schon lange einen Einschub vermutet hat. Lässt man ihn
einmal unberücksichtigt, dann ergibt sich ein klarer Aufbau:[32]

I persönlich (1.Person sing.)	A 46f:	Lob Gottes (subjektiv) im Parallelismus membrorum (mit "und" verbunden)
	B 48a:	Begründung im Par. membr. a: "weil...*seiner Magd*..."
	49a	b: "weil er mir...*getan hat*"

II allgemein (3.Person sing.)	A'49b.50:	Lob Gottes (objektiv) im Par. membr. (mit "und" verbunden)
	B'b 51:	Begründung im Par. membr.: "er *hat getan*..."
	C 52f:	Rückverweis auf das biblische Gesetz (1. Sam.2,7) im chiastischen Par. membr. (a-b/b-a)
III geschichtlich (1.Person plur. = Israel)	a 54:	Begründung im Par. membr.: "...*seines Knechtes*..."
	C'55:	Rückverweis auf die Verheissung an die Väter

Natürlich ist dies kein Beweis für die spätere Zufügung von V. 48b. Selbst wenn der Aufbau den Gedankenfluss des Dichters richtig wiedergäbe, wäre noch nicht sicher, dass er nicht selbst schon in V.48b einen Zwischengedanken (gewissermassen in Klammern) eingeschoben hätte, der dann freilich auch die Funktion von V.49a verändert hätte (da dieser jetzt eher V.48b als V.46f begründet). Immerhin zeigt sich, dass die Annahme einer redaktionellen Zufügung, die vielleicht erst einen Elisabet-Hymnus als Maria-Hymnus deutlicher charakterisiert, nicht unvernünftig ist. Sie könnte durch Lukas selbst eingeführt worden sein, da "von nun an" typische lukanische Floskel ist; doch könnte er natürlich ein einfacheres "nun" durch seine Wendung wiedergegeben haben. Erkennt man, dass dieser Hymnus ohne Gegenstück in 2,41-52 bleibt und dass vor allem das Vokabular (abgesehen von den besonders dem Hannalied verwandten Versen 52f) dem des Benedictus sehr gleicht,[33] wird man vermuten können, dass auch hier ein schon vorliegendes Traditionsstück aus Täuferkreisen aufgenommen worden ist. Freilich könnte es kaum vom gleichen Verfasser stammen wie das Benedictus, da dieses im Satzbau viel weniger durchsichtig ist als das Marialied.

Wichtig ist der Gedankengang, der durch die Struktur des Loblieds sichtbar wird. Die persönliche Erfahrung der Gotteshilfe wird sofort ins Allgemeine ausgeweitet, wie es alttestamentlicher Ueberlieferung entspricht.[34] Aber es bleibt auch nicht bei einigen zeitlos gültigen Sätzen über eine Umwertung aller Werte; im letzten Teil wird das wiederum konkret, jetzt

aber nicht mehr individuell, sondern auf das Schicksal Israels
in der jetzt angebrochenen messianischen Zeit bezogen, was
Lukas und wahrscheinlich schon sein Vorgänger, der das Lied
hier eingeschlossen hat, auf die Gemeinde Jesu bezieht. In
ihr wird soziale Wirklichkeit, was der einzelne als Gottesgnade erlebt und besungen hat.[35]

Auch die Geschichte vom Zwölfjährigen im Tempel dient als
Verbindungsstück. Sie verknüpft zwar nicht Täufer- und Jesustradition, wohl aber das von Profeten schon über Jesus Gesagte
mit dem, was das Evangelium von seinem Wirken (und dem des
Täufers) berichten wird. Man kann sie gliedern:

A Zug nach Jerusalem (41f)

   B Jesu Zurückbleiben ohne Wissen der Eltern (43)

      C Ihr Suchen und Finden (44-46a)

         X Jesus unter den Gelehrten (46b.47)

      C' Vorwurf der Eltern (48)

   B' Jesu Antwort, den Eltern unverständlich (49f)

A' Rückkehr von Jerusalem (51).

Dann steht Jesu Weisheit in der Mitte, hervorgehoben durch
V.47, der freilich deutlich sekundär ist.[36] So versteht es
wohl Lukas. Lässt man ihn und damit das Motiv aussergewöhn-
licher Weisheit weg, zeigt sich der Ablauf anders:

A Einleitung: Personen, Ort, Zeit, Charakterisierung
     (in Nebensätzen, 41f)

B Notlage: Aktion Jesu (Zurückbleiben, 43) -
     Reaktion der Eltern (Suchen, Finden, 44-46a)

C Vorläufige Lösung: Aktion Jesu (Lernen, 46b) -
     Reaktion der Eltern (Vorwurf, 48)

D Eigentliche Lösung: Aktion Jesu (Wort, 49) -
     Reaktion der Eltern (Unverständnis, 50)

E Abschluss: Rückkehr (51a, Jesus Subjekt wie V.42).

Dann liegt alles Gewicht auf der Aussage Jesu über seinen Vater (V.49). V.51b korrigiert V.50; die darin genannten "Worte" sind nicht das V.50 genannte "Wort", sondern alles in Kap.1f Erzählte im Sinne von "Begebenheiten".[37] Ausserdem ist V.51a der übliche Perikopenschluss (vgl.1,23.38.56; 2,20.39). So schliesst der 2,19 wiederholende und wohl vom gleichen Autor zugefügte Halbvers mit V.52 zusammen die ganzen Kindheitsgeschichten ab.

5. *Folgerungen*

Wie immer man traditionsgeschichtlich einteilt--die Abgrenzungen sind hier besonders schwierig durchzuführen, weil Lukas übernommene Traditionen einerseits mit seinem Stil weithin durchdringt, andererseits sich als Vorbild nimmt, wie der Vergleich mit Markus und Q zeigen kann -,[38] klar ist jedenfalls, dass es Täufertraditionen gab, die diesen noch als Vorläufer des endzeitlichen Kommens Gottes sahen, ohne mit einer anderen messianischen Gestalt zu rechnen, und daneben verschiedene Jesusgeschichten. Jene standen in betonter Kontinuität zur Geschichte Israels, zu den davidisch-messianischen Hoffnungen im Fall der beiden Hymnen, zur priesterlich-jerusalemitischen Welt im Fall der beiden Erzählungen. Die Jesustradition war in den Erzählungen von der Darstellung und vom Zwölfjährigen ebenso sehr am engen Zusammenhang mit Israels Geschichte, insbesondere mit Jerusalem und seiner Tempelfrömmigkeit interessiert; nur dass dabei profetische Gestalten und Kreise der auf die Endzeit Wartenden noch stärker hervorgehoben werden. In dieser Schicht werden auch die Eltern Jesu als gesetzestreue Fromme geschildert, die freilich das Neue, das mit Jesus hereinbricht, noch nicht recht verstehen.

Deutlich ist weiter, dass schon vor Lukas die beiden Ueberlieferungsgruppen mit einander verknüpft wurden und dabei Maria besonders hervorgehoben wurde. Hier ist ihre Gesetzesfrömmigkeit nicht erwähnt; sie erscheint auch durchwegs als die Verstehende oder für zukünftiges volles Verstehen Offene (1,38.45.46a.48b; 2,19.[34f]51b). Die Geschichte von der Ankündigung der Geburt Jesu ist dabei so stark auf Maria ausgerichtet, dass vermutlich auch die Verheissung der Empfängnis durch den heiligen Geist in V.34f von Anfang an dazu gehörte.[39] Die Zwischenbemerkungen 1,48b; 2,19 (34f?) 51b scheinen aus sprachlichen Gründen von Lukas zu stammen. Freilich hebt er sonst abgesehen von der kurzen Notiz Apg.1,14 Maria nicht hervor; doch ist sie ihm in Kap.1f offenbar als Urbild eines nur von Gottes Gnadenzusage lebenden Glaubens wichtig.

Weit entscheidender sind aber die theologischen Aussagen.
Das Erstaunlichste ist die Zusammenstellung dieser Johannes-
und Jesustraditionen überhaupt. In einer eigentlich unerhör-
ten Weise wird die Täufertradition von dem, der *Gott* dem Herrn
voran den Weg bereitet (1,16f), auf den Vorgänger *Jesu* bezogen.
Darin geschieht etwas von dem, was Markus Barth einmal vom Verfasser des Hebräerbriefs gesagt hat: der in die Welt kommende
Herr ist der Kanon im Kanon; darum schaut der Verfasser, wo er
ihn in der Geschichte Israels, in dem Dialog zwischen Gott und
seinem Volk entdecken kann, und dies nicht in zeitlosen Ideen,
wohl aber in Gottes lebendiger Stimme.[40] Was aber darüber hin-
ausgeht, ist nicht nur die Tatsache, dass hier nicht einfach
ein Text, sondern die Geschichte Gottes als solche in Anspruch
genommen wird - das tut der Hebräerbrief in gewisser Weise
auch, wenn er über Melchisedek nachdenkt -; es ist vor allem
die Tatsache, dass es eine Geschichte ist, die sich zeitlich
völlig mit derjenigen Jesu verschränkt. Ja, es ist sogar so,
dass mindestens die Erzählung von der Ankündigung der Geburt
Jesu völlig der Geschichte Gottes mit dem Täufer nachgestaltet
ist. Was bedeutet das theologisch?

Schon dass überhaupt Geschichten aus der Kindheit Jesu
und erst recht des Täufers erzählt werden, ist beachtenswert.
Markus und Johannes, aber auch die Kurzzusammenfassungen des
christlichen Glaubens in den Predigtender Apostelgeschichte
und die Autoren der neutestamentlichen Briefe (Paulus inbe-
griffen) scheinen das nicht für notwendig zu halten. Erzäh-
lend will Lukas auf seine Weise festhalten, was Markus mit
seinem betonten Hinweis auf die Erfüllung der Schrift, Johannes mit seinem Prolog und Paulus mit der Rede von der Sendung
des präexistenten Sohnes aussagen wollen. Darum ist bei ihm
zuerst von Kleinkindern die Rede, die passives Objekt des Geschehens sind, nicht aktives Subjekt eines glaubenden Existenz-
verständnisses.[41] Darum setzt von allem Anfang an der Engel
Gottes alles in Bewegung, erscheint dieser dann als allererster
auf dem Plan bei der Ankündigung der Geburt Jesu und deutet er
erst das an sich unverständliche Zeichen der Geburt in der
Krippe. Darum werden beide Schwangerschaften als Wunder
Gottes erzählt, wird der kommende Weg des noch kleinen Kindes
vorweg profetisch beschrieben, und enden die Vorgeschichten
mit dem Wort Jesu von seinem Vater. An der Stelle, an der der
eigentliche, der von Gott gemeinte Sinn des Lebens Jesu mar-
kiert, wo dieses also als "eschatologisches" verkündet werden
soll, begnügt sich Lukas nicht mit dem noch so hervorgehobenen
Rückverweis auf erfüllte Schrift, auch nicht mit dem noch so
hoch greifenden Begriff eines ewigen Logos oder mit einer noch
so mythisch verklärten Rede von einer Sendung eines himmlischen Sohnes. Er erzählt im Gegenteil Geschichten, die sich
auf dieser Erde abspielen mitten zwischen all den Menschen,
die sich eben dort aufhalten mit all dem, was so ein Menschen-

leben in sich enthält. Nur wird immer deutlicher, dass diese
eigentlich eine einzige, alles entscheidende Geschichte sind,
deren Herr und verantwortliches Subjekt Gott selbst ist.
Liessen sich Schrifterfüllung, Logoslehre und Sendung eines
präexistenten Himmelswesens noch als zeitlose Ideen missver-
stehen - gnostische Systeme zeigen dies -, so kann man auf
alle Fälle die sehr konkreten und in vielem sehr menschlich-
irdischen Geschichten des Lukas nicht mehr so interpretieren.[42]
Gottes eschatologisches Handeln vollzieht sich also als sehr
konkrete, sich im Israel einer ganz bestimmten Zeit abspielende
Geschichte.

Aber noch erregender ist die andere, schon genannte Tatsache. Die Täufergeschichte geht hier derart in die Jesusgeschichte über, dass sie diese sogar überhaupt erst gestaltet oder doch in vielen Einzelheiten prägt. Eschatologisch
ist das Jesusgeschehen für Lukas demnach in dem Sinn, dass,
was sich in Israel, insbesondere in der Geburt des Täufers und
in den diese umrahmenden Ereignissen als Handeln Gottes erkennen lässt, in Jesus seine letzte Erfüllung findet.[43] Mindestens von der Art des Erzählens her lässt sich nicht sagen,
dass die Jesusgeschichte auf einer völlig anderen Ebene spielt
als die Johannesgeschichte; sie überbietet diese nur. Umgekehrt ist es aber auch nicht so, dass Gottes Handeln sich hier
ausschliesslich sub contrario verbirgt, ohne irgend welche
Zeichen in der konkreten Geschichte zu hinterlassen, sodass
sein eschatologischer Charakter nur rein-kerygmatisch verkündet werden kann. Die Geschichten beider Gestalten sind
"Evangelium"; freilich so, dass dieses Stichwort bei Johannes
die Ankündigung der Geburt, bei Jesus die Nachricht von der
erfolgten Geburt selbst bezeichnet (1,19; 2,10). Beide verden
später als Verkünder des Evangeliums vorgeführt; freilich so,
dass Johannes dies als, Mahner zu einem Gott wohlgefälligen
Wandel ist, Jesus als Künder des Reiches Gottes (1,19; 3,18;
4,43; vgl. 20,1).[44] Erst das Wort des heiligen Geistes und
der Engel stellt jenen in die Kategorie des Profeten, diesen
in die des Gottessohnes und Retters, der Israel- und Täufergeschichte zu ihrem Ziel bringt.[45] Für die in Luk. 1-2 er-
scheinende Tradition, aber auch für Lukas selbst, der sie
übernimmt, ist das freilich nicht etwa das Ende der Geschichte
Israels, die dann von gar keiner Geschichte mehr oder doch von
einer Geschichte eines anderen, neuen Volkes abgelöst würde.
Zwar bricht mit Jesus das Heil "vor allen Völkern" an und kommt
in ihm "das Licht zur Erleuchtung der Heiden"; aber es kommt
so, dass damit die "Herrlichkeit Israels" offenbar wird,
weil "viele in Israel zu Fall und Auferstehung kommen und ihre
Herzen aufgedeckt werden sollen" (2,31-35). Israelgeschichte
und Jesusgeschichte bleiben in einander verschränkt, wie sie
es im Kommen von Johannes und Jesus waren.[46] "Die Hoffnung
der an die Väter ergangenen Verheissung", der "das Zwölfstäm-

mevolk in Tag und Nacht eifrig vollzogenem Gottesdienst zu begegnen hofft", wird darin erreicht, dass auch die Heiden "ein Erbteil unter den Geheiligten"[47] finden (Apg. 26,6f.18).

"Eschatologisch" ist das Jesusgeschehen für Lukas also nicht in dem Sinn, dass es analogielos gewissermassen wie ein Meteor vom Himmel her in die irdische Geschichte einbräche. Es ist es nicht einmal in dem heilgeschichtlichen Sinn, dass sich Analogien nur in einer achon kanonisch gewordenen, offiziell durch die heilige Schrift interpretierten Geschichte fänden. Sie zeigen sich im zeitgenössichen Erleben anscheinend zufällig auftretender Menschen. "Eschatologisch" ist Jesu Geschichte insofern, als bisherige Erfahrungen Israels erst darin ihren Sinn und ihr Ziel finden. Dabei ist nicht von einer in irgendeiner Weise kontinuierlichen Geschichte die Rede, wie das der mattäische Stammbaum konzipiert (Mt. 1,1-17). Wie Lukas in bunter Fülle und ohne sichtbare systematische Ordnung Geschichten erzählt, in denen Gottes Heilshandeln dem Glauben sichtbar wird, so sind es in Israel einzelne Geschichten, die jetzt ihren Sinn bekommen, ohne dass dabei bestimmte Entwicklungslinien von der Früh- bis zur Spätzeit deutlich würden. Die Analogien zwischen dem Erleben Elisabet und Marias einerseits, dem Saras, Rahels, der Frau Manoachs und Hannas andererseits zeigen mehr oder weniger gleichwertig die Einübung des Glaubens in Israel. So hat Israel gelernt, auf jenes Handeln Gottes zu warten, das in noch ganz anderer Weise, alles Vorangegangene überbietend, reines Gnadenhandeln war, das der Mensch nur glaubend und lobpreisend empfangen kann wie Maria. Lukas hat verstanden, dass Gott, wenn er nicht - im Sinn des Doketismus - ein Himmelswesen bleibt, das sich bloss verkleidet, in Jesus eingehen muss in die ganze, kontingente Fülle dessen, was menschliches Erfahren und Erleiden ist.[48]

Was ist inhaltlich diese letzte Ueberbietung aller bisherigen Geschichte im Jesusgeschehen? Der, der zuerst die Ankündigung der Geburt Jesu an Maria gestaltet hat, hat sie ja nicht nur der vorliegenden Erzählung von Zacharias nachgebildet. Er hat das, was jetzt als Ziel alles Handelns Gottes in Israel erscheint, hervorgehoben. In Israel gibt es Gesetzes- und Tempelfrömmigkeit, z.B. bei den Eltern des Johannes und den Eltern Jesu. Menschen haben also schon freudig und lobpreisend etwas von Gottes gutem Tun verstanden. Die Erfüllung dieses Tuns aber kommt als reine Begnadigung. Das gilt so absolut, dass von Maria, die zeichenhaft das von Jesus bestimmte Gottesvolk abbildet, nicht einmal mehr gesagt werden kann, dass sie fromm und gesetzestreu gewesen sei. So völlig erscheint sie als die, an der sich Gottes alle Erwartungen übersteigende, alle überraschende Gnade vollzieht. Sie ist nicht mehr selbst die Gerechte, Fromme und Wissende; sie ist nur die auf Gottes zu ihr kommendes Gnadenwort und sein zukünftiges Handeln hin Lauschende. Eben darin bildet sich in ihr schon jenes Israel ab, zu dem sich dann die Völker gesellen werden, die lernen dürfen, ganz auf Gottes Gnade zu trauen.

NOTES

1. Israel und die Kirche im Brief des Paulus an die
Epheser, TEH 75 (1959), 9: Die Kirche ist nicht "die al-
leinige Besitzerin und Hüterin der Wahrheit"; ebenda 17-20,
24: nach Eph.2,15 werden die Heiden Glieder Christi durch
ihre Zusammenfassung mit Israel, womit nicht nur das christliche Israel gemeint ist(!, ähnlich schon The Ecumenical Dialogue at Cornell University, New York 1962, 33; ferner: Das
Volk Gottes. Juden und Christen in der Botschaft des Paulus,
in: Paulus - Apostat oder Apostel? Jüdische und christliche
Antworten, Regensburg 1977, 98-101, wo S.106 sogar vom "character indelebilis" des jüdischen Volkes die Rede ist.) Etwas
zurückhaltender ist: Ephesians, AncB 34 (1974) I 253-325.
"In ihm" bedeutet: in seinem gekreuzigten Leib, der der Leib
eines Juden ist (298,303); darum müssen Juden nicht Heiden
werden, so wenig Heiden Juden werden müssen; beide brauchen
einander, auch in der Kirche Jesu Christi (310f). So ist die
Taufe das Ereignis, das Heiden mit Israel verbindet (Sieben
Sätze zur Taufe nach dem Neuen Testament, in: D. Schellong,
Warum Christen ihre Kinder nicht mehr taufen lassen, Antwor-
ten 18, Frankfurt/Main 1969, 92-97). Die Heiden werden so zu
"Mitmenschen der Juden" mit allen daraus folgenden sozialen
Konsequenzen (Gottes und des Nächsten Recht, in: ΠΑΡΡΗΣΙΑ,
FS K. Barth, Zürich 1966, 455-457). Vgl. auch: Die Einheit
des Galater- und Epheserbriefs, ThZ 32 (1976), 90.

2. Ebd. (Einheit..[Anm.1]) 83f; Der gute Jude Paulus,
in: FS H. Gollwitzer, München 1976, 112-123; Jesus, Paulus
und die Juden, ThSt(B) 91 (1967), 60-67: nach J. Munck und
W. D. Davies ist Christus Ziel, nicht Ende des Gesetzes; 70:
Paulus versteht sich als Erfüllung der Mission Israels unter
den Heiden, nicht als Judenmissionar. Vgl. auch die Betonung
der Gemeinschaft von Juden und Heiden unter Gericht und Gnade
in: Rechtfertigung. Versuch einer Auslegung paulinischer
Texte im Rahmen des AT und NT, in: Foi et salut selon S. Paul,
AnBib 46 (1970, = ThSt(B) 90, 1969) 149-156, 185-187. Es ist
dies ein Vortrag, der "narrative" Theologie zu verwirklichen
sucht (ebd. 148).

3. Dass er gerade der Vierzigste ist, dem ich mit einem
Aufsatz zum Geburtstag grüssen darf, und dass es auf den Tag
genau vierzig Jahre her sind, seit sein Vater als Dekan mir
eine sehr beherzigenswerte Rede zur Doktorpromotion in Basel
(am 2.7.1938) gehalten hat, wollen wir - trotz der grossen Bedeutung der Zahl 40 im AT - nicht typologisch ausdeuten.

4. H. Schürmann, Das Lukasevangelium, Freiburg 1969, 20f: Homologese.

5. Ebd. 25, vgl. 28.

6. Das Evangelium nach Lukas, ThHK (1971), 46.

7. Die theologische Struktur der Komposition des Lukas-evangeliums, ThZ 34 (1978), 1-3 (im Wesantlichen nach R. Laurentin, Structure et théologie de Luc I-II [Etudes bibliques, Paris 1957] 32f, dessen Einteilung in 14 Szenen (S.25) freilich sehr fraglich bleibt).

8. R. E. Brown, The Birth of the Messiah, New York 1977, 294f stellt nicht nur Parallelen mit Einzelheiten neben einander, sondern vergleicht vor allem (S.156) die Engelerscheinungen in Gen. 16; 17 und Ri. 13 mit der gleichen Folge von Erscheinung, Verwirrung des Menschen, Botschaft, Frage des Menschen und Zeichen mit Lk 1f.

9. Wörtlich wiederholen sich: "wurde verwirrt" (in V.29 Compositum); "sprach der Engel (zu) ihm/ihr: Fürchte dich nicht (+ Name)".

10. Wörtlich wiederholen sich: "Sie wird dir/du wirst einen Sohn(gebären) und du wirst seinen Namen...nennen"; "er wird gross sein". "Er wird Sohn des Höchsten genannt werden" ist zu vergleichen mit 1,76: "du wirst Prophet des Höchsten genannt werden".

11. Wörtlich wiederholen sich: "...sprach zum Engel"; "und siehe,..." Beidemal ist der Name des Engels Gabriel.

12. Grundmann (Anm.6) 48: Rahmung, beide Abschnitte sind von gleicher Länge.

13. W. B. Tatum, The Epoch of Israel: Luke I - II and the Theological Plan of Luke-Acts, NTS 13 (1966/67) 187; W. Klaiber, Eine lukanische Fassung des sola gratia. Beobachtungen zu Lk 1,5-56, in: Rechtfertigung, FS E. Käsemann, Tübingen 1976, 217.

14. Die nächste sprachliche Parallele im AT ist daher Gen. 16,11 (Hagar), wo bei und nach der Geburt kein Vater anwesend ist. Der Lk 1,31 verwendete Ausdruck ist eine Mischung aus dem in der LXX (auch Ri. 13,3; Jes 7,14) und dem in der B-version von Ri. 13,3 auftauchenden. Benennung durch die Mutter freilich auch Gen.30,21; Ri.13,24.

15. Die Schrift "lässt nämlich Sara dann schwanger werden,

als Gott...auf sie schaut..."; "Gott öffnete ihren (Leas)
Mutterschoss - den Mutterschoss öffnen ist aber Sache des
Mannes"; Rebekka "wird von dem Angeflehten (Gott) schwanger";
"Mose...findet...Zippora schwanger, keinesfalls von einem Ster-
blichen" (Cher.45-47). Gewiss versteht Philo selbst dies al-
legorisch; er stützt sich dabei aber fast sicher auf Versionen
dieser Geschichten der Patriarchenfrauen, die keineswegs Alle-
gorien waren.

16. 4Q243 (NTS 20 [1973/74] 391-394 [J. A. Fitzmyer, The
Contribution of Qumran Aramaic to the Study of the NT]), 2,1;
lQGenApocr 2,1; lQSa 2,11f; 4Q243, 1,1.

17. Vgl. auch Brown (Anm. 8) 409.

18. Structure du "Benedictus", NTS 12 (1965/66) 382-389.

19. Note sur la structure littéraire de Lc I.68-79, NTS
24 (1977/78) 248-258.

20. So Auffret ebd. 253. Man könnte sogar noch "besuchen"
in V.68 und 78 vor (a) und nach (a') zufügen; vgl. das Schema
von Vanhoye (Anm. 18).

21. Brown (Anm. 8) 385-391 grenzt V.68b-71(I)/72-75(II)/
76f(III)/78f(Abschluss)ab.

22. V.68: Herr, Gott, tat (mit Akkusativobjekt); V.69:
Heil, sein Knecht; V.70: wie er sprach; V.72: tat (mit Akkusativobjekt), Barmherzigkeit, unsere Väter, gedenken; V.73:
(unser Vater). Ferner entsprechen sich "er besuchte" (V.68)
und "er schaute auf" (V.48), "alle unsere Tage" (V.75) und
"von Geschlecht zu Geschlecht" (V.50). "Feinde" (V.71.74) ist
der Ausdruck, der Ps.88,11 LXX steht, während "Hochfahrende"
(V.51) dort im Parallelismus membrorum erscheint.

23. V.76 = Mk.1,2 = Lk.7,27; vgl.3,4. V.79 = Mt.4,16
(wo die auffällige Form Nazara in V.13 mit Lk.4,16 über-
einstimmt und vielleicht noch auf eine auch Lukas bekannte
Ueberlieferung hinweist, s. meinen Kommentar in NTD 2 z.St.).
2,30 = 3,6 (in Fortsetzung des schon Mk.1,3 zitierten Wortes
zum Vorläufertum des Johannes). 2,31 = Apg.13,47.

24. Gegen Ph. Vielhauer, Das Benedictus des Zacharias,
ZThK 49 (1952) 255-272, mit J. Gnilka, Der Hymnus des Zacharias, BZ 6 (1962) 215-238.

25. Die Beziehung auf die 1.Person Plural fehlt in dem
Ausdruck "in Vergebung ihrer (!) Sünden", der vielleicht erst
lukanische Einfügung ist (vgl. Lk.24,47; Apg.2,38; 5,31; 10,

43; 13,38; 26,18; sonst nur Mk.1,4 = Lk.3,3; Mt.26,28; ähnlich Kol.1,14; nicht in LXX).

26. Vielleicht ist sogar parallel zu V.25 "Israel" zu lesen, was freilich schlecht bezeugt ist.

27. So meistens; z.B. K. H. Rengstorf, NTD 3; H. Schürmann (Anm.4, anch S.426); J. Ernst, RNT z.St.

28. Röm.9,33; 1.Petr.2,6-8 und dazu B. Lindars, New Testament Apologetic, London 1961, 169-188, besonders 175-179.

29. 1QH 2,8f; 1QM 14,10f; vgl. 1QH 2,29 und W. Grundmann, Stehen und Fallen im qumrānischen und neutestamentlichen Schrifttum, in: Qumran-Probleme, ed. H. Bardtke, Berlin 1963, 147-166, besonders 164, Anm. 10.

30. Die Funktion des Schwertes ist dabei nicht die Scheidung wie in Hebr.4,12. Jüdisch liegt das Bild in 3.Sib. 316 vor: "das Schwert wird mitten durch dich hindurchgehen" (nämlich: durch Aegypten, vgl. Ez.14,17 LXX, allgemein verstanden).

31. J. Jervell, Luke and the People of God. A New Look at Luke-Acts, Minneapolis 1972, besonders 41-55, 101f, 153-177. Nach Lukas lehnt nicht ganz Israel Jesus ab, sondern nur seine Führer (z.B. Lk.7,30, vgl.9 und 31; 23,1ff; Schürmann [Anm. 4] 406; R. Schnackenburg, Das Johannesevangelium, HThK, III [Freiburg 1975], 284).

32. Brown (Anm. 8) 358 teilt ein: V.48-50 (I)/ 51-53 (II)/ 54f (Abschluss).

33. Vgl. Anm. 22.

34. L. Schottroff, Das Magnificat und die älteste Tradition über Jesus von Nazareth, EvTh 38 (1978), 298-313, ist der Meinung, dass gerade mit den Versen 51-53 die entscheidende, ins Sozialgefüge eingreifende Aussage aus der frühen Jesustradition aufgenommen ist, während der Kontext diese schon spiritualisiere. Man wird aber im Blick auf den Hymnus wie im Blick auf Jesus selbst betonen müssen, dass diese Sätze vom Lob der Gottesgnade in V.46-50 herkommen und in den Ausblick auf das erlöste Israel (im Sinne des Lukas: auf die Gemeinde Jesu) ausmünden.

35. Auch hier wäre an M. Barth zu erinnern (besonders deutlich etwa: Rechtfertigung [Anm.2] 186f, auch Einheit [Anm.1] 90f).

36. So H. J. de Jonge, Sonship, Wisdom, Infancy: Luke II.41-51a, NTS 24 (1977/8), 339; zu V.47 ebd. 342f und Schürmann (Anm.4) z.St. V.48 sind die Eltern wieder Subjekt wie V.46, ohne aber neu genannt zu werden. Während V.46 vom lernbegierigen Fragen des Schülers spricht, denkt V.47 an belehrende Antworten.

37. So übersetzt H. Schürmann (Anm.4), obwohl er in 2,19 das gleiche griechische Wort mit "Worte" wiedergibt. Auch 1, 37 ist der Ausdruck in einer alttestamentlichen Wendung wie in 2,51 verstanden.

38. Mein Vorschlag wäre: Ia Täufertraditionen: 1,5-25. 57-66; dazu die Hymnen 1,46b-55 (ohne 48b).67-75 - In Jesustradition: Jungfrauengeburt in Betlehem (vgl. Mt.1f); 2,8-20 (ohne V.19) wohl erst mündlich überliefert; 2,22-39 (ohne V. 34f?).41-46.48-51a(52?) - II Verknüpfung beider Traditionen: 1,26-38.39-45.56.76-79(80?); 2,3-7.21(34f?)(40?) - III Lukanische Redaktion durchwegs in Einzelformulierungen; am stärksten 2,1f, wohl auch 1,48b(80?); 2,19(34f)(40?).51b.

39. Man wird zwar den Tonunterschied zwischen der davidisch-nationalen Erwartung in V.32f und dem in V.34f Gesagten nicht übersehen können, muss sich aber klar sein, wie sehr auch die Aussagen von V.35 schon ins Judentum übernommen worden sind (Anm.15 und 16) und wie stark Maria schon in V.27-31 herausgehoben ist.

40. The Old Testament in Hebrews, in: Current Issues in NT Interpretation, FS O. Piper, ed. W. Klassen/G. F. Snyder, New York 1962, 57, 76f.

41. Natürlich findet sich ein solches auch bei den Zeugen dieser Ereignisse, den beiden Elternpaaren, den Hirten, den Jerusalemer Propheten in allen möglichen Schattierungen. Doch zeigen auch diese Stellen Maria als Empfängerin göttlichen Gnadenhandelns, die Hirten als Hörer, die Profeten als vom heiligen Geist Bewegte, andere, z.B. auch die Eltern Jesu als mehr oder weniger unverständige, staunende Zeugen eines "fremden" Geschehens, das sich jedenfalls nicht einfach in ihren Herzen vollzieht.

42. Selbstverständlich könnte das umgekehrt dahin missverstanden werden, dass das Heil durch eine bestimmte Geschichtskonzeption bewältigt werden könnte. Doch ist es Mt. 1,1-17, der die Vorstellung einer völlig auf die Erscheinung Jesu hin strukturierten Heilsgeschichte vertritt (wie ähnlich schon vor ihm Q!), während Lk. 3,23-38 die ursprüngliche Aufgliederung der Geschichte in elfmal sieben Generationen mit Jesus als dem Anfänger der zwölften "Woche" fallen gelassen

hat, bzw. überhaupt nicht mehr kennt. Gott kann zwar die Profangeschichte benützen, um sein Heil zu schaffen (2,1f); aber die bunte Fülle des Geschehens lässt jedenfalls kein heilsgeschichtliches Schema zu, auf das hin dieses reduziert werden könnte.

43. Vielleicht lässt sich damit vergleichen, dass bei Lukas das ganze Leben Jesu als Dienst an den Niedrigen und Schwachen konzipiert ist (19,10 und 22,27 treten an die Stelle von Mk. 10,45!), der seine letzte Erfüllung in der Kreuzigung findet, bei der sich Jesus noch immer seinen Feinden und dem neben ihm hängenden Verbrecher zuneigt, ohne dass aber sein Kreuzestod (etwa im Sinne von Gal.3,13) auf einer anderen Ebene läge.

44. Ich meine auch nicht, dass 3,19f einen Abschluss der Periode des Täufers vor dem Beginn des Wirkens Jesu markieren will, sondern eher, dass das Schicksal des Johannes als Hinweis auf das parallele Schicksal Jesu verstanden ist. In 7, 18f tritt der Täufer ja wieder in Aktion, und von seinem Tod hören wir erst 9,7-9.

45. Zu vergleichen ist die Q-Tradition, die Johannes und Jesus als Boten der Weisheit nebeneinander stellt (Lk.7,33-35).

46. Vgl. am Ende von 3d.

47. Der Ausdruck stammt aus Deut.33,3. Die "Heiligen" sind zwar 26,10 wie 9,13.32,41 Judenchristen; doch ist der Ausdruck in 20,32 so allgemein verwendet, dass Lukas damit schwerlich eine Eingliederung in Israel (von der er nie explizit redet) aussagen will. Jedoch vermeidet Lk.4,33.44; 12,11(Mt.10,17!), von "ihren" Synagogen zu sprechen (anders nur 4,15; vgl. aber Apg.13,5; 14,1; 17,1). Die glaubenden Heiden gehören mit denen zusammen, die in der Synagoge "richtig" auf Mose hören (Apg.13,14-41; 15,21). Heiliges "Volk" (λαός) bleibt Israel (gut 80mal, selbst wo nur von einer Volksmenge die Rede ist; Ausnahmen sind nur Apg.15,14;18,10). Darum ist bei Lukas die Gemeinde nie das neue Israel, sondern hat teil an Israels Segen(Apg. 3,25f; P. Borgen, Von Paulus zu Lukas, StTh 20, 1966, 147f; für die Stephanusrede V. Hasler, Jesu Selbstzeugnis und das Bekenntnis des Stephanus vor dem Hohen Rat, SThU 36, 1966, 41f). Vgl. noch Anm.31 hier.

48. Hier wäre weiter nachzudenken darüber, wie sich das Handeln Gottes im neutestamentlichen Gottesvolk nach Lukas von dem im alttestamentlichen unterscheidet, und ob nicht jenes weit stärker mit dem Jesusgeschehen zusammen eine Einheit bildet, die Israel als Vor-geschichte charakterisiert

(z.B. E. Rasco, La teologia de Lucas: Origen, Desarollo,
Orientaciones, AnGr 201 [1976] 142-147; H. Schürmann, Evange-
lienschrift und kirchliche Unterweisung, in: Das Lukasevangelium, ed. G. Braumann, Darmstadt 1974 (WdF 280), 157, sieht
sogar die Kirche als die lukanische "Mitte der Erfüllungszeit"
und verweist dafür auch in seinem Kommentar [Anm.4] z.St. auf
Lk.1,1 ["unter *uns* vollendet"]). Es wäre auch darüber nachzudenken, wie sich nach Lukas Gottes Handeln in der Weltgeschichte zur Heilsgeschichte verhält, ob es nur insofern relevant ist, als es der Geschichte des Gottesvolkes dient (wie
etwa der Zensus, die römische Appellationspraxis, die Paulus
nach Rom bringt, der Schiffbruch und die Rettung daraus).
Aber das alles kann hier nicht mehr geleistet werden.

16

THE HALAKHAH OF JAMES[*]

Phillip Sigal

The Epistle of James has been studied from various per-
ceptions and on different levels. It is considered wisdom
literature by some, parenetic by some, Christian by some, un-
datable by some, Palestinian by some. All of these views have
degrees of truth.[1] The Epistle of James certainly has affini-
ties with wisdom literature and resembles other parenetic
tracts, but contains material of other substantive value. It
is certainly Christian, for although it contains no Christology it has two references to Jesus (1:1, 2:1) which imply a
faith in which Jesus has a special place, and both times Jesus
is referred to as the Christ or the Anointed One. The ambience
appears certainly to be Palestinian. The dating game may conceivably be an exercise in futility when one notes that scholars have ranged from the year 40 to 150, as well as ascribing
it to a pre-Christian period.[2] Like the Book of Ruth in the
Old Testament which transcends history, James defies dating
partially because there is here no quarrel between Christian
Jews and other Jews, and the epistle makes no reference to
significant events of the first or second century. The ad-
dressees worship in a synagogue (2:2) which indicates the
writer does not feel the urgency of Paul to distinguish the
place of gathering of the community as an *ekklēsia* and points
to a Christian Jewish Palestinian community rather than a diaspora community where the distinction may have seemed more
appropriate. The writer unselfconsciously refers to Abraham
as "our father" (2:21). There can be little doubt that W. O.
E. Oesterley was correct a long time ago when he expressed the
view that the thoroughly Judaic qualities of the epistle make
it quite likely that it was written by James, the brother of
Jesus, and therefore dates to a very early time, perhaps being
the earliest work of the New Testament. Despite all that has

---

[*]This essay is substantially the paper originally delivered
before the Annual Meeting of the Eastern Great Lakes Biblical Society, April 11, 1980, at Duquesne University, Pittsburgh, Pennsylvania.

been written since, there is still no truly persuasive reason
to doubt what we read in the *Didascalia Apostolorum* of James:
"...James, the Bishop of Jerusalem, who is our Lord's brother
after the flesh...".[3] Oesterley was also correct in calling
attention to the epistle's keen interest in what he called
"the Jewish doctrine of works". But Oesterley did not see
that this indicated a distinct interest in halakhah on the
part of James and did not proceed to examine the halakhah of
James. Similarly, Dibelius rejected the notion that James'
teaching on "works" was Judaic, emphasizing rather that it was
related to a new Christian "spiritual nomism".[4]

It is useful at this juncture to define the term halakhah.
I use this term both to describe a general process and an individual norm of conduct. To be halakhic, therefore, means to
affirm the idea that right conduct is significant in the religious life. Furthermore, the term applies both to conduct per-
taining to the human's relationship with God, ritual, and the
human's relationship with other humans, ethics. And finally,
one may express oneself in moralistic tones without invoking
the more precise language of halakhah, what to do now and how
to do it, and yet be engaged in halakhic method by virtue of
the implications of one's moralistic sermon or one's wisdom
discourse. The Book of Wisdom and Proverbs are not generally
regarded as halakhic works. But they are every bit as significant halakhically as long exhortative passages of Deuteronomy. This is also the case with James. And while James
does not present a staccato roster of apodictic commands, one
must infer from his sermonic, midrashic mode a larger number
of strong recommendations for right conduct. This is halakhah.

Intimately related to this halakhah of James is his underlying theology, that salvation is connected with the halakhic
process, with the way one lives. This is conventionally referred to as the doctrine of "faith and works", and a great
dichotomy is normally suggested between James and Paul on this
subject, and between Paul and Judaism. It is unfortunately
not within the scope of this paper to explore comprehensively
the interesting question of "faith and works" in James, or its
relationship to the same doctrine in Paul's writings. Nevertheless, this is at the heart of the whole question, and I
proceed on the premise that both James and Paul agreed with
antecedent proto-rabbinic and Qumran teaching that both faith
and works are a desideratum.[5] For James, the climax to the
Sermon on the Mount is Jesus' warning that calling out "Lord,
Lord", that is, vigorously expressing faith, is not sufficient
to enter the Kingdom of Heaven, but rather by doing the will
of the Father, that is, fulfilling good works. For Jesus it
is the hearing and the doing of his sayings that count, and to
hear and not to do is to build the house of faith on sand.[6]

One cannot read the Sermon as representing only the proto-rabbinic stage of Jesus' ministry and argue for his teaching another view after the resurrection, for we find that Mt. 28: 20, purporting to be a post-resurrection statement, emphasizes that the disciples are to teach proselytes *terein*, to *observe* the teachings. Furthermore, M. H. Shepherd has shown that in James there is a high degree of parallelism with the Sermon on the Mount.[7] This does not hint at dependence upon Matthew. It merely indicates that both James and Matthew used the Sermon.

Just as the Sermon is a major halakhic statement, so too is the Epistle of James, although the halakhah is cloaked in the style of wisdom literature, sounds much like a homily, and is what Kümmel has referred to as a random succession of admonitions and sayings, a parenetic tract.[8] In many ways it resembles Pirke Abot, a most unusual tractate of the Mishnah; although stylistically it is quite different. Since most of the epistle consists of numerous individual sayings, space would not permit me here to review the halakhic particulars. Although such an examination would indicate a hypothesis that the halakhah of James is pietistic and partakes of the quality of Qumran, it is nevertheless also proto-rabbinic because of James' long period of pragmatic leadership in Jerusalem where he was distant from the monastic and pietistic ambience of Qumran, and alienated from those circles that were part of the large Essene and Qumranite movements.[9]

In his proto-rabbinic mode, James emphasizes the centrality of Torah in the life of the Christian Jew, although for our purposes we need not define the content of Torah. He accompanies this emphasis with the admonition that the love command must underlie this Torah, as I shall soon explain. James 1: 22-25 is a basic passage that clarifies James' halakhic approach. The main verses read:

v. 22 "Become doers of the word, and not only listeners, deceiving oneself...."

v. 25 "The one who looks intently into the perfect law of freedom and abides by it, not having become a forgetful listener, but a doer of the deed, this one will be blessed in the doing of it."

James' language in v. 22 is quite illuminating. He uses a strong imperative, *ginesthe*, "become", or as Dibelius translates, "be", in a tone which is obviously a command; and as Dibelius also pointed out, "to do" the Torah is a traditional expression of the idea of observing the norms and precepts in an active way.[10] This is the articulation of a halakhah which believers are to follow. This nuance is supported by the prohibitive nature of the term *mē* which soon follows. They are to become doers of the word, and *mē*, they are not to be mere hearers. The stringency involved in the combination of *ginesthe* and *mē* is further supported by the statement that if they were mere hearers they would deceive themselves.

Listening to or hearing the word of God linked to the doing of the word of God is not only indigenous to the pre-Jesus Judaic tradition, but also endemic to the teachings of Jesus. It is not a matter of option or theological preference. The "listener" or believer must be a *poiētēs*, a "doer" of the deed.[11] "Hearing" and "doing" the will of God have a consistent relationship in the teachings of Jesus, and even where the "hearing" is omitted, the "doing" is highlighted.[12] Even more interesting is the coincidence of Paul's teaching with that of James. This need not occasion any great surprise since both are Jews brought up in the tradition of doing the will of God and both are teaching that same tradition in the sayings of Jesus. Yet, the myth of Paul's anti-nomianism in which both Christian and Jewish scholars revel, often obscures the obvious truth that for Paul too *hoi akroatai nomou*, those who hear the *nomos* are not righteous in the sight of God, are not *dikaioi*, not subjects of salvation, for only *hoi poiētai nomou*, the doers of the *nomos*, *dikaiōthēsontai*, will be vindicated at judgment, or attain salvation (Rom. 2:13).

Both Paul and James agreed with their proto-rabbinic tradition that not inquiry or study, "hearing" the word, is what is fundamental, *haikar*, but the doing of it, *hamaàseh* (M. Ab. 1:17). Along with this emphasis upon doing, the mishnaic teacher in the same pericope warned that whoever proliferates talk brings on sin, and here James too (1:26) links loose speech, the failure to control the tongue as contrary to sound religion. Another citation in the name of Shammai and therefore pre-James, formulates it in this way: say little and do much (M. Ab. 1:15). We find also that at Lydda a group of rabbis discussed what is greater, study or doing. R. Tarfon said that action, doing *mizvot* takes priority over study. R. Akiba argued that study takes priority over action. Others present sided with Akiba because, they argued, study will lead to action (Sifre Deut. 41). But if study does not lead to action, that is, to know or to hear the word and not to do it, it is deceptive, as James makes clear.

James, furthermore, indicates that at the basis of all "doing" must be the love command. This is emphasized at v. 25 to which we must give special attention.

1:25 reads,

> "The one who contemplates [looks intently
> into] the perfect *nomos* of freedom and
> remains with it, who does not become a
> forgetful hearer but is a doer of the
> deed, this one is divinely favored [or
> acclaimed] in the doing."

Like Jesus and Paul, James is concerned that in the new movement or The Way--literally, the *halakhah*--the believer or ad-
herent be a *poiētēs*, a "doer" of the deed and not a mere listener. At 1:25 he is emphasizing that one must contemplate
deeply the perfect *nomos* of freedom and remain attached to it,
which is the meaning of *parameinas*. The word *parakyptō* must
be understood in the sense of going out of one's way to look
deeply into something since its primary meaning is "to stoop
sideways". It therefore signifies one is to peruse carefully.
Thus at Jn. 20:5 *parakypsas* means "stooping forward" and at
v. 11 again it means Mary looked carefully into the tomb as
the context of vv. 11-12 require.[13] Thus the believer is not
merely to hear it, study it, know it or pay lip service to the
word in an indifferent fashion, which is the thrust of *akroa-
tēs epilēsmonēs*, "forgetful listener". He is to be a *poiētēs
ergou*, a doer of the deed. And it is not in the hearing of it,
but in the *doing* of it that he is *makarios*, fortunate or
blessed in the Hebrew sense of *ashrai haish*, that that person
is divinely favored (Ps. 1:1-3) who walks in God's ways. For
ashrai, targum at Ps. 1:1 reads *tooveh* and LXX reads *makarios*,
all signifying one who is entitled to divine acclaim. James
here harks back to Jesus' sayings at Mt. 5:3-10 where all the
makarios sayings are bracketed by vv. 3 and 10 with the assurance that those who are in the category of divine *makarioi*
will enter the kingdom of heaven, which is also clearly the
conclusion of the Psalmist at Ps. 1:5f. for the person who is
ashrai.[14]

The Greek text bears out carefully what the proto-rabbi
James is saying: that one must mediate intently upon the
Torah as at Ps. 1:2, such study taking priority over any other
mizvah (M. Peah 1:1). Thus, to engage in this *midrash*, to
contemplate with great concentration, *parakyptō*, means that
the righteous person will examine minutely what is required of
him by the "perfect *nomos* of freedom". But the quintessential
purpose of peering into this perfect *nomos* is not to be an intellectual exercise. Rather it is to be able to engage in
deeds, for as another proto-rabbinic contemporary of James,
Simon, son of Hillel, admonished, "not the *midrash* is quintessential but the doing" (M. Ab. 1:17). Like Simon, James

argues that "to listen and not to obey" is inadequate. Hearing, even affirmations of belief, is only preparation for doing. The hearers must be doers of the word (*poiētai logou*). One must bear in mind that Deut. 6:3 reads that Israel is to hear in order to *do* God's word, and again at 6:4, the creedal affirmation of "Hear, O Israel" is immediately followed by one part of the love command. There too, at v. 12 Israel, the "hearer" is admonished not to be forgetful of the Lord, the Redeemer, as James warns the "hearer" not to be forgetful.

James is therefore making a basic proto-rabbinic statement. Scholars like Bo Reicke who run off in other directions are missing this real *sitz im leben* of James' espistle.[15] Reicke argues that the *nomos* in this verse (1:25) is the gospel of love, and not any attempt "to reintroduce external observances". This kind of statement highlights the presuppositions that are a disaster for modern scholarship.[16] For one thing, Reicke implies that there is something wrong with "external observances", and we have no evidence at all that either Jesus or James felt that way in any comprehensive way regardless of, for example, Jesus' negative view of the pietist requirement to wash the hands before meals (Mt. 15:1-20). Secondly, one must distinguish between "external observances" which are hypocritical (as at Is. 1:10-17 or Mt. 23) and those that are sincerely motivated and consistent with God's will. Thirdly, Reicke implies that "doing" must refer to what he calls "external observances". Not at all. "Doing" can as easily refer to what Jesus insisted upon as the source of purity at Mt. 15:19, a perfectly proper proto-rabbinic ethical program, somewhat peppered by something at least remotely connected with the ritual side of life, to refrain from blasphemy. There is no basis on which to define the Christian *nomos*, the Way, literally, the halakhah of Jesus, as divorced from the Judaic meaning of *nomos*; and not only Matthew, but Paul and James make it very clear that the gospel of love requires a large amount of "observance" whether we tack on the loaded code-word "external" with Bo Reicke or not. Judaism of the first century, whether in its Christian form or in its proto-rabbinic form made great demands upon the believer. As Jesus is reported to have said his yoke is light (Mt. 11:30), rabbinic literature emphasized that no practice should be imposed that people find too onerous;[17] and Paul's teacher, Gamaliel I, is reported to have taught that "he who has compassion upon people, upon him will they have compassion from the heavens", as James indicates at 2:13.[18] Here, interestingly, we have an example of the love command expressed in a positive way in a Judaic source and a negative way in a Christian source. Jesus, Paul, and Gamaliel all maintained the need to translate faith into action as James emphasized (2:14-26).[19]

An important aspect to understanding James is to perceive his meaning at 1:25 of "the perfect *nomos* of freedom
[or liberty]". Beginning with the presupposition that the
Christian gospel is what is meant by James, Bo Reicke argues
backwards that the attributes of "perfect" and "liberty" make
this self-evident, for the gospel "leads to perfection and
gives its adherents freedom", and in accordance with v. 21,
saves their souls.[20] For Reicke "the law of liberty" is the
gospel of salvation, and he believes that this is what James
has in mind at 2:12 where he writes of those who will be
judged by "the law of freedom". There is no necessary connection between James' "law of freedom" and the Christian gospel, for the *nomos eleutherias*, the "freedom *nomos*" of James
can mean something that comes out of his Judaic matrix like so
much else in his epistle. Reicke sees in this phrase "law of
liberty" something "partly reminiscent of Stoic phraseology".
Reicke goes on to discuss how "the law", whatever that is, was
used as an excuse to persecute Jesus, Stephen, Paul and the
Jerusalem Church, and as a stimulus for aggressive zealotry
(the Maccabees, the Zealots), and that James expresses "a
sharp difference with Jewish national fervor" by calling "the
perfection of the law which is found in the gospel of love,
'the law of freedom'".[21] What Reicke says expresses the consensus of error that dominates a segment of modern scholarship, but does not resemble the thought of Jesus, Paul or
James. Reicke cites verses from Paul that appear to postulate
a *nomos* which has no action to express it, but conviently omits
all of the halakhah that requires serious restraint and positive action that is scattered throughout Paul's letters. At
this juncture it is important to note that the use of *nomos* by
Paul is an interesting subject in itself.[22] It must suffice
here to say that Paul's rejection of the need for *nomōn ergōn*
refers to salvific cultic acts and not all halakhah. For Paul
the death of Jesus frees the believer from the need to gain
salvation through the cultic acts of Judaism. Paul uses the
term *ergōn* in the same way as it is used at I Macc. 14:42,
where it represents the *'abodah* or temple cult. Paul believes
that because the believer *participates in the death of Jesus*
through his or her baptism, the believer is free from the cultic *mizvot*, and in Paul's terminology, from the *nomos*. The
person who emerges from baptism, in Paul's thinking, is as
newborn or resurrected, sharing in Jesus' resurrection. This
person has the status of the resurrected Jew in Paul's own Judaic tradition: namely, he is free of *mizvot*.[23]

Psalm 88:6 (LXX 87:5) which literally reads, "among the
dead, free", is taken in rabbinic exegesis to declare that
"when one dies he is free of Torah".[24] The Greek also translates "among the dead, free" (*en nekrois eleutheros*). Thus
too, Paul at Rom. 7:1 indicates the *nomos* is lord over the

person as long as he lives, and that, for example, a widow is *eleuthera*, is free of the law that governs husband and wife. So too, he argues (v. 4) the believer is dead to the *nomos* because of the death of Jesus, and becomes subject to the resurrected Jesus. This signifies that salvation comes from faith and participation in that death and resurrection process. But it in no way abandons the need to continue to live the ethical and moral principles which Jesus taught. Both rabbinic Judaism and the transmuted Judaism which became Christianity contained the triad of faith, works, and grace. James simply spends more energy asserting this because he had to deal with the historical reality that the Christian synagogues or the Christian communities that still shared synagogues with non-Christian Jews, were becoming increasingly populated by former pagans who did not have the same attachment to Judaism.

We may now turn to another aspect of James 1:25, the phrase "perfect *nomos* of freedom", *nomon teleion ton tēs eleutherias*. James is here sharing with us his interpretation of a well-known proto-rabbinic usage. Like Reicke who sees here Stoic terminology, C. H. Dodd looks to other pagan writers as the background for James' statement. Dodd says specifically that James 1:25 does not allude to Ps. 19:8 (LXX 19:7). But it is quite puzzling why Dodd should bother denying it unless he realized that the possibility is very great that James does indeed here allude to Ps. 19:8, and that this allusion in itself highlights the proto-rabbinic approach of James, an approach modern scholarship seems determined to obfuscate.[25]

The Hebrew text reads: *Torat Yhwh temimah meshibat nefesh*, which is best translated as "The Torah of Yhwh is perfect, setting the soul at ease" [or, setting a person at ease, or restoring the soul].

LXX reads: *ho nomos tou kyriou amōmos, epistrefōn psychas* which we may translate as, "the *nomos* of the Lord is spotless, restoring souls". Actually James does a better translation by using *teleion* rather than LXX's *amōmos* because James has in mind the Hebrew *temimah*, the "perfect *torah*". For the Hebrew *meshibat* James also improves over the LXX by using *eleutheras*, for while the LXX hews closely to the Hebrew it does not express the midrashic exegesis which James seeks to apply. James has in mind *meshibat* in the sense of restoring, refreshing or allowing the *nefesh* to take a new breath, metaphorically to find new freedom or renewal of life. This nuance of "restore, refresh", goes well with *nefesh* and occurs also at Ps. 23:3 and Ruth 4:15.

What James has in mind here is the midrash reflected at M. Ab. 6:2 which comments upon Ex. 32:16 which refers to the two tablets containing the ten words. Ex. 32:16 states, "the writing was the writing of God engraved upon the tablets". The Hebrew for engraved is *harut*. The rabbinic exegesis is to read *herut* "freedom" and so, in reading "the writing was the writing of God, *herut* upon the tablets", the exegetes were saying "the only free person, *horin*, is he who occupies himself with *torah*". And here, of course, rabbinic *torah* must be understood in lower case, and referring to both the written torah and the interpretive or so-called "oral" torah. As Travers Herford well understood, bondage is in ignoring the word of God, freedom is in living it.[26]

Furthermore, Torah is said to free Israel from subjugation, from the angel of death, and from suffering.[27] All in all, this rabbinic exegesis of the freedom bestowed by the Torah is clearly illustrative of a "perfect torah [*nomos*] of freedom which restores the person". James is here reflecting this midrash upon Ps. 19:8. The *torah temimah* is the *nomon teleion*, and this torah of Yhwh *herut* upon the tablets, is a torah which is *ton tēs eleutherias*, *herut*, a gift of ultimate freedom. The only reason Dodd could not see this is because he begins with the same unfortunate presuppositions as Reicke, and because he did not bother to inquire into the real possibility of the term *meshibat nefesh*, signifying that the torah gives ultimate freedom, the refreshment of the whole being, by its putting an end to subjugation, the angel of death and all suffering. In other words, the torah's effect is as paradigm of the eschaton.

Philo refers to the teaching of Moses as *hoi nomoi kallistoi*, "the most excellent of laws", and uses the Sabbath as an example of the type of thing among these excellent *nomoi* that attracts Gentiles to Judaism.[28] Philo explains that the Sabbath allows for every segment of nature, human, animal, and vegetable to live in freedom, *eleutherion*. And again Philo repeats that the teachings of Moses make the people *eleutherois*, and not *doulois*, free, not slaves, as the rabbis teach that the torah on the tablets is *herut*, freedom. So too, for James, the *doing* of the halakhah, albeit the new Christian Judaic halakhah, is the opportunity to live in freedom. The idea and the imagery is Judaic and highlights James' emphasis upon a traditional approach to the meaning of religion.

Philo emphasizes this elsewhere too in his lengthy discussion of the freedom of the one who lives the righteous life.[29] He points to the friend of God as one who is free (*tous philous tou theou eleutherous einai*). He calls the one who is subject to passion and vice a slave, while "those who live by *nomos* are free" (*hossi de meta nomou zōsin eleu-*

theroi).[30] Similarly R. Elazar ben R. Yosi Hagelili teaches that only those to whom *ḥerut* (freedom) is given, that is, the Torah, are delivered from the sway of the angel of death (Ex. R. 41:7). This obviously has reference to ultimate freedom from death, that is, resurrection and the eternal bliss of the righteous. Torah or *nomos* is therefore equated with salvation, precisely what James does with the *nomos*.[31]

The same proto-rabbinic teaching is transmitted by a first-century scholar, Nehunyah b. Hakanah (M. Ab. 3:6). He says *kol hamekabel àlav òl torah maàvirin mimenu òl milkhut veòl derekh erez*, "whoever receives upon himself the yoke of Torah, is relieved of the yoke of government and mundane life". In effect, becoming subject to Torah is a liberating act and state of being. Nehunyah was of the circle of Yoḥanan b. Zakkai, and in my opinion, discussed elsewhere, Yohanan was a contemporary of Jesus in Galilee and had knowledge of, and interacted with the proto-rabbi of Nazareth.[32] James and Nehunyah were contemporaries in the same pre-60 circles of Galilee, and as Yohanan moved to Jerusalem, so probably did James sometime in the early 30's.

One can go on in great length to define points of contact between James and rabbinic literature in matters that reflect norms of conduct or halakhah. Although James is a pietist who emphasizes *doing* of *miẓvot*, he can understand as well as Paul that grace is needed for salvation, as Yoḥanan b. Zakkai also taught.[33] Thus James is anxious about the kind of person he calls a *threskos*, a "formal worshiper", that is, one who engages in the pietistic rites and cultus, but is without the merit of the ethical life (1:26). In this James is akin to Isaiah, Micah, Zekhariah and others, whose ethical passion was taken up into rabbinic emphasis upon the doing of *miẓvot* and not only the believing of doctrine.[34] James, therefore, calls Lev. 19:18 *nomon basilikon*, the "royal" or "supreme" norm of religion, as Akiba called it when he referred to it as *kelal gadol batorah*, "the supreme principle of Torah".[35] By referring to one's being judged by the *nomou eleutherias*, "the *nomos* of freedom", James is alluding back to 1:25, and with these emphases in Chapter Two James orients the entire chapter to his Judaic thought which can be paralleled from Intertestamental literature and Mishnah and midrash. Contrary to Ropes in the International Critical Commentary, James, Chapter Two is *not* what Ropes calls it (p. 185), "more original and less a repetition of current Jewish ideas than any other part of the epistle". In the history of religious thought it is not originality which counts, but how the religious teacher drew upon and applied the reservoir of spiritual teaching which he inherited. This is true of the New Testament writers as well as of the proto-rabbis. One of the hang-ups we all will have to overcome is the superficial notion that the ancient spiritual teachers of Judaism and Christianity must be original or unique in the sense of saying what has not been said previously. What we really must learn to appreciate is how they synthesized what had already been revealed, and how through the help of the holy spirit they made viable the ancient traditions within new contexts. In Chapter Two, as throughout his work, James' teachings can be paralleled comprehensively. Even v. 1 sets the tone for that when he expresses anxiety over partiality in their way of life, a take-off from Lev. 19:15 where LXX uses the same term as James.[36] The parallel between James 2:13 and Gamaliel I has been referred to earlier. At P. B. K. 6c Gamaliel is quoted almost exactly like James, "If you are not merciful, God will not be merciful to you."[37]

An analysis, and even only a mere listing and cataloguing of many of these items belongs more to the field of *àgadah* than to halakhah, and I should constrain myself from further examples. But as is the case in rabbinic literature, so with James, there is a fine line between *àgadah* and halakhah. The *àgadah* of James leads to halakhic affirmations. Thus, in a homily on faith, *pistis*, James teaches that *pistis* without *erga* is insufficient (2:14, 17, 26), and that a believer must go as far as Abraham in offering up Isaac to show through *erga* that his *pistis* is real.[38] At Mt. 23:3 Jesus accuses the so-called Pharisees of being *legousin*, those who profess faith, but are not *poiousin ta erga*, doers of the deed. James similarly deplores the practice of *legē*, professing faith and then not conducting oneself properly. He is therefore in the tradition of M. Ab. 4:13, that every *miẓvah* is a paraclete, a view given in the name of R. Eliezer b. Jacob, a first century contemporary of Yohanan b. Zakkai, Jesus, and James.[39] It is understandable, therefore, if each *miẓvah* is a paraclete, that a person is *dikaioutai*, vindicated or saved (James 2:24) *ex ergōn* because of the deeds, and not *ek pisteōs monon*, as a product of faith alone.

It is of some interest that James refers to the *àkedah*, the binding of Isaac, as the testimony to Abraham's faith which led to his being called *philos theou*, "a friend of God". One might argue that in the *àkedah* story at Gen. 22:12 Abraham is called *yerai elohim*, "a God-fearer". But the connection James makes is quite within the bounds of tradition where it is taught that the *yeerah*, the fear or reverence of Abraham connotes "love" in accord with Is. 41:8 which refers to Abraham as God's beloved or friend. This rabbinic passage uses one verse of scripture in typical midrashic form to interpret another, seeing *yerai elohim* of Gen. 22:12 as friend of God, just as James does.[40] In this way also Philo relates Abra-

ham's love of God with the *àkedah*.[41] This tradition relating
Abraham's faith reported at Gen. 15:6 with the *àkedah* is reflected by Pseudo-Philo when that work sees Abraham's vision
of Gen. 15 as being a vision of the *àkedah*. Pseudo-Philo ends
this particular passage by citing Gen. 18:17, that God will
reveal to Abraham what he is about to do.[42] And at that same
verse the P. Targ. adds the word *rahami*, "my beloved", to the
name of Abraham, as does Philo.[43] Taking all of these items
together leads one to the conclusion that James is in the tradition.[44]

It might be pertinent to note that at Gen. 22:9 the masoretic text reads that Abraham "bound" Isaac upon the altar·and
never specifies that Abraham offered him as a burnt-offering
which is the term used by God at v. 2. Yet when James refers
to the event, and specifically to what Abraham did, at 2:21,
he uses the term *anenegkas* which is appropriate for the Hebrew
"offer up as a burnt offering" and frequently so used in the
LXX. The masoretic text is careful to distinguish between the
verbs used by Abraham when "binding" Isaac (*vayaàked*) at v. 9
and when offering up the ram (*vayaàlehu*) at v. 13. This leads
me to the supposition that James was aware of the tradition
that Abraham actually sacrificed Isaac and explains the tradition that Isaac was Israel's future atonement lamb, and in
Christian exegesis, the prefiguration of Jesus, a matter I
discuss elsewhere with numerous references to other scholars
who both affirm and deny the pre-Christian provenance of this
tradition. It is important in a discussion of the halakhah of
James only because James uses the *àkedah* as the centerpiece of
his teaching that faith must express itself in *miẓvah*.[45] It
is, therefore, no accident that James closes his epistle with
a halakhic program (5:1-15) and finally a call for repentance
with allusion to Elijah, the harbinger of the messiah.

NOTES

1. J. A. T. Robinson, *Redating the New Testament* (Philadelphia: Westminster, 1976), pp. 118-120; Martin Dibelius, *James*, trans. Michael A. Williams, ed. Helmut Koester (Philadelphia: Fortress, 1976), pp. 3-11.

2. D. Y. Hadidian, "Palestinian Pictures in the Epistle of James," *Expository Times* 63 (1951-52), 227f. See also J. H. Ropes, *A Critical and Exegetical Commentary on the Epistle of James. The International Critical Commentary* (New York: Charles Scribner's Sons, 1916), 295-297. For a critique of dating views see *The Epistle of St. James*, ed. Joseph B. Mayor, 2nd ed. (London: Macmillan, 1897), Chapter VII, parts I and II, pp. cxxi-clxxviii; Gerald H. Rendall, *The Epistle of St. James and Judaic Christianity* (Cambridge: University Press, 1927).

3. See W. O. E. Oesterley, *The General Epistle of James, The Expositors Greek Testament*, 5 vols. (Grand Rapids, Mich.: Wm. B. Eerdmans, 1974 Rpt.) IV, 385-476. See pp. 392-397, 405, 408-413. Cf. Dibelius, *op. cit.*, pp. 11-21 for another view. See also Joseph B. Mayor, *op. cit.*, pp. xxxvi, xliiiff. See also *The Didascalia Apostolorum in Syriac* II, *Corpus Scriptorum Christianorum Orientalium* (Louvain: Secretariat Du Corpus SCO, 1979) vols. 407, p. 233; 408, p. 215.

4. *Ibid.*, pp. 411ff. But Oesterley, p. 413, is wrong in differentiating James from Paul and arguing that Paul rather than James is in accord with Jesus at I Cor. 10:13; Rom. 2:4. These sayings of Paul do not contravene James. James does not deny that God helps the person repent. He does not address that question. If James wrote the epistle and if his ideas are thoroughly Judaic, as Oesterley argues, James would also agree that "whoever comes to purify himself is helped", that is, a repentant person is aided by God's love and grace: B. Shab. 104a; Yom 38b; Z.A. 55a; Men. 29b. Luke James at 4:6 the talmudist uses Prov. 3:34 to support his teaching on the same general subject. At B.B.B. 55a, Meg. 6b and Ket. 63b we also have a distinct category of *seeyata deshmaya*, "divine help" that intrudes in favor of those upon whom God decides to aid in any given situation. Since it may be unearned grace it falls into the same category of the previous statement. Cf. Dibelius, *op. cit.*, pp. 21-26.

5. I Macc. 2:51f; IQ p. Hab. 8:1-3. If Paul argues that people are saved by faith he does not deny that they are judged by works, Rom. 2:13, 25.

6. Mt. 7:21-27. The use of *poiōn* and *poiei* at vv. 21, 24 emphasizes the carrying out of the teachings in tandem with hearing them, as was the case with Israel at Ex. 24:7 where "doing" even precedes "hearing", thus emphasizing the nuance of "obedience" contained in the Hebrew word "to hear". Cf. Deut. 5:1, 6:24 where "hearing" and "doing" are related. See also I Q P. Hab. 7:11, 8:1; 12:4 IQS 2:25-3:12. At I Ki 3:9 *leb shomeà* "an understanding heart" emphasizes the association of hearing and comprehension.

7. M. H. Shepherd, "Epistle of James and Mt.," *JBL* 75 (1956), p. 42.

8. Werner G. Kümmel, *Introduction to the New Testament*, Rev. ed. trans. Howard Clark Kee (Nashville: Abingdon, 1975), pp. 404, 408.

9. Phillip Sigal, *The Emergence of Contemporary Judaism* (Pittsburgh: Pickwick Press, 1980) vol. I, pt. 1, pp. 422-426.

10. Dibelius, *op. cit.*, p. 114. The root *àso* "to do" is used numerous times in scripture with the meaning of actively fulfilling *mitzvot, torah, mishpatim*, etc. cf. M. Ab. 4:6; Philo, *On Rewards and Punishments* 14 (79). See Mayor, *op. cit.*, p. 66 for the idea that *ginesthe* is even more than the stringent command "be", having also the connotation "show yourselves more and more".

11. See n. 6. Cf. Mt. 11:15; Mk. 4:9, 23; 7:16, all of which associate hearing and comprehension, the latter essential for doing. (Many texts omit Mk. 7:16.)

12. Mt. 7:24; Lk. 6:47; 8:21. For a negative view of hearing and not doing see Mt. 7:26; Lk. 6:49. Cf. Mt. 12:50; Mk. 3:35.

13. See also I Peter 1:12.

14. The words *àshrai, tooveh*, and *makarios* are all defined in the dictionaries and are related to one another. See for these terms Brown, Driver and Briggs, p. 807 for *àshrai*; Jastrow, p. 521b for *tooveh* and Arndt-Gingrich, p. 486b for *makarios*.

15. Bo Reicke, *The Epistles of James, Peter and Jude*, Anchor Bible (Garden City, N.Y.: Doubleday, 1964), pp. 23f. Dibelius, *op. cit.*. p. 117 does better by citing Seneca, *De vita beata* 15:7, "to obey God is freedom". But note also

Philo, *EVERY GOOD MAN IS FREE* 7 (45, 50); see below, and nn. 28-30.

16. See Sigal, *Emergence* I, Pt. 1, p. 378 and references at p. 452, n. 4.

17. References *ibid.*, Pt. 2, p. 89, n. 20.

18. B. Shab. 151b; the translation in the text of this paper is literal, but actually means "God will have compassion upon one who has compassion upon people." See also T. B. K. 9:30 which reads "As long as you are one of compassion, the compassionate one will have mercy upon you."

19. See Thorwald Lorenzen, "Faith Without Works Does Not Count Before God! James 2:14-26," *The Expository Times* 89 (1977-78), 231-235.

20. *Op. cit.*, pp. 22f.

21. *Ibid.*, p. 24.

22. This is discussed in my unpublished paper, "A Brief Inquiry into the Meaning of *Nomos*," delivered at the Annual Meeting of the Eastern Great Lakes Biblical Society, Duquesne University, April, 1977.

23. See for example II Cor. 5:14-21 and Rom. 7:1-6. See Sigal, *Emergence* I, Pt. 1, p. 487f., nn. 125, 126; B. Nid. 61b; Shab. 151b; M. Kil. 9:4; B. Pes. 40b; P. Ket. 34d, etc.

24. B. Nid. 61b; Shab. 30a; 151b; Pes. 40b. Cf. also P. Kil. 32a; Ket. 34d. While not all medieval Jewish commentaries make this connection, the notable Abraham ibn Ezra states in comment to the "free", "from all the *miẓvot*...".

25. C. H. Dodd, *The Bible and the Greeks* (London: Hodder and Stoughton, 1935), pp. 39f.

26. Travers Herford, *Pirke Aboth* (New York: Jewish Institute of Religion, 1925), p. 152. While it is a 2nd-3rd century scholar, R. Joshua b. Levi who is cited at Aḅot, it is given anonymously at Ex. R. 41:7. The term *hakhamim* cited there can easily refer to proto-rabbinic and pre-Christian tradition. The interpolations at Aḅot, in fact, imply that the version at Ex. R. is the earlier saying.

27. B. Er. 54a; A.Z. 5a; Num. R. 16:24.

28. Philo, *Moses* II, 3(12); 4(21-22).

29. Philo, *Every Good Man is Free* 7 (42, 45, 50).

30. *Ibid.*, 45; James 1:19-21.

31. At 2:8-12 we see that basic Torahitic norms are important to James.

32. Phillip Sigal, *The Halakhah of Jesus of Nazareth According to the Gospel of Matthew*. Dissertation, University of Pittsburgh, Pittsburgh, Pa.: 1979, pp. 54, 166f. *Emergence* I, Pt. 1, 393f., 474; Pt. 2, pp. 21f.

33. *Emergence, ibid.*, p. 483, n. 107; Yohanan's anxiety over grace is at B. Ber. 28b.

34. Is. 1:10-17; 58; Mic. 6:6-8; Zekh. 7:4-10.

35. See *TDNT* I, 591 for a discussion of *basilikon* as used here to denote "supreme". See also Ropes, *op. cit.*, p. 198.

36. LXX Lev. 19:15 *ou lēpsē prosōpon*; James 2:1 *en prosopolempsiais*.

37. See n. 17; also Ps. 18:25f., Ben Sira 28:2ff.; Test. Zeb. 5:8, P. B. K. 6c; B. R. H. 17a. So too at M. Peah 1:1, salvation is won by acts of love, *gemilut hasadim*.

38. On James 2:14-26, see Dibelius, *op. cit.*, pp. 149-180.

39. See also Ab. de R. N. B., 35.

40. See Irving Jacobs, "The Midrashic Background for James 2:21-23," *NTS* 22 (1976) 457-464; M. Sot. 5:5; B. Sot 31a.

41. Philo, *On Abraham* 37 (170); see also 45 (262). Jub. 19:9 also refers to Abraham as friend of God, as does CDC 3:2-3, both of which allude to II Chron. 20:7. See also Philo, *ibid.*, 19 (89); cf. *On Sobriety* 11 (56), and P. Targ. to Gen. 18:17.

42. *The Biblical Antiquities of Philo*, trans. M. R. James (New York: Ktar, 1971), 18:5.

43. Philo, *On Sobriety*, 11 (56).

44. See Dibelius, *op. cit.*, p. 165, where he sees James 2:23 dependent upon Jewish biblical interpretation; but Dibelius misses the mark in thinking Judaism does not see faith

and works as two elements, as does James, even if they stand "in a very close relationship" (p. 178).

45.   Sigal, *Emergence* I, Pt. 1, pp. 387, 395, 467f., n. 50; 398ff., 470f., n. 62; 401, 418f., 485f., n. 118.   See also Shalom Spiegel, *The Last Trial* (Philadelphia: JPS, 1967) and Geza Vermes, *Scripture and Tradition in Judaism* (Leiden: E. J. Brill, 1961).

17

THE SERVANT OF THE LORD, ISRAEL, THE JEWS AND THE PEOPLE OF GOD

H. Eberhard von Waldow

Ever since the historical critical approach became the preferred method in biblical scholarship, tremendous advances have been made in our knowledge about the history of the people of Israel and in the development of her religion and culture. However, the theological yield that would justify the Old Testament as part of the Christian canon and Old Testament study as a discipline among other traditional theological disciplines has been deficient. With this poor yield as a weak point in Christian theology, it is quite understandable that the Nazi ideology in Hitler Germany with its call for the abolition of the O.T. launched an attack exactly at this point.

The most important effort to re-establish the theological importance of the Old Testament in the Christian canon was made by the Systematic Theologian, Karl Barth. His main thrust is that the Holy Scripture, Old and New Testament, contains the testimony of the primary witnesses of God's revelation. The O.T. was included in the scriptural norm of Christian theology.[1] The historical critical approach becomes an essential theological necessity with Barth's contention that the Bible itself is not identical with the revelation of God but rather the testimony of the witnesses. The result is a new interest in the theology of the O.T. instead of the traditional emphasis on the religion of Ancient Israel.[2] This new theological interest focused primarily on the Christian aspect. Thus, the long standing tradition in Christianity to exclude Judaism was continued.[3] Historically, there have been areas of silence in Christian scholarship: church history did not include the study of Judaism; homiletics or catechetics did not consider the rich Jewish preaching and teaching tradition; systematic theology showed little interest in the role of the Jewish people as a theological phenomenon. Finally, neither O.T. nor N.T. scholarship concerned itself with the fact that the people whose religion and culture are the background of the two parts of the Christian canon did not fade out after the conversion of the apostle Paul.

This situation changed when the terrible extent of the catastrophe which we call today "Holocaust" became known.

Under the impression of the inescapable weight of this disaster, it became clear to more and more Christian theologians that the thread of the history of Israel as a viable entity and a theological phenomenon was not cut off by the Romans when they put down the Jewish insurrections in the years 66 through 70 and 132 through 135.[4] Rather, what in Biblical times was called the chosen people of God continued to exist and was always present at the side of the Christian church. In the light of this discovery, the Holocaust assumed monumental existential dimensions that opened up a new realm of theological inquiry. When the theological interpretation of the O.T. stressed the fact that God speaks through events in human history, it became increasingly clear that this speaking did not stop with the events that are reported in the Gospels of the N.T. Rather what began with the exodus from Egypt and the Babylonian exile, and what continued with the Christ events in the N.T. happened again and again in later events in the history of the people of God. It becomes theologically necessary to ask: what does God say through human suffering in the Holocaust? And in turn, it should be asked: in the light of the word of God, what can be said theologically about the Holocaust? It is intended with this essay to honor Markus Barth upon his sixty-fifth birthday. In the pursuit of his Biblical-theological studies, the topic, "Christianity and Judaism" has always played an important role.[5] Friends and colleagues are indebted to him because he stimulated their interest. For this reason it seems quite appropriate to dedicate this essay, which deals with a small aspect of this area, to him.

This exegetical study attempts to include the Jewish people in Christian Biblical-theological considerations. The focus is on the topic, "the suffering of the people of God" and the textual basis is the Ebed Yahweh Songs in the book of Deutero-Isaiah.

I

The so-called Ebed Yahweh Songs in the book of Deutero-Isaiah are Isa 42:1-9 (or 1-5, 5-9); 49:1-6; 50:4-9; 52:13-53:12. These units have in common the "servant" ('ebed) of Yahweh who is chosen and appointed by Yahweh to bring mišpāṭ to the Gentile nations (Isa 42:1-9). Mišpāṭ with the original meaning, "judgment, justice, just claim" is in the context of Deutero-Isaiah Yahweh's justified claim to be the only and true God.[6] Or in turn, it is rejection of the gentile's claim that their gods are real and divine: "Behold, you are nothing, and your work is naught; an abomination is he who chooses you"

(Isa 41:24). As missionary to the gentiles, the 'ebed encounters from song to song increasing difficulties and opposition until in the last unit he suffers personal humiliation
and dies as a martyr for his witness (Isa 53:8f.). However,
in their confession, some converts express their recognition
that this death is not the climax of failure, rather the beginning of his restoration to honor and exaltation by Yahweh.
His suffering and death in shame is explained as a sacrifice
of expiation and vicarious suffering for his persecutors (Isa
53:5, 11f.).

The traditional question of biblical exegesis is: Who is
this Ebed Yahweh?[7] When we take the four units as a group in
isolation from the rest of the book of Deutero-Isaiah, the
impression which intrudes upon the reader is that the Ebed
must be an individual and this individual must be identified.
The Ethiopian official in Acts 8:34 is asking the typical
question of the individualistic interpretation: "Of whom is
the prophet saying this? of himself or of someone else?"
Here the Ethiopian is considering the autobiographical interpretation. This was hardly a new suggestion. The oldest evidence of this understanding was probably given 500 years earlier when the unknown prophet of Isa 60:1-3 was expressing his
conviction that he was called as a prophet in terms of Isa 42:
1-4 and 49:1-6. With this he sees himself as a successor of
Deutero-Isaiah whom he understood as the Ebed of the Songs.
In his reply, Philip adds, in v. 35, to the suggested autobiographical interpretation or the identification with any
other suitable figure of the history of Israel his own christological interpretation. The context of the Deutero-Isaiah
book, however, leads into another direction. Here, in Isa.
41:8f; 42:19; 44:1-2, 21; 45:4 and 45:11, Israel is called the
Ebed Yahweh. From here a strong case can be built for the
identification of the Ebed of the Songs with the Ebed of the
context. This would be the collective interpretation. Apparently the first exegete to do this was the unknown person
who inserted into Isaiah 49:3, "Israel"[8] as an explicative.

Exegesis of these Ebed-Yahweh texts must always take into
account these two conflicting characteristics of the Ebed,
namely, collective or individualistic. Coming from the context the exegete is led to the collective interpretation which
in the songs collides with the individualistic traits. On the
other hand, starting with the songs as a distinct group of
units within the book, one is inclined to follow the individualistic interpretation which is bound to clash with collective
Ebed-Israel of the context. Traditional Protestant exegesis of
the past decades was more inclined to follow the latter. From
here it was easier to draw lines to a messianic or christological concept. The problem raised by the context was either in-

terpreted away with the help of literary-critical theories[9] or it was not discussed at all.

This basic choice, individualistic or collective interpretation led into a dead end road. The reason is that the alternative is wrong. It does not take into account that O.T. thinking does not differentiate so much between the individual and his community as modern western thinking does particularly after the Renaissance. In the O.T. world, the communal concept is the principal aspect. Separation from one's community would result in a crisis for the individual.[10] The community stands up for the individual, and what happens to the individual member happens to the entire community. In turn, the entire community is represented by the individual. What he does, right or wrong, reflects upon the entire community.[11] Because of this close connection a community can be represented and characterized by an individual, real or fictional. For example, Jacob/Israel represents the community of the twelve tribes,[12] and Adam stands for the entire human race.

This way of thinking provides a key for the interpretation of the Ebed Yahweh Songs. The collective characteristics of the Ebed of the context and the individual of the songs are not mutually exclusive, rather they must be combined.[13] But in order to understand this combination of the communal-centered individual, the Ebed of the Songs must first be identified. Even though the author of the Songs seems to be making a deliberate attempt to keep the identity of the Ebed in the dark, he does not hide the fact that the Ebed is a prophet.[14] He is elected, called and appointed by Yahweh (49:1), is equipped with his spirit (42:1), his task is to speak with the word of his mouth (49:2, 50:4), and to teach (42:4), what he has been taught by Yahweh (50:4f.). In this manner, he is to bring Israel back to Yahweh (49:6) and eventually to bring Yahweh's covenant to all nations (41:6). This is the climax of his mission in which the Ebed-prophet appears as a certain parallel to the first prophet Moses, who brought Yahweh's covenant to Israel.[15]

For identification of the Ebed, the next question is: Who is this prophet? In order to avoid wild guessing, one should return to the N.T. and heed the suggestion in Acts 8:34 that this mysterious prophet is the prophet Deutero-Isaiah himself.[16] Understood in this manner, the second Isaiah is speaking in the Ebed Yahweh Songs about himself, his mission as a prophet, the burden of his office and his frustrations and sufferings. These Songs are autobiographical material which shed some light on the cryptic and veiled language and places these units in parallel to the so-called confessions of Jeremiah.[17] Deutero-Isaiah sees himself as the typical prophet

of Yahweh. Being called by Yahweh into this office means confronting opposition, suffering and eventually death.[18]

With this prophetic self-understanding Deutero-Isaiah was
seen as symbolizing the role of Israel in her mission to the
gentile nations. The suffering of this prophet became a symbol for the suffering of the people of God in the world. This
is the way the compiler of the book of Deutero-Isaiah wanted
these songs to be understood. That is why he included them in
his book suggesting to the reader the equation of the Ebed-
Israel of the context with the Ebed-prophet of the Songs. The
later interpolation of "Israel" in Isa 49:3 is an indication
that the intention of the compiler was understood. Now these
texts are a testimony of Israel's self-understanding in the
exilic period when the people of God had to cope with the
series of disasters in their new situation: loss of statehood
and independence; destruction of the temple, the place chosen
by Yahweh to make his name available; occupation by imperial-
istic gentiles; and dispersion of a portion of the people
throughout the ancient world. In this national, theological
and spiritual crisis, the Ebed-Yahweh Songs answered two
questions: 1. What does it mean to be the chosen people of
God? 2. What can the chosen people of God expect from the
future?

II

What does it mean to be the chosen people of God? The
book of Deutero-Isaiah with the inclusion of the servant songs
gives the answer through Deutero-Isaiah's reflections about
his own role and fate as a prophet of Yahweh.

To be chosen by God means to be appointed to fulfill a
task. In autobiographical terms this means to be a prophet.
All characteristics of the Ebed of the Sons point to the office of a prophet of Yahweh. The exilic age saw the prophetic
office with a twofold function: a. The prophet is sent to
Israel (Jer. 1:18). In Isa 49:5 this is specified: "To raise
up the tribes of Jacob, and to restore the preserved of
Israel." b. He is sent to the nations of the world "as a
light to the nations, that my (Yahweh's) salvation may reach
to the end of the earth", v. 6.[19] The mode of the prophet's
operation is low key (Isa 42:2) because his only tool is the
word of his mouth (49:2). However, what he proclaims is the
word from God (Jer 1:7-9; Isa 50:4).

This prophet is no ordinary prophet like his predecessors.

The crisis of his time places him in a special role. He is
appointed *běrît 'ām* = "Covenant of the people" [20] (Isa 42:6).
With this he represents the continuance of the covenant in the
time after the catastrophe of 587 when the covenant appears in
the minds of many to be revoked or invalidated (Isa 50:1).
This Ebed-prophet and the covenant belong together as in the
past on Mount Sinai Moses and the covenant belong together.
Therefore, in this context the Ebed appears in the role of the
prototype of all prophets, Moses (Deut 18:18).

When we follow the collective line this sheds light on
the role of Israel as God's elect. To be the chosen people
means not only to be singled out for God's blessings, or to
receive the promised land, help, assistance, protection, but
also for God's punishment. It means also to be appointed to
a mission to the other nations of the world. Whenever Israel
confesses that she is the chosen people of God she accepts the
role as God's prophet to the nations with the assignment to
bring to them knowledge of the only true God and to proclaim
His praise.[21] Thus, what Moses was to Israel when he brought
her God's covenant, Israel as the second Moses is to the nations of the world, "a light to the nations" (Isa 49:6), a
běrît 'ām = "a covenant for the peoples".[22] Through the
prophetic witness of the Ebed-Israel the Moses-covenant will
be amended to include all nations. This enlarged self-understanding reminds one of the Abraham promise, "be a blessing,--
and in you shall be blessed all the families of the earth"
(Gen 12:3).

What can the chosen people of God expect from the future?
Israel's future as God's messenger, witness or prophet to the
gentiles is symbolized by the fate of the Ebed Deutero-Isaiah.
He met with the opposition of the ones to whom he was sent.
He was "stricken", his "beard was plucked out", he was subjected to "humiliations", he was tortured (Isa 53:5, 7), put
to death (v. 8) and buried with the criminals or outlaws (v. 9).
What Israel did to the Ebed Deutero-Isaiah, the gentiles will
do to the Ebed-Israel.

The experience of Deutero-Isaiah as prophet sent to Israel
was not unique. According to the exilic tradition it is a
characteristic of the true prophet of Yahweh to be rejected
(Jer 7:25f.), and the passion of Jeremiah and his lesser known
colleague, Uriah, (Jer 26:20-23) was well remembered.[23] The
pre-exilic prophets were announcing God's punishment. This
could explain their rejection. But Deutero-Isaiah's message
was exclusively salvation. Why did he meet opposition? Salvation in the expectation of the exiles meant return and restoration. That is what Deutero-Isaiah told them.[24] What was
probably wrong was that Deutero-Isaiah announced this in the

framework of eschatological events.[25] This was not in accordance with the more realistic expectation of the people, it was too different. However, the primary reason for the rejection lies probably deeper. It is not so much the content, be it judgment or salvation, rather it is the message with the claim to be the word of God. The true scandalon is the *kōh 'āmar yhwh* = "thus says Yahweh".

Nevertheless, the rejection of the Ebed and his tragic end which superficially considered could be understood as failure, did not conclude his mission, because he was not an Ebed of the people, but an Ebed of God. As God's official envoy his death was the climax and successful completion of his mission and this in two ways: It reveals the true character of the persecutors, and it was a vicarious death intended for the salvation of the world.

A messenger in an official mission represents his master. Whatever happens to the messenger, or is being done to him happens to the master.[26] The tragic fate of the Ebed symbolizes the collective ignorance of either Israel or of the gentiles. They are hostile to the true God and in dire need for truth and salvation. In his sufferings the Ebed reveals the true character of his opponents in a way that cannot be surpassed. On the other hand, the suffering of God's envoy is actually God's own suffering. The Lord God suffers under the hands of the ones who are supposed to serve him.

The second way in which Ebed's death becomes the climax of his mission is the interpretation as vicarious death. The text states explicitly that this death was understood as death for the benefit of the ones who rejected him (Isa 53:5-4). If carried through to a final conclusion, in a very subtle way, this text seems to intimate somehow that actually God himself must die for the salvation of the world. However, it was left to the N.T. to develop this thought explicitly. This O.T. text continues only with the idea that after his vicarious death the Ebed will continue to live in the ones who accept his sacrifice (Isa 53:10) (or is the idea of resurrection implied?), and in this fashion God's plan will succeed.

What does all this mean for Israel's future as the chosen people of God along the lines of the collective interpretation? It means first of all that Israel's position as the chosen people of God must be interpreted as chosen to fulfill a task. This will prompt severe opposition. Israel's future as Yahweh's prophet to the nation or as *bĕrît 'ām* will be a *via dolorosa* leading through suffering and persecution to near extermination. In a mysterious way, this *via dolorosa* is Israel's path to eventual success. This is in the future of the chosen people of God in a sinful world in dire need of God's salvation and this salvation will be brought about by Israel as "light of the nations" (Isa 49:5) faithfully walking her *via dolorosa* (Isa 50:5f.).

Implied is the idea that whenever Israel is suffering persecution it becomes evident to her as well as to others that she is the chosen people of God. On the other hand, as chosen people Israel is not better than the non-Israelites, rather she shares in the sin of the world (Isa 43:8). When Israel, as the prophet to the nations, will suffer persecution she will only be experiencing what she herself did to her own prophets--persecuting and killing them.[27] This is the way she certified them as true prophets. In this context, Israel's suffering in the world will establish her as the true prophet of the only and true God.

Whenever Israel is suffering persecution she is suffering as God's prophet to the world. Whatever the given reason for a persecution may be, political, ideological or economic, explicitly or tacitly somewhere in the background will be that other reason: Israel is different. And different she always was. After the occupation of the promised land, Israel lived for about 300 years without state order and king because she believed her God was her ruler (Judg 8:23). The prophets expected Israel as a political entity to act differently with no political alliances (Isa 30:1-5; 31:1; Jer 37:1-10); her national security was not based on strong fortifications (Isa 7:1-9) or modern weaponry (Isa 31:1); and when the enemy was attacking Jerusalem the prophet Jeremiah's instruction was: Surrender (Jer 38:2). The roots of these particularities lie in Israel's character as God's chosen people. But when Israel is suffering, God is suffering with her. Thus, whoever participates in the persecution of Israel represents the fallen world. Interestingly, the classical exceptions from this rule in the O.T. are the Assyrians (Isa 8:5-8) and the Babylonians whose king is called *'abdî* = "my servant Nebuchadnezzar" (Jer 25:9; 27:6). They are used as Yahweh's agents to punish his unfaithful chosen people, but as soon as they overstep their assignment they too become sinful world and are held accountable for that (Jer 10:5-11, Jer 50:51).

In all these persecutions and sufferings Israel will not and cannot perish. Whatever may happen to Israel in her future, be it suffering or salvation, it will enable the gentiles eventually to recognize the true God: "that they may know and believe me and understand that I am He. Before me no god was formed nor should there by any after Me",[28] or as expressed in the frequent recognition formula: "And they shall recognize

that I am the Lord."[29]   This recognition is part of biblical
eschatology.

These general theological considerations should lead to
the more specific question which is: How does biblical theology help to understand the plight of the contemporary Jewish
people?

III

Two preliminary remarks are called for before any answer
to the above question is attempted:

a.   No secular attempt, be it undertaken in the area of
history of religion, sociology, biology, philosophy of history, etc., to explain the phenomenon of Israel and the Jews
or the event of the Holocaust has been completely successful.
The only statement that can be made in such a context is:
Israel always was and the Jews still are a phenomenon *sui
generis*,[30] and any purely secular attempt to logically explain the Holocaust must necessarily belittle this event.

The only plausible explanation of the Israel-phenomenon
can be given on the basis of the Bible. But this means, Israel
and her history in this world is first of all a theological
phenomenon that can only be explained when the God of the
Bible is taken into account. Just how "plausible" such an
explanation will be may be left undecided. As a theological
phenomenon the existence of the Jewish people does not so much
call for logical or rational explanation but for meditation and
theological contemplation.

b.   The attempt of Christian theologians to deal with the
Jewish people as a theological problem and to do so on the
basis of a Christian understanding of the Bible will necessarily lead to a Christian concept. With this, however, Christians should not try to tell the Jews how they should understand themselves and their history. A Christian understanding
can only be meant for Christian consumption. However, with
loving respect it should take into account that Jews have their
own self-understanding. This difference could be the subject
of a fruitful dialogue.

A Christian understanding of the Jewish people as God's
Elect must begin with the O.T. where the people of Israel enter
history as God's own people and the line must be drawn all the
way through to include the Holocaust. Christian understanding

of the Jewish people is based on the fact that God made a covenant with Israel that is everlasting and irrevocable.[31] This covenant could or can be broken by Israel, but never by God. If God could revoke his covenant with Israel he could as well one day revoke his covenant with the Gentiles.[32] This means all catastrophies which Israel experienced during her long history such as subjugation by the Philistines, destruction of the Northern Kingdom, Babylonian exile, persecution under Antiochus IV Epiphanes, destruction of the Jewish communities by the Romans in AD 66-70 and 132, medieval pogroms and eventually the Holocaust must be seen as events within God's covenant and not against it.

Christian interpretation of the O.T., including, of course, the Ebed Yahweh Songs is based on the conviction that Christ is the center of all Scripture. Christian exegesis of the Ebed Yahweh Songs must by definition be christological. However, any form of christological exegesis that does not take into account the historical dimension with the focus on Israel and the setting of these texts in O.T. theology would do more harm than good. The christological interpretation has its legitimate basis in the individual and prophetic character of the Ebed. Since this Ebed is neither a king nor an offspring of the House of David, a messianic interpretation would be out of place. Rather the lines should be drawn to the *munus propheticum* (prophetic office) and based on Isa 53 to the *munus sacerdotale* (priestly office) of Christ.

More important is the ecclesiological interpretation, which would continue the collective interpretation of the Songs. The Christian church does not replace the Ebed Israel of the Songs in his prophetic mission to the nations, rather she joins O.T. Israel. Since the establishment of the Church, Jews and Christians are fellow prophets sent by the same God into the world. In this context Christian mission to the Jews becomes a contradiction in terms, because two prophets working on each other would have no credibility to the world.[33] Nevertheless, some questions need to be raised: how would Jews today and how would Christians define the Jewish mission to bring light and *mišpāṭ* to the nations? Is there a legitimate, possibly, complimentary relationship, or are they mutually exclusive?

It could be shown that the collective interpretation saw the fate of the Ebed-Israel on his *via dolorosa* typified in the personal experience of the prophet Deutero-Isaiah. This is the point at which Christians see their christological and ecclesiological interpretation as one. The passion of Jesus of Nazareth typifies the way of his church. By definition the way of the church in her mission to the world is a way of suffering. However, what does it mean when today in our western culture, the church no longer suffers? Does this mean the biblical model is not valid any longer or could it mean that instead of confronting the world the Ebed-Church has chosen the path of compromise and accommodation? The prophet Deutero-Isaiah suffered resistance from his own people, the people of God. In the context of the ecclesiological exegesis, this should be more than a mere historical fact. In view of the cross of Christ, Christians have no reason to put the blame for the crucifixion on the Jews. Rather, the question to the Church and her theologians is: Where are they crucifying Christ today? Strange as it may sound in the face of a deplorable Christian tradition, the crucifixion of Christ or the events of Good Friday do not separate Jews from Christians rather they bind them together.

As it seems, a full understanding of the Church of Jesus Christ or Christian ecclesiology is not possible without a full understanding of the role of the Jewish people. When a Christology that does not take into account that Jesus was a Jew becomes necessarily docetic, an ecclesiology disregarding the Jews as fellow brothers in God's covenant becomes docetic as well. Its focus would be on a church without roots.

"Christians represent together with the Jews the one people of God on Earth."[34] This statement with all its ramifications has its scriptural basis in the Servant Songs of Deutero-Isaiah. If this is so than everything that happens to the Jews in this world has a theological dimension and therefore is of vital interest to the Christian Church because in one way or another, the Church is involved. Recognition of this fact gives us the Christian approach to the Holocaust. It is not enough as a not participating Christian bystander to show one's indignation over this terrible event and express sympathy for the poor victims. The Church is involved. She is involved on the side of the guilty. Through the neglect of Christian teaching and preaching to include the Jews in the *communio* of God's chosen people, the Jews were left to secular philosophies and ideologies which when combined with antisemitic bias did provide the spiritual basis for the Holocaust. The Church is involved on the side of the victims because when one part of the people of God is suffering the other part is suffering too. Above all, the Church is involved because of her *communio* with the Son of God. When he is suffering in this world under the uproar of human sin the entire people of God is suffering as well.

NOTES

1. Karl Barth. *Das Wort Gottes und die Theologie*. Ge-
sammelte Vorträge (München: Chr. Kaiser, 1926); *Church Dogmatics*. Vol. 1, 2, "The Doctrine of the Word of God" (New
York: Scribner, 1956), pp. 457ff. It should be noted that
Hans-Joachim Kraus hails Barth's new approach as a "stormy
gale roaring through OT studies" (*Geschichte der historisch-
kritischen Erforschung des Alten Testaments*. [Neukirchen:
Neuk Verlag, 2nd ed., 1969], p. 417), but on the other hand
in Ronald E. Clement's discussion Barth's contribution is not
mentioned at all (*One Hundred Years of Old Testament Interpretation*. [Philadelphia: Westminster, 1976], pp. 118-38).

2. E.g. Walter Eichrodt. *Theology of the Old Testament*.
Trans. J. A. Baker (Philadelphia: Westminster, 1961); Gerhard
von Rad. *Old Testament Theology*. Trans. D. M. G. Stalker
(New York: Harper, Vol. I, 1962, Vol. II, 1965).

3. An important exception is Wilhelm Vischer. *Das
Christuszeugnis des Alten Testaments* (Zürich: Evang. Verlag,
Vol I and II, 2nd ed., 1946); English translation of Vol I.
The Witness of the Old Testament to Christ. Trans. A. B.
Crabtree (London: Lutterworth, 1949).

4. Martin Noth. *The History of Israel*. Trans. P. R.
Ackroyd (New York: Harper, 2nd ed., 1960), p. 7.

5. See Markus Barth. "Was the Apostle Paul an Anti-
Semite?" *JES* 5 (1968), pp. 78-104; repr. in *Israel and the
Church* (Richmond: Knox, 1969), pp. 43-78; *Jesus the Jew*.
Trans. Fred. Prussner (Atlanta: Knox, 1978); *Ephesians*. *AB*,
Vol. I and II (Garden City, New York: Doubleday, 1974).

6. Claus Westermann. *Isaiah 40-66*. Trans. David M. G.
Stalker (Philadelphia: Westminster, 1969), p. 95.

7. For a full discussion of the history of interpreta-
tion with the various attempts to identify the Ebed see:
Christopher R. North. *The Suffering Servant in Deutero-
Isaiah* (London: Oxford University Press, 1948); H. H. Rowley.
"The Servant of the Lord in the Light of Three Decades of
Criticism." *The Servant of the Lord* (Oxford: Blackwell, 2nd
ed., 1965), pp. 3-60.

8. See BHK.

9. The first to do this was Bernhard Duhm. *Das Buch*

Jesaja (Göttingen: Vandenhoeck, 4th ed., 1922), pp. 14f.

10. Hans Walter Wolff. *Anthropology of the Old Testament*. Trans. Margaret Kohl (Philadelphia: Fortress, 1974), pp. 214ff. See also H. Wheeler Robinson. "The Hebrew Conception of Corporate Personality." *Werden und Wesen des Alten Testaments*. *BZAW*, 66, 1936, pp. 49-62. Reprint, *Corporate Personality in Ancient Israel*. Facet Books, Bibl. Series 11 (Philadelphia: Fortress, 1964).

11. A good example in the OT tradition is the story of Achan's theft in Josh 7. The entire people is under the verdict "the people of Israel broke the faith", v. 1, because of the transgression of the one man Achan.

12. On Jacob/Israel see H. Eberhard von Waldow. " - - denn ich erlöse dich." *Biblische Studien* 29 (Neukirchen: Neukirchen Verlag, 1960), pp. 17ff.

13. This has been called "the fluid or integral interpretation", Georg Fohrer. *Introduction to the Old Testament*. Trans. David Green (Nashville: Abingdon, 1968), p. 380.

14. The details have frequently been pointed out, most recently Claus Westermann in his commentary (see note 6) on the individual songs. On the other hand, Ivan Engnell ("The Ebed Yahveh Songs and the Suffering Messiah in Deutero-Isaiah." *Bulletin of the John Rylands Library* 31, 1948, pp. 54-93) places heavy emphasis on the royal characteristics of the Ebed. To a lesser degree this is also done by Otto Kaiser (*Der Königliche Knecht*. *FRLANT* 70 (Göttingen: Vandenhoeck, 1959); cp. also Westermann. There are indeed some features that are known from a royal setting, such as presentation as Yahweh's elect, or equipment with his spirit. This is, however, what all persons who are called by Yahweh have in common. This does not make them royal.

15. Aage Bentzen. *Introduction to the Old Testament*. (Copenhagen: G. E. C. Gad, 6th ed., 1961), Vol. II, p. 112.

16. For recent representatives of this view see Georg Fohrer, *op. cit.*, pp. 379ff.

17. Jer 11:18-23; 12:1-4; 15:10-12, 15-21; 17:12-18; 18:18-23; 20:7-18.

18. Westermann is trying to back away from the identification of the Ebed with Deutero-Isaiah and suggests that the songs speak of office and ministry of Israel's prophets (pp. 211f.). However, it is doubtful if an OT author could have

spoken in such an abstract fashion, as a German Lutheran pastor discussing his *"Amtsbegriff"*.

19. Cp. also Isa 42:1.4 and Jer 1:4.10.

20. This term is difficult both in terms of grammar and translation, see Karl Elliger. *Jesaja II*. *BKAT* XI (Neukirchen: Neukirchener Verlag, 1971), pp. 233ff.; and Delbert R. Hillers *"Běrît 'ām*: 'Emancipation of the People'." *JBL* 97, 1978, pp. 172-182. However, most likely we have here a reference to the Sinai covenant.

21. Isa 43:21; 45:6.23; 49:26.

22. So Westermann. The Zürcher Bible has *"Bundesmittler für das Menschengeschlecht"*.

23. Cp. also I Kings 19:10; Neh 9:26; Jer 2:30.

24. Isa 43:5-7; 49:16-19; 55:12.

25. Isa 41:18f.; 42:15f.; 43:19f.

26. In later Judaism it was frequently stated: *"šelūhtō šel ādām kěmôtô"* = the one sent by a man is like the man himself. This means there is no difference between the *šōlēaḥ* and the *šālîaḥ* = between the sender and the one who is sent, K. H. Rengstorf, "apostolos", *Theological Dictionary of the New Testament*, ed. G. Kittel, trans. Ed. Geoffrey W. Bromiley. Vol. I, Grand Rapids, 1964, p. 415.

27. See note 23.

28. Isa 43.10, textual emendation; see BHK and John L. McKenzie. *Second Isaiah*. *AB* (New York: Doubleday, 1968), p. 52.

29. Isa 45:3.6; 49:23.26; 52:6, or 54 times in Ezek.

30. See Karl Barth. *Church Dogmatics*. Vol. III, 3, "The Doctrine of Creation", pp. 210ff.

31. Gen 17:7.13.19; Exod 31:16 (cp. Gen 9:16).

32. Markus Barth. *Jesus the Jew* (note 5), 38f.

33. See the extensive discussion in Karl Barth. *Church Dogmatics*. Vol. IV, 3, "The Doctrine of Reconciliation", 2nd half, pp. 876ff.

34. Markus Barth, *op. cit.*, 39.